e Flag

nd art by

KAITO

7

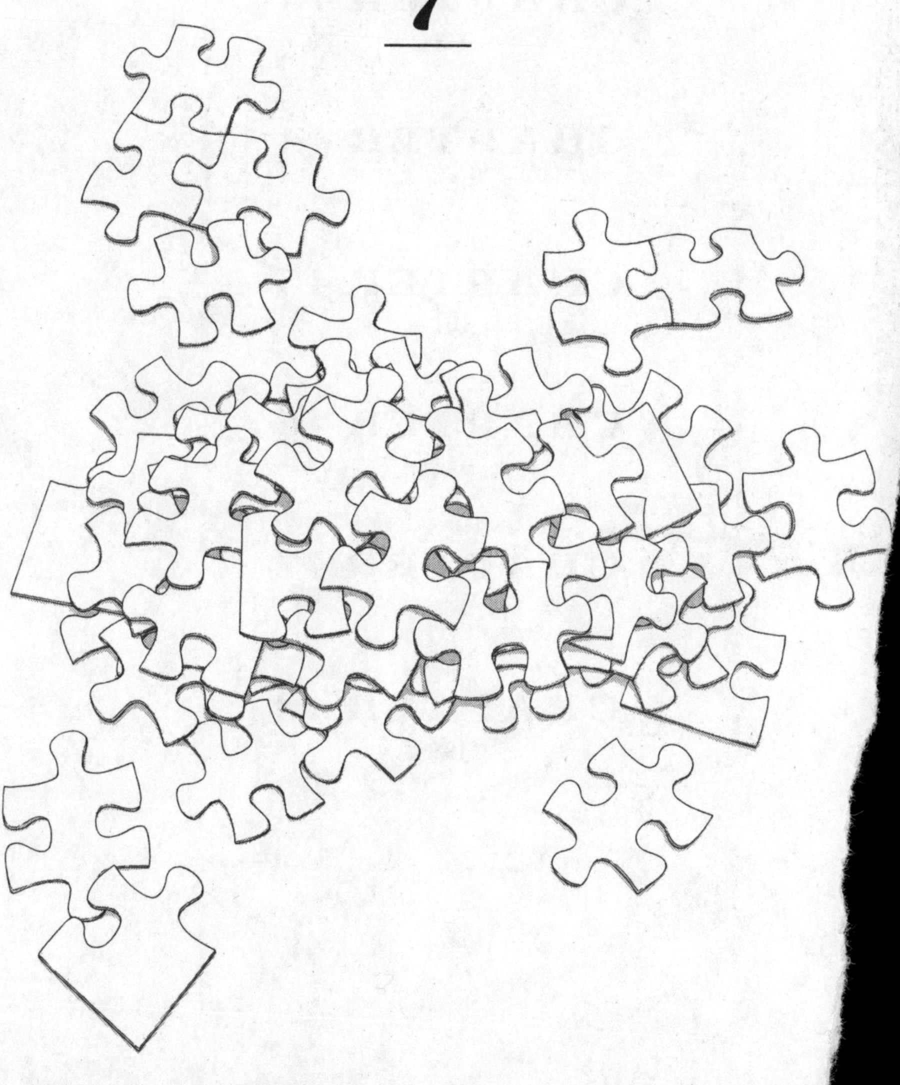

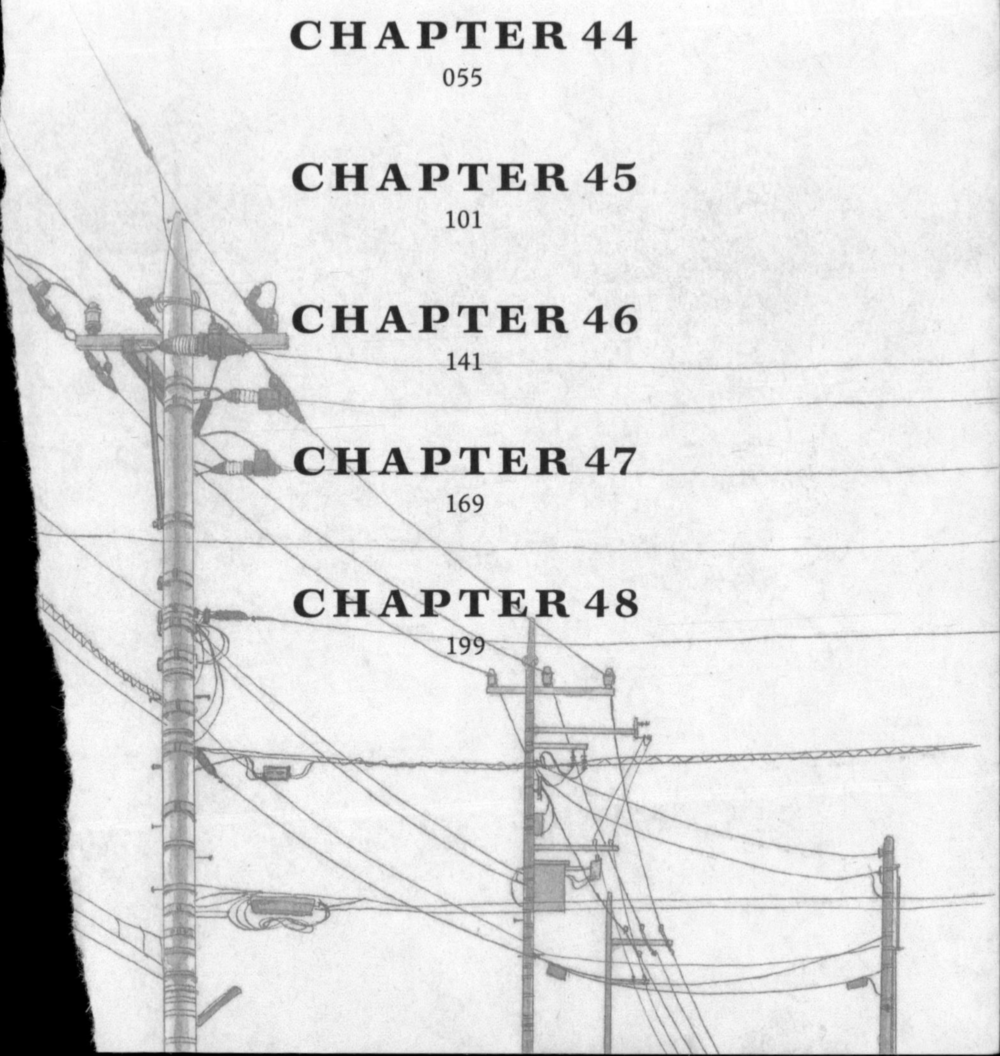

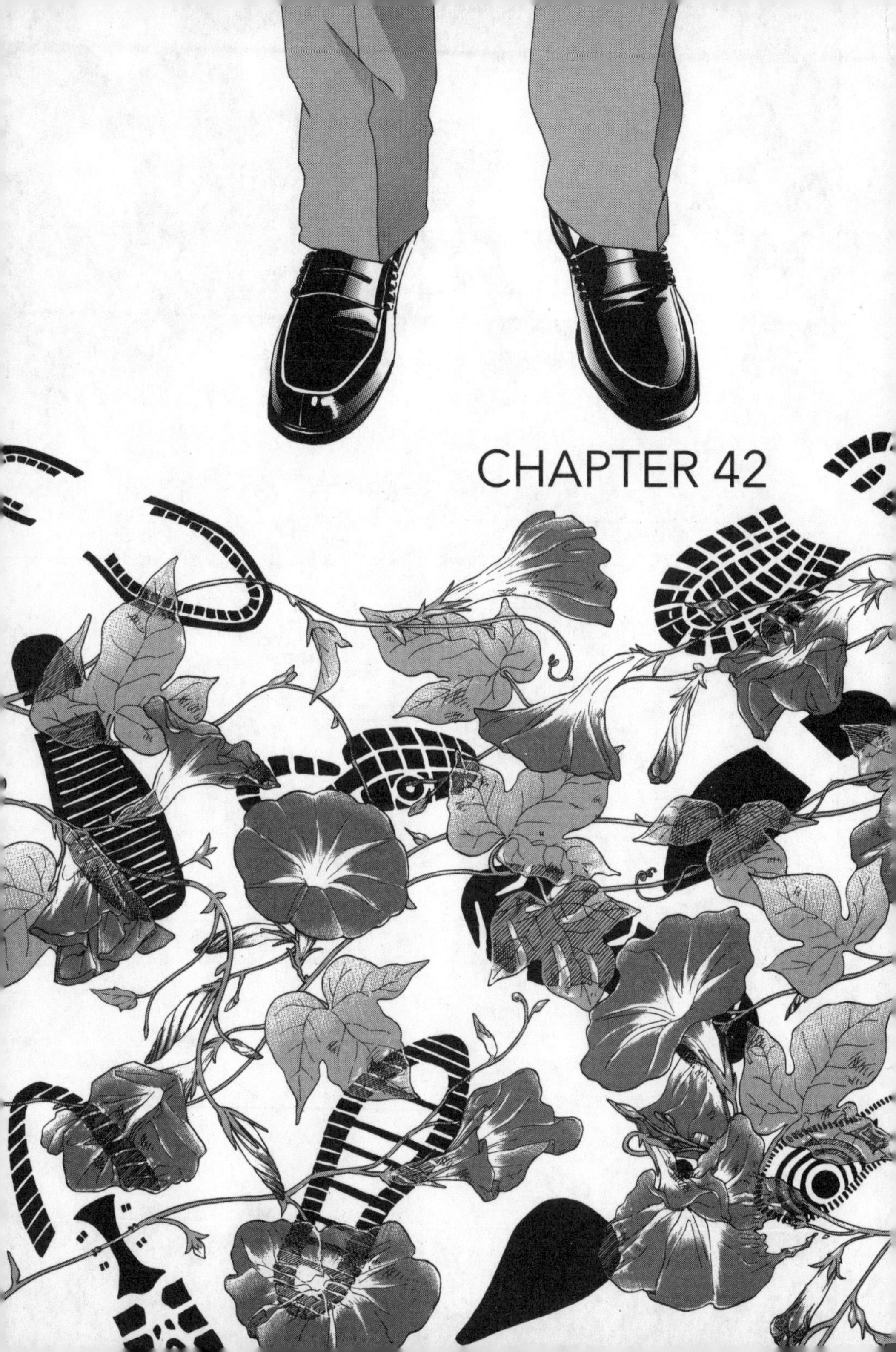
CHAPTER 42

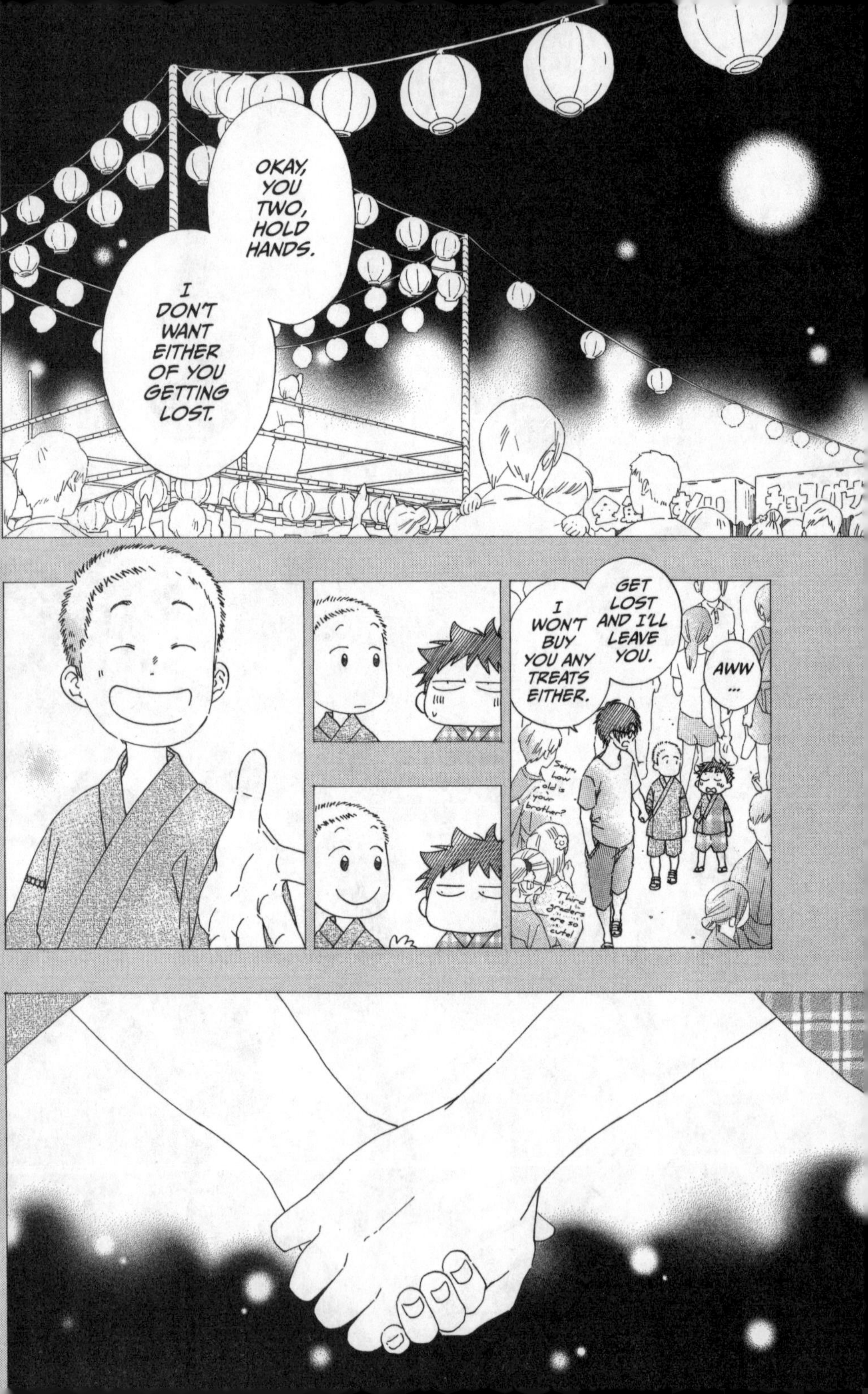
OKAY, YOU TWO, HOLD HANDS.
I DON'T WANT EITHER OF YOU GETTING LOST.
GET LOST AND I'LL LEAVE YOU.
I WON'T BUY YOU ANY TREATS EITHER.
AWW ...
Seiya, how old is your brother?
Third graders are so cute!

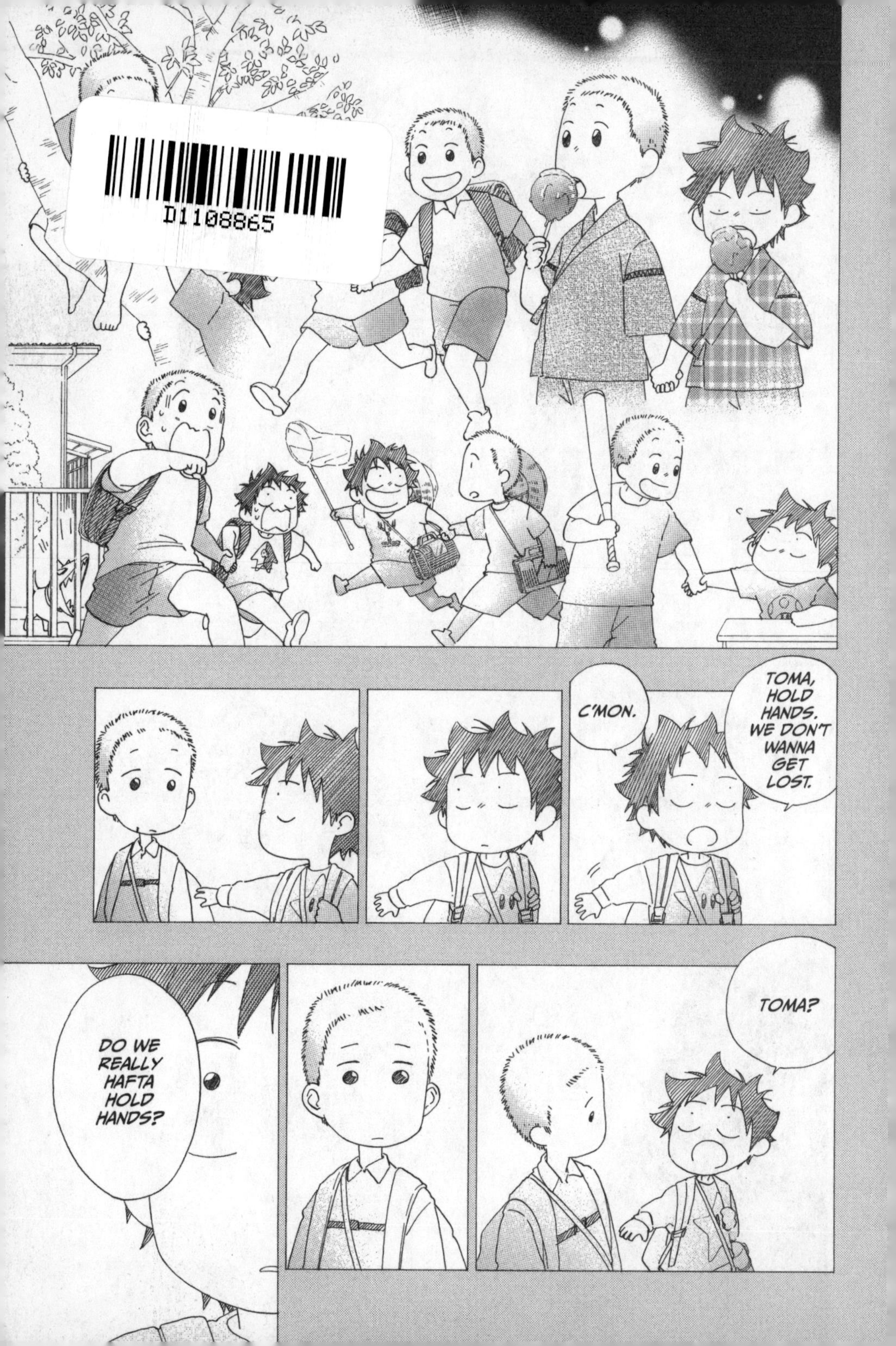
TOMA, HOLD HANDS. WE DON'T WANNA GET LOST.
C'MON.
TOMA?
DO WE REALLY HAFTA HOLD HANDS?

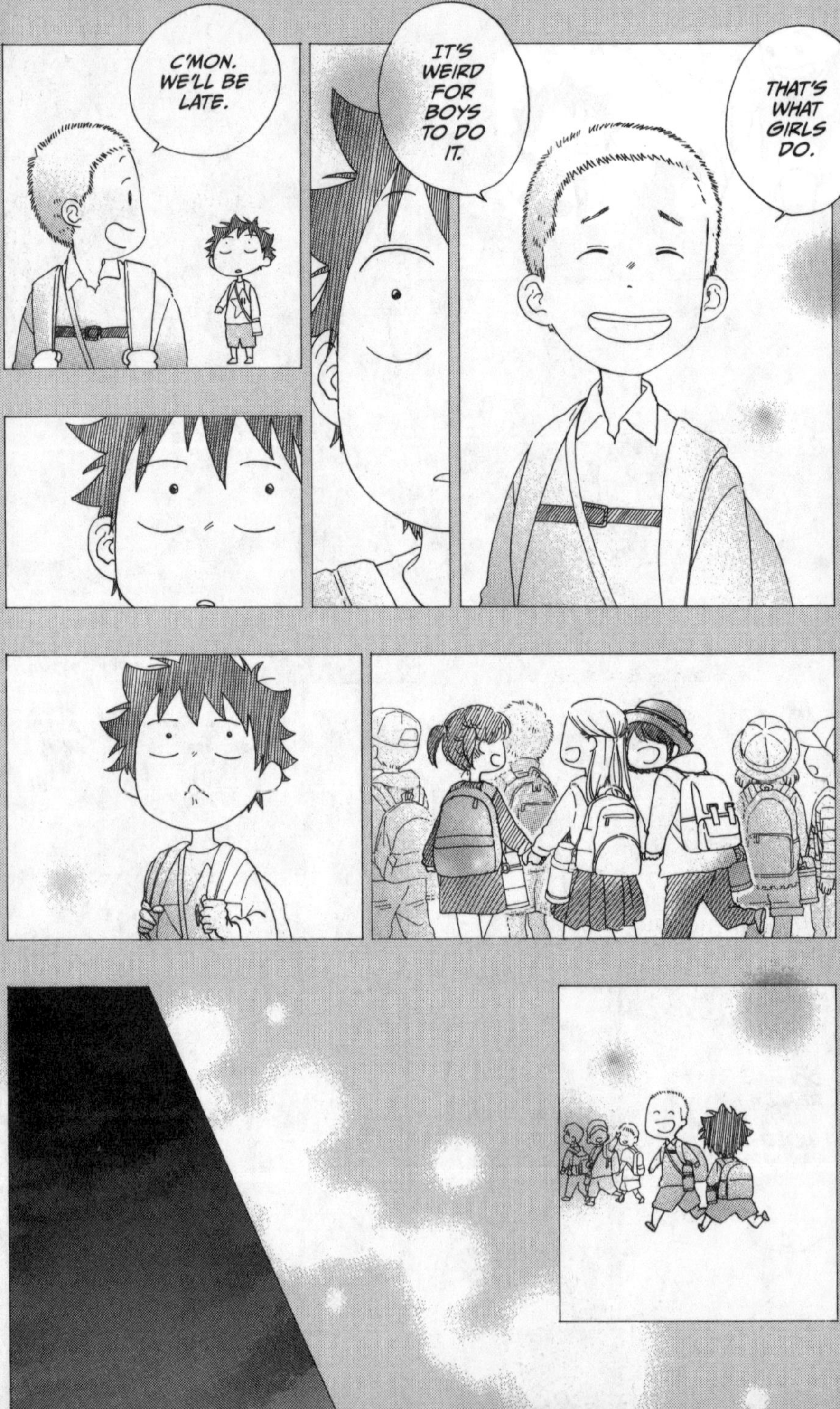
THAT'S WHAT GIRLS DO.
IT'S WEIRD FOR BOYS TO DO IT.
C'MON. WE'LL BE LATE.

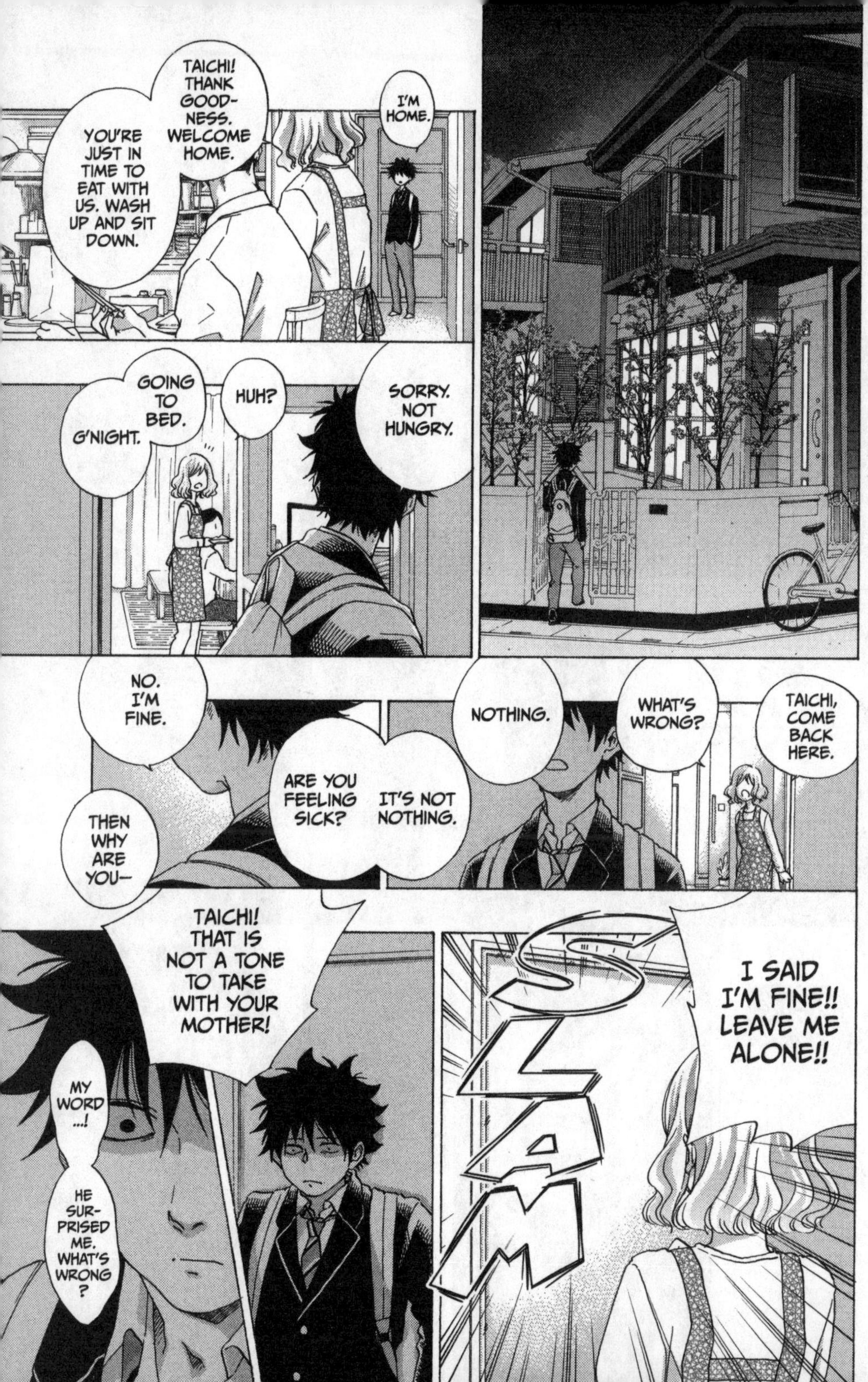
I'M HOME.
TAICHI! THANK GOODNESS. WELCOME HOME.
YOU'RE JUST IN TIME TO EAT WITH US. WASH UP AND SIT DOWN.
SORRY. NOT HUNGRY.
HUH?
GOING TO BED. G'NIGHT.
TAICHI, COME BACK HERE.
WHAT'S WRONG?
NOTHING.
IT'S NOT NOTHING.
ARE YOU FEELING SICK?
NO. I'M FINE.
THEN WHY ARE YOU—
I SAID I'M FINE!! LEAVE ME ALONE!!
SLAM
TAICHI! THAT IS NOT A TONE TO TAKE WITH YOUR MOTHER!
MY WORD...!
HE SURPRISED ME. WHAT'S WRONG?

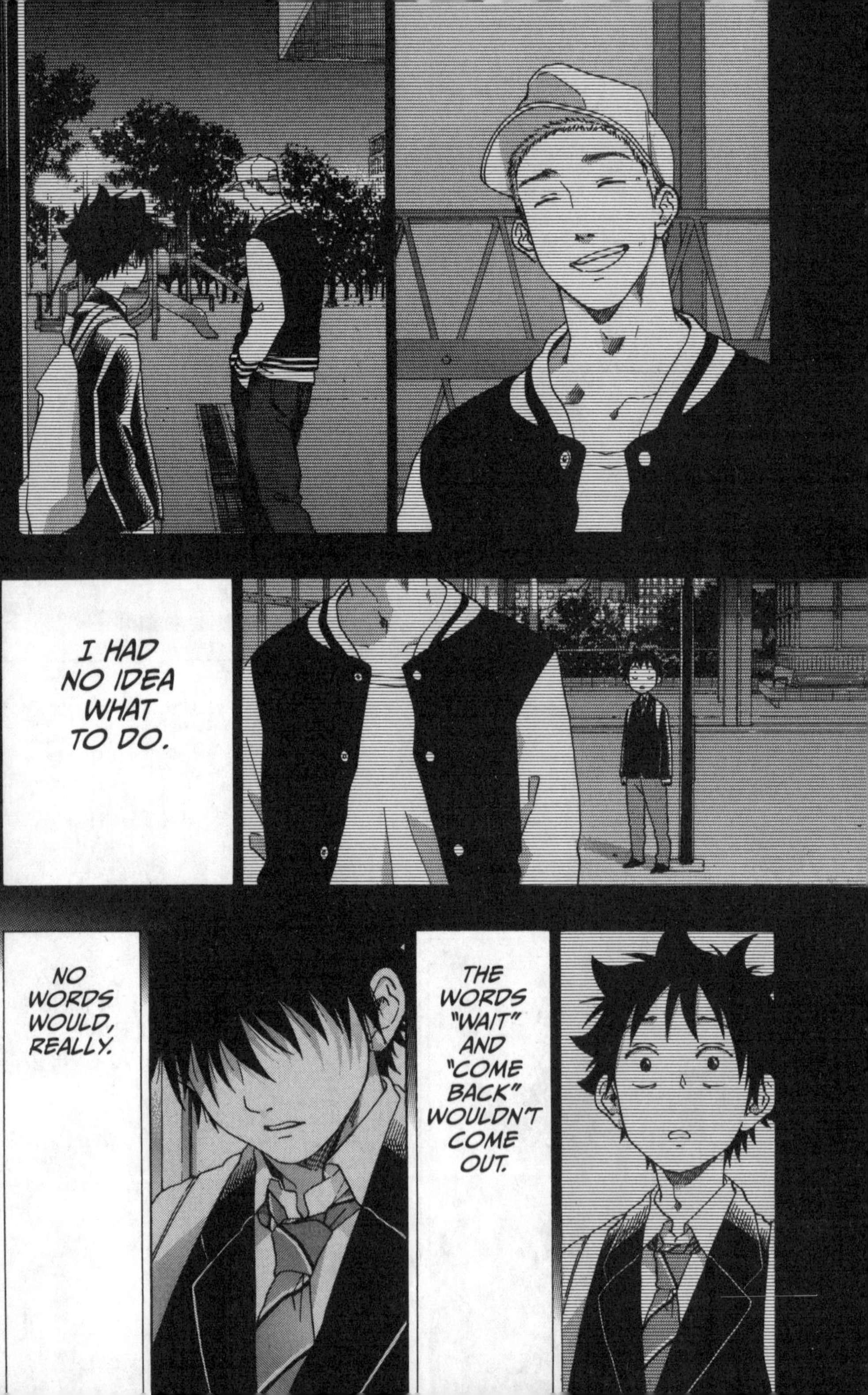
I HAD NO IDEA WHAT TO DO.
THE WORDS "WAIT" AND "COME BACK" WOULDN'T COME OUT.
NO WORDS WOULD, REALLY.

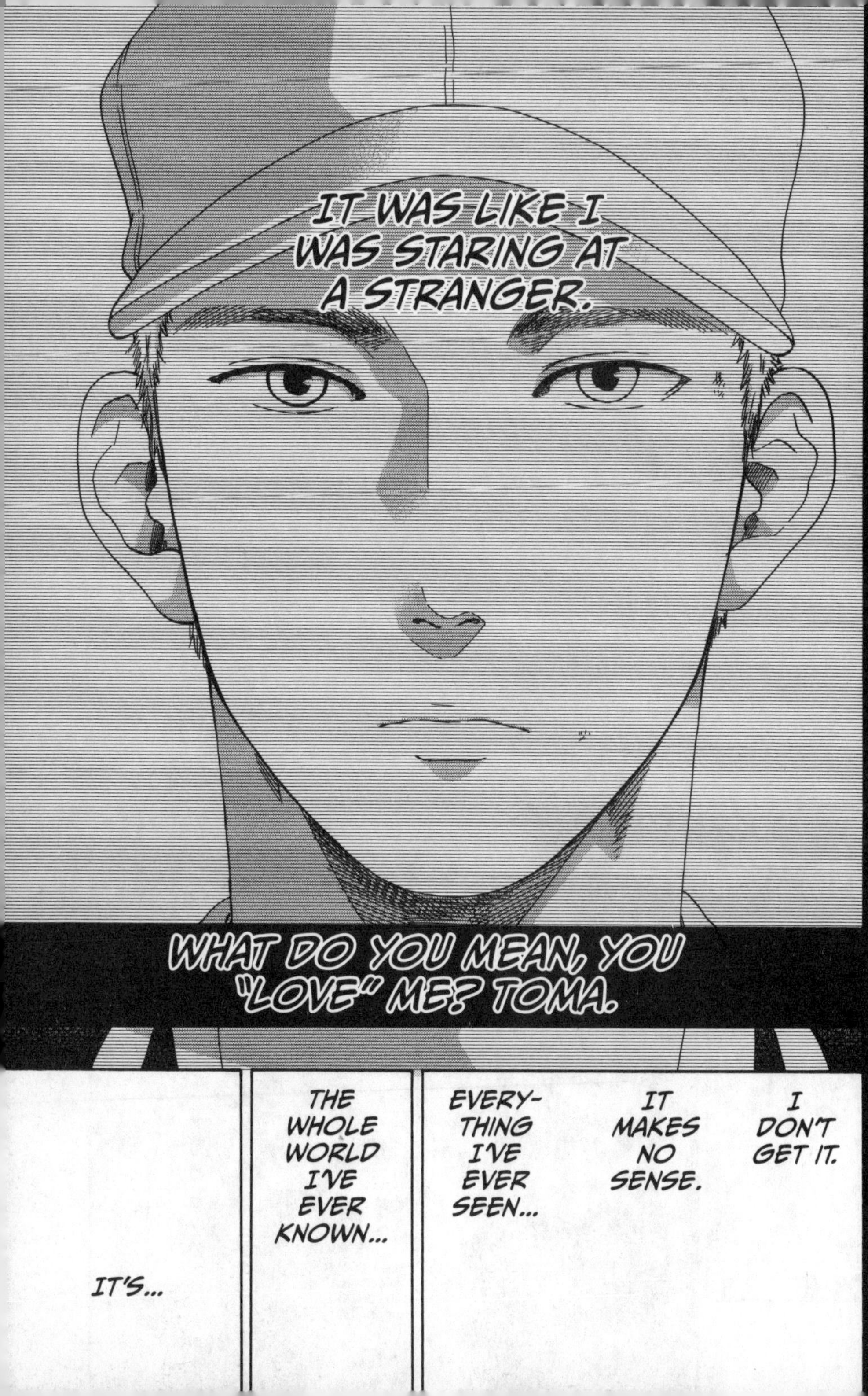
IT WAS LIKE I WAS STARING AT A STRANGER.
WHAT DO YOU MEAN, YOU "LOVE" ME? TOMA.
I DON'T GET IT.
IT MAKES NO SENSE.
EVERY-THING I'VE EVER SEEN...
THE WHOLE WORLD I'VE EVER KNOWN...
IT'S...

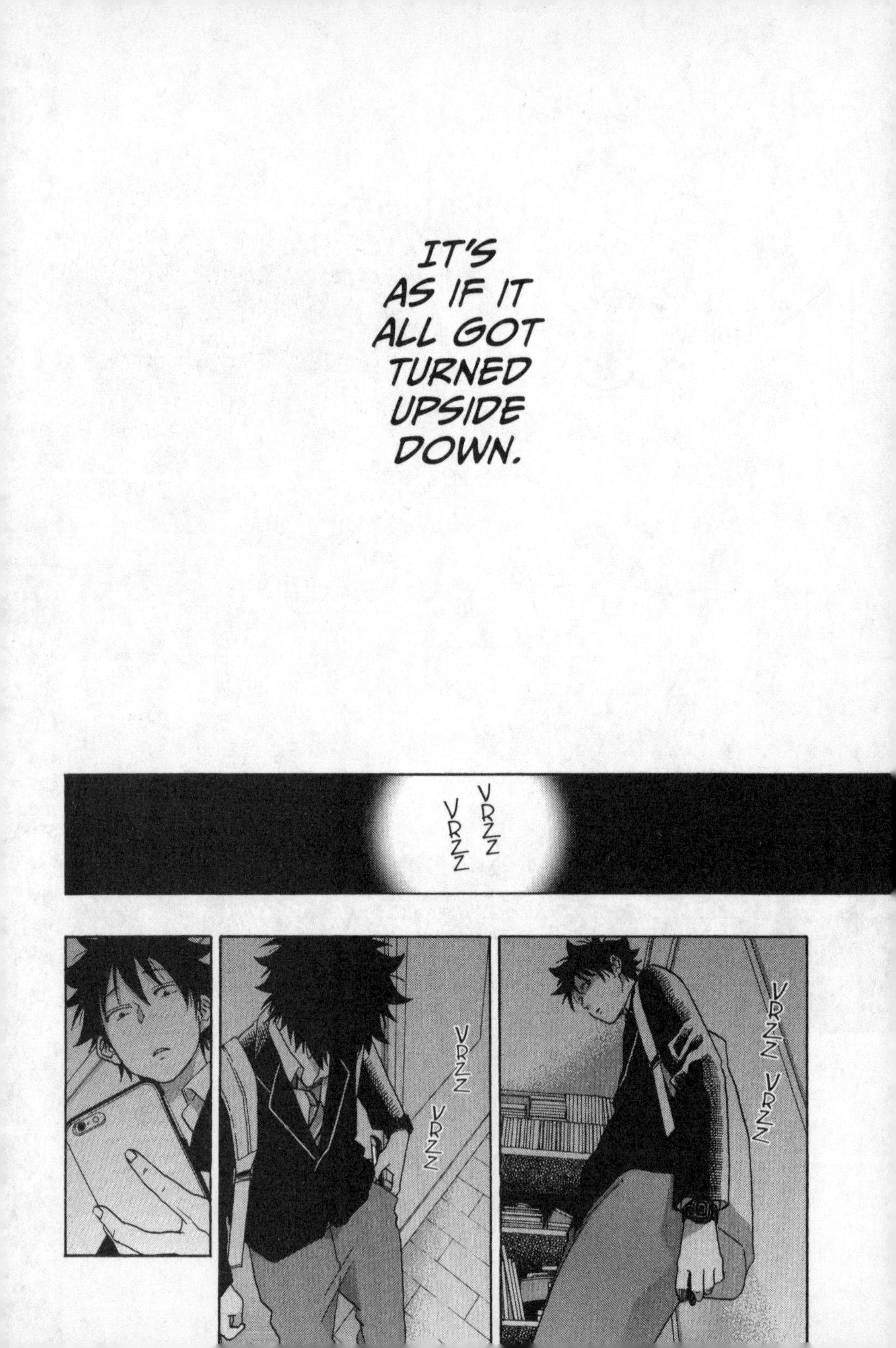
IT'S AS IF IT ALL GOT TURNED UPSIDE DOWN.
VRZZ
VRZZ
VRZZ
VRZZ
VRZZ
VRZZ

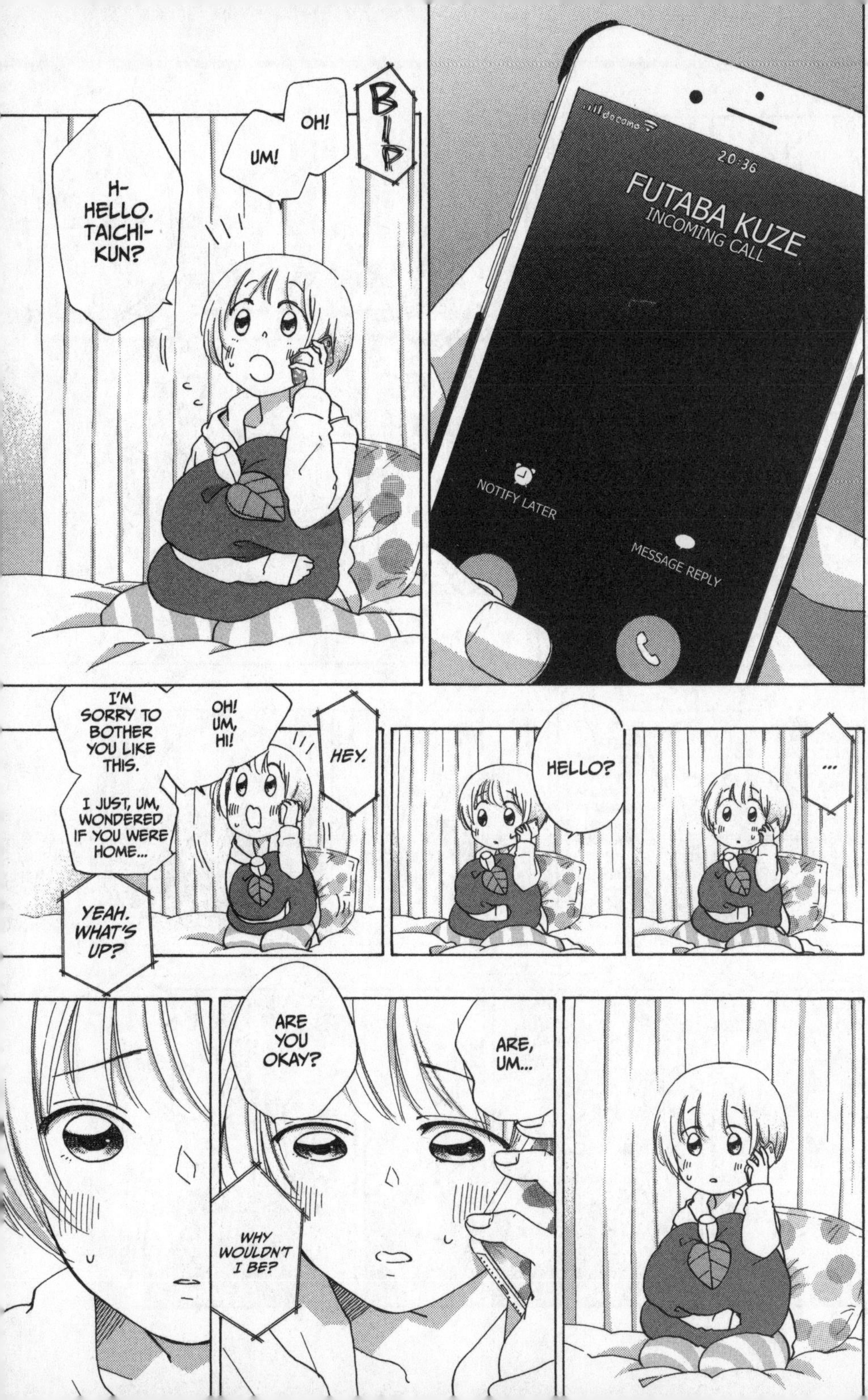
docomo
20:36
FUTABA KUZE
INCOMING CALL
NOTIFY LATER
MESSAGE REPLY
BIP
OH!
UM!
H-HELLO. TAICHI-KUN?
...
HELLO?
HEY.
OH! UM, HI!
I'M SORRY TO BOTHER YOU LIKE THIS.
I JUST, UM, WONDERED IF YOU WERE HOME...
YEAH. WHAT'S UP?
ARE, UM...
ARE YOU OKAY?
WHY WOULDN'T I BE?

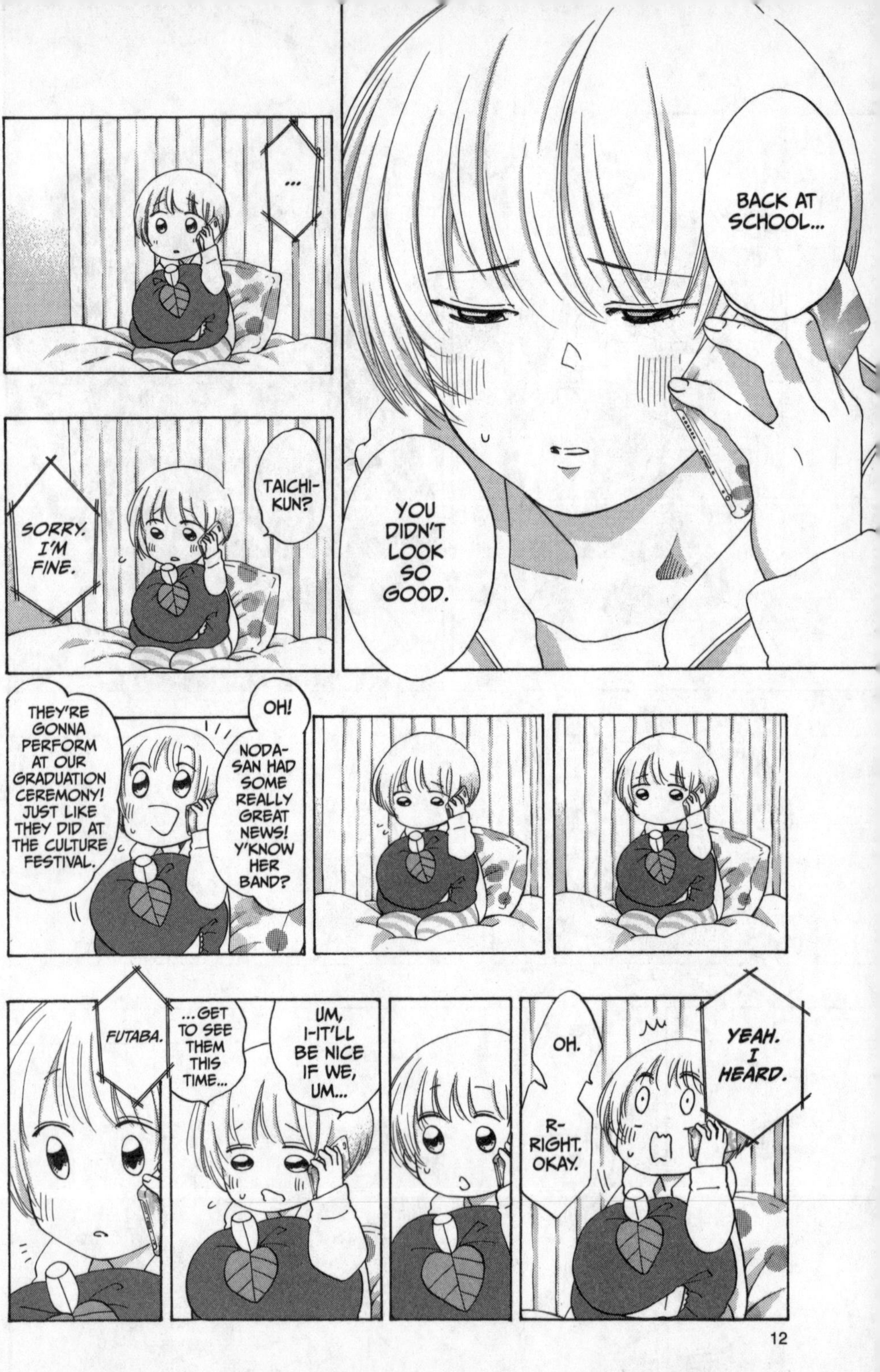
BACK AT SCHOOL...
YOU DIDN'T LOOK SO GOOD.
...
TAICHI-KUN?
SORRY. I'M FINE.
OH!
NODA-SAN HAD SOME REALLY GREAT NEWS! Y'KNOW HER BAND?
THEY'RE GONNA PERFORM AT OUR GRADUATION CEREMONY! JUST LIKE THEY DID AT THE CULTURE FESTIVAL.
YEAH. I HEARD.
OH.
R-RIGHT. OKAY.
UM, I-IT'LL BE NICE IF WE, UM...
...GET TO SEE THEM THIS TIME...
FUTABA.

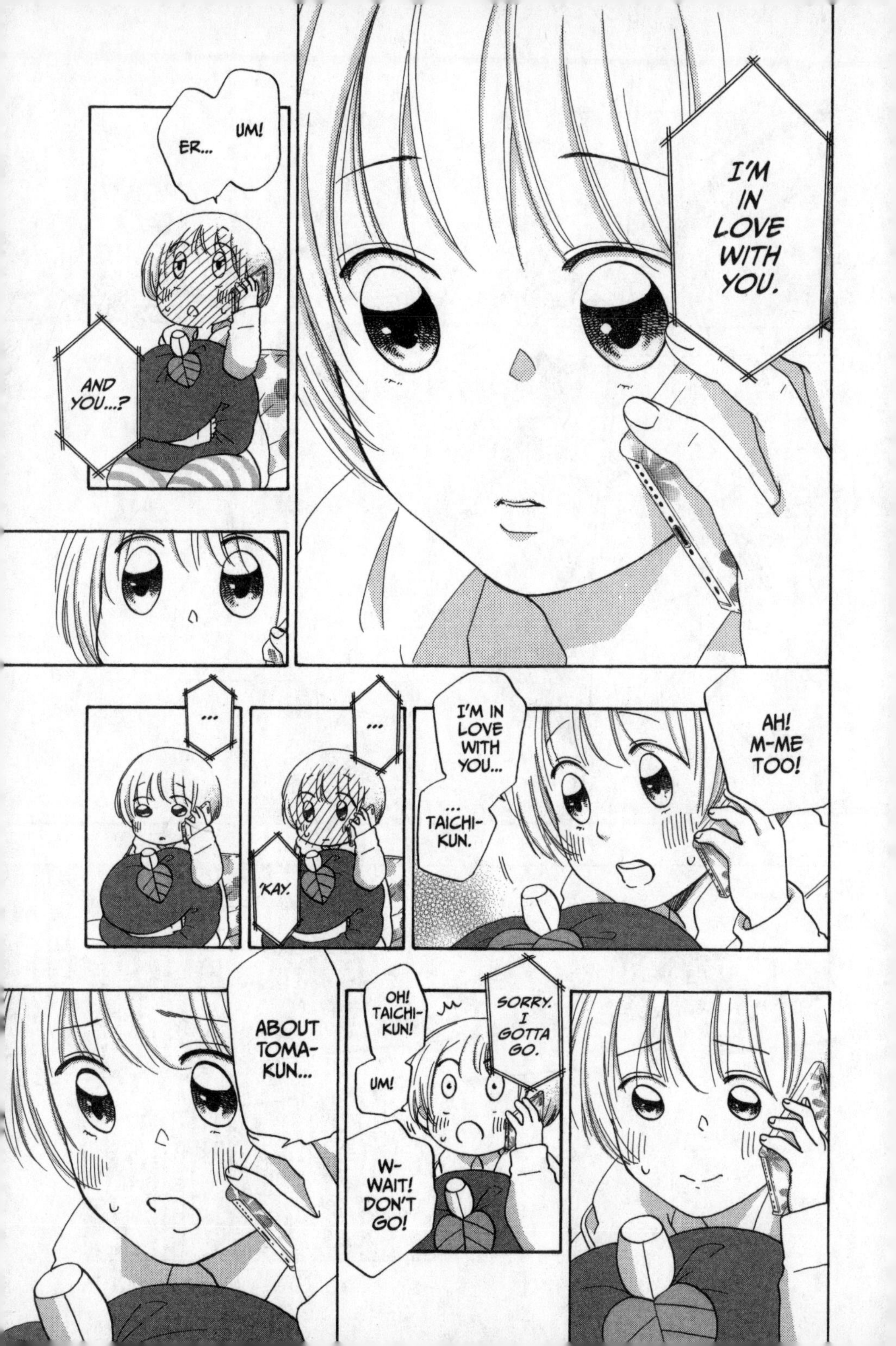
I'M IN LOVE WITH YOU.
UM!
ER...
AND YOU...?
AH! M-ME TOO!
I'M IN LOVE WITH YOU... ...TAICHI-KUN.
...
'KAY.
...
SORRY. I GOTTA GO.
OH! TAICHI-KUN!
UM!
W-WAIT! DON'T GO!
ABOUT TOMA-KUN...

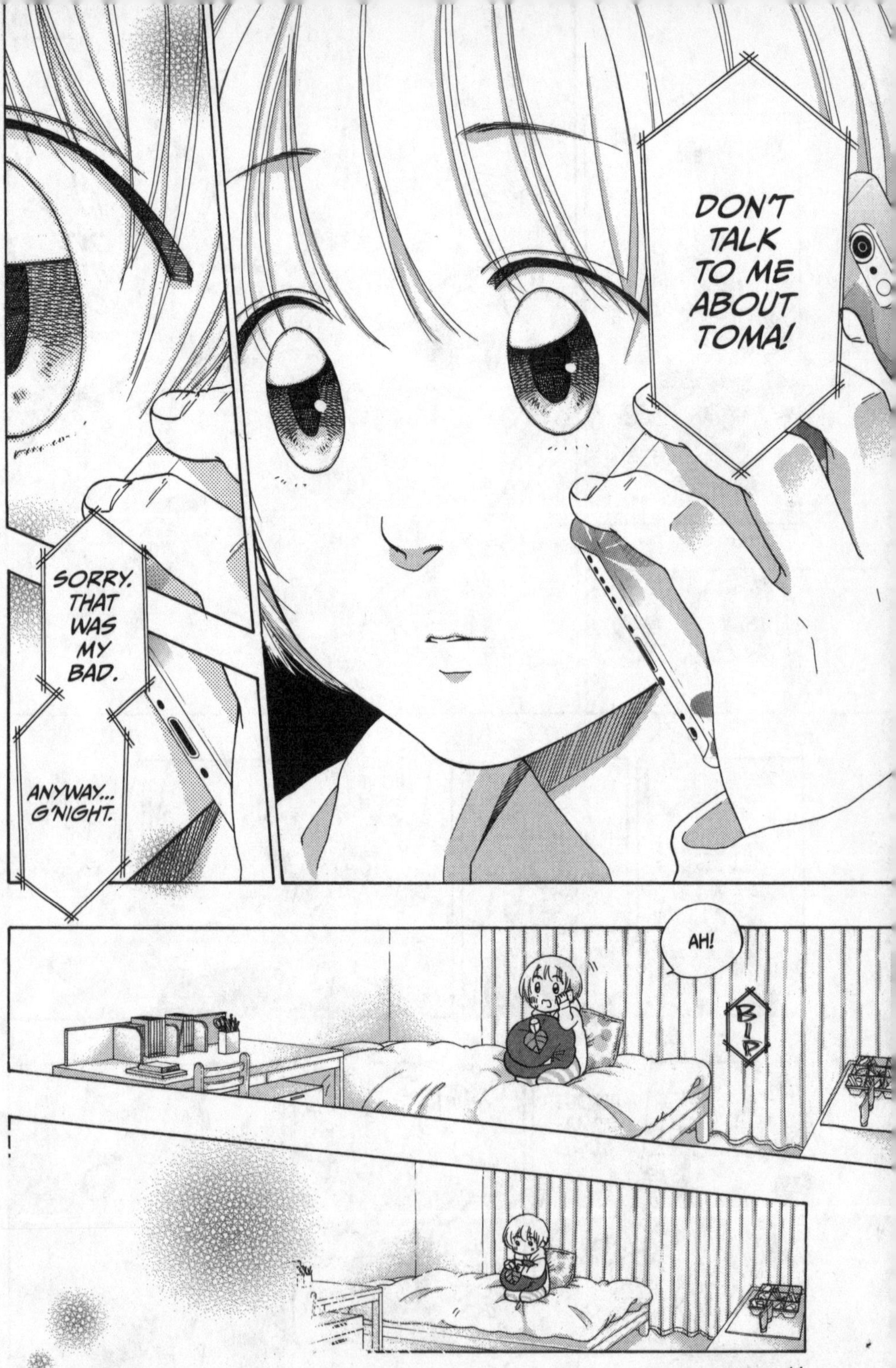
DON'T TALK TO ME ABOUT TOMA!
SORRY. THAT WAS MY BAD.
ANYWAY... G'NIGHT.
AH!
BIP

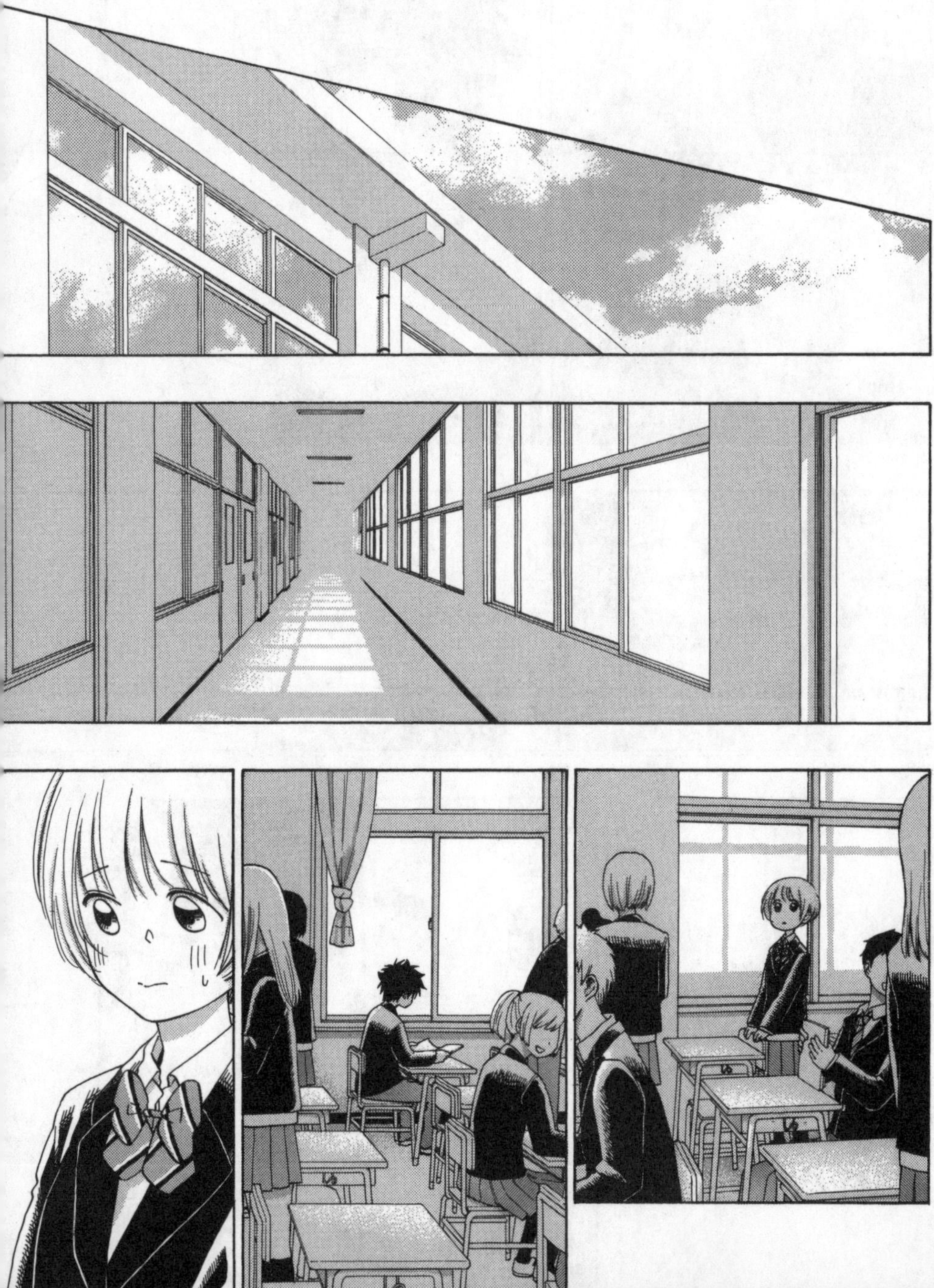

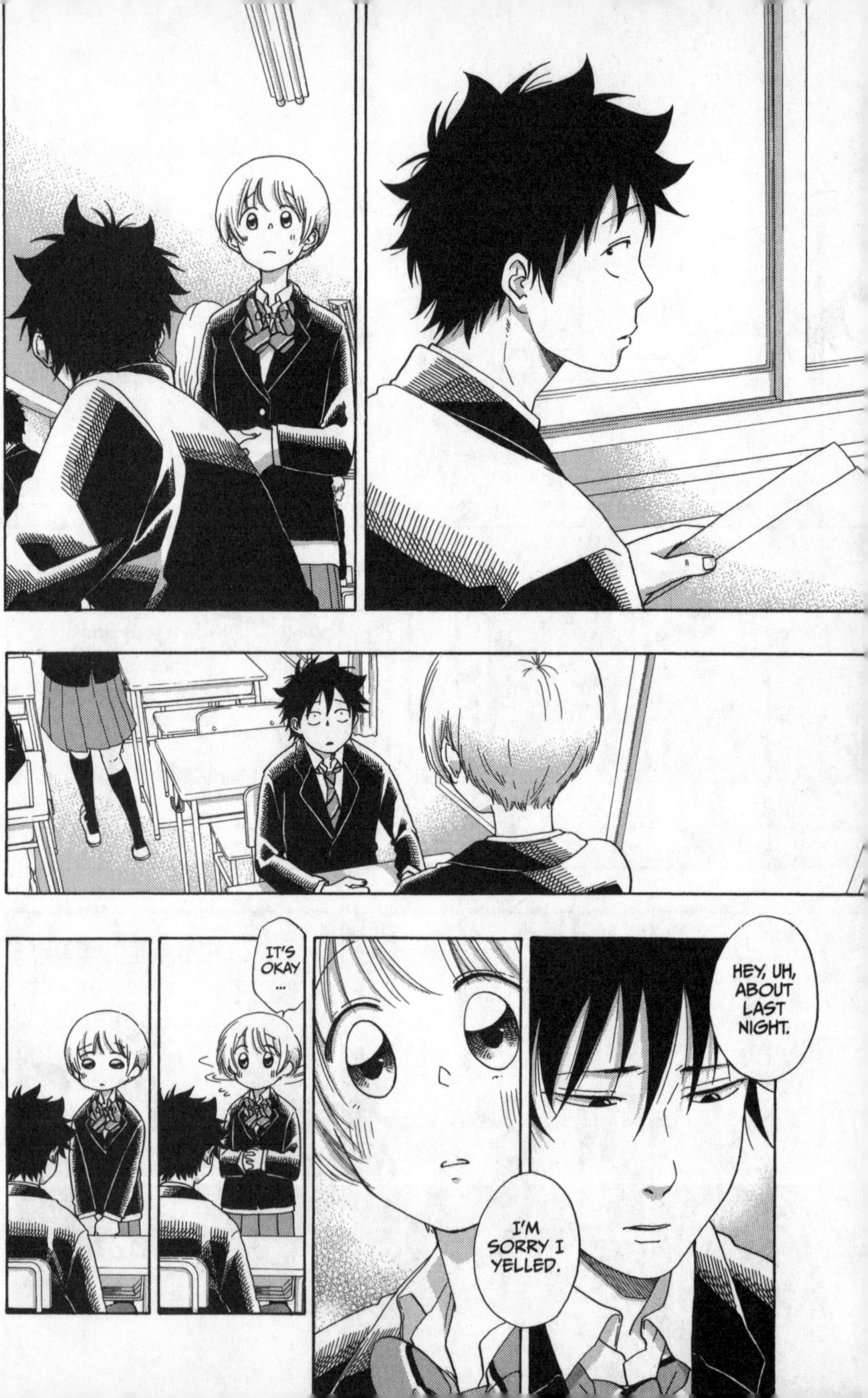
HEY, UH, ABOUT LAST NIGHT.
I'M SORRY I YELLED.
IT'S OKAY...

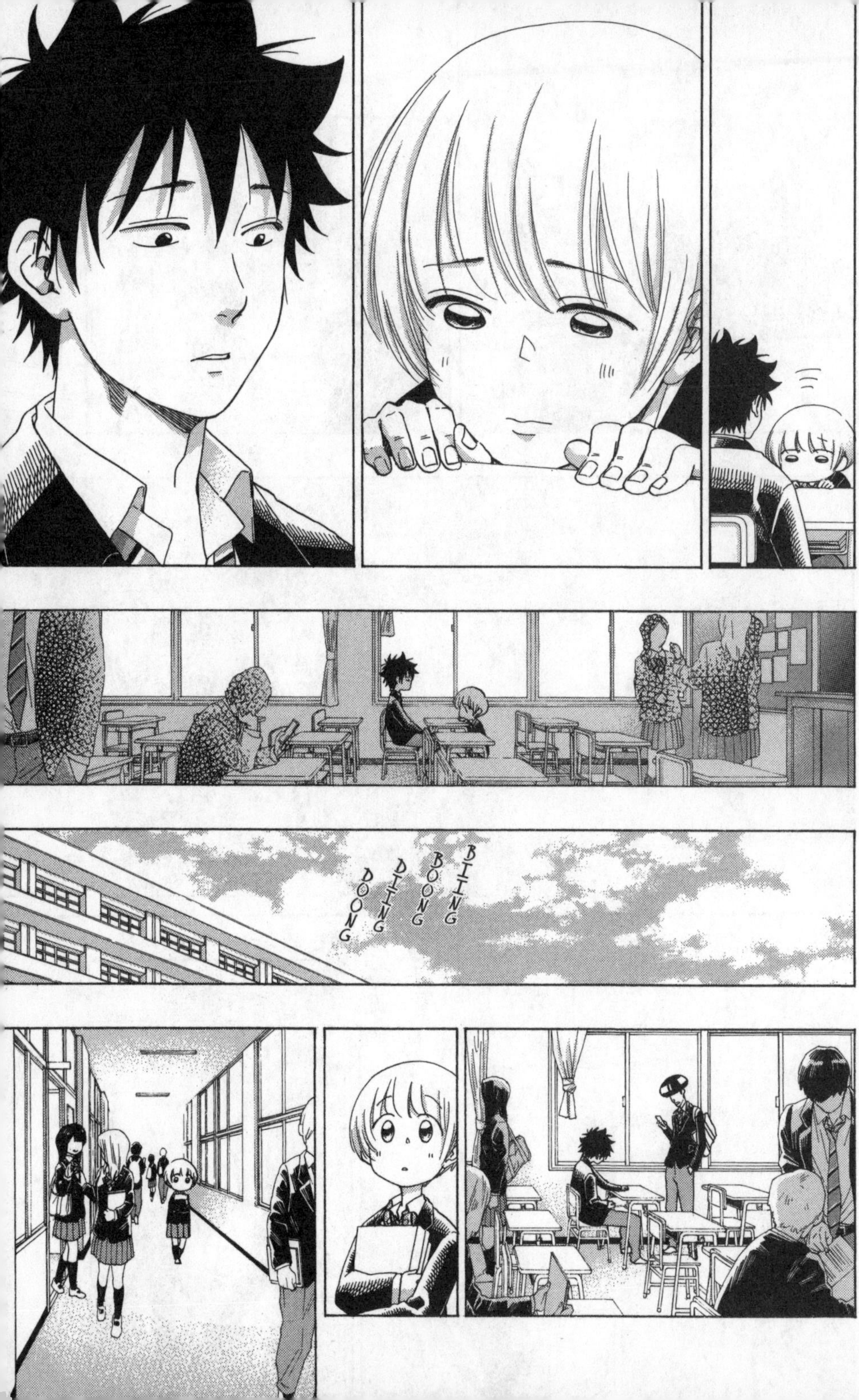
BIING
BOONG
DIING
DOONG

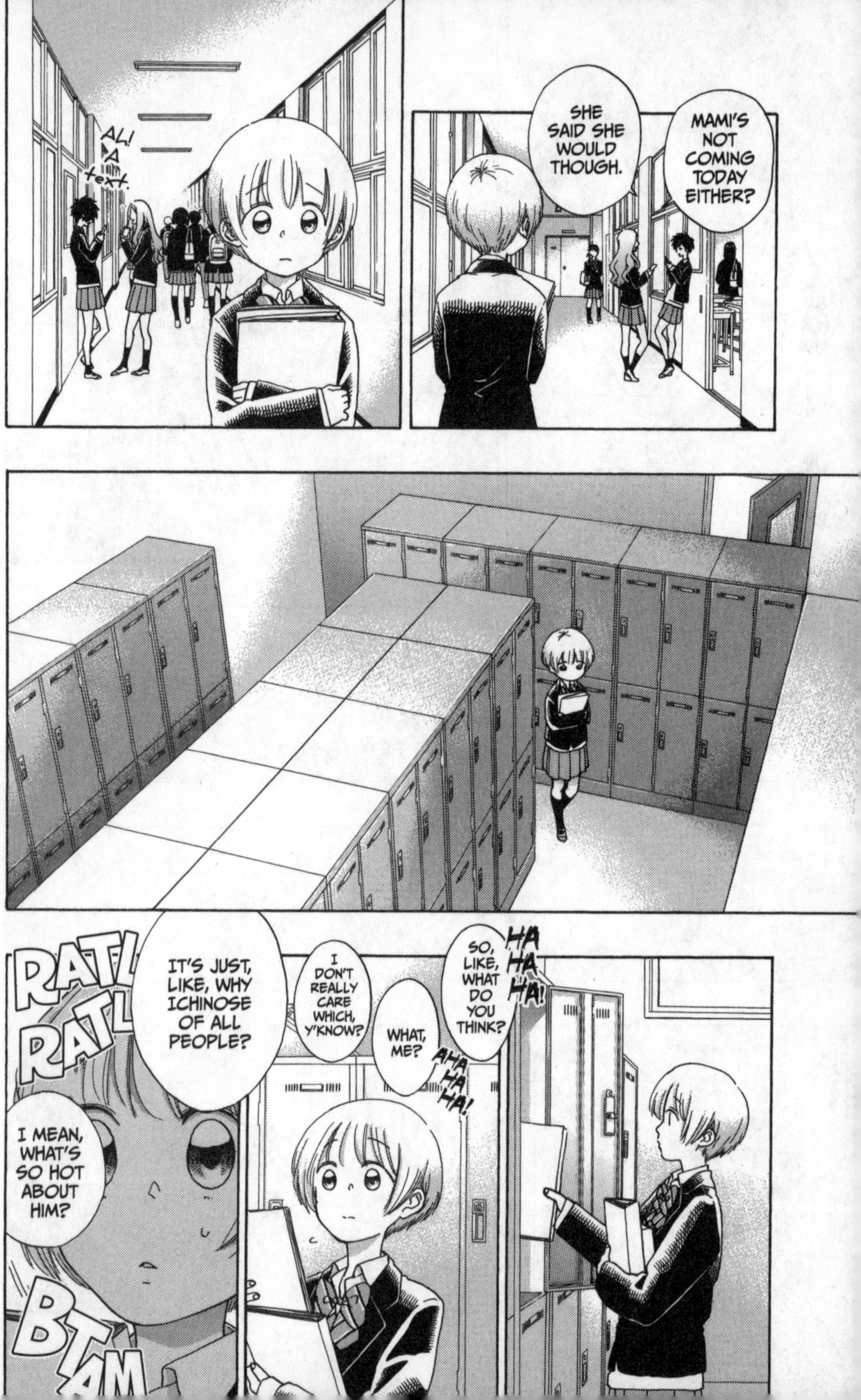

MAMI'S NOT COMING TODAY EITHER?
SHE SAID SHE WOULD THOUGH.
AH! A text.
HA HA HA!
SO, LIKE, WHAT DO YOU THINK?
AHA HA HA!
WHAT, ME?
I DON'T REALLY CARE WHICH, Y'KNOW?
IT'S JUST, LIKE, WHY ICHINOSE OF ALL PEOPLE?
RATL
RATL
I MEAN, WHAT'S SO HOT ABOUT HIM?
BTAM

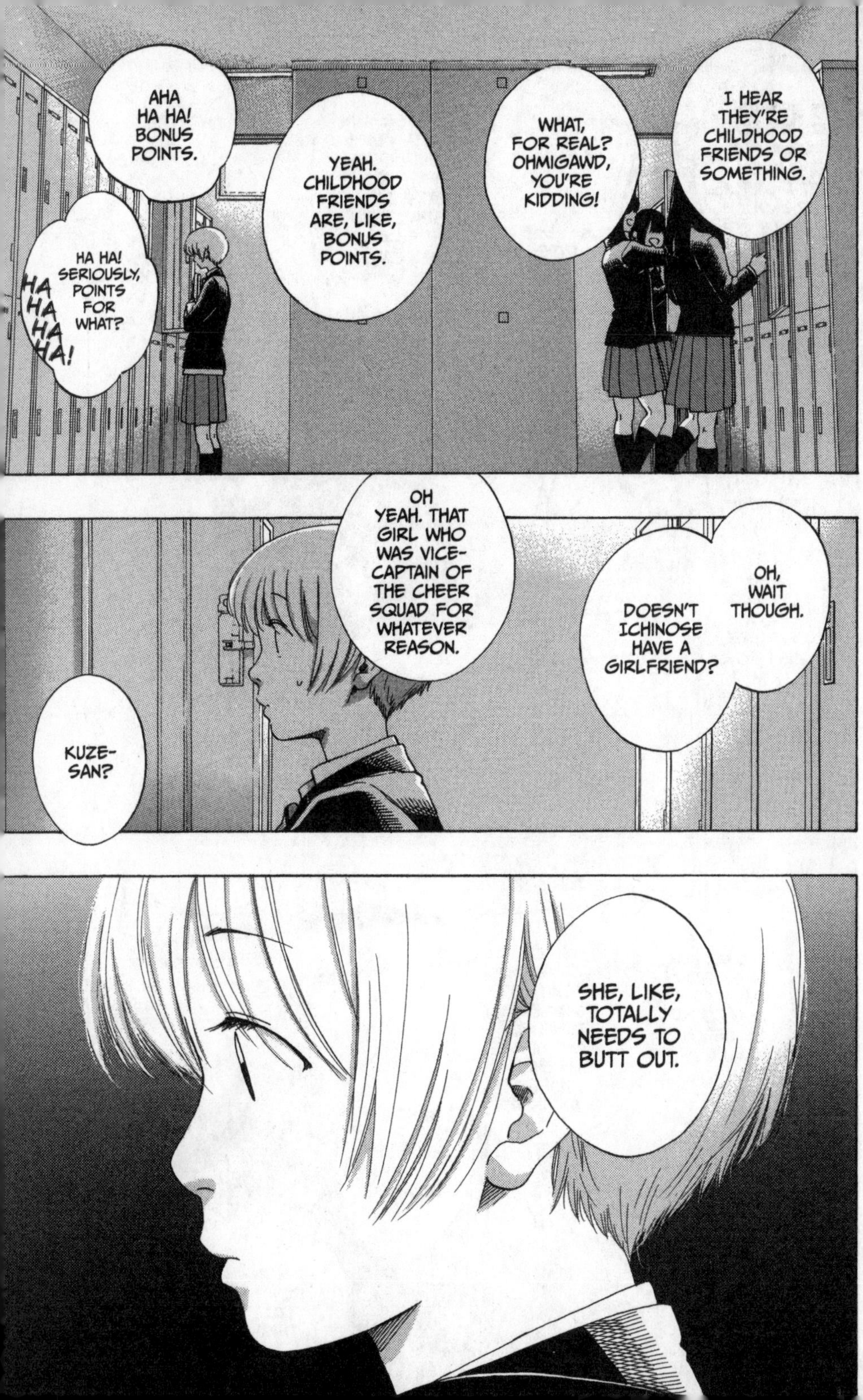
I HEAR THEY'RE CHILDHOOD FRIENDS OR SOMETHING.
WHAT, FOR REAL? OHMIGAWD, YOU'RE KIDDING!
YEAH. CHILDHOOD FRIENDS ARE, LIKE, BONUS POINTS.
AHA HA HA! BONUS POINTS.
HA HA! SERIOUSLY, POINTS FOR WHAT?
HA HA HA HA!
OH, WAIT THOUGH.
DOESN'T ICHINOSE HAVE A GIRLFRIEND?
OH YEAH. THAT GIRL WHO WAS VICE-CAPTAIN OF THE CHEER SQUAD FOR WHATEVER REASON.
KUZE-SAN?
SHE, LIKE, TOTALLY NEEDS TO BUTT OUT.

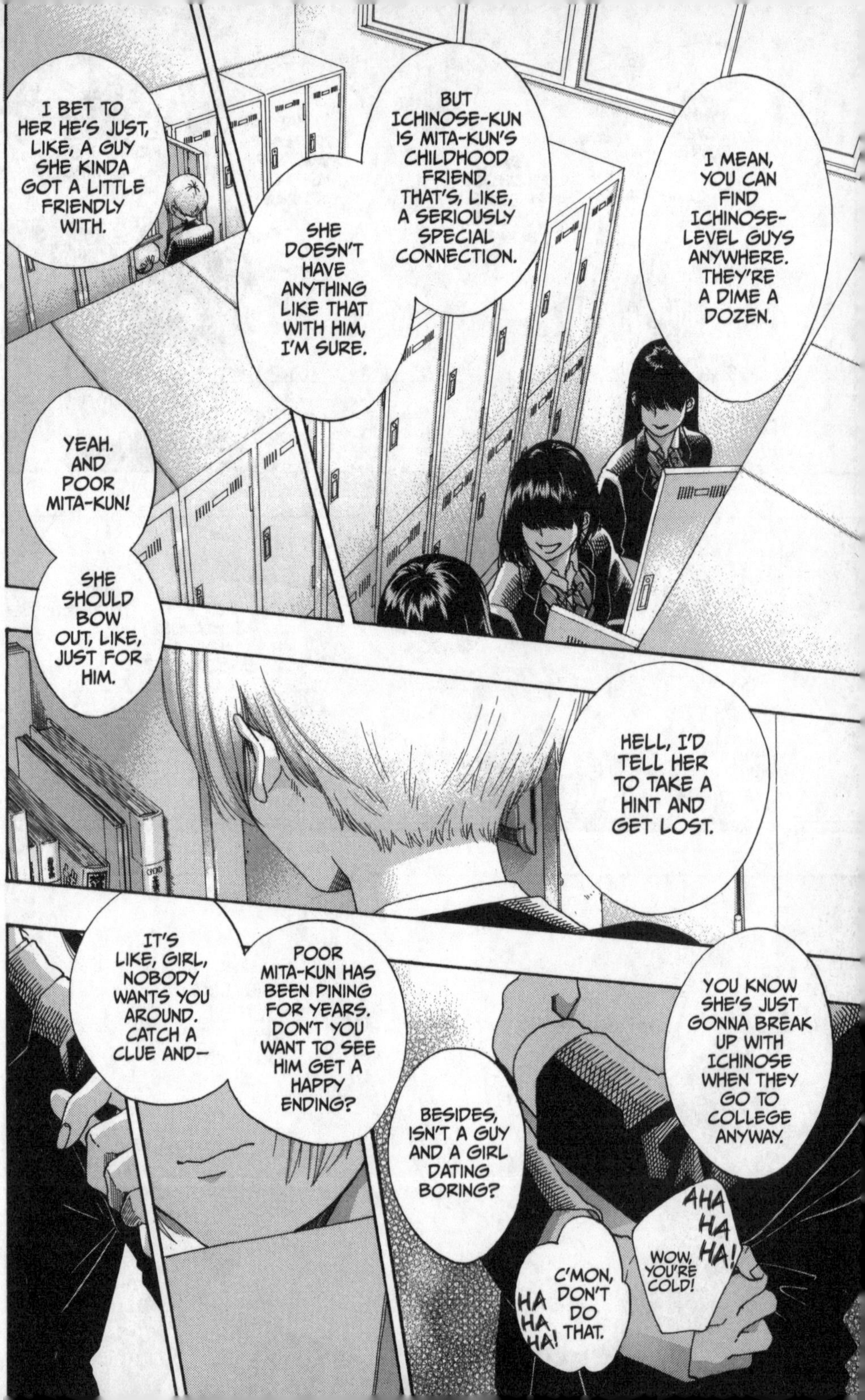
I MEAN, YOU CAN FIND ICHINOSE-LEVEL GUYS ANYWHERE. THEY'RE A DIME A DOZEN.
BUT ICHINOSE-KUN IS MITA-KUN'S CHILDHOOD FRIEND. THAT'S, LIKE, A SERIOUSLY SPECIAL CONNECTION.
SHE DOESN'T HAVE ANYTHING LIKE THAT WITH HIM, I'M SURE.
I BET TO HER HE'S JUST, LIKE, A GUY SHE KINDA GOT A LITTLE FRIENDLY WITH.
YEAH. AND POOR MITA-KUN!
SHE SHOULD BOW OUT, LIKE, JUST FOR HIM.
HELL, I'D TELL HER TO TAKE A HINT AND GET LOST.
YOU KNOW SHE'S JUST GONNA BREAK UP WITH ICHINOSE WHEN THEY GO TO COLLEGE ANYWAY.
POOR MITA-KUN HAS BEEN PINING FOR YEARS. DON'T YOU WANT TO SEE HIM GET A HAPPY ENDING?
IT'S LIKE, GIRL, NOBODY WANTS YOU AROUND. CATCH A CLUE AND—
BESIDES, ISN'T A GUY AND A GIRL DATING BORING?
AHA HA HA!
WOW, YOU'RE COLD!
C'MON, DON'T DO THAT.
HA HA HA!

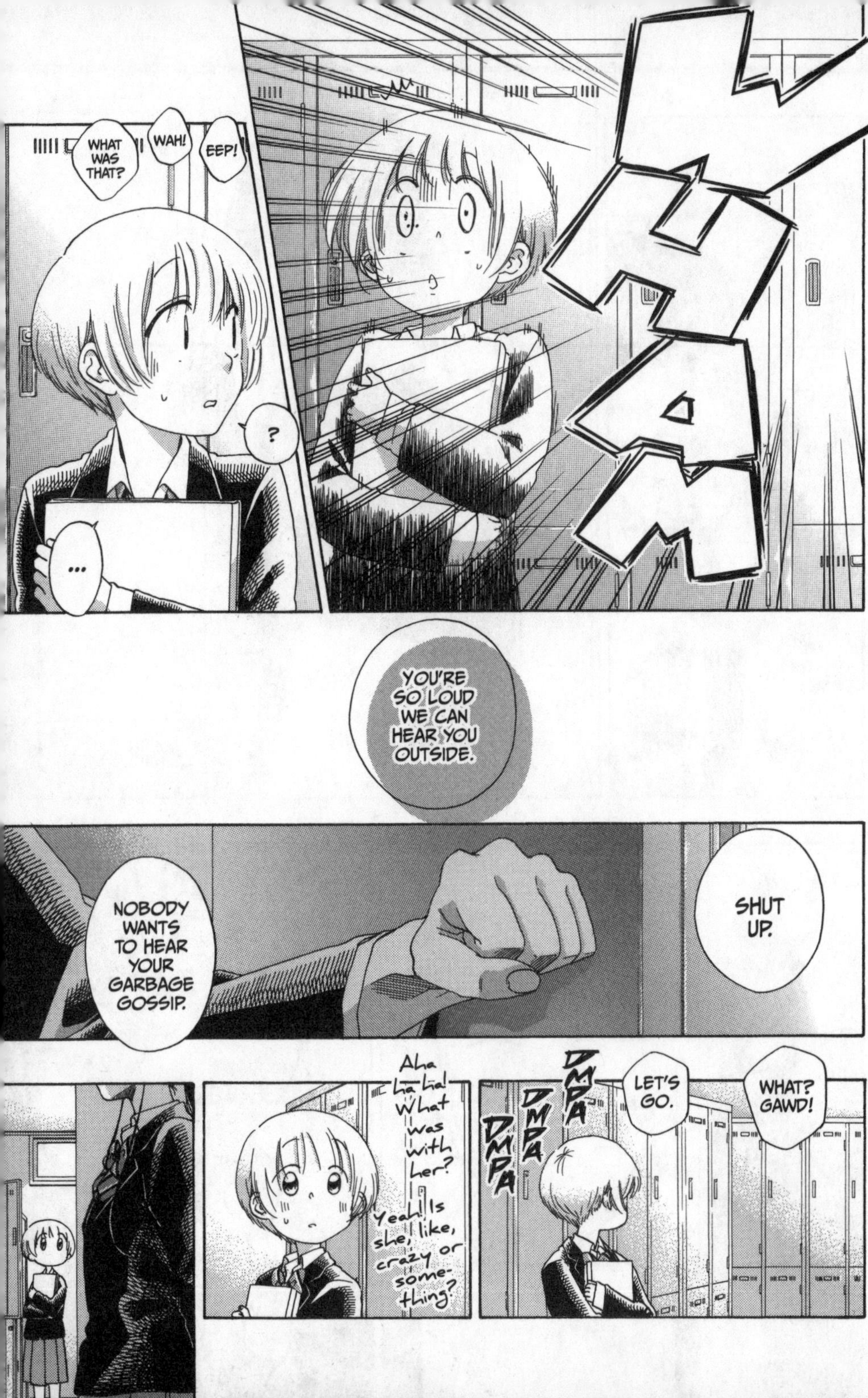
EEP!
WAH!
WHAT WAS THAT?
?
...
YOU'RE SO LOUD WE CAN HEAR YOU OUTSIDE.
SHUT UP.
NOBODY WANTS TO HEAR YOUR GARBAGE GOSSIP.
WHAT? GAWD!
LET'S GO.
DMPA DMPA DMPA
Aha ha ha! What was with her?
Yeah! Is she, like, crazy or something?

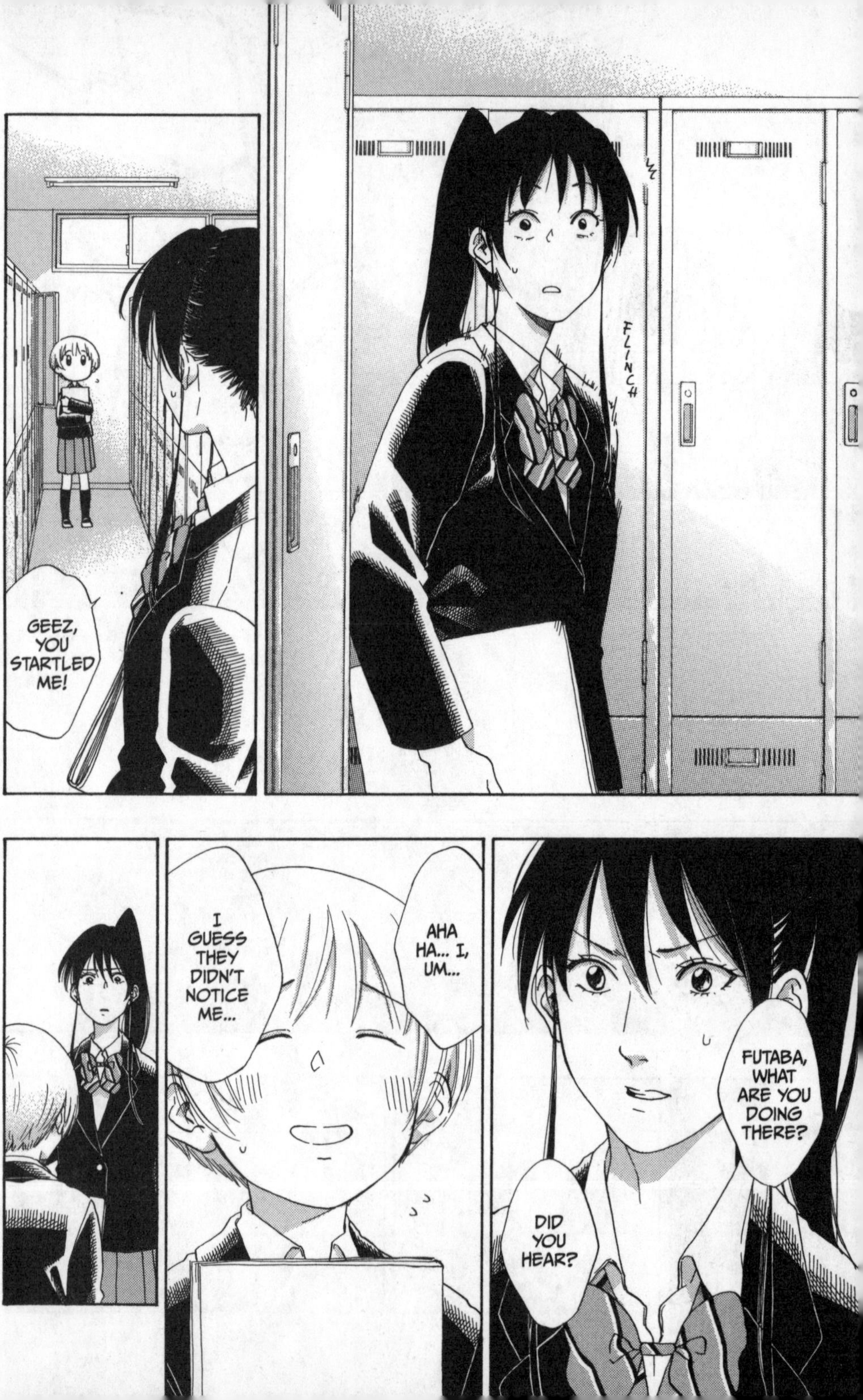
FLINCH
GEEZ, YOU STARTLED ME!
FUTABA, WHAT ARE YOU DOING THERE?
DID YOU HEAR?
AHA HA... I, UM...
I GUESS THEY DIDN'T NOTICE ME...

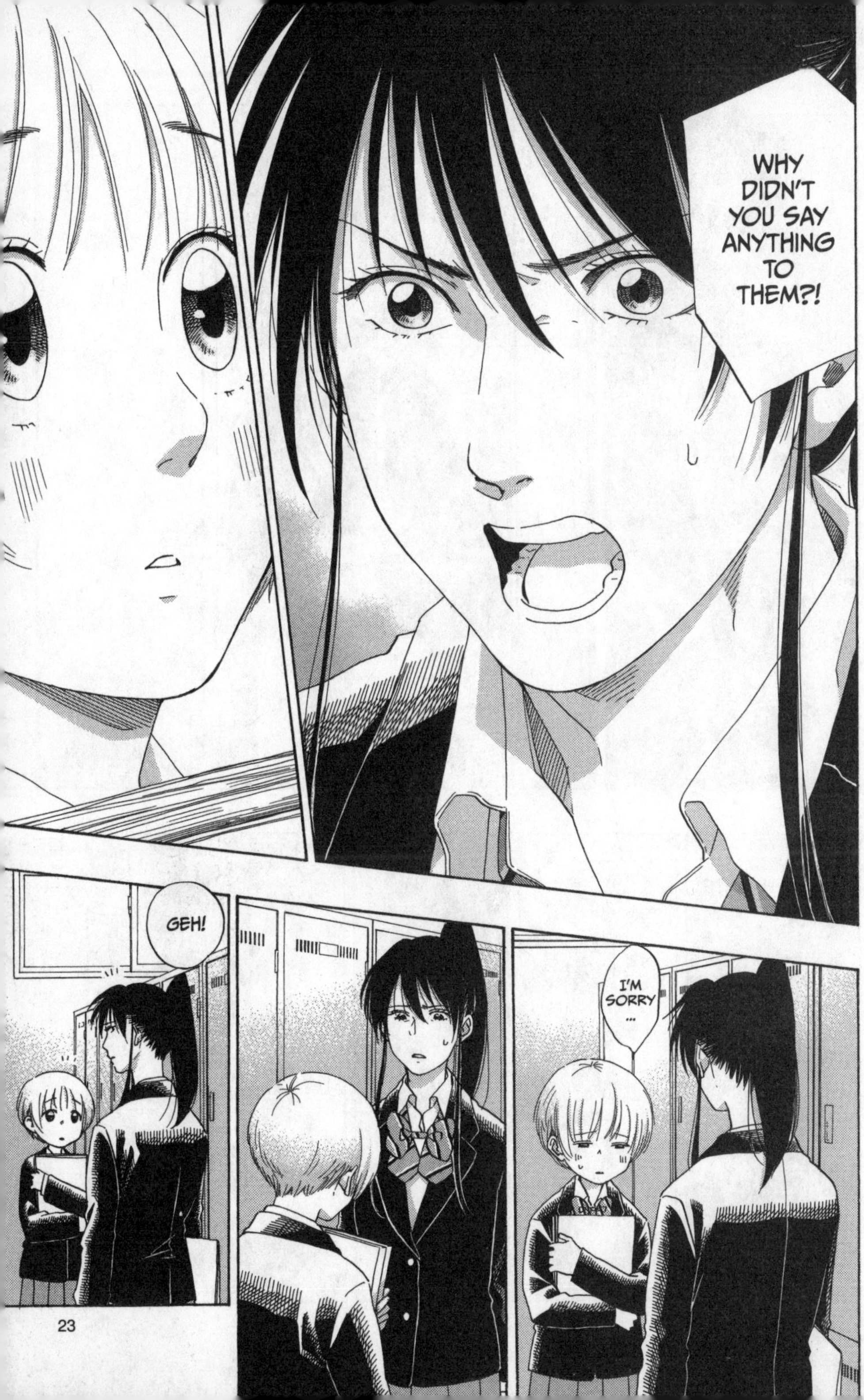
WHY DIDN'T YOU SAY ANYTHING TO THEM?!
I'M SORRY ...
GEH!

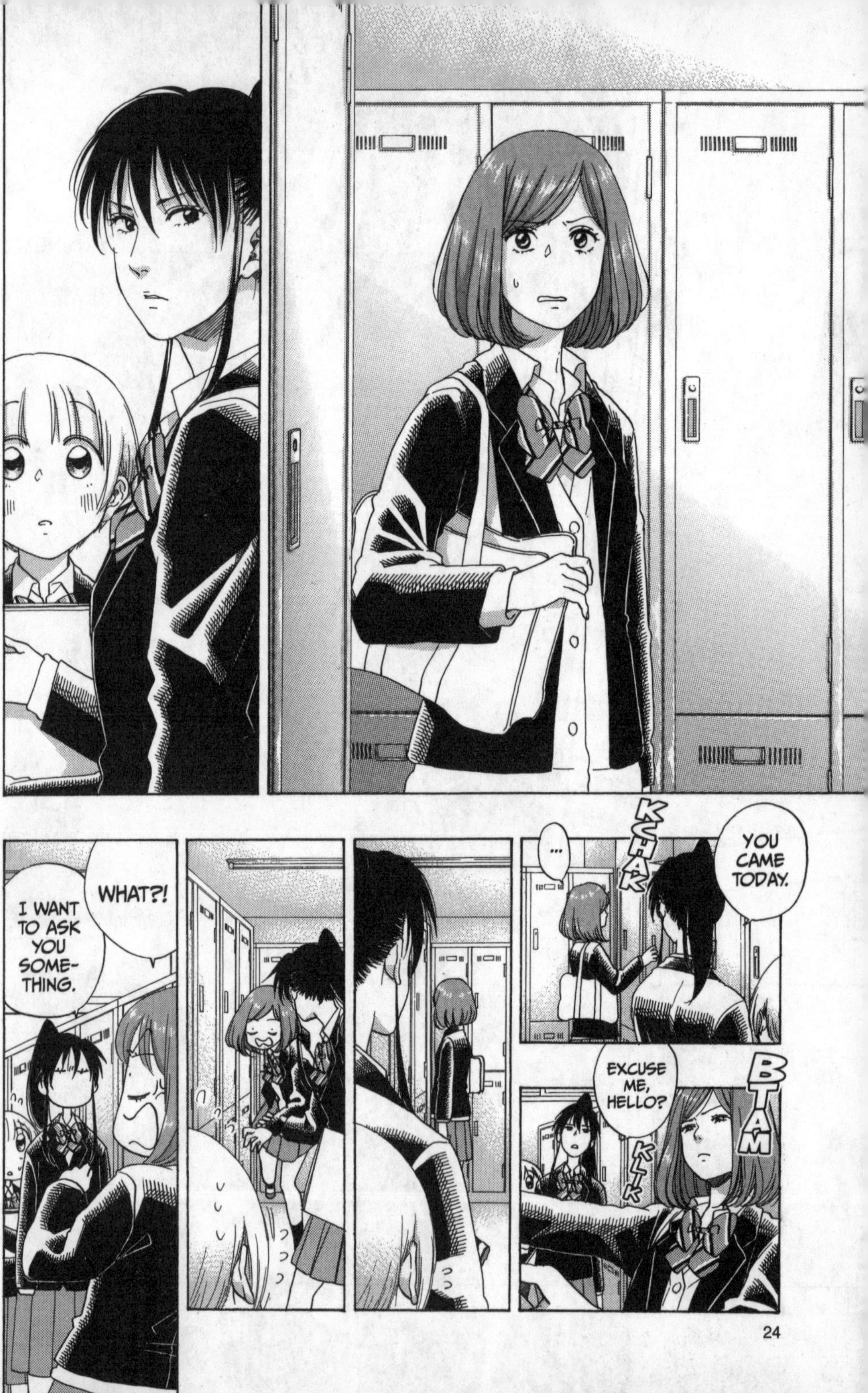
YOU CAME TODAY.
KCHAK
...
BTAM
EXCUSE ME, HELLO?
KLIK
WHAT?!
I WANT TO ASK YOU SOME-THING.

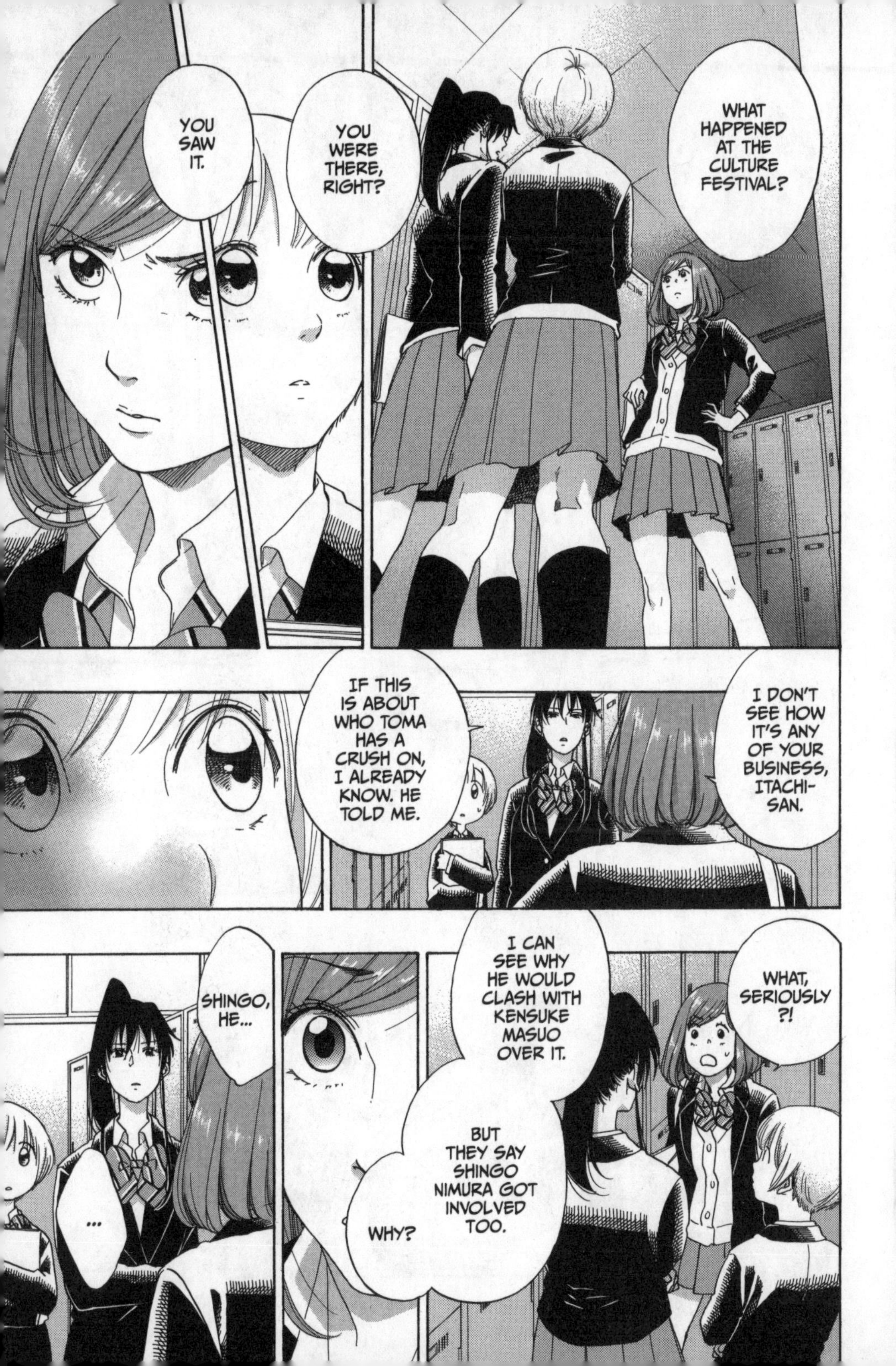
WHAT HAPPENED AT THE CULTURE FESTIVAL?
YOU WERE THERE, RIGHT?
YOU SAW IT.
I DON'T SEE HOW IT'S ANY OF YOUR BUSINESS, ITACHI-SAN.
IF THIS IS ABOUT WHO TOMA HAS A CRUSH ON, I ALREADY KNOW. HE TOLD ME.
WHAT, SERIOUSLY?!
I CAN SEE WHY HE WOULD CLASH WITH KENSUKE MASUO OVER IT.
BUT THEY SAY SHINGO NIMURA GOT INVOLVED TOO.
WHY?
SHINGO, HE...
...

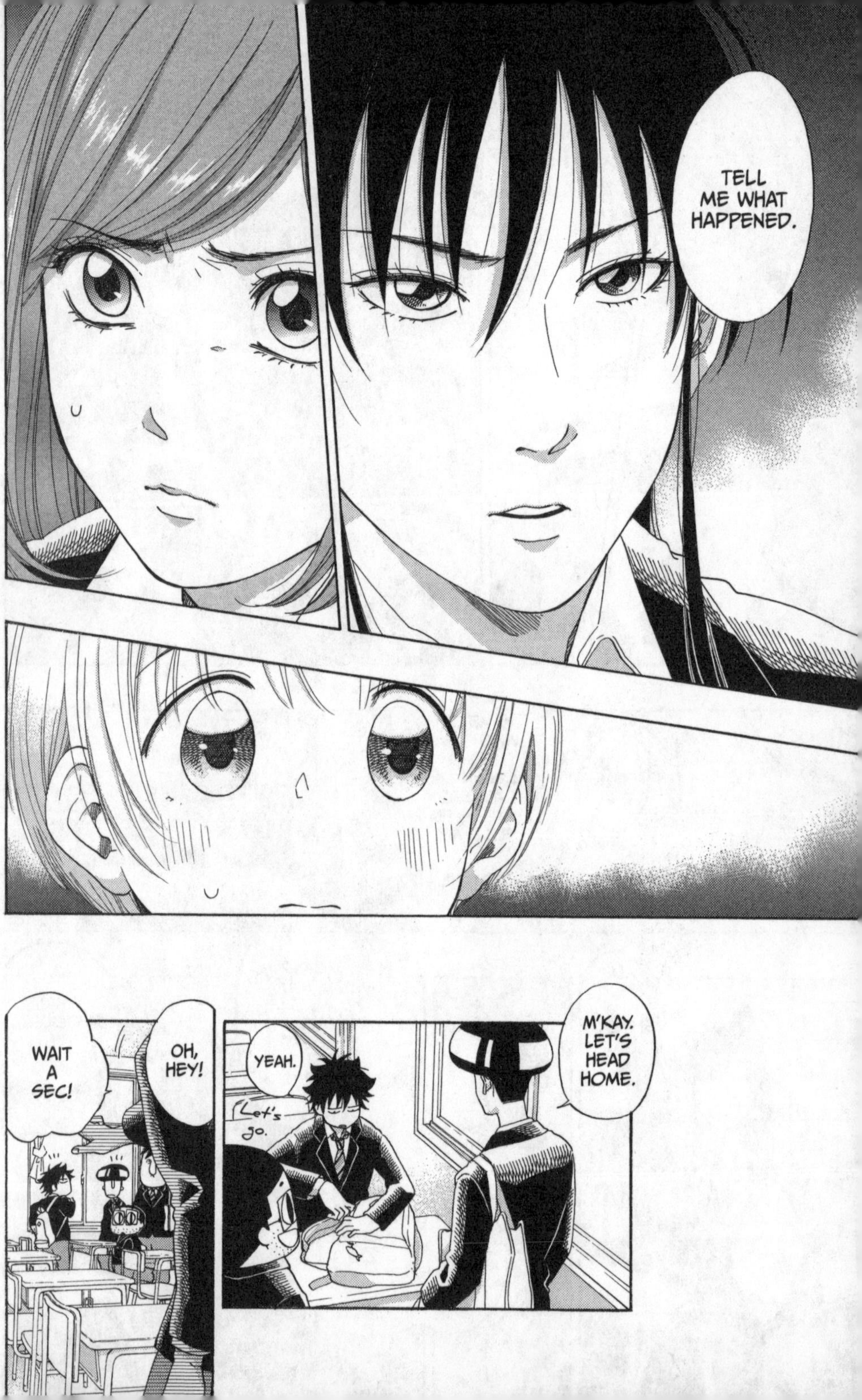
TELL ME WHAT HAPPENED.
M'KAY. LET'S HEAD HOME.
YEAH.
Let's go.
OH, HEY!
WAIT A SEC!

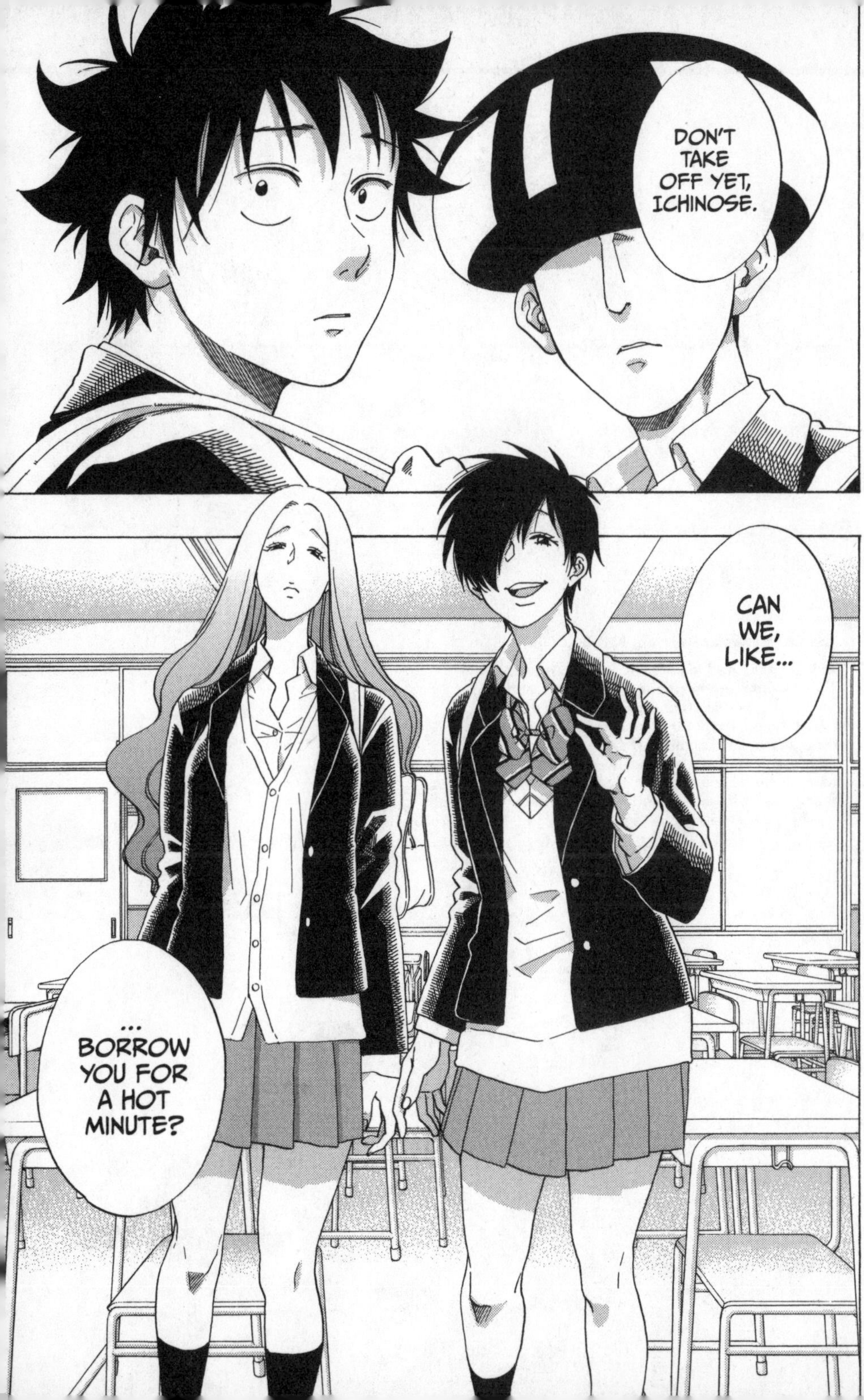
DON'T TAKE OFF YET, ICHINOSE.
CAN WE, LIKE...
... BORROW YOU FOR A HOT MINUTE?

The Characters as Animals, Part 6

At first I imagined Mami's two friends as cats.
Then I wound up making Mami, Kensuke and
Shingo raptors, so I thought it best to stick with
a bird theme. I'm not too familiar with birds,
though. I looked up this and that and went
off of appearance in the end, making Shoko a
flamingo and Saya a toucan. Having looked into
them, though, I have to say toucans are cute.
Really, really cute. Almost too cute.

CHAPTER 43

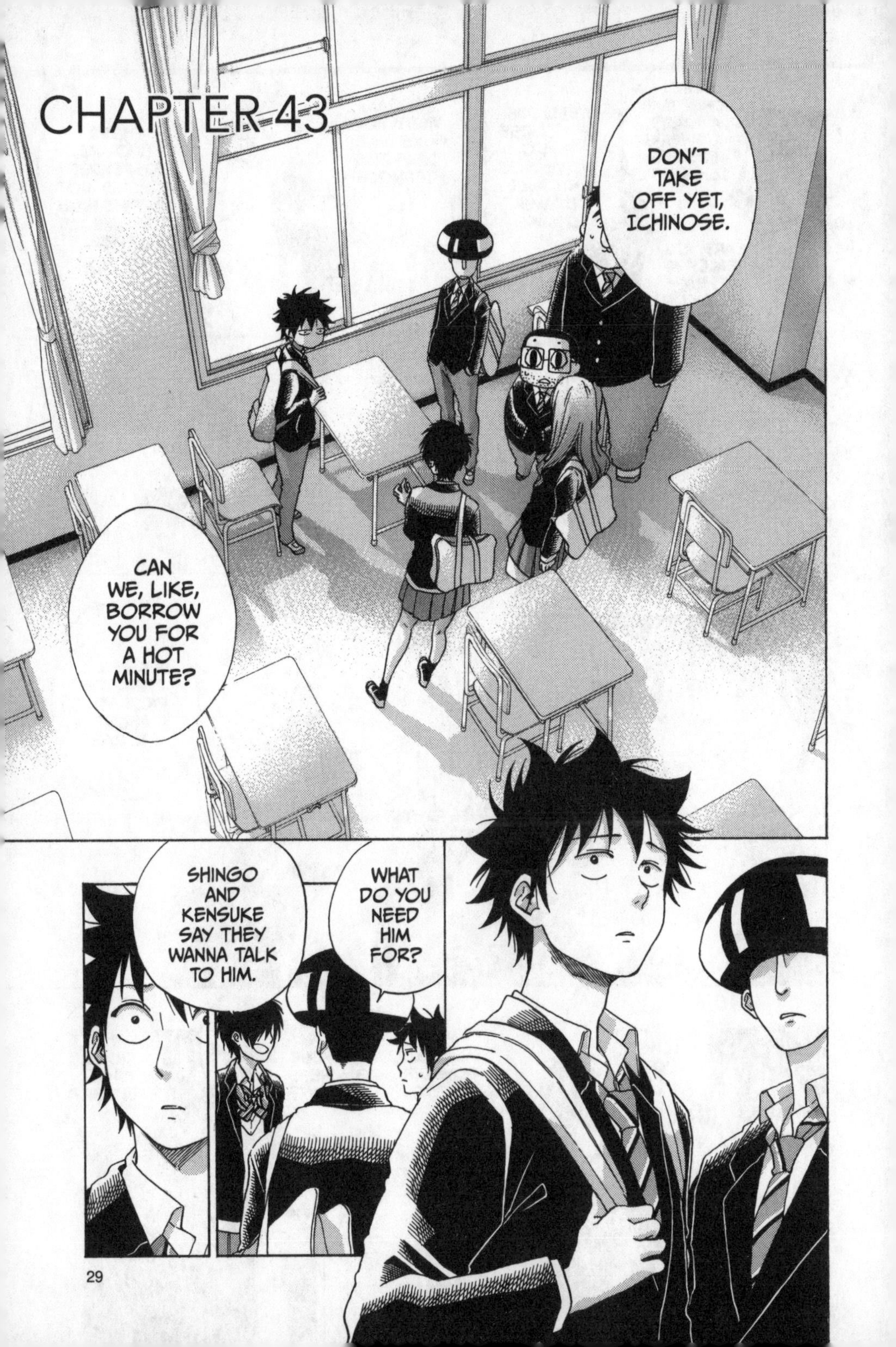
DON'T TAKE OFF YET, ICHINOSE.
CAN WE, LIKE, BORROW YOU FOR A HOT MINUTE?
WHAT DO YOU NEED HIM FOR?
SHINGO AND KENSUKE SAY THEY WANNA TALK TO HIM.

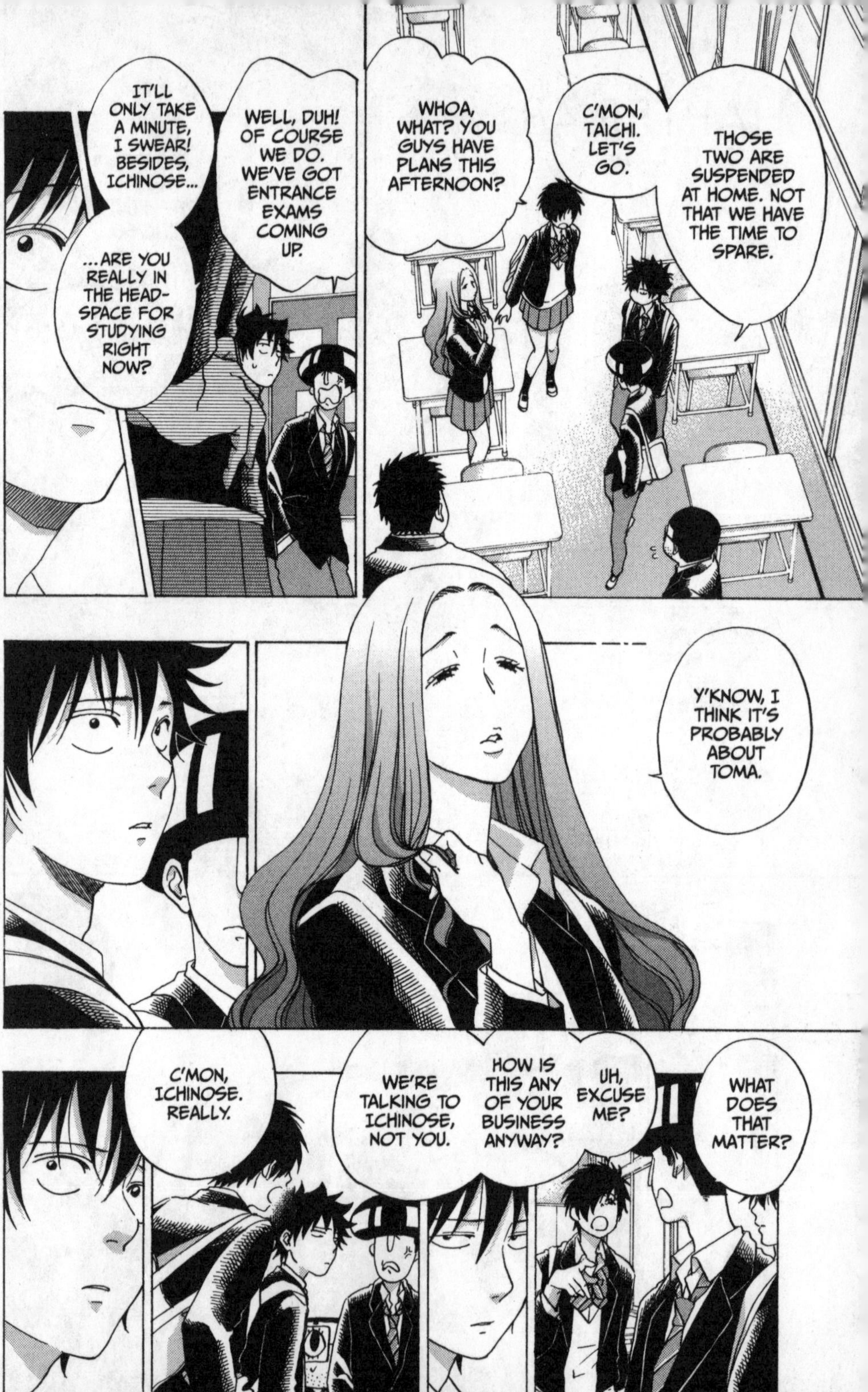
THOSE TWO ARE SUSPENDED AT HOME. NOT THAT WE HAVE THE TIME TO SPARE.
C'MON, TAICHI. LET'S GO.
WHOA, WHAT? YOU GUYS HAVE PLANS THIS AFTERNOON?
WELL, DUH! OF COURSE WE DO. WE'VE GOT ENTRANCE EXAMS COMING UP.
IT'LL ONLY TAKE A MINUTE, I SWEAR! BESIDES, ICHINOSE...
...ARE YOU REALLY IN THE HEAD-SPACE FOR STUDYING RIGHT NOW?
Y'KNOW, I THINK IT'S PROBABLY ABOUT TOMA.
WHAT DOES THAT MATTER?
UH, EXCUSE ME?
HOW IS THIS ANY OF YOUR BUSINESS ANYWAY?
WE'RE TALKING TO ICHINOSE, NOT YOU.
C'MON, ICHINOSE. REALLY.

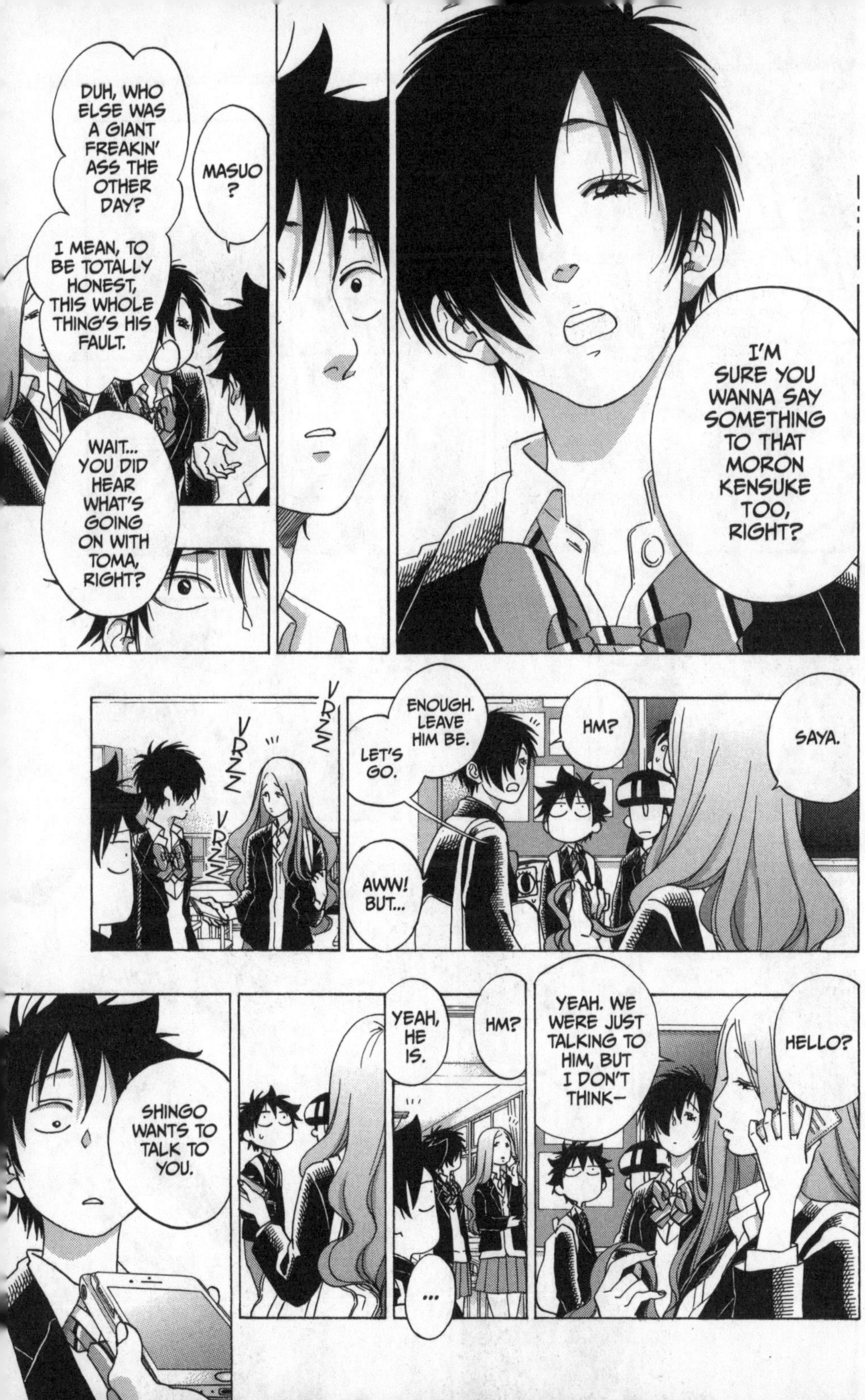
I'M SURE YOU WANNA SAY SOMETHING TO THAT MORON KENSUKE TOO, RIGHT?
MASUO?
DUH, WHO ELSE WAS A GIANT FREAKIN' ASS THE OTHER DAY?
I MEAN, TO BE TOTALLY HONEST, THIS WHOLE THING'S HIS FAULT.
WAIT... YOU DID HEAR WHAT'S GOING ON WITH TOMA, RIGHT?
SAYA.
HM?
ENOUGH. LEAVE HIM BE.
LET'S GO.
AWW! BUT...
VRZZ
VRZZ
VRZZ
HELLO?
YEAH. WE WERE JUST TALKING TO HIM, BUT I DON'T THINK–
HM?
YEAH, HE IS.
...
SHINGO WANTS TO TALK TO YOU.

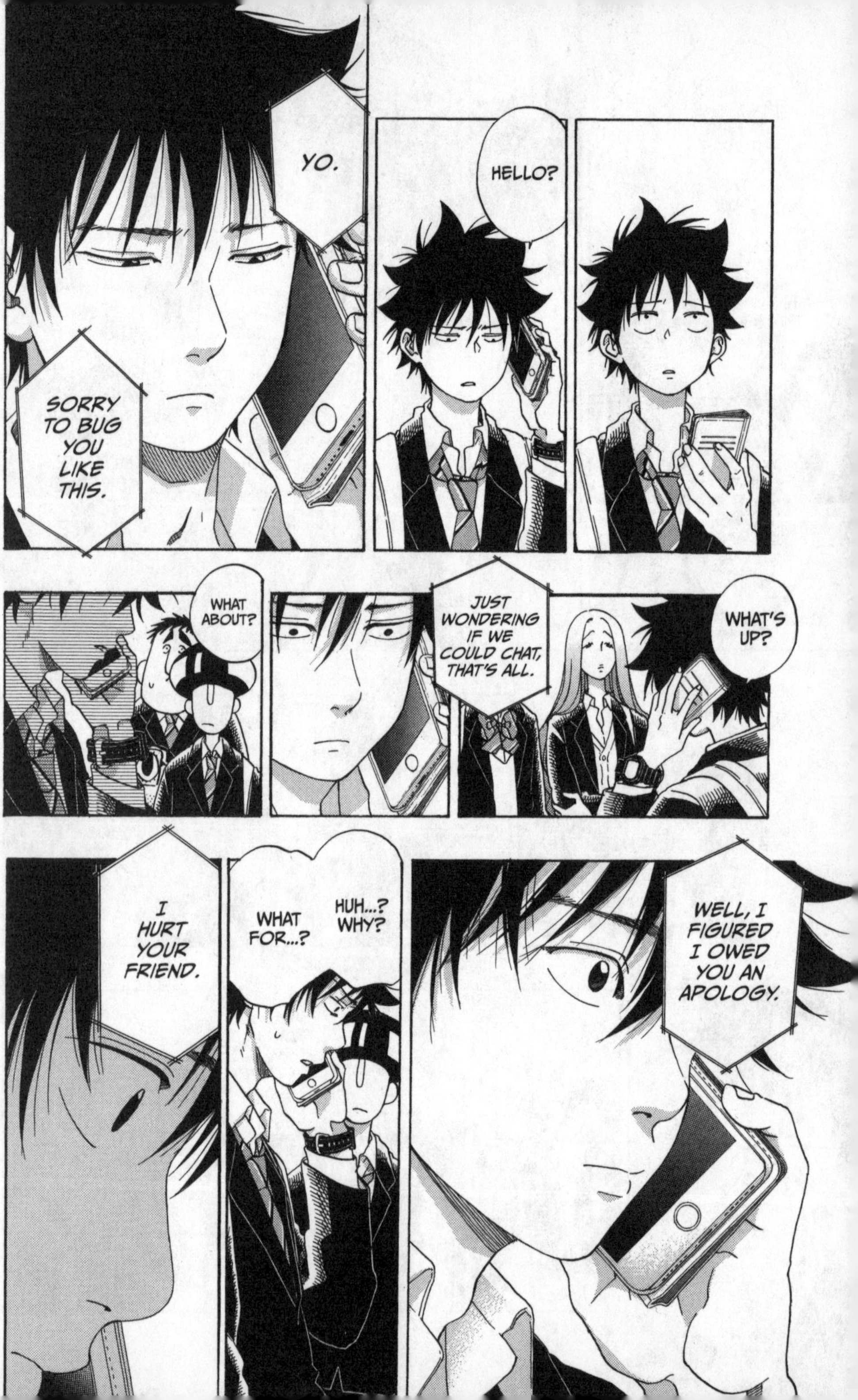
HELLO?
YO.
SORRY TO BUG YOU LIKE THIS.
WHAT'S UP?
JUST WONDERING IF WE COULD CHAT, THAT'S ALL.
WHAT ABOUT?
WELL, I FIGURED I OWED YOU AN APOLOGY.
HUH...? WHY?
WHAT FOR...?
I HURT YOUR FRIEND.

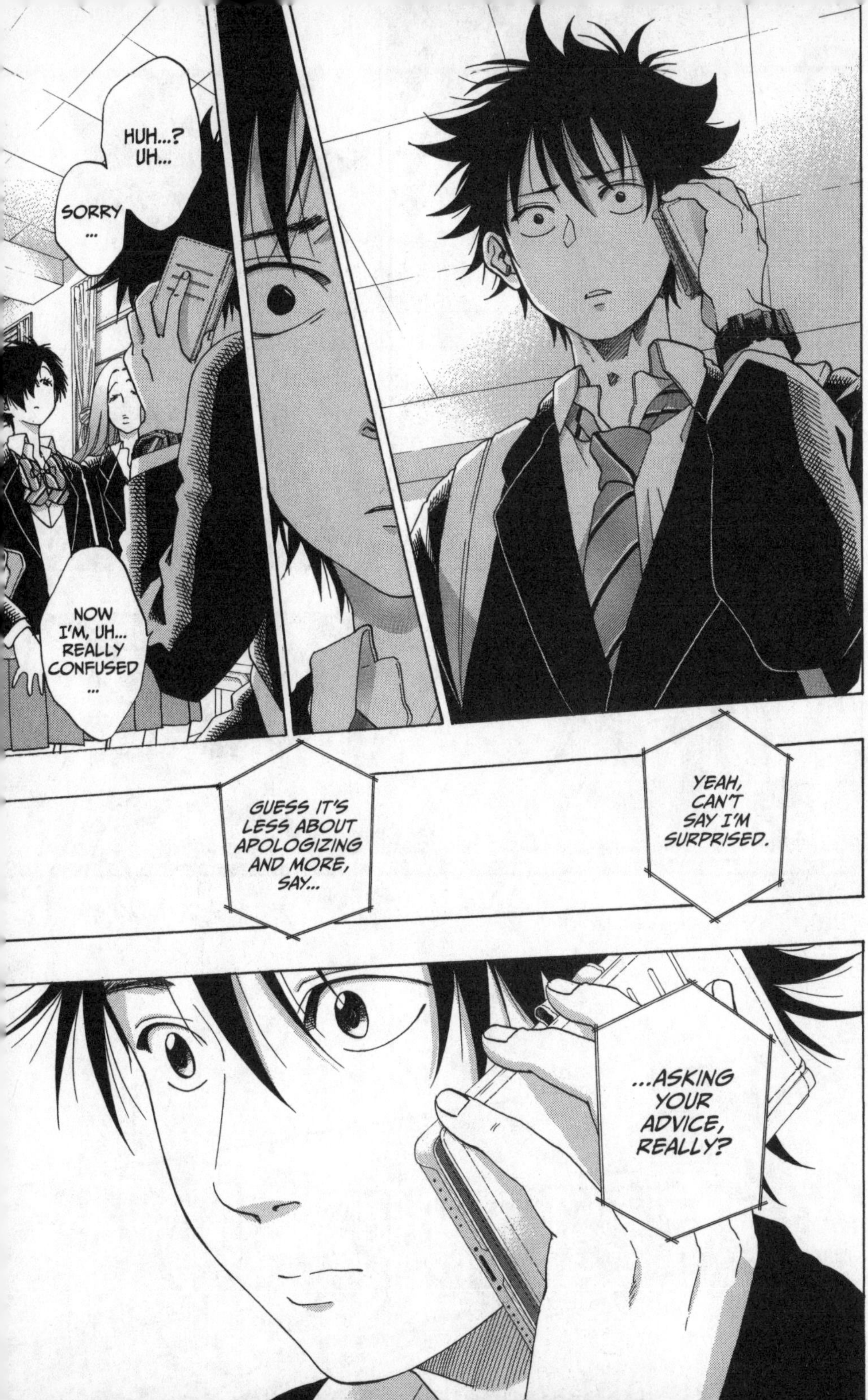
HUH...? UH...
SORRY...
NOW I'M, UH... REALLY CONFUSED...
YEAH, CAN'T SAY I'M SURPRISED.
GUESS IT'S LESS ABOUT APOLOGIZING AND MORE, SAY...
...ASKING YOUR ADVICE, REALLY?

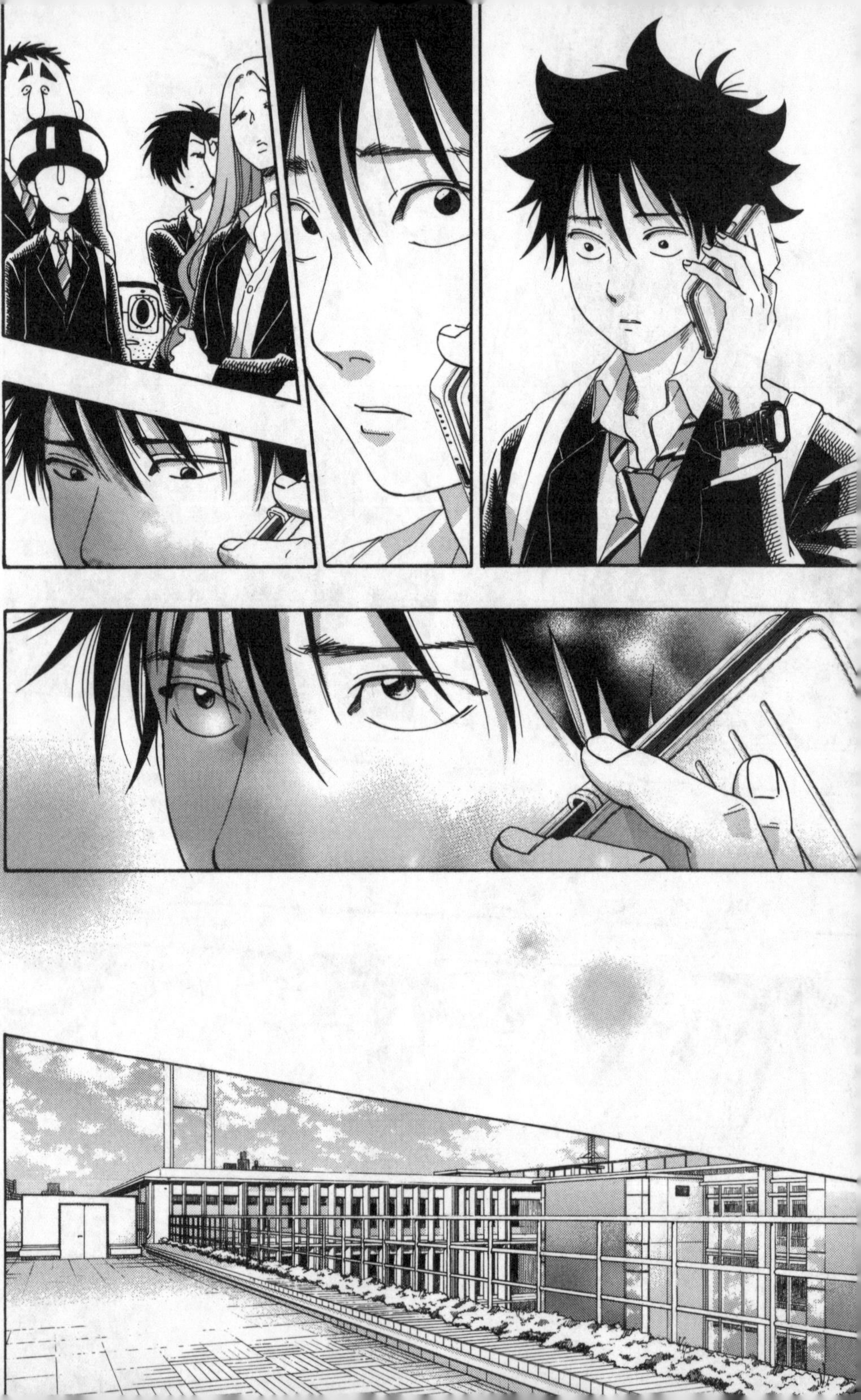

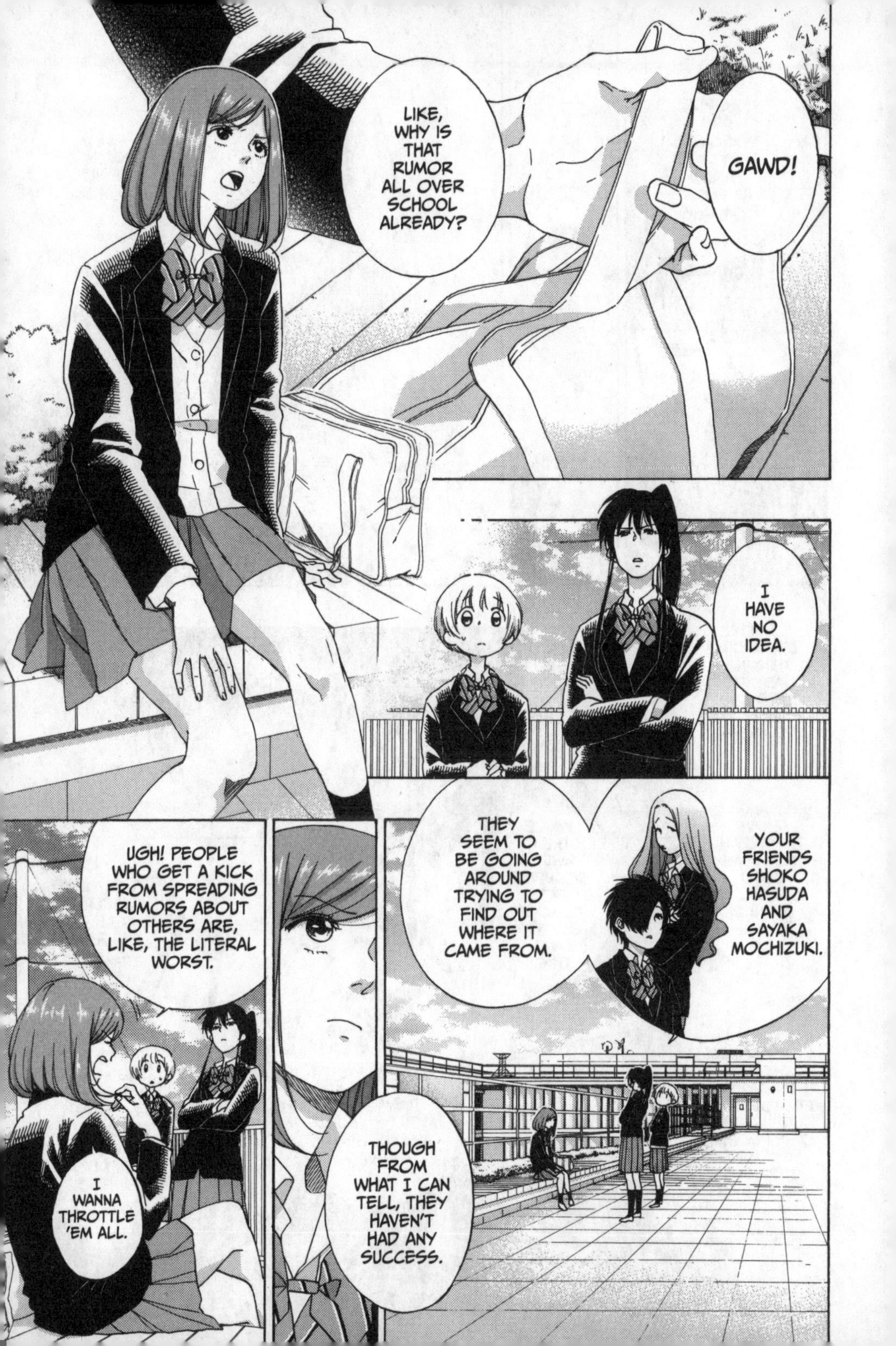
GAWD!
LIKE, WHY IS THAT RUMOR ALL OVER SCHOOL ALREADY?
I HAVE NO IDEA.
YOUR FRIENDS SHOKO HASUDA AND SAYAKA MOCHIZUKI.
THEY SEEM TO BE GOING AROUND TRYING TO FIND OUT WHERE IT CAME FROM.
THOUGH FROM WHAT I CAN TELL, THEY HAVEN'T HAD ANY SUCCESS.
UGH! PEOPLE WHO GET A KICK FROM SPREADING RUMORS ABOUT OTHERS ARE, LIKE, THE LITERAL WORST.
I WANNA THROTTLE 'EM ALL.

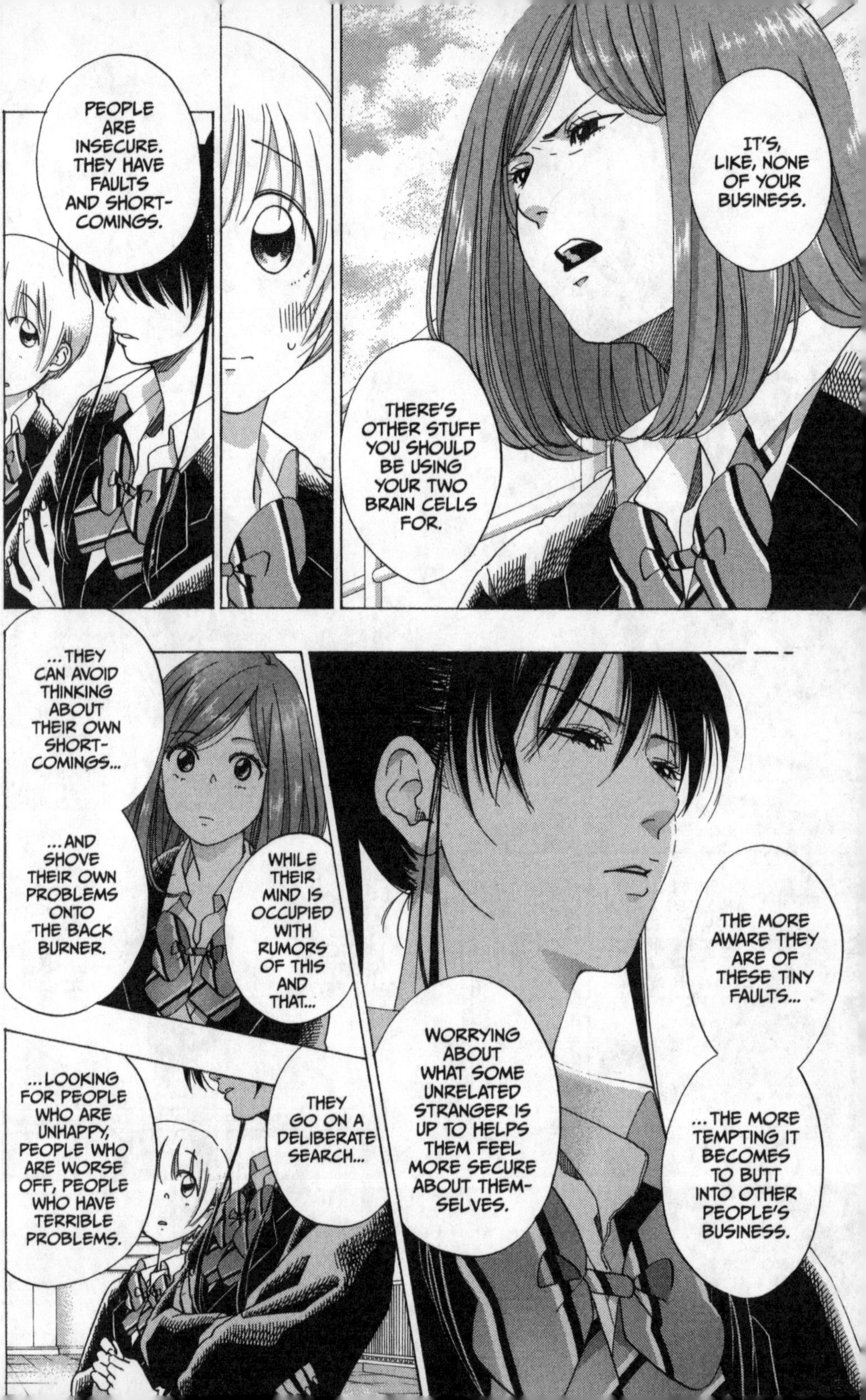
IT'S, LIKE, NONE OF YOUR BUSINESS.
THERE'S OTHER STUFF YOU SHOULD BE USING YOUR TWO BRAIN CELLS FOR.
PEOPLE ARE INSECURE. THEY HAVE FAULTS AND SHORT-COMINGS.
THE MORE AWARE THEY ARE OF THESE TINY FAULTS...
...THE MORE TEMPTING IT BECOMES TO BUTT INTO OTHER PEOPLE'S BUSINESS.
WORRYING ABOUT WHAT SOME UNRELATED STRANGER IS UP TO HELPS THEM FEEL MORE SECURE ABOUT THEM-SELVES.
WHILE THEIR MIND IS OCCUPIED WITH RUMORS OF THIS AND THAT...
...THEY CAN AVOID THINKING ABOUT THEIR OWN SHORT-COMINGS...
...AND SHOVE THEIR OWN PROBLEMS ONTO THE BACK BURNER.
THEY GO ON A DELIBERATE SEARCH...
...LOOKING FOR PEOPLE WHO ARE UNHAPPY, PEOPLE WHO ARE WORSE OFF, PEOPLE WHO HAVE TERRIBLE PROBLEMS.

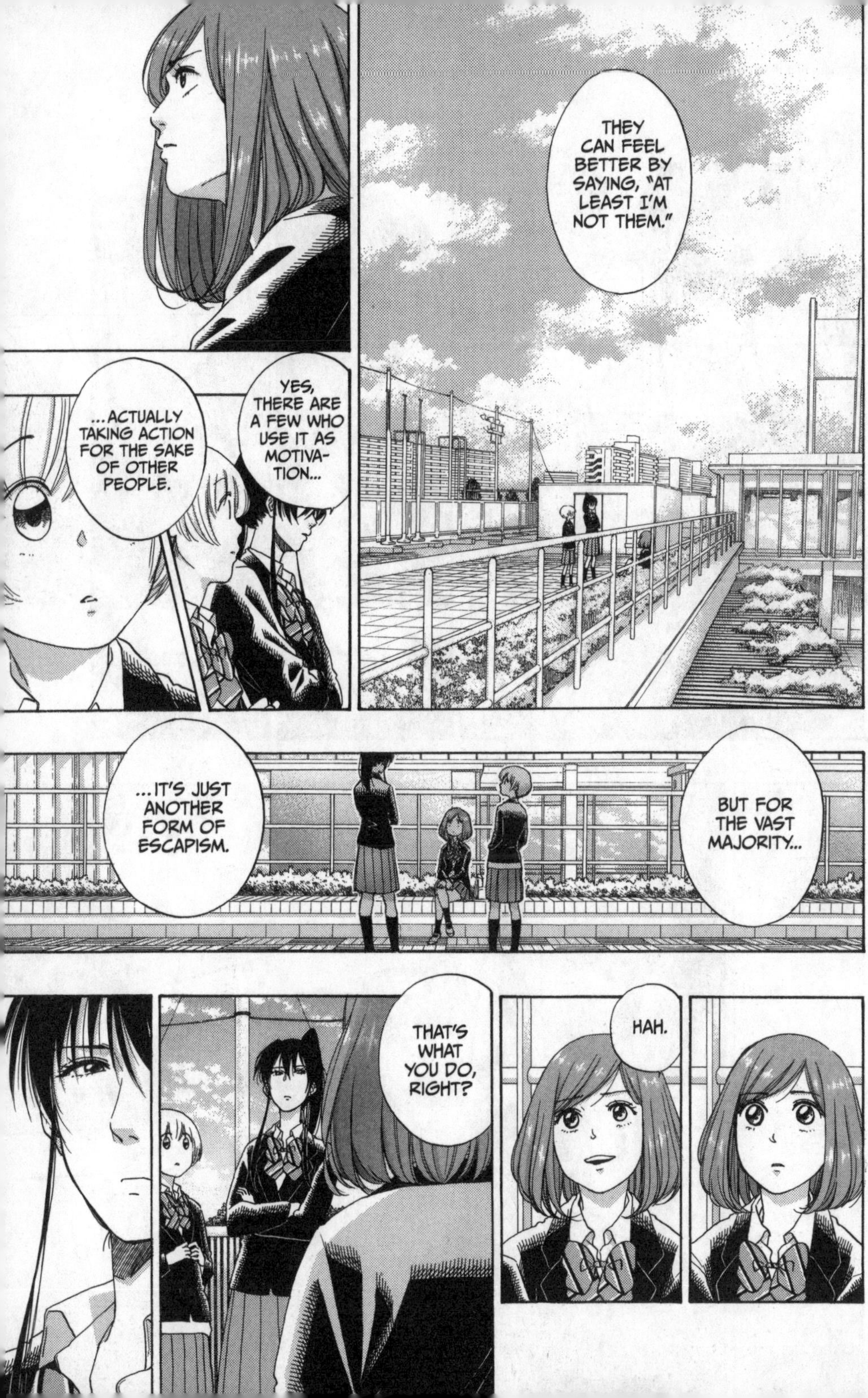
THEY CAN FEEL BETTER BY SAYING, "AT LEAST I'M NOT THEM."
YES, THERE ARE A FEW WHO USE IT AS MOTIVATION...
...ACTUALLY TAKING ACTION FOR THE SAKE OF OTHER PEOPLE.
BUT FOR THE VAST MAJORITY...
...IT'S JUST ANOTHER FORM OF ESCAPISM.
HAH.
THAT'S WHAT YOU DO, RIGHT?

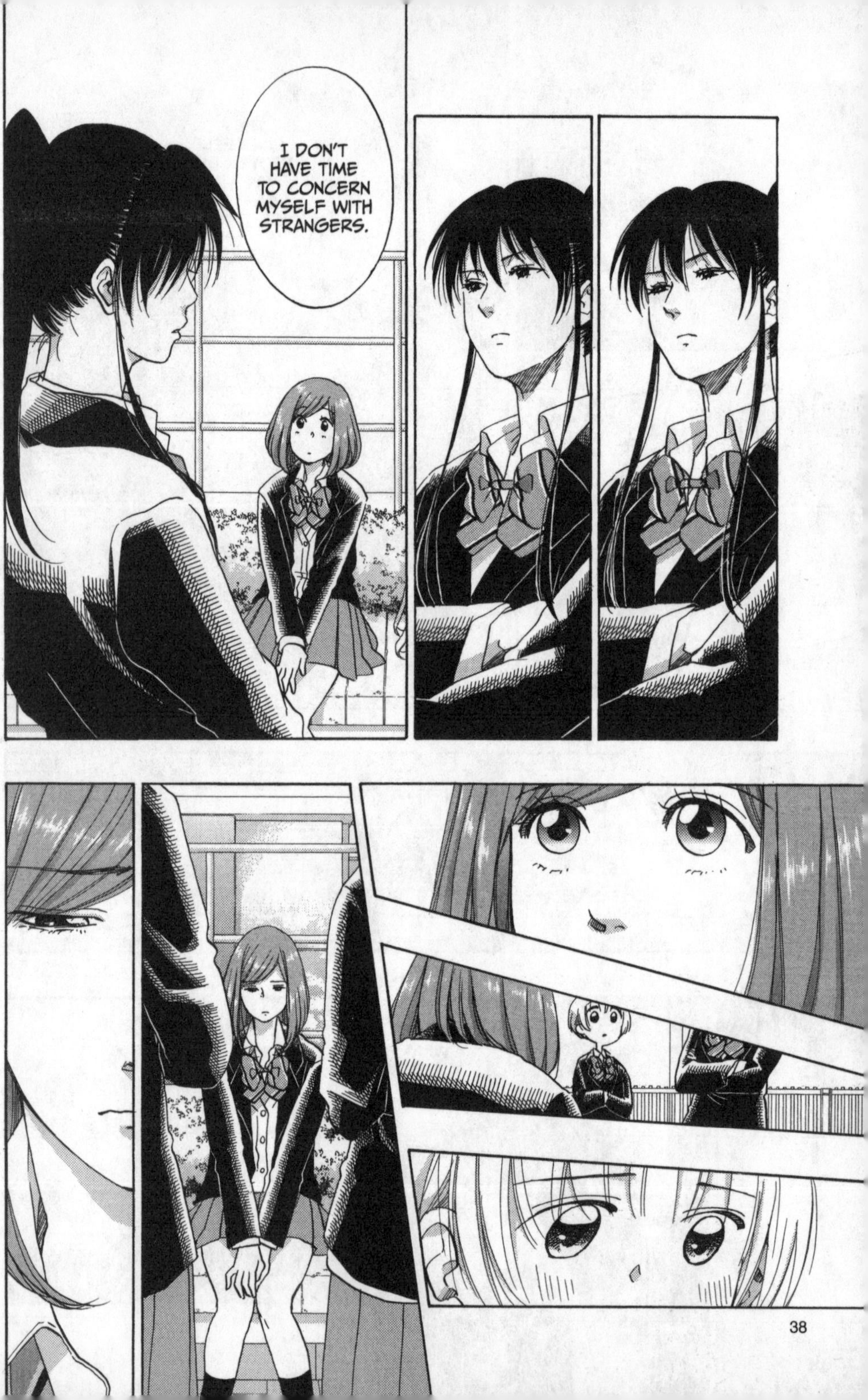
I DON'T HAVE TIME TO CONCERN MYSELF WITH STRANGERS.

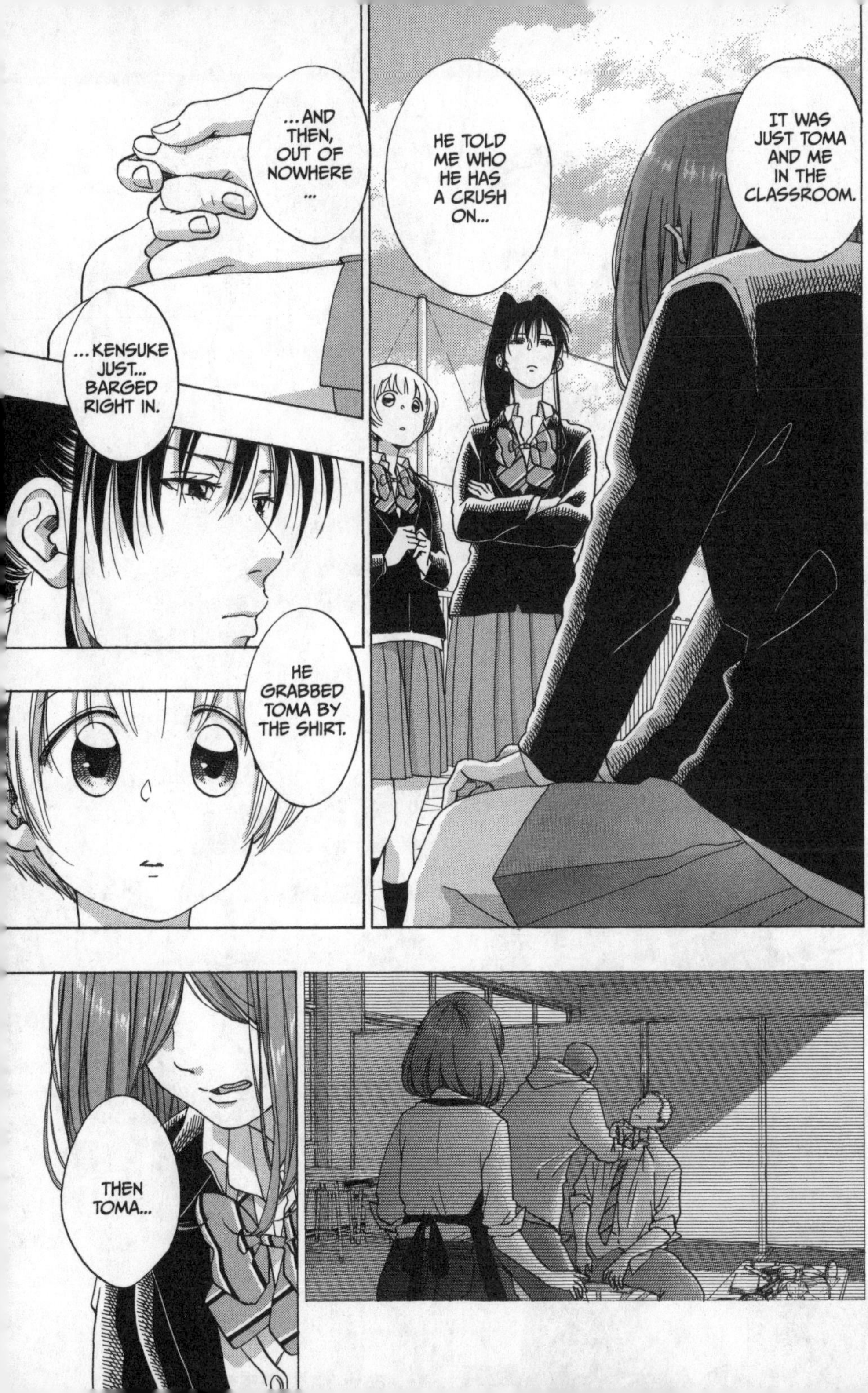
IT WAS JUST TOMA AND ME IN THE CLASSROOM.
HE TOLD ME WHO HE HAS A CRUSH ON...
...AND THEN, OUT OF NOWHERE...
...KENSUKE JUST... BARGED RIGHT IN.
HE GRABBED TOMA BY THE SHIRT.
THEN TOMA...

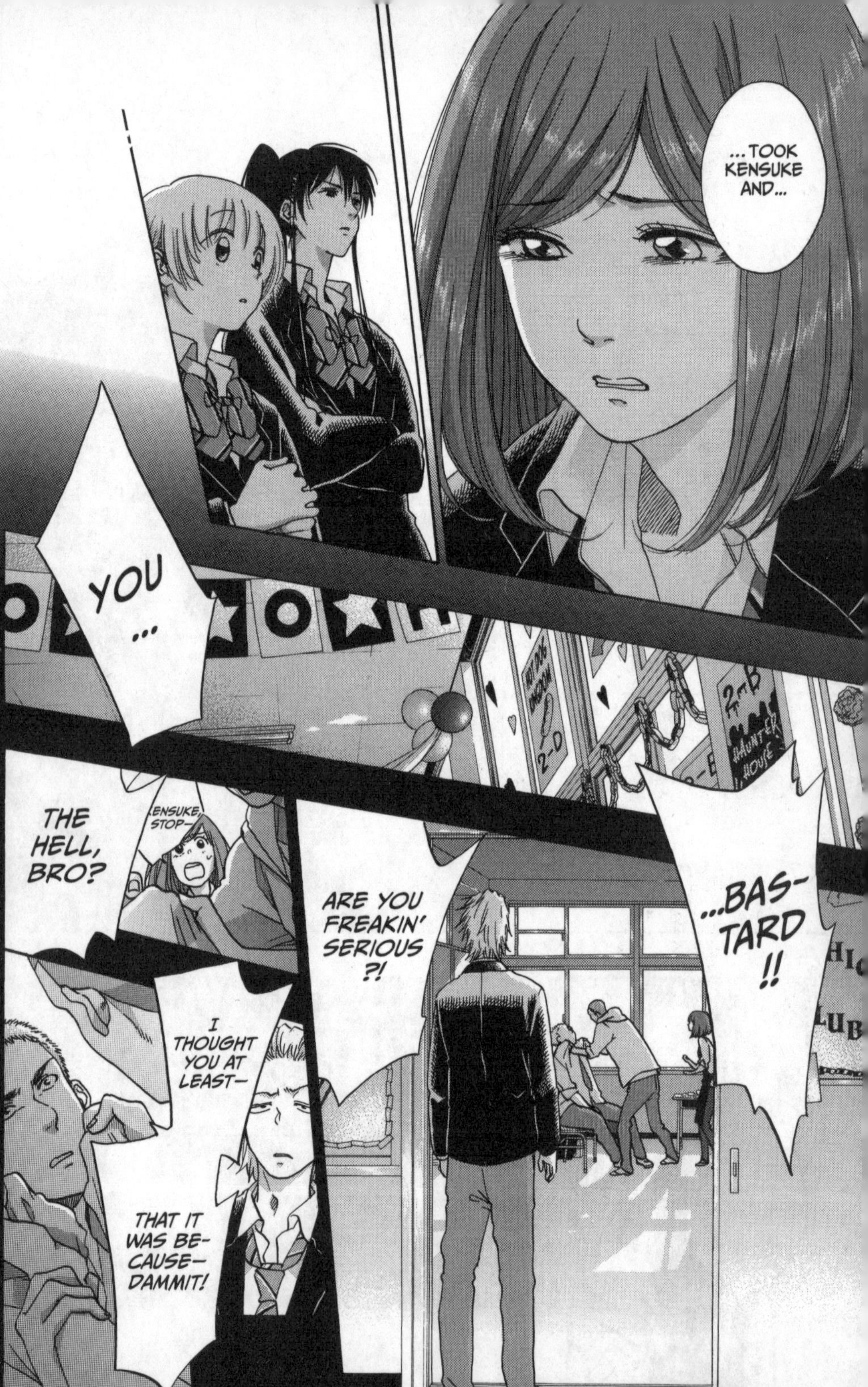
...TOOK KENSUKE AND...
YOU ...
...BAS- TARD !!
ARE YOU FREAKIN' SERIOUS ?!
KENSUKE, STOP—
THE HELL, BRO?
I THOUGHT YOU AT LEAST—
THAT IT WAS BE- CAUSE— DAMMIT!

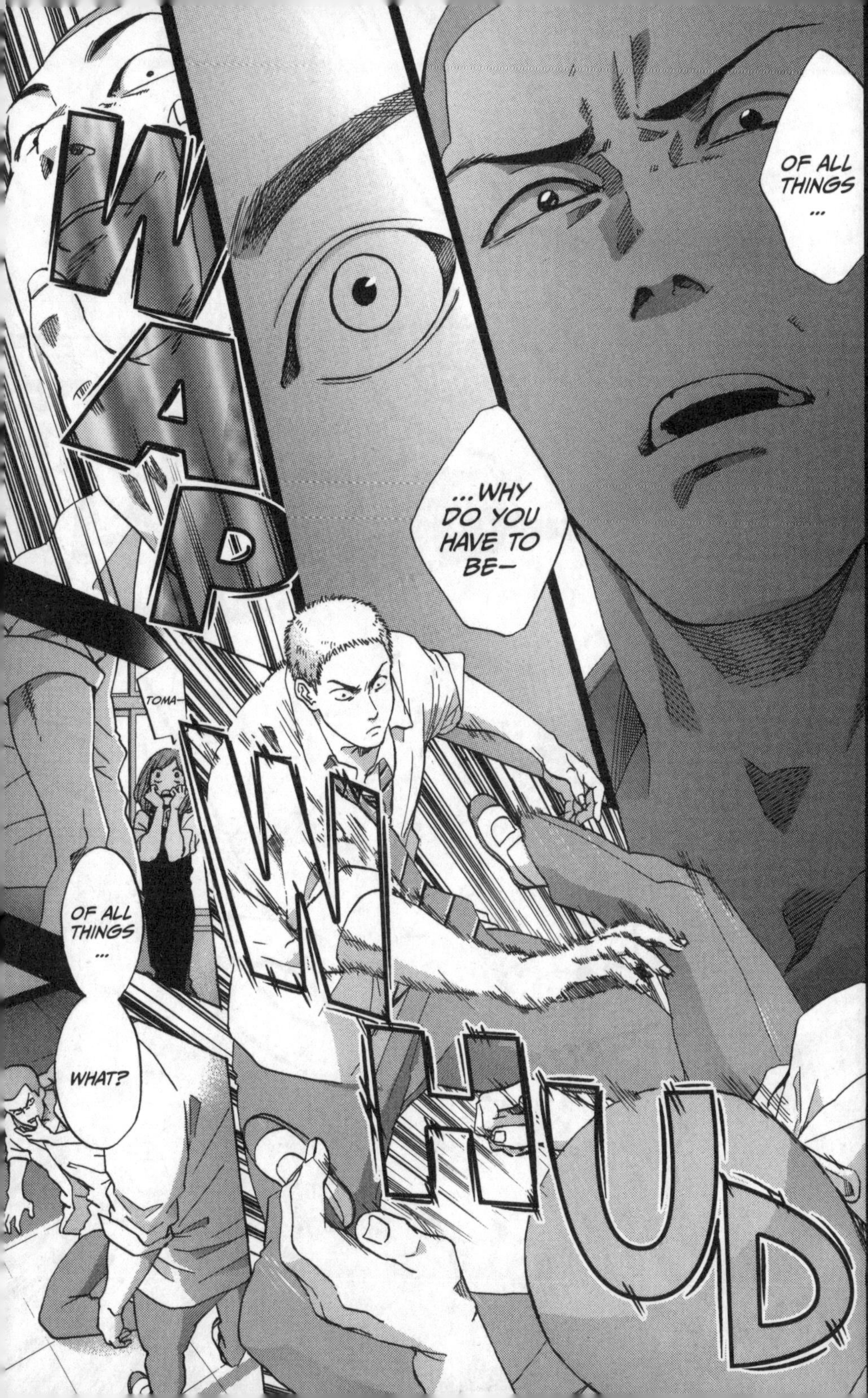
OF ALL THINGS ...
...WHY DO YOU HAVE TO BE—
WHAP
TOMA—
THUD
OF ALL THINGS ...
WHAT?

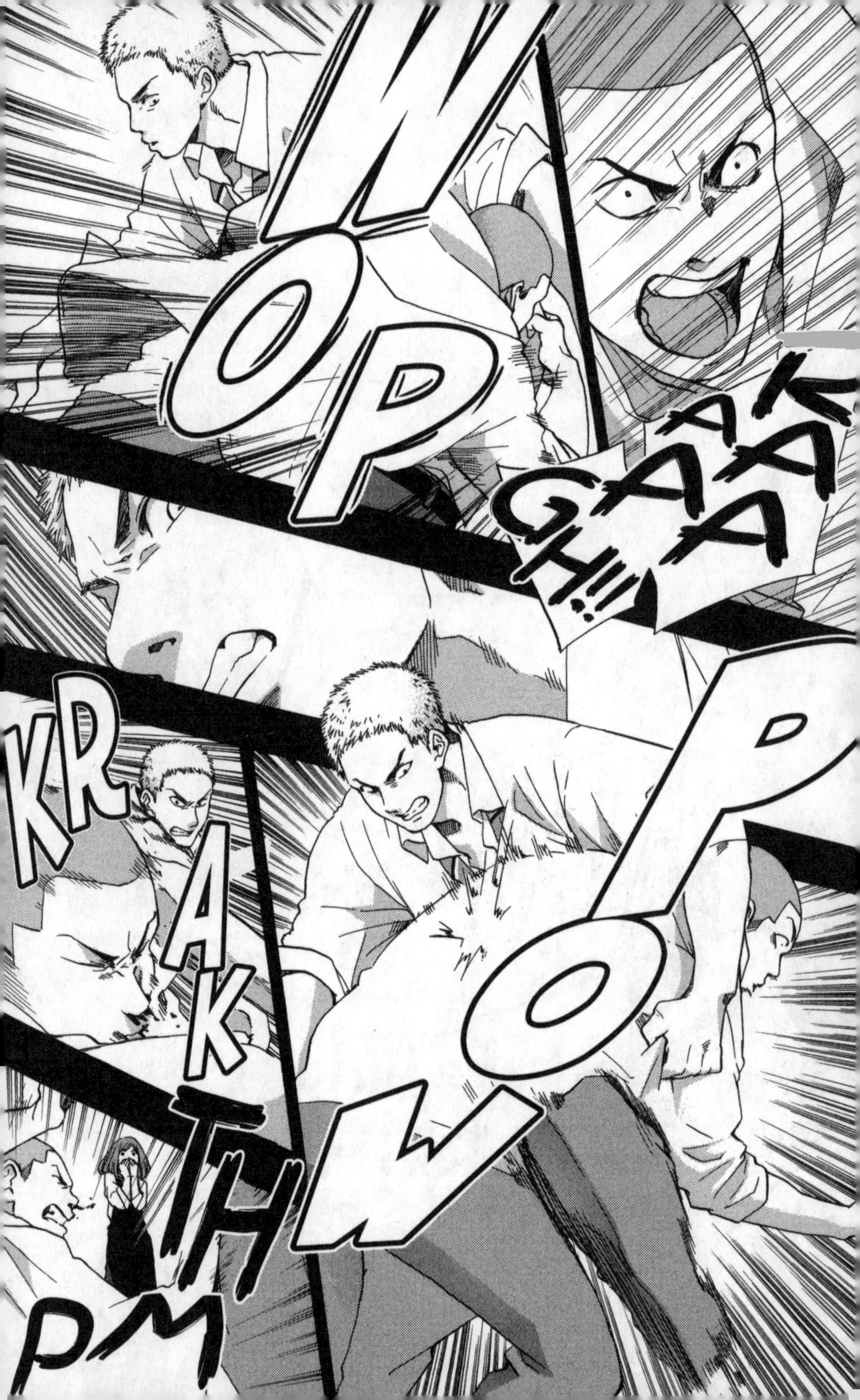
WOP
KAAAAGH!!!
WOP
KRAK
THTH
PM

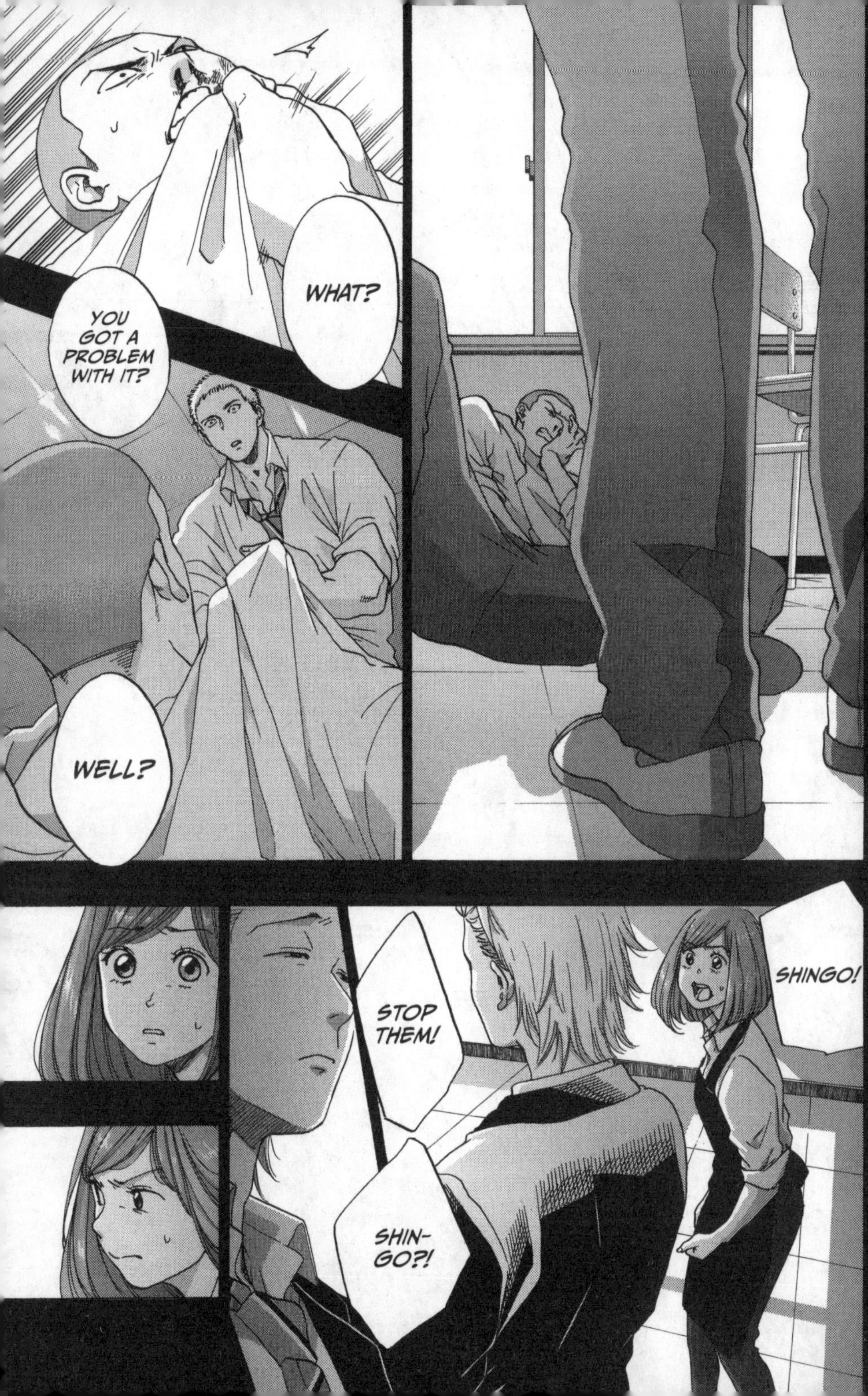
WHAT?
YOU GOT A PROBLEM WITH IT?
WELL?
SHINGO!
STOP THEM!
SHIN-GO?!

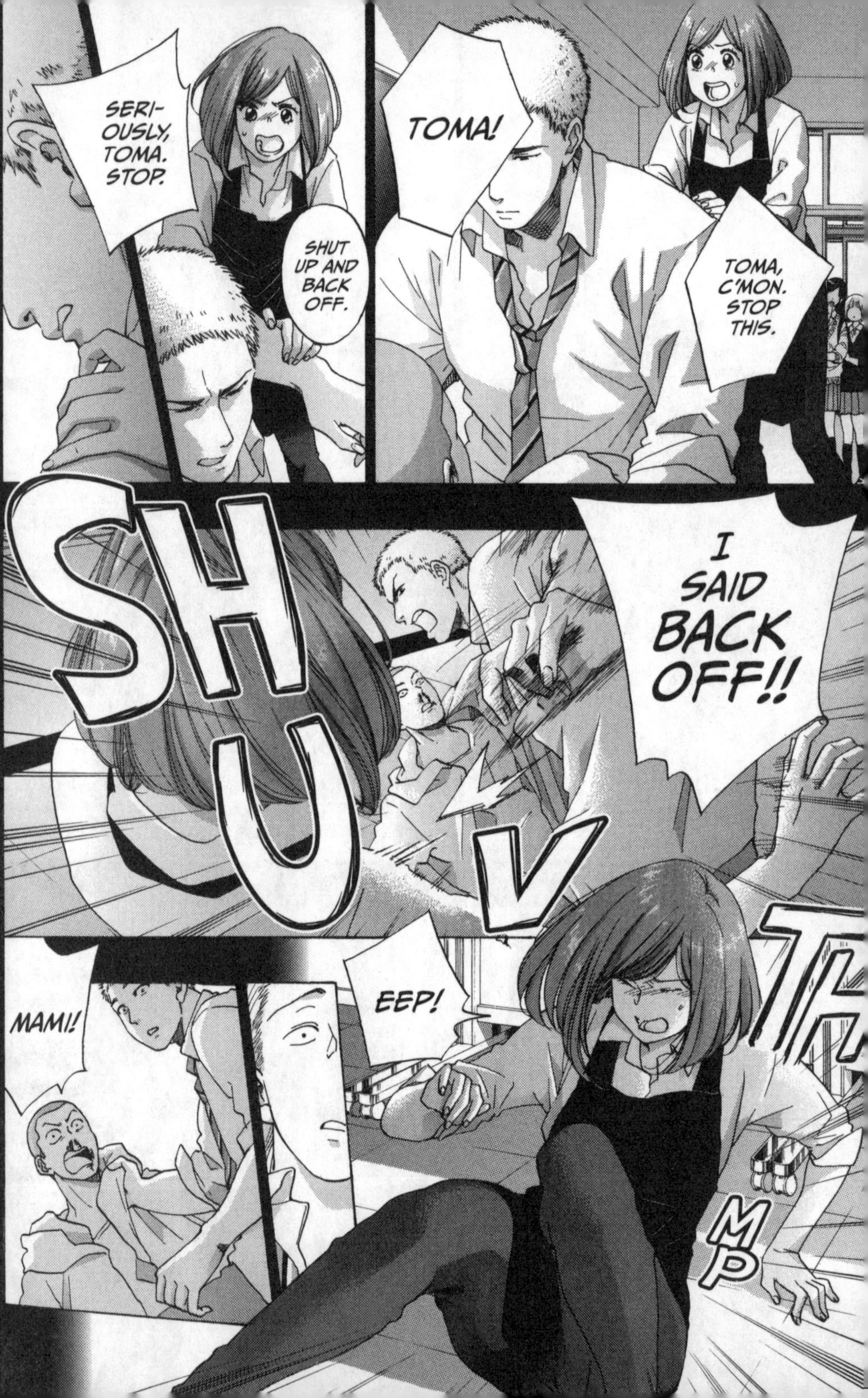
TOMA!
TOMA, C'MON. STOP THIS.
SERI-OUSLY, TOMA. STOP.
SHUT UP AND BACK OFF.
I SAID BACK OFF!!
SHUV
THUMP
EEP!
MAMI!

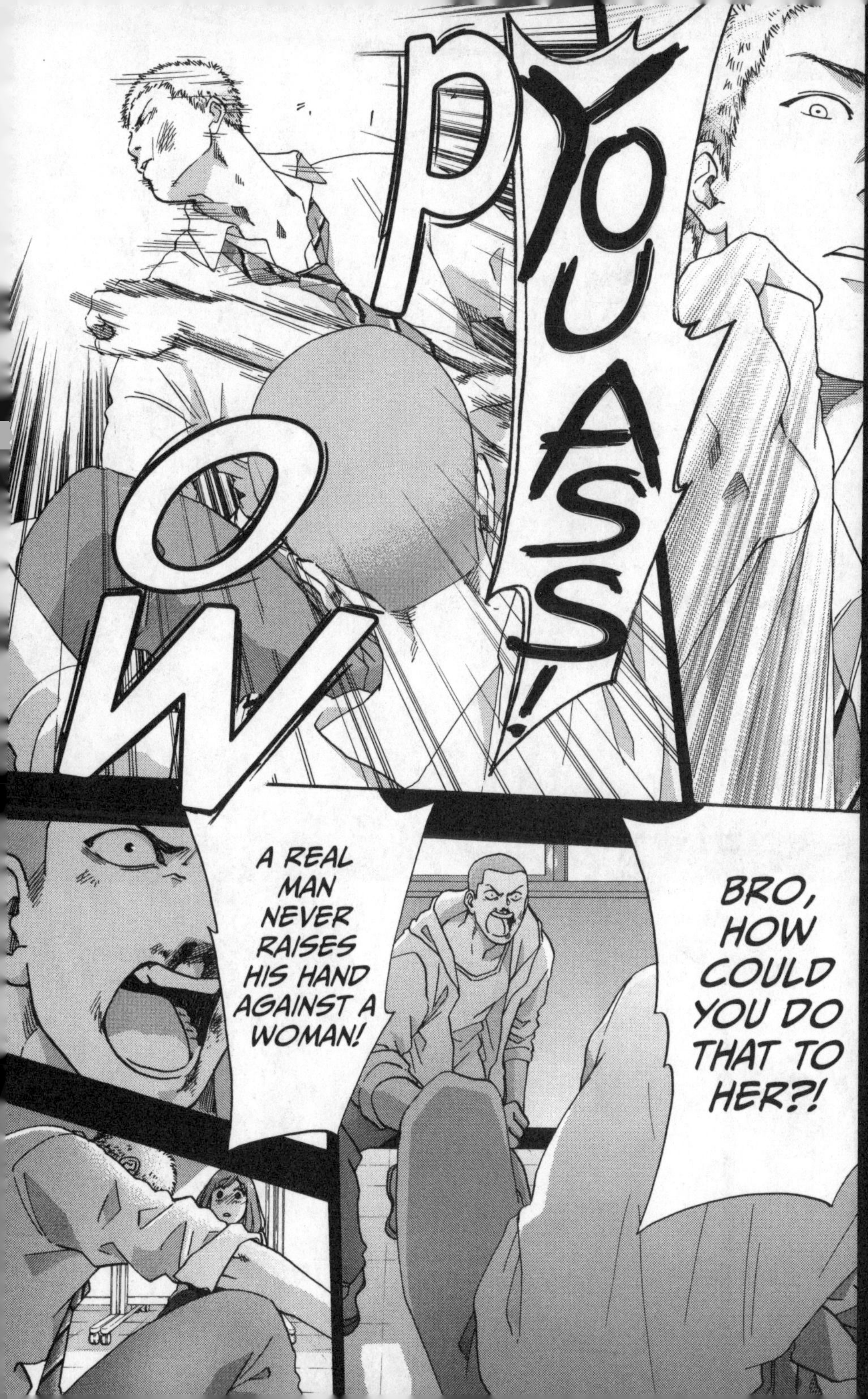
YOU ASS!
POW
BRO, HOW COULD YOU DO THAT TO HER?!
A REAL MAN NEVER RAISES HIS HAND AGAINST A WOMAN!

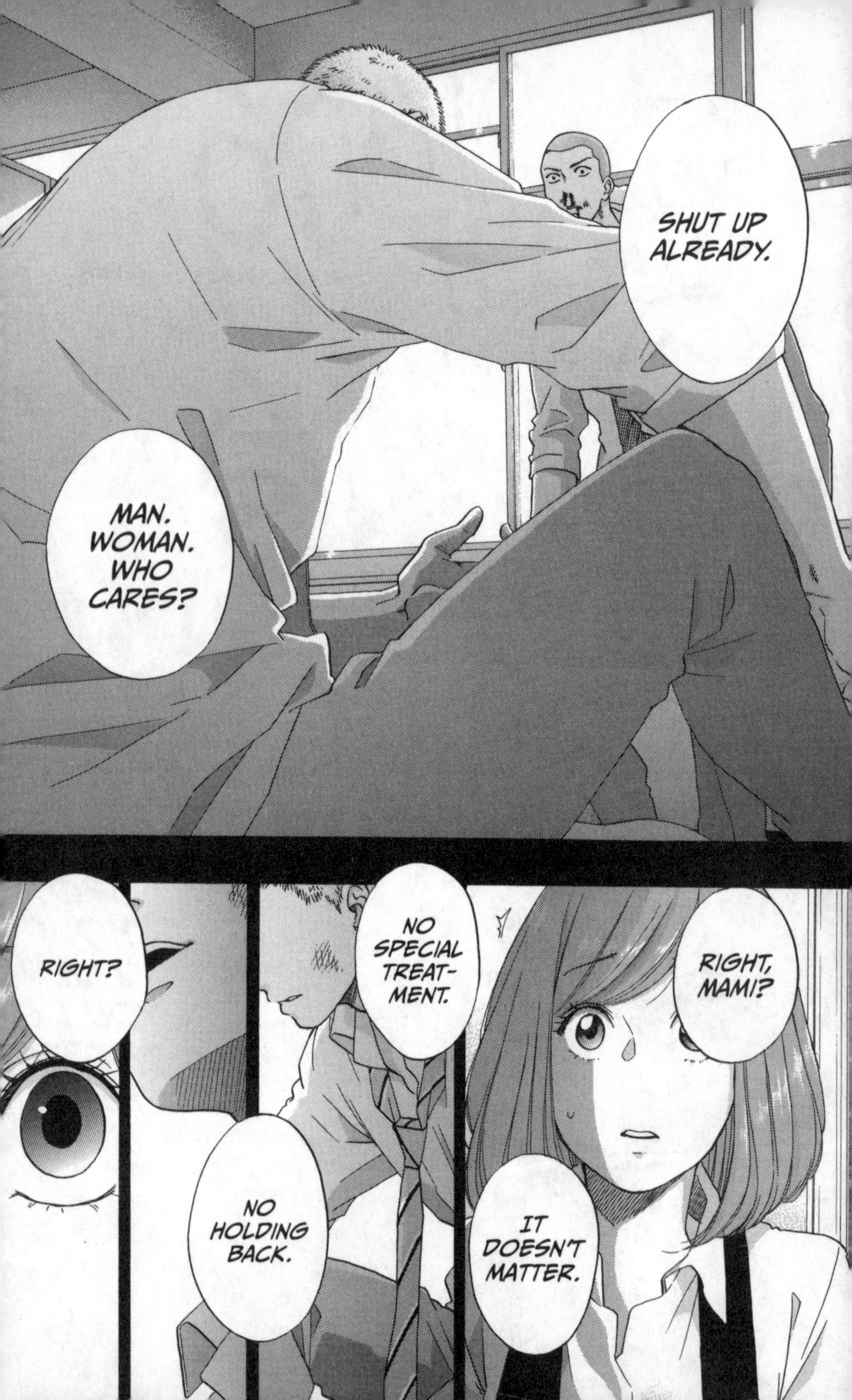
SHUT UP ALREADY.
MAN. WOMAN. WHO CARES?
RIGHT, MAMI?
IT DOESN'T MATTER.
NO SPECIAL TREAT-MENT.
NO HOLDING BACK.
RIGHT?

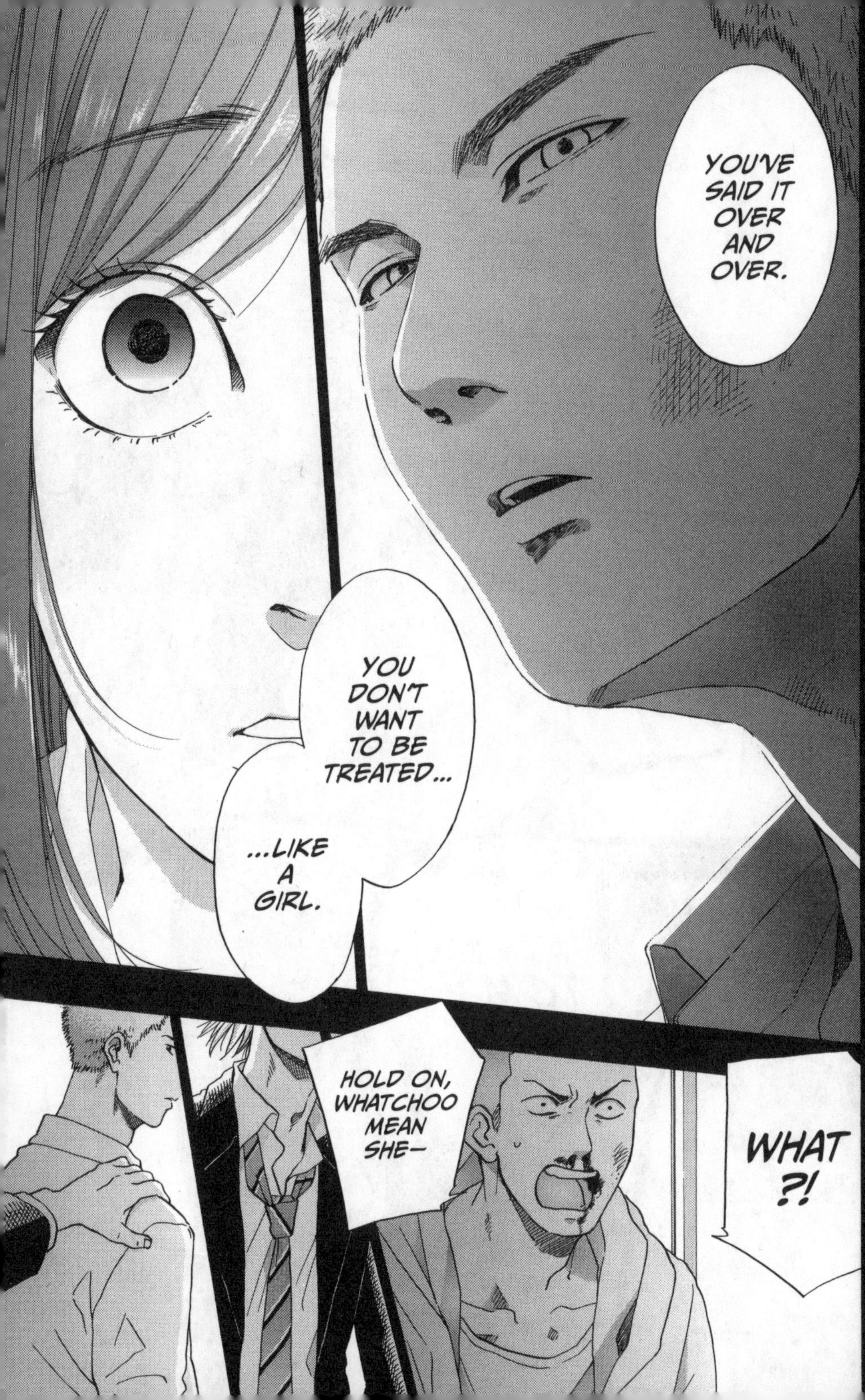
YOU'VE SAID IT OVER AND OVER.
YOU DON'T WANT TO BE TREATED...
...LIKE A GIRL.
WHAT ?!
HOLD ON, WHATCHOO MEAN SHE—

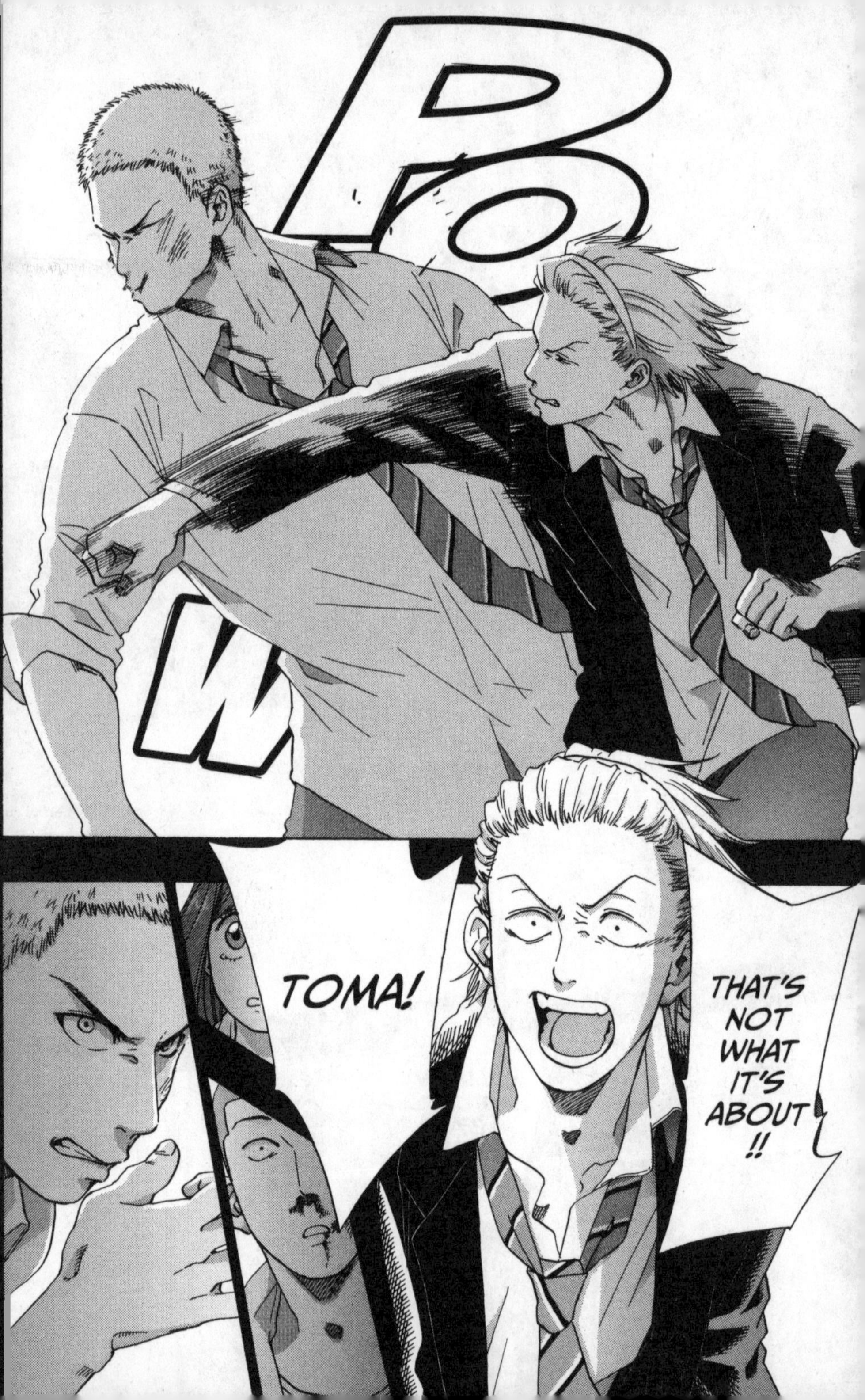
POW
TOMA!
THAT'S NOT WHAT IT'S ABOUT !!

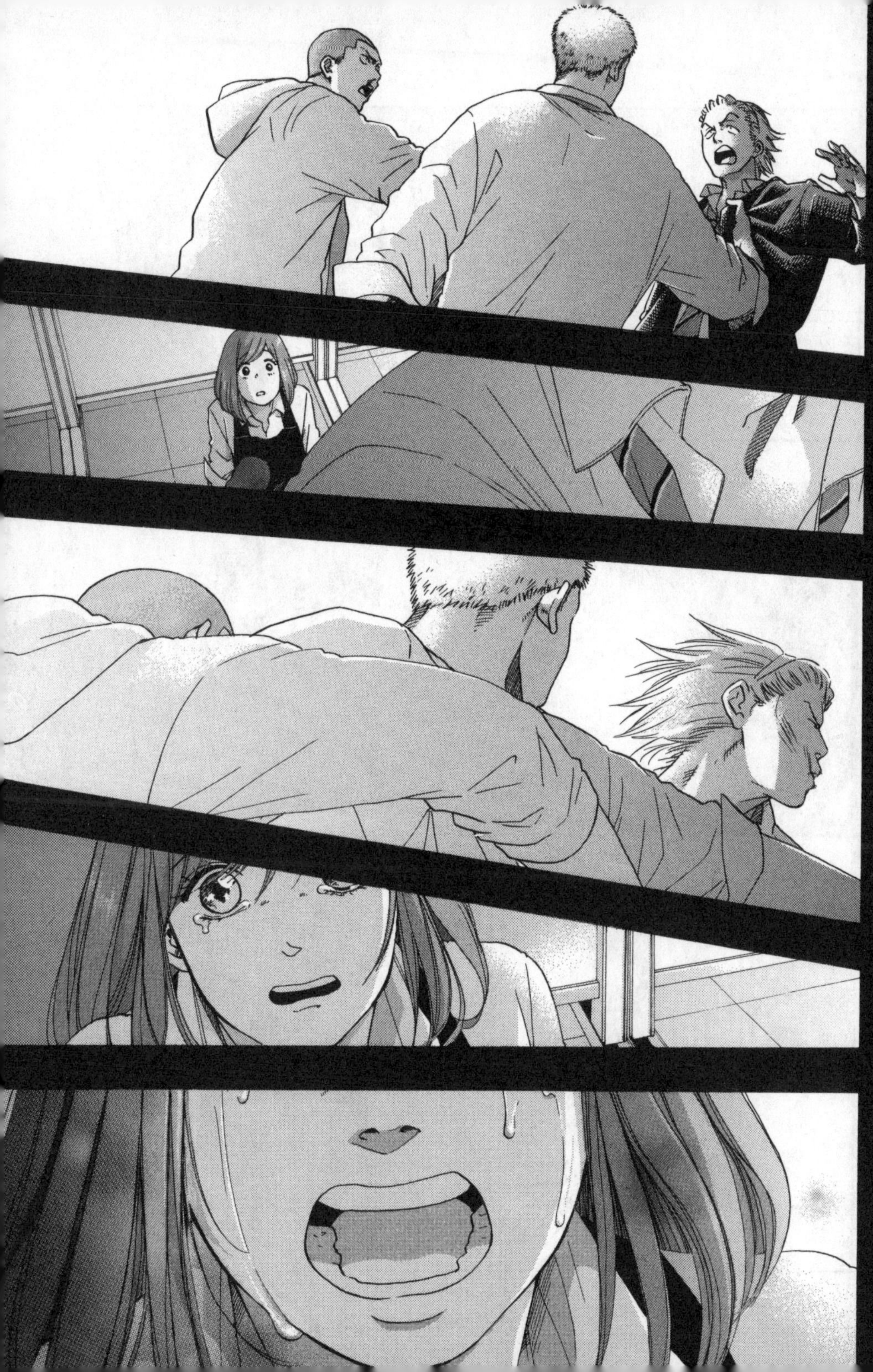

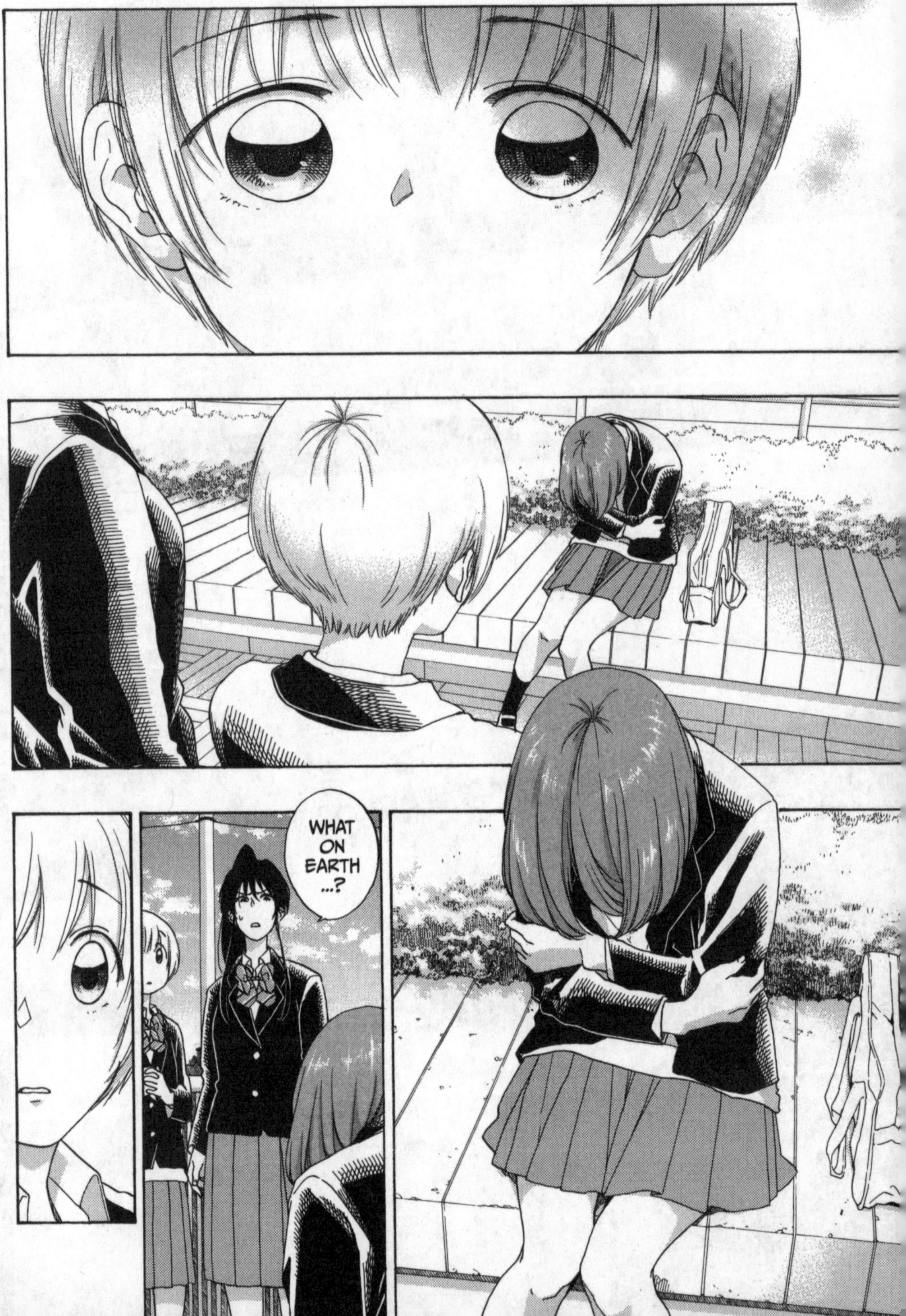
WHAT ON EARTH ...?

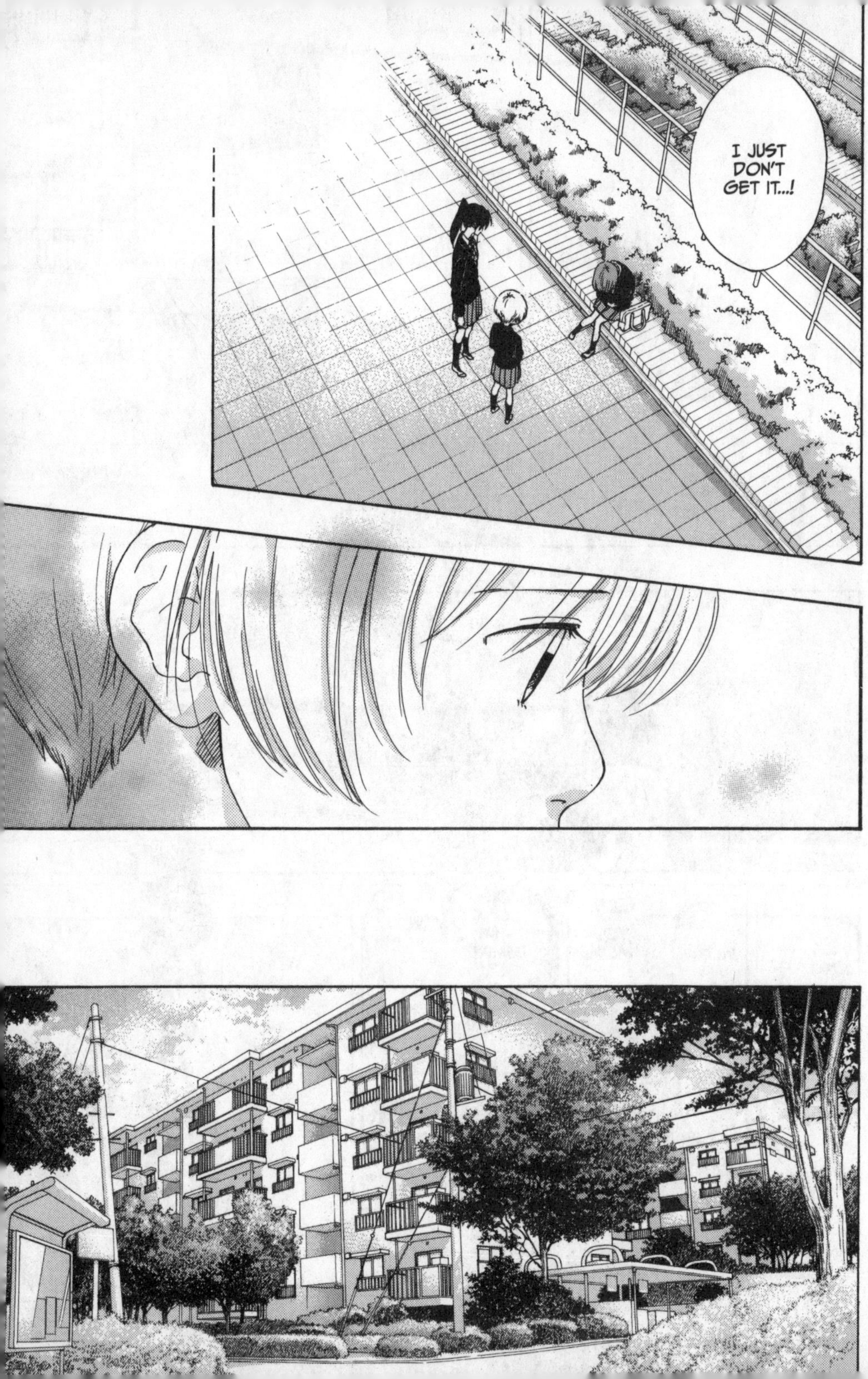
I JUST DON'T GET IT...!

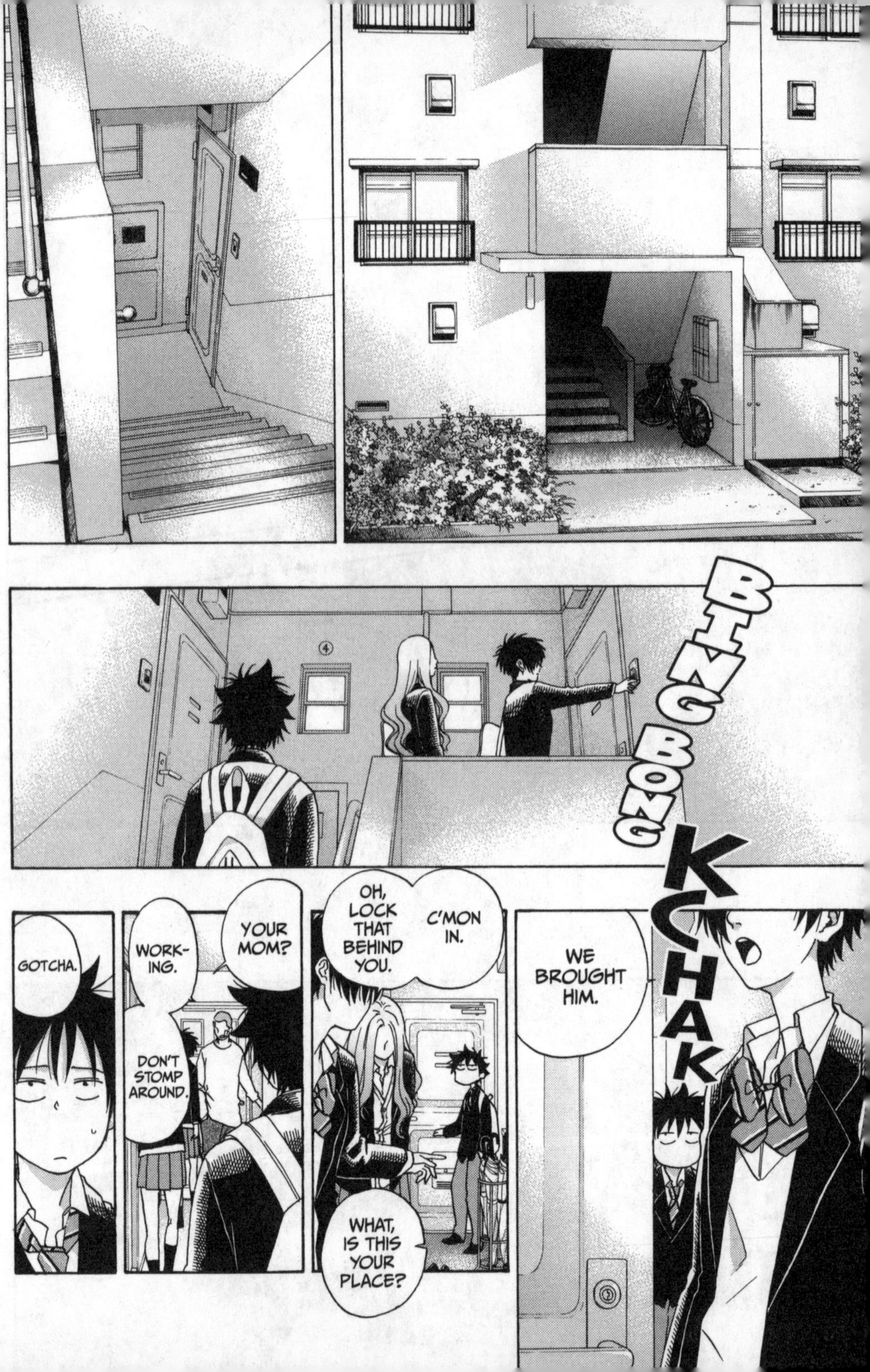
BING BONG
KCHAK
WE BROUGHT HIM.
C'MON IN.
OH, LOCK THAT BEHIND YOU.
WHAT, IS THIS YOUR PLACE?
YOUR MOM?
WORKING.
DON'T STOMP AROUND.
GOTCHA.

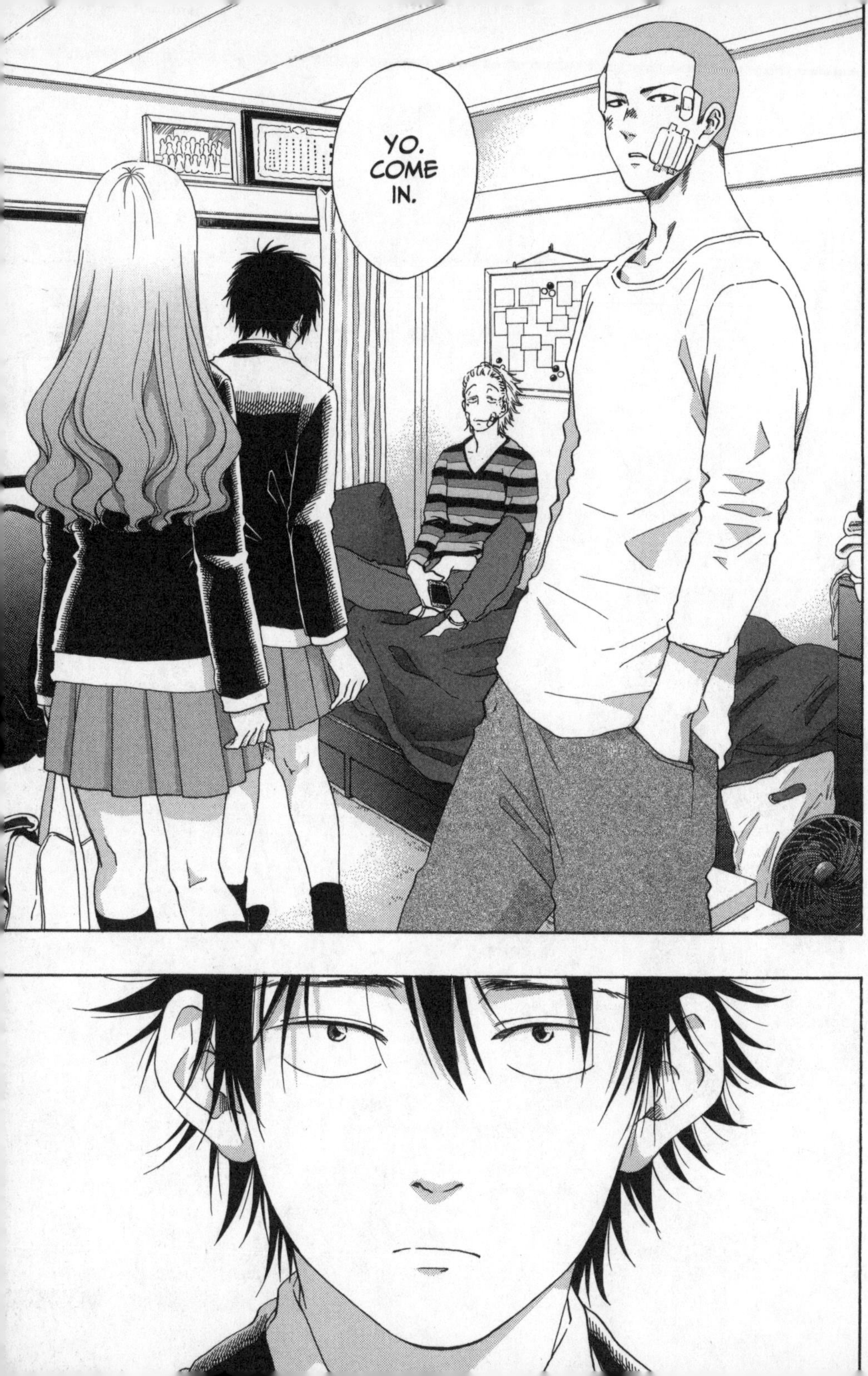
YO. COME IN.

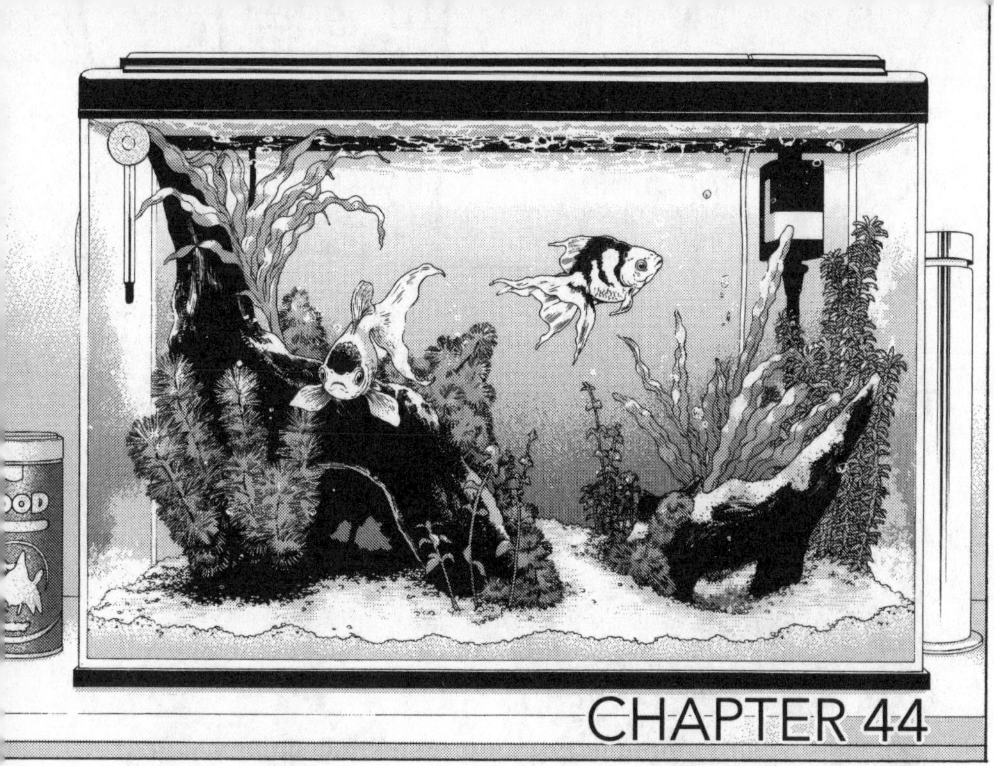
CHAPTER 44

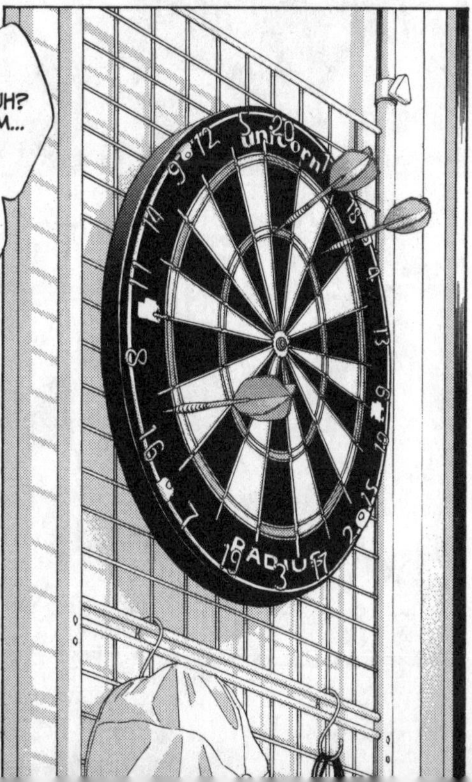
unicorn

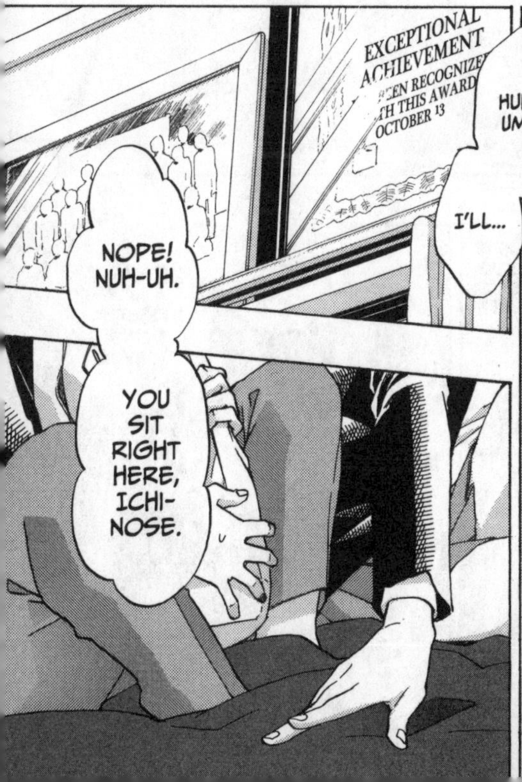
EXCEPTIONAL
ACHIEVEMENT
OCTOBER 13
HUH? UM...
I'LL...
NOPE! NUH-UH.
YOU SIT RIGHT HERE, ICHINOSE.

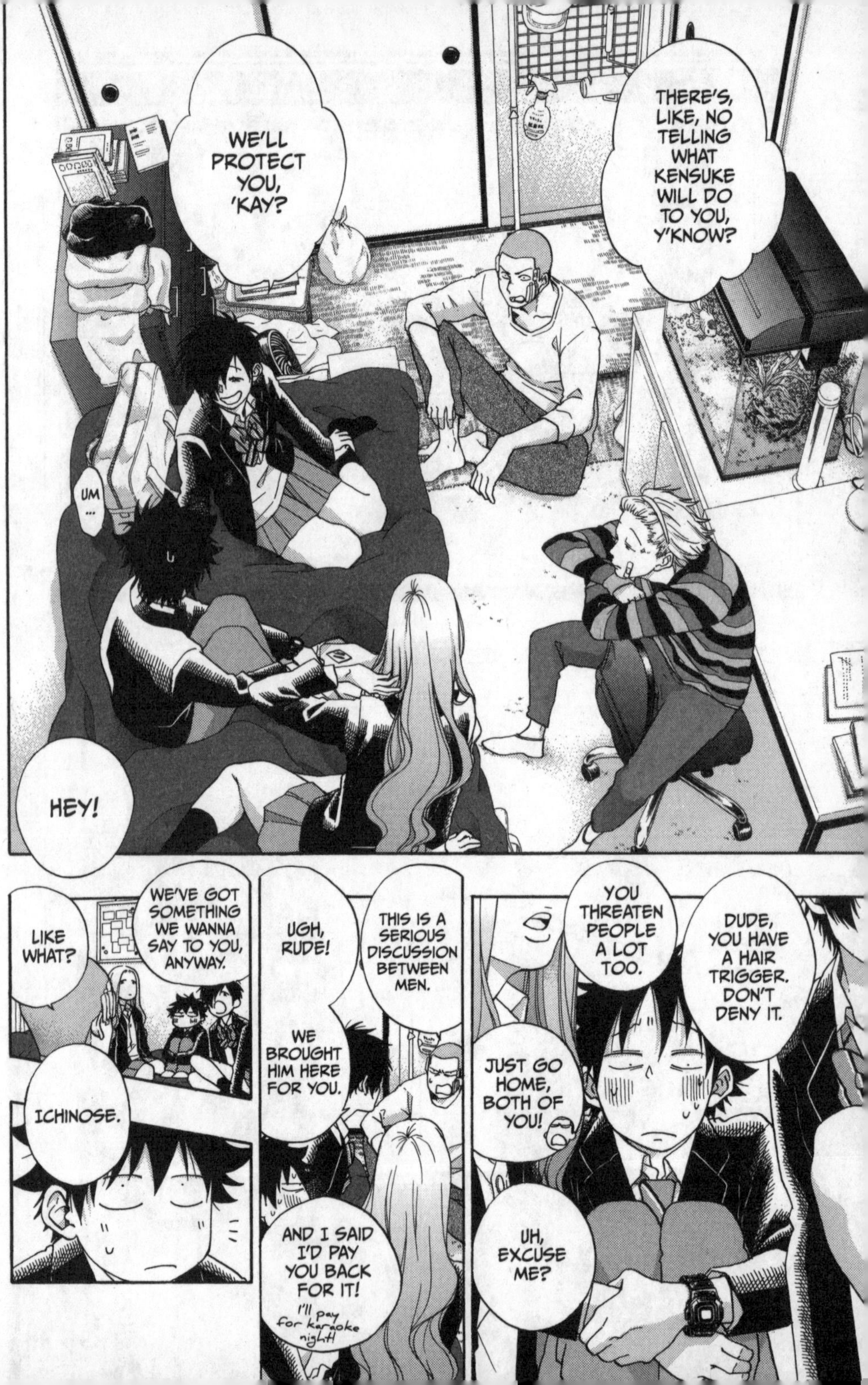
THERE'S, LIKE, NO TELLING WHAT KENSUKE WILL DO TO YOU, Y'KNOW?
WE'LL PROTECT YOU, 'KAY?
UM ...
HEY!
DUDE, YOU HAVE A HAIR TRIGGER. DON'T DENY IT.
YOU THREATEN PEOPLE A LOT TOO.
JUST GO HOME, BOTH OF YOU!
UH, EXCUSE ME?
THIS IS A SERIOUS DISCUSSION BETWEEN MEN.
UGH, RUDE!
WE BROUGHT HIM HERE FOR YOU.
AND I SAID I'D PAY YOU BACK FOR IT!
I'll pay for karaoke night!
WE'VE GOT SOMETHING WE WANNA SAY TO YOU, ANYWAY.
LIKE WHAT?
ICHINOSE.

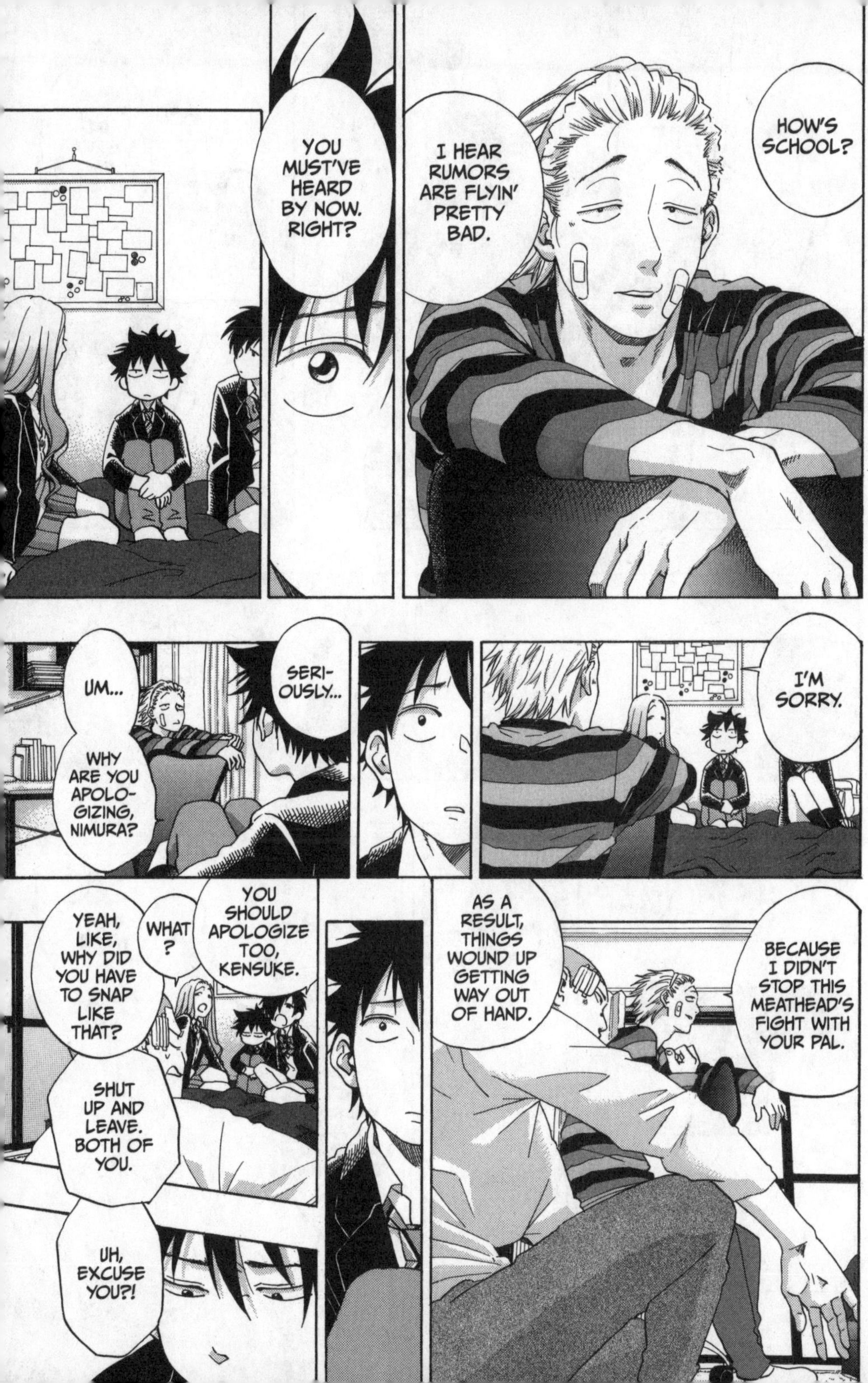
HOW'S SCHOOL?
I HEAR RUMORS ARE FLYIN' PRETTY BAD.
YOU MUST'VE HEARD BY NOW. RIGHT?
I'M SORRY.
SERI-OUSLY...
UM...
WHY ARE YOU APOLO-GIZING, NIMURA?
BECAUSE I DIDN'T STOP THIS MEATHEAD'S FIGHT WITH YOUR PAL.
AS A RESULT, THINGS WOUND UP GETTING WAY OUT OF HAND.
YOU SHOULD APOLOGIZE TOO, KENSUKE.
WHAT?
YEAH, LIKE, WHY DID YOU HAVE TO SNAP LIKE THAT?
SHUT UP AND LEAVE. BOTH OF YOU.
UH, EXCUSE YOU?!

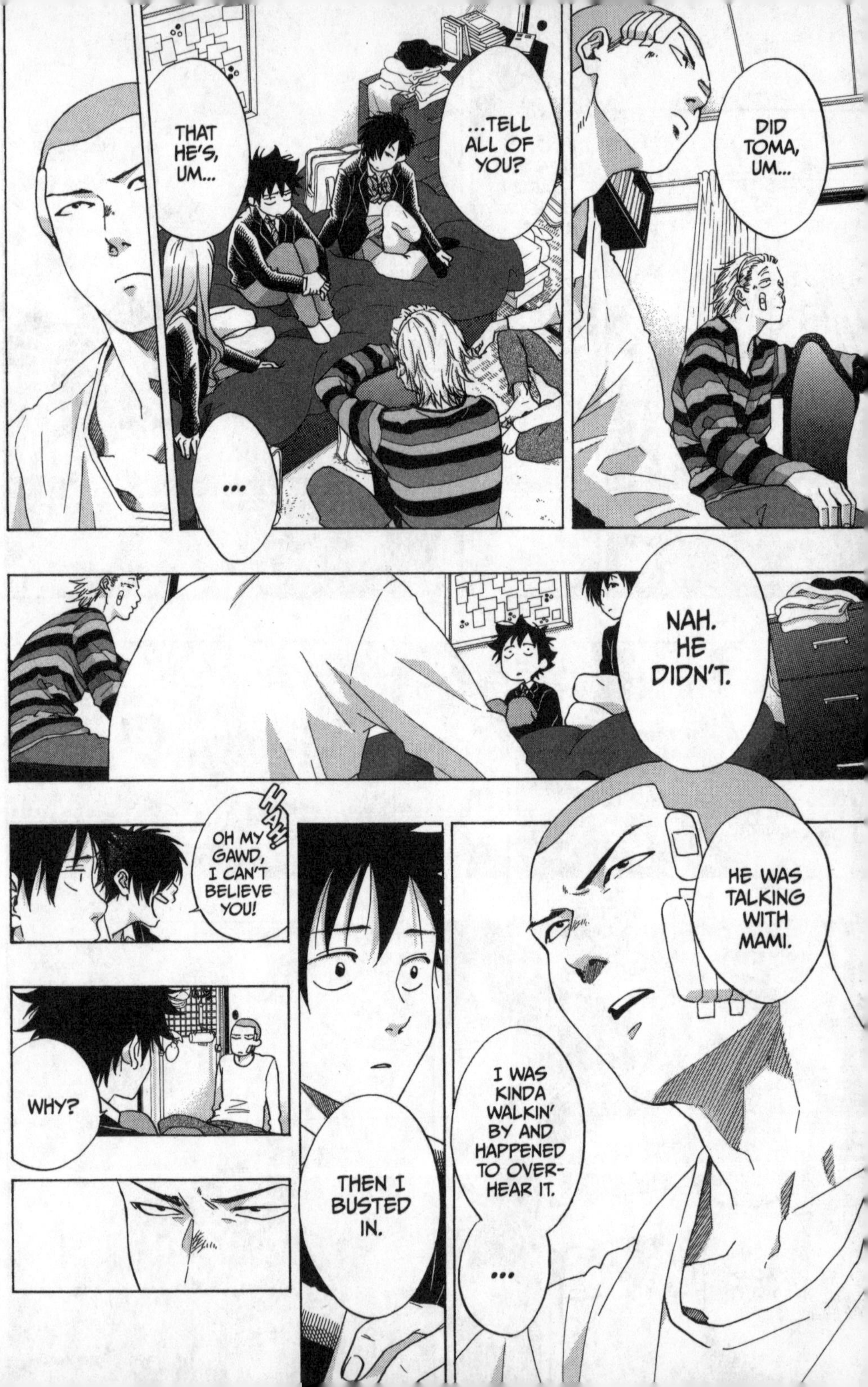
DID TOMA, UM...
...TELL ALL OF YOU?
...
THAT HE'S, UM...
NAH. HE DIDN'T.
HE WAS TALKING WITH MAMI.
I WAS KINDA WALKIN' BY AND HAPPENED TO OVER-HEAR IT.
...
THEN I BUSTED IN.
HAH!
OH MY GAWD, I CAN'T BELIEVE YOU!
WHY?

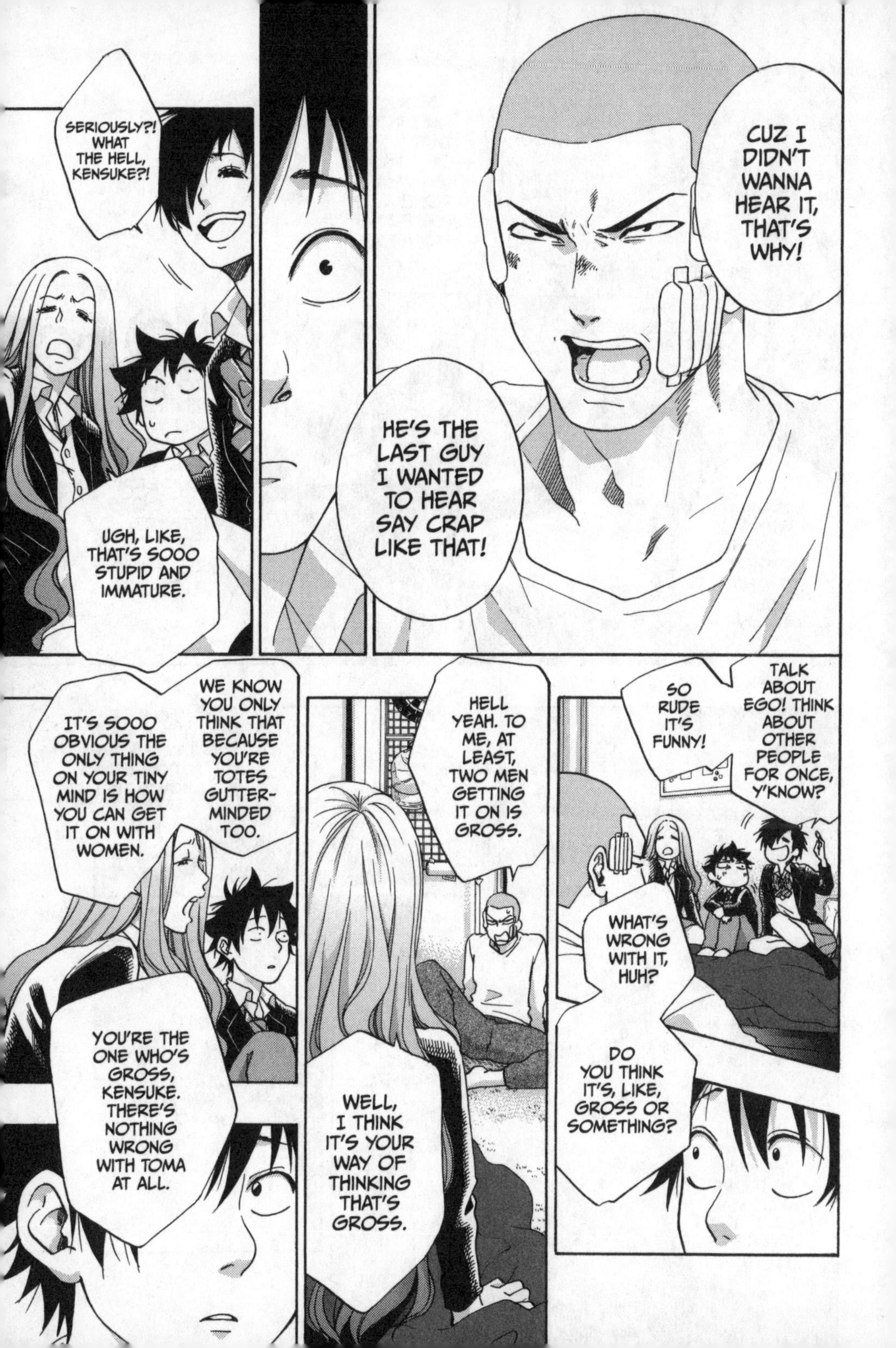
CUZ I DIDN'T WANNA HEAR IT, THAT'S WHY!
HE'S THE LAST GUY I WANTED TO HEAR SAY CRAP LIKE THAT!
SERIOUSLY?! WHAT THE HELL, KENSUKE?!
UGH, LIKE, THAT'S SOOO STUPID AND IMMATURE.
TALK ABOUT EGO! THINK ABOUT OTHER PEOPLE FOR ONCE, Y'KNOW?
SO RUDE IT'S FUNNY!
WHAT'S WRONG WITH IT, HUH?
DO YOU THINK IT'S, LIKE, GROSS OR SOMETHING?
HELL YEAH. TO ME, AT LEAST, TWO MEN GETTING IT ON IS GROSS.
WELL, I THINK IT'S YOUR WAY OF THINKING THAT'S GROSS.
WE KNOW YOU ONLY THINK THAT BECAUSE YOU'RE TOTES GUTTER-MINDED TOO.
IT'S SOOO OBVIOUS THE ONLY THING ON YOUR TINY MIND IS HOW YOU CAN GET IT ON WITH WOMEN.
YOU'RE THE ONE WHO'S GROSS, KENSUKE. THERE'S NOTHING WRONG WITH TOMA AT ALL.

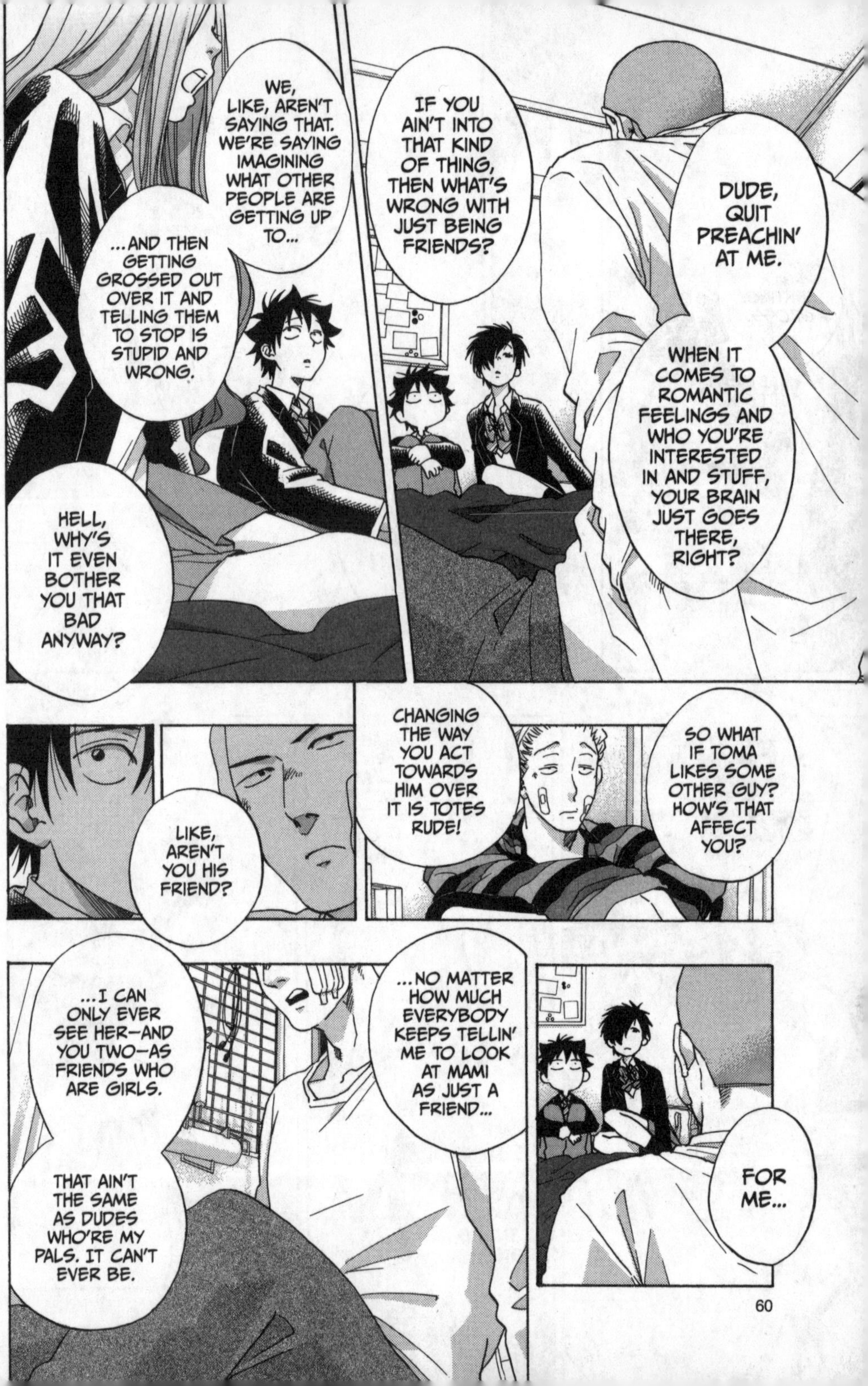
DUDE, QUIT PREACHIN' AT ME.
WHEN IT COMES TO ROMANTIC FEELINGS AND WHO YOU'RE INTERESTED IN AND STUFF, YOUR BRAIN JUST GOES THERE, RIGHT?
IF YOU AIN'T INTO THAT KIND OF THING, THEN WHAT'S WRONG WITH JUST BEING FRIENDS?
WE, LIKE, AREN'T SAYING THAT. WE'RE SAYING IMAGINING WHAT OTHER PEOPLE ARE GETTING UP TO...
...AND THEN GETTING GROSSED OUT OVER IT AND TELLING THEM TO STOP IS STUPID AND WRONG.
HELL, WHY'S IT EVEN BOTHER YOU THAT BAD ANYWAY?
SO WHAT IF TOMA LIKES SOME OTHER GUY? HOW'S THAT AFFECT YOU?
CHANGING THE WAY YOU ACT TOWARDS HIM OVER IT IS TOTES RUDE!
LIKE, AREN'T YOU HIS FRIEND?
FOR ME...
...NO MATTER HOW MUCH EVERYBODY KEEPS TELLIN' ME TO LOOK AT MAMI AS JUST A FRIEND...
...I CAN ONLY EVER SEE HER—AND YOU TWO—AS FRIENDS WHO ARE GIRLS.
THAT AIN'T THE SAME AS DUDES WHO'RE MY PALS. IT CAN'T EVER BE.

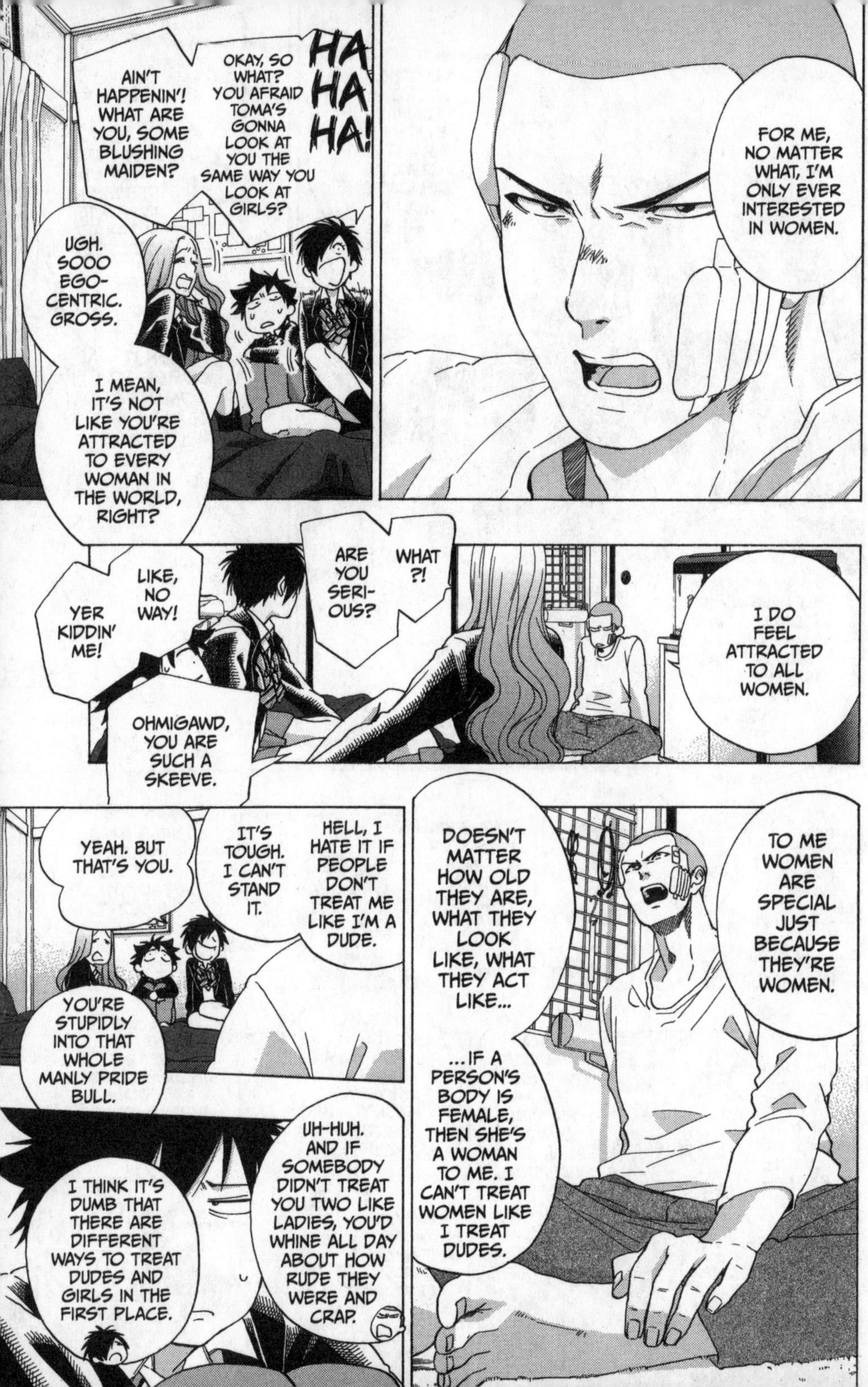
FOR ME, NO MATTER WHAT, I'M ONLY EVER INTERESTED IN WOMEN.
HA HA HA!
OKAY, SO WHAT? YOU AFRAID TOMA'S GONNA LOOK AT YOU THE SAME WAY YOU LOOK AT GIRLS?
AIN'T HAPPENIN'! WHAT ARE YOU, SOME BLUSHING MAIDEN?
UGH. SOOO EGO-CENTRIC. GROSS.
I MEAN, IT'S NOT LIKE YOU'RE ATTRACTED TO EVERY WOMAN IN THE WORLD, RIGHT?
I DO FEEL ATTRACTED TO ALL WOMEN.
WHAT?!
ARE YOU SERI-OUS?
LIKE, NO WAY!
YER KIDDIN' ME!
OHMIGAWD, YOU ARE SUCH A SKEEVE.
TO ME WOMEN ARE SPECIAL JUST BECAUSE THEY'RE WOMEN.
DOESN'T MATTER HOW OLD THEY ARE, WHAT THEY LOOK LIKE, WHAT THEY ACT LIKE...
...IF A PERSON'S BODY IS FEMALE, THEN SHE'S A WOMAN TO ME. I CAN'T TREAT WOMEN LIKE I TREAT DUDES.
HELL, I HATE IT IF PEOPLE DON'T TREAT ME LIKE I'M A DUDE.
IT'S TOUGH. I CAN'T STAND IT.
YEAH. BUT THAT'S YOU.
YOU'RE STUPIDLY INTO THAT WHOLE MANLY PRIDE BULL.
UH-HUH. AND IF SOMEBODY DIDN'T TREAT YOU TWO LIKE LADIES, YOU'D WHINE ALL DAY ABOUT HOW RUDE THEY WERE AND CRAP.
I THINK IT'S DUMB THAT THERE ARE DIFFERENT WAYS TO TREAT DUDES AND GIRLS IN THE FIRST PLACE.

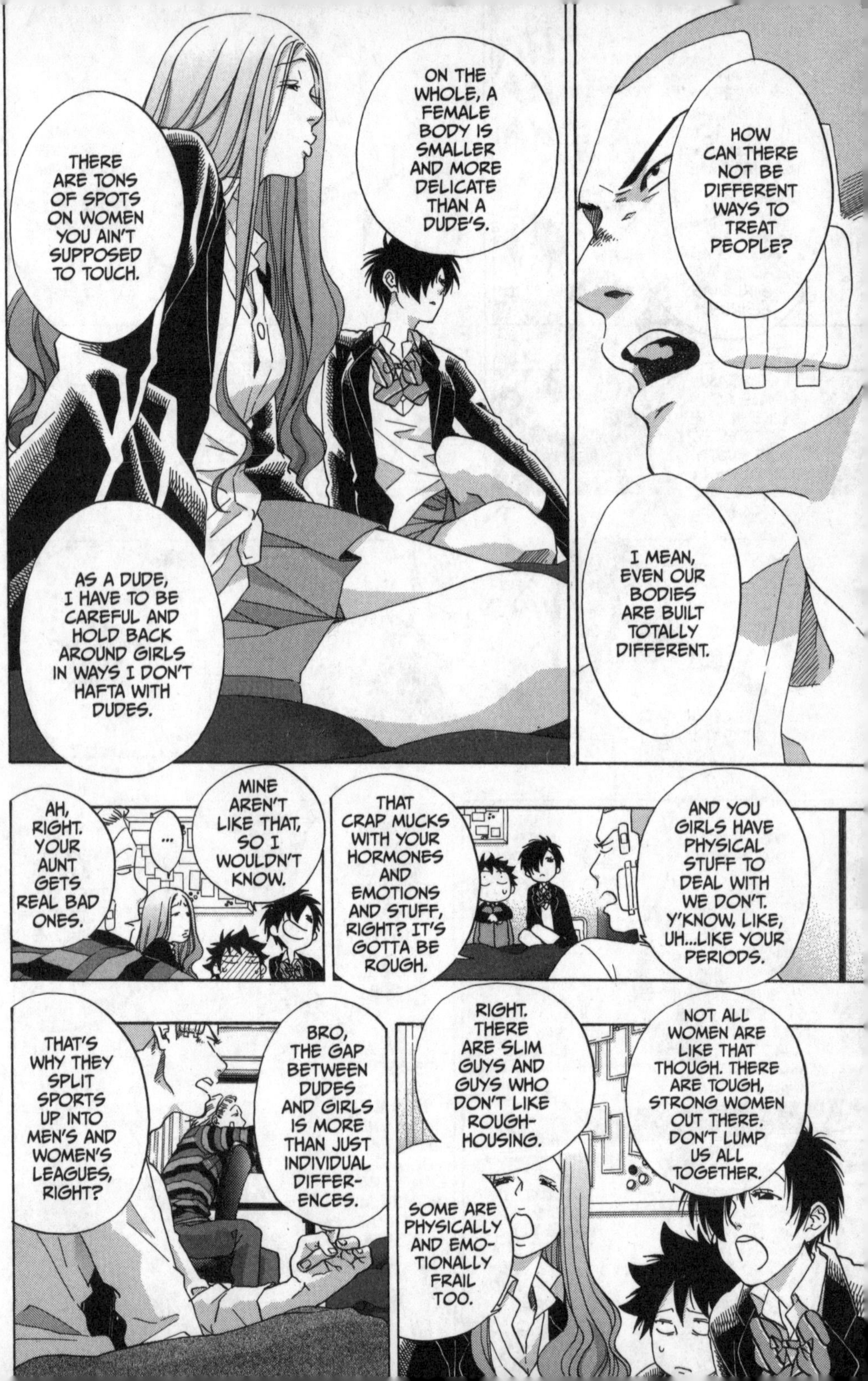
HOW CAN THERE NOT BE DIFFERENT WAYS TO TREAT PEOPLE?
I MEAN, EVEN OUR BODIES ARE BUILT TOTALLY DIFFERENT.
ON THE WHOLE, A FEMALE BODY IS SMALLER AND MORE DELICATE THAN A DUDE'S.
THERE ARE TONS OF SPOTS ON WOMEN YOU AIN'T SUPPOSED TO TOUCH.
AS A DUDE, I HAVE TO BE CAREFUL AND HOLD BACK AROUND GIRLS IN WAYS I DON'T HAFTA WITH DUDES.
AND YOU GIRLS HAVE PHYSICAL STUFF TO DEAL WITH WE DON'T. Y'KNOW, LIKE, UH...LIKE YOUR PERIODS.
THAT CRAP MUCKS WITH YOUR HORMONES AND EMOTIONS AND STUFF, RIGHT? IT'S GOTTA BE ROUGH.
MINE AREN'T LIKE THAT, SO I WOULDN'T KNOW.
...
AH, RIGHT. YOUR AUNT GETS REAL BAD ONES.
NOT ALL WOMEN ARE LIKE THAT THOUGH. THERE ARE TOUGH, STRONG WOMEN OUT THERE. DON'T LUMP US ALL TOGETHER.
RIGHT. THERE ARE SLIM GUYS AND GUYS WHO DON'T LIKE ROUGH-HOUSING.
SOME ARE PHYSICALLY AND EMO-TIONALLY FRAIL TOO.
BRO, THE GAP BETWEEN DUDES AND GIRLS IS MORE THAN JUST INDIVIDUAL DIFFER-ENCES.
THAT'S WHY THEY SPLIT SPORTS UP INTO MEN'S AND WOMEN'S LEAGUES, RIGHT?

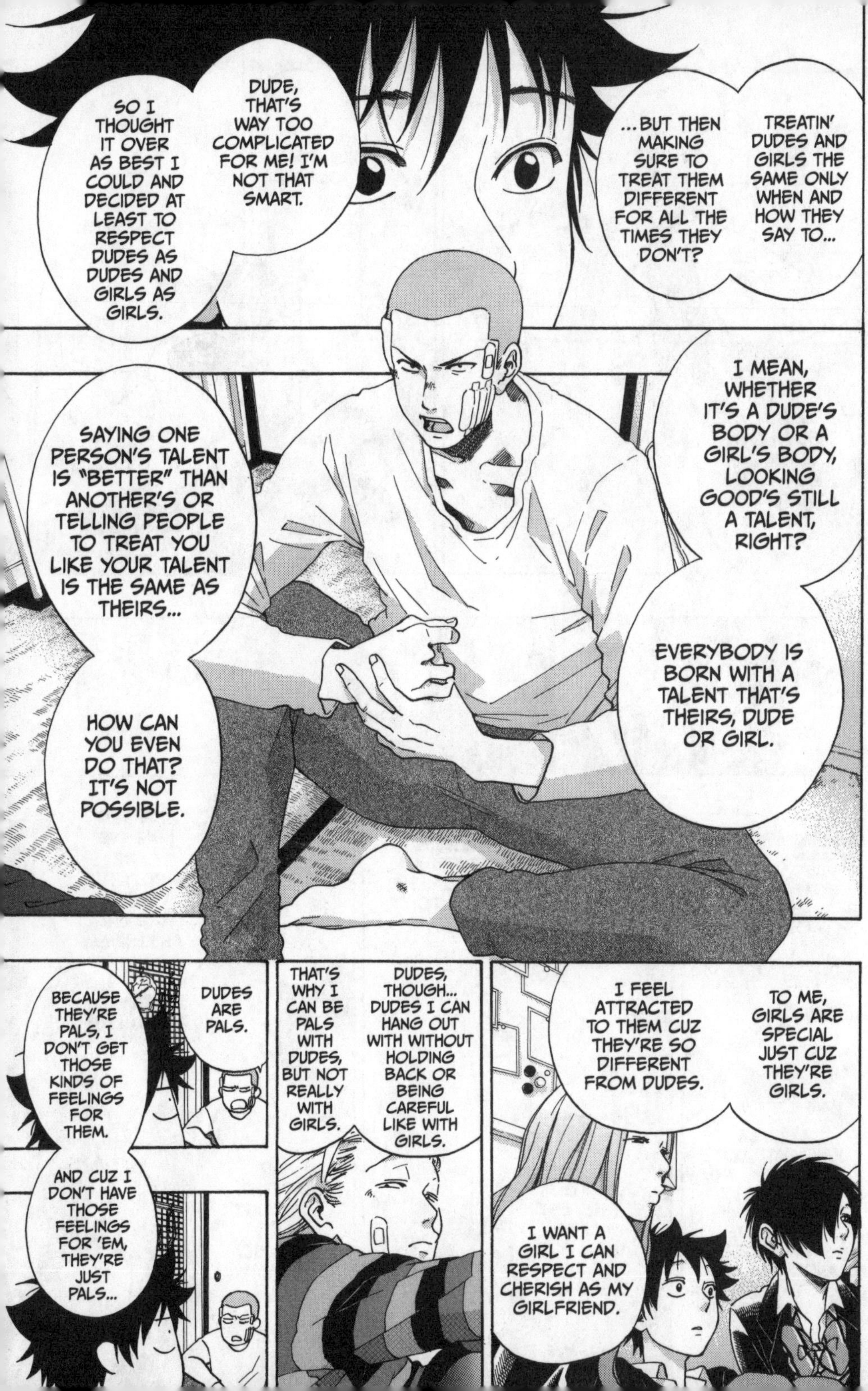
TREATIN' DUDES AND GIRLS THE SAME ONLY WHEN AND HOW THEY SAY TO...
...BUT THEN MAKING SURE TO TREAT THEM DIFFERENT FOR ALL THE TIMES THEY DON'T?
DUDE, THAT'S WAY TOO COMPLICATED FOR ME! I'M NOT THAT SMART.
SO I THOUGHT IT OVER AS BEST I COULD AND DECIDED AT LEAST TO RESPECT DUDES AS DUDES AND GIRLS AS GIRLS.
I MEAN, WHETHER IT'S A DUDE'S BODY OR A GIRL'S BODY, LOOKING GOOD'S STILL A TALENT, RIGHT?
EVERYBODY IS BORN WITH A TALENT THAT'S THEIRS, DUDE OR GIRL.
SAYING ONE PERSON'S TALENT IS "BETTER" THAN ANOTHER'S OR TELLING PEOPLE TO TREAT YOU LIKE YOUR TALENT IS THE SAME AS THEIRS...
HOW CAN YOU EVEN DO THAT? IT'S NOT POSSIBLE.
TO ME, GIRLS ARE SPECIAL JUST CUZ THEY'RE GIRLS.
I FEEL ATTRACTED TO THEM CUZ THEY'RE SO DIFFERENT FROM DUDES.
I WANT A GIRL I CAN RESPECT AND CHERISH AS MY GIRLFRIEND.
DUDES, THOUGH... DUDES I CAN HANG OUT WITH WITHOUT HOLDING BACK OR BEING CAREFUL LIKE WITH GIRLS.
THAT'S WHY I CAN BE PALS WITH DUDES, BUT NOT REALLY WITH GIRLS.
DUDES ARE PALS.
BECAUSE THEY'RE PALS, I DON'T GET THOSE KINDS OF FEELINGS FOR THEM.
AND CUZ I DON'T HAVE THOSE FEELINGS FOR 'EM, THEY'RE JUST PALS...

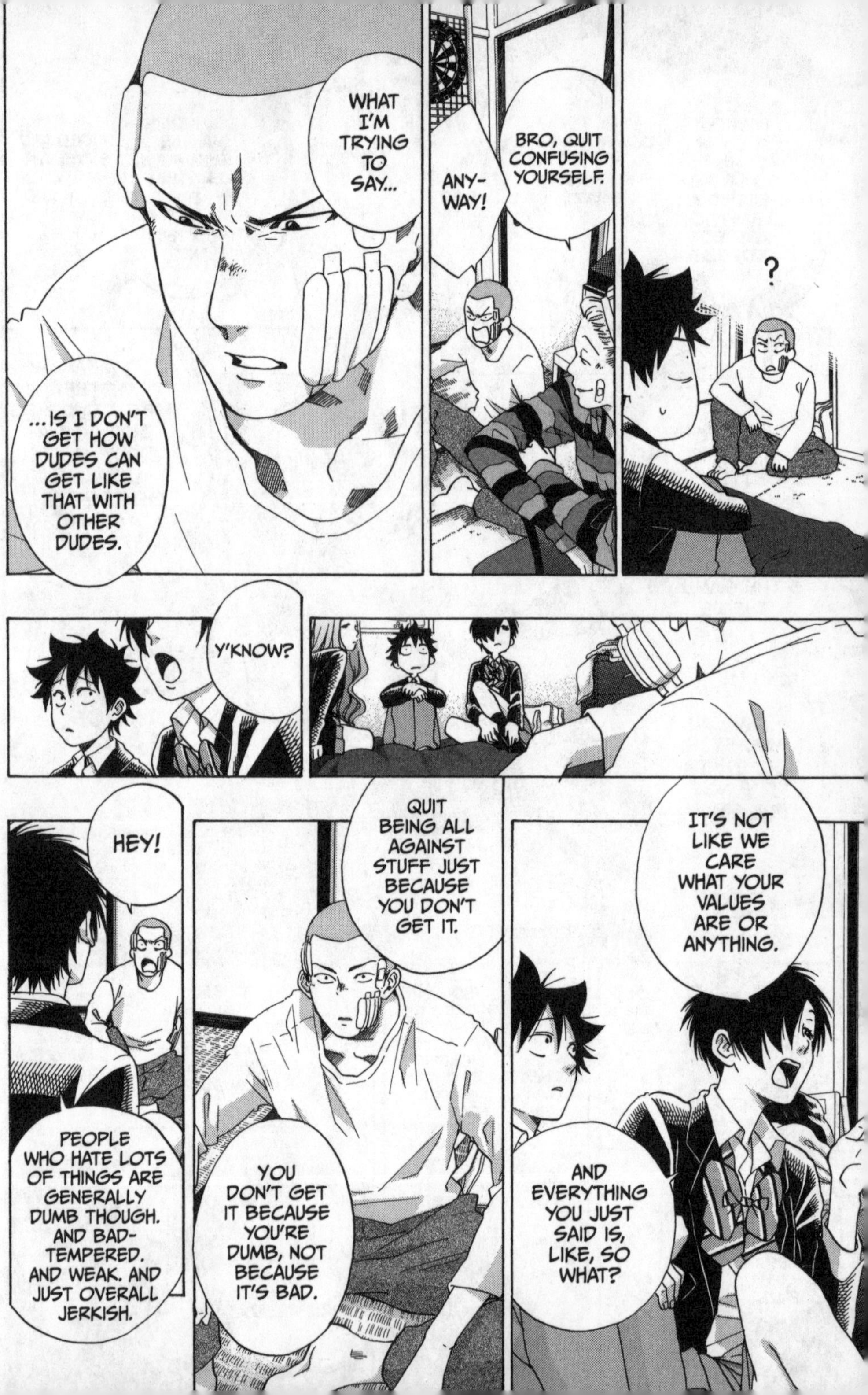
?
BRO, QUIT CONFUSING YOURSELF.
ANY-WAY!
WHAT I'M TRYING TO SAY...
...IS I DON'T GET HOW DUDES CAN GET LIKE THAT WITH OTHER DUDES.
Y'KNOW?
IT'S NOT LIKE WE CARE WHAT YOUR VALUES ARE OR ANYTHING.
AND EVERYTHING YOU JUST SAID IS, LIKE, SO WHAT?
QUIT BEING ALL AGAINST STUFF JUST BECAUSE YOU DON'T GET IT.
YOU DON'T GET IT BECAUSE YOU'RE DUMB, NOT BECAUSE IT'S BAD.
HEY!
PEOPLE WHO HATE LOTS OF THINGS ARE GENERALLY DUMB THOUGH. AND BAD-TEMPERED. AND WEAK. AND JUST OVERALL JERKISH.

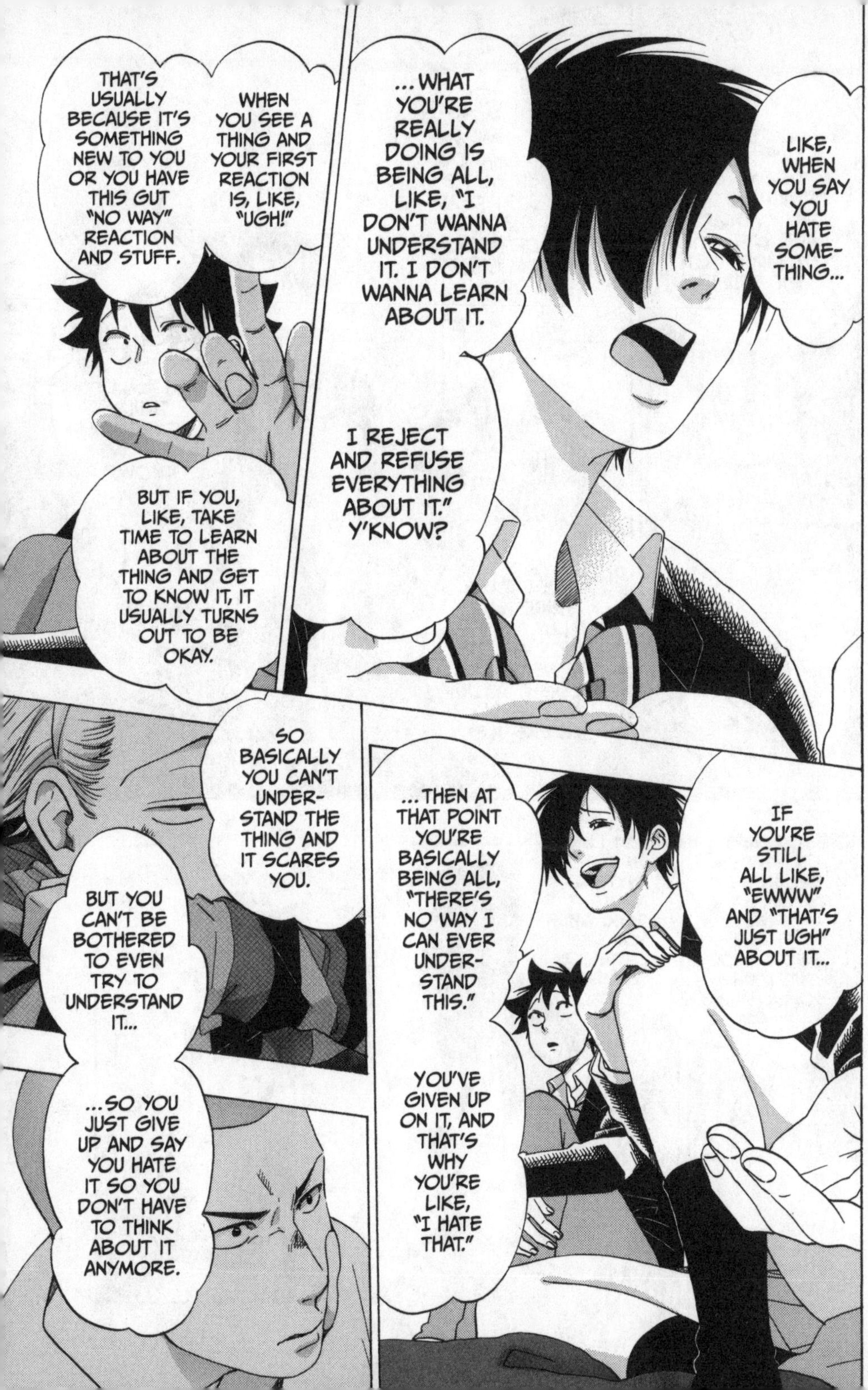
LIKE, WHEN YOU SAY YOU HATE SOMETHING...
...WHAT YOU'RE REALLY DOING IS BEING ALL, LIKE, "I DON'T WANNA UNDERSTAND IT. I DON'T WANNA LEARN ABOUT IT.
I REJECT AND REFUSE EVERYTHING ABOUT IT." Y'KNOW?
WHEN YOU SEE A THING AND YOUR FIRST REACTION IS, LIKE, "UGH!"
THAT'S USUALLY BECAUSE IT'S SOMETHING NEW TO YOU OR YOU HAVE THIS GUT "NO WAY" REACTION AND STUFF.
BUT IF YOU, LIKE, TAKE TIME TO LEARN ABOUT THE THING AND GET TO KNOW IT, IT USUALLY TURNS OUT TO BE OKAY.
IF YOU'RE STILL ALL LIKE, "EWWW" AND "THAT'S JUST UGH" ABOUT IT...
...THEN AT THAT POINT YOU'RE BASICALLY BEING ALL, "THERE'S NO WAY I CAN EVER UNDERSTAND THIS."
YOU'VE GIVEN UP ON IT, AND THAT'S WHY YOU'RE LIKE, "I HATE THAT."
SO BASICALLY YOU CAN'T UNDERSTAND THE THING AND IT SCARES YOU.
BUT YOU CAN'T BE BOTHERED TO EVEN TRY TO UNDERSTAND IT...
...SO YOU JUST GIVE UP AND SAY YOU HATE IT SO YOU DON'T HAVE TO THINK ABOUT IT ANYMORE.

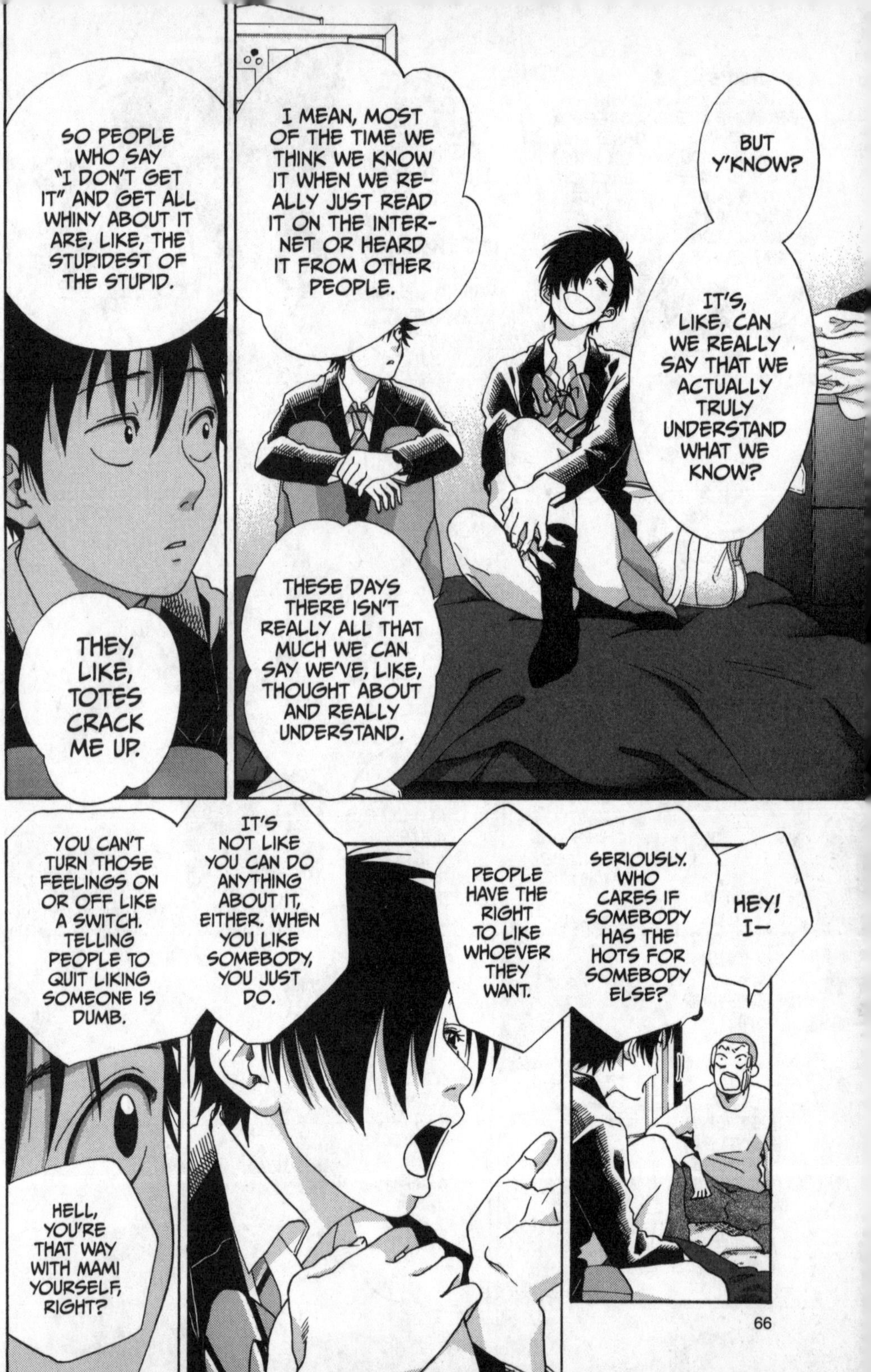
BUT Y'KNOW?
IT'S, LIKE, CAN WE REALLY SAY THAT WE ACTUALLY TRULY UNDERSTAND WHAT WE KNOW?
I MEAN, MOST OF THE TIME WE THINK WE KNOW IT WHEN WE RE-ALLY JUST READ IT ON THE INTER-NET OR HEARD IT FROM OTHER PEOPLE.
THESE DAYS THERE ISN'T REALLY ALL THAT MUCH WE CAN SAY WE'VE, LIKE, THOUGHT ABOUT AND REALLY UNDERSTAND.
SO PEOPLE WHO SAY "I DON'T GET IT" AND GET ALL WHINY ABOUT IT ARE, LIKE, THE STUPIDEST OF THE STUPID.
THEY, LIKE, TOTES CRACK ME UP.
HEY! I—
SERIOUSLY. WHO CARES IF SOMEBODY HAS THE HOTS FOR SOMEBODY ELSE?
PEOPLE HAVE THE RIGHT TO LIKE WHOEVER THEY WANT.
IT'S NOT LIKE YOU CAN DO ANYTHING ABOUT IT, EITHER. WHEN YOU LIKE SOMEBODY, YOU JUST DO.
YOU CAN'T TURN THOSE FEELINGS ON OR OFF LIKE A SWITCH. TELLING PEOPLE TO QUIT LIKING SOMEONE IS DUMB.
HELL, YOU'RE THAT WAY WITH MAMI YOURSELF, RIGHT?

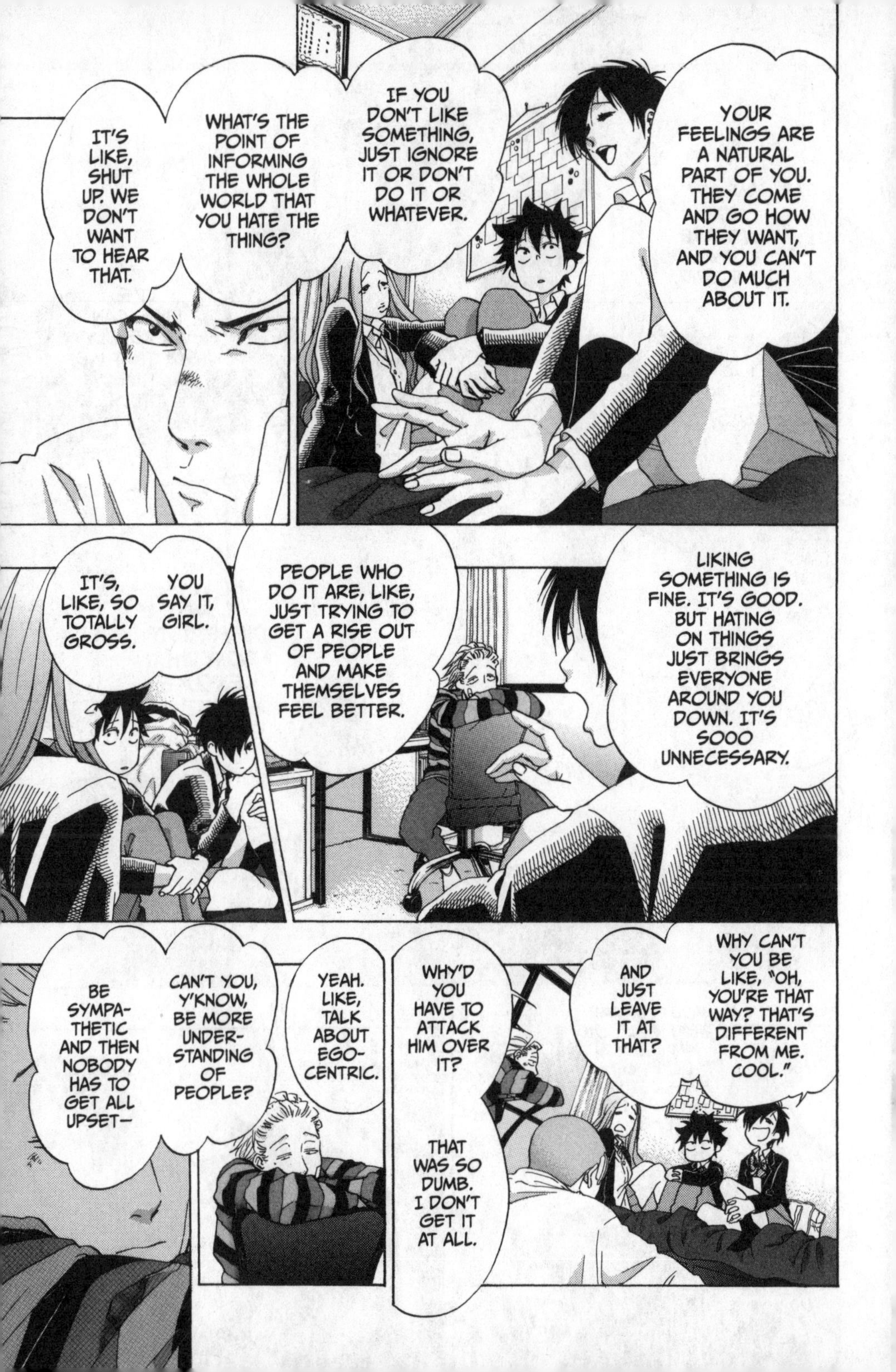
YOUR FEELINGS ARE A NATURAL PART OF YOU. THEY COME AND GO HOW THEY WANT, AND YOU CAN'T DO MUCH ABOUT IT.
IF YOU DON'T LIKE SOMETHING, JUST IGNORE IT OR DON'T DO IT OR WHATEVER.
WHAT'S THE POINT OF INFORMING THE WHOLE WORLD THAT YOU HATE THE THING?
IT'S LIKE, SHUT UP. WE DON'T WANT TO HEAR THAT.
LIKING SOMETHING IS FINE. IT'S GOOD. BUT HATING ON THINGS JUST BRINGS EVERYONE AROUND YOU DOWN. IT'S SOOO UNNECESSARY.
PEOPLE WHO DO IT ARE, LIKE, JUST TRYING TO GET A RISE OUT OF PEOPLE AND MAKE THEMSELVES FEEL BETTER.
IT'S, LIKE, SO TOTALLY GROSS.
YOU SAY IT, GIRL.
WHY CAN'T YOU BE LIKE, "OH, YOU'RE THAT WAY? THAT'S DIFFERENT FROM ME. COOL."
AND JUST LEAVE IT AT THAT?
WHY'D YOU HAVE TO ATTACK HIM OVER IT?
THAT WAS SO DUMB. I DON'T GET IT AT ALL.
YEAH. LIKE, TALK ABOUT EGO-CENTRIC.
CAN'T YOU, Y'KNOW, BE MORE UNDER-STANDING OF PEOPLE?
BE SYMPA-THETIC AND THEN NOBODY HAS TO GET ALL UPSET—

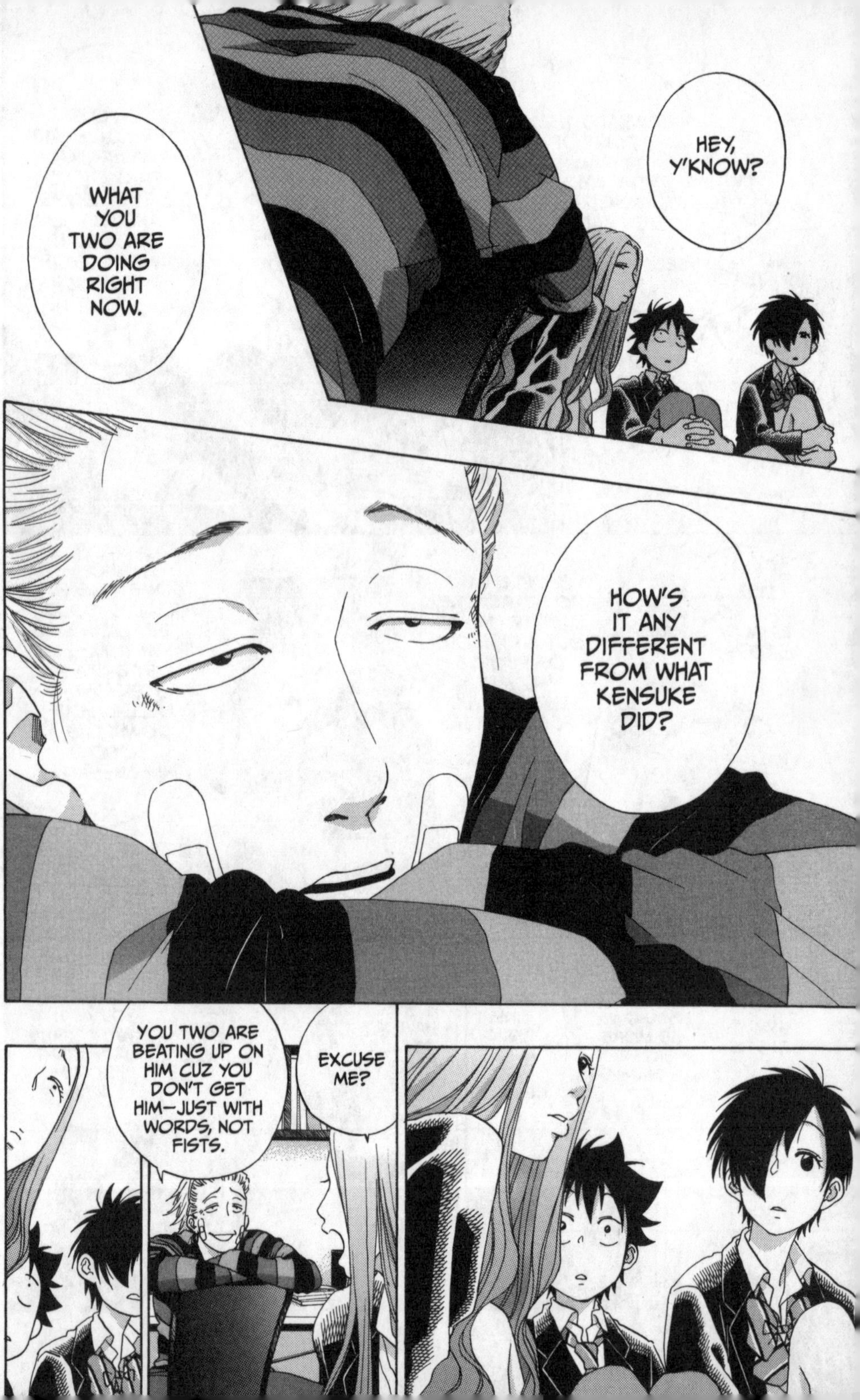
HEY, Y'KNOW?
WHAT YOU TWO ARE DOING RIGHT NOW.
HOW'S IT ANY DIFFERENT FROM WHAT KENSUKE DID?
EXCUSE ME?
YOU TWO ARE BEATING UP ON HIM CUZ YOU DON'T GET HIM—JUST WITH WORDS, NOT FISTS.

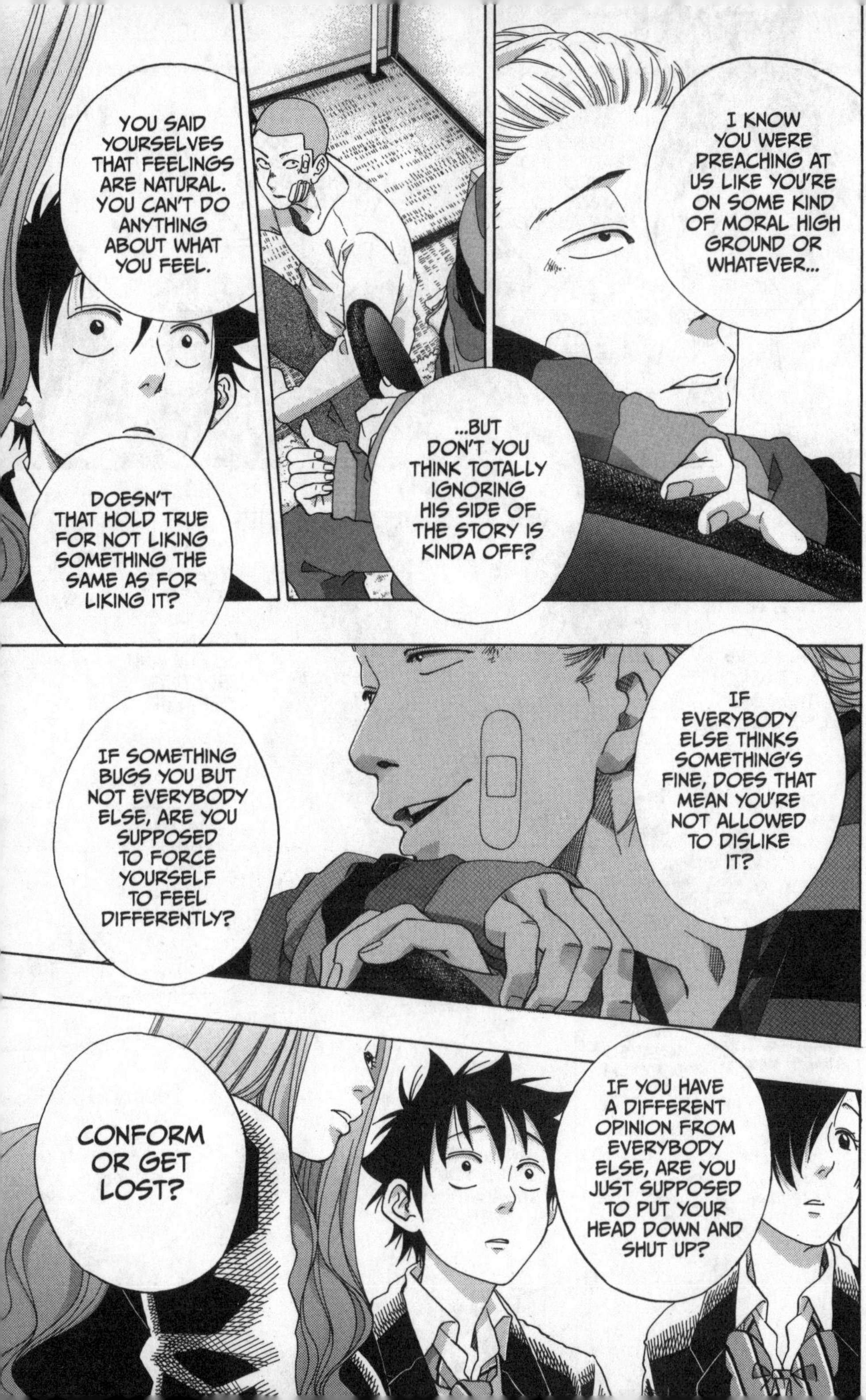
I KNOW YOU WERE PREACHING AT US LIKE YOU'RE ON SOME KIND OF MORAL HIGH GROUND OR WHATEVER...
...BUT DON'T YOU THINK TOTALLY IGNORING HIS SIDE OF THE STORY IS KINDA OFF?
YOU SAID YOURSELVES THAT FEELINGS ARE NATURAL. YOU CAN'T DO ANYTHING ABOUT WHAT YOU FEEL.
DOESN'T THAT HOLD TRUE FOR NOT LIKING SOMETHING THE SAME AS FOR LIKING IT?
IF EVERYBODY ELSE THINKS SOMETHING'S FINE, DOES THAT MEAN YOU'RE NOT ALLOWED TO DISLIKE IT?
IF SOMETHING BUGS YOU BUT NOT EVERYBODY ELSE, ARE YOU SUPPOSED TO FORCE YOURSELF TO FEEL DIFFERENTLY?
IF YOU HAVE A DIFFERENT OPINION FROM EVERYBODY ELSE, ARE YOU JUST SUPPOSED TO PUT YOUR HEAD DOWN AND SHUT UP?
CONFORM OR GET LOST?

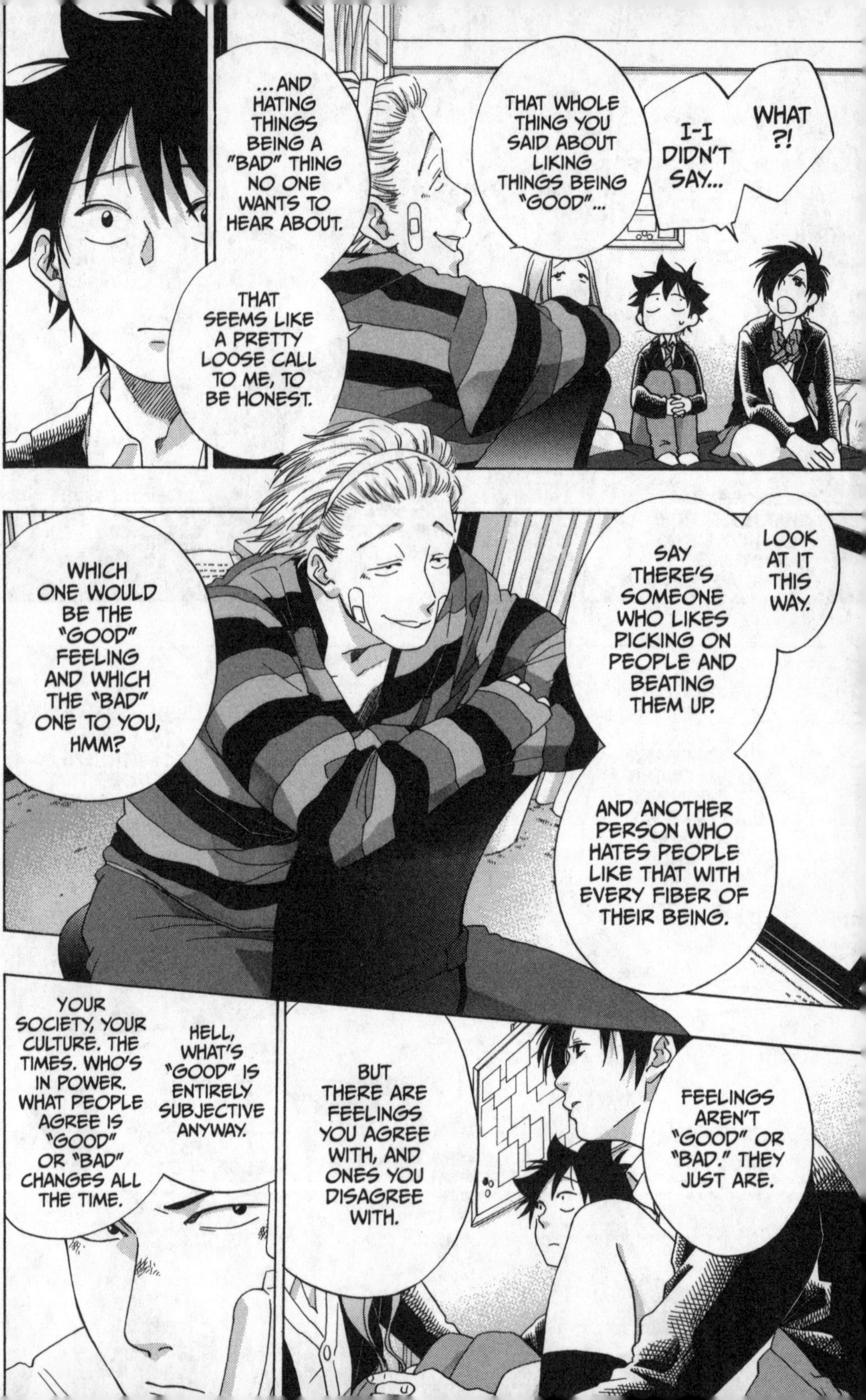
WHAT ?!
I-I DIDN'T SAY...
THAT WHOLE THING YOU SAID ABOUT LIKING THINGS BEING "GOOD"...
...AND HATING THINGS BEING A "BAD" THING NO ONE WANTS TO HEAR ABOUT.
THAT SEEMS LIKE A PRETTY LOOSE CALL TO ME, TO BE HONEST.
LOOK AT IT THIS WAY.
SAY THERE'S SOMEONE WHO LIKES PICKING ON PEOPLE AND BEATING THEM UP.
AND ANOTHER PERSON WHO HATES PEOPLE LIKE THAT WITH EVERY FIBER OF THEIR BEING.
WHICH ONE WOULD BE THE "GOOD" FEELING AND WHICH THE "BAD" ONE TO YOU, HMM?
FEELINGS AREN'T "GOOD" OR "BAD." THEY JUST ARE.
BUT THERE ARE FEELINGS YOU AGREE WITH, AND ONES YOU DISAGREE WITH.
HELL, WHAT'S "GOOD" IS ENTIRELY SUBJECTIVE ANYWAY.
YOUR SOCIETY, YOUR CULTURE. THE TIMES. WHO'S IN POWER. WHAT PEOPLE AGREE IS "GOOD" OR "BAD" CHANGES ALL THE TIME.

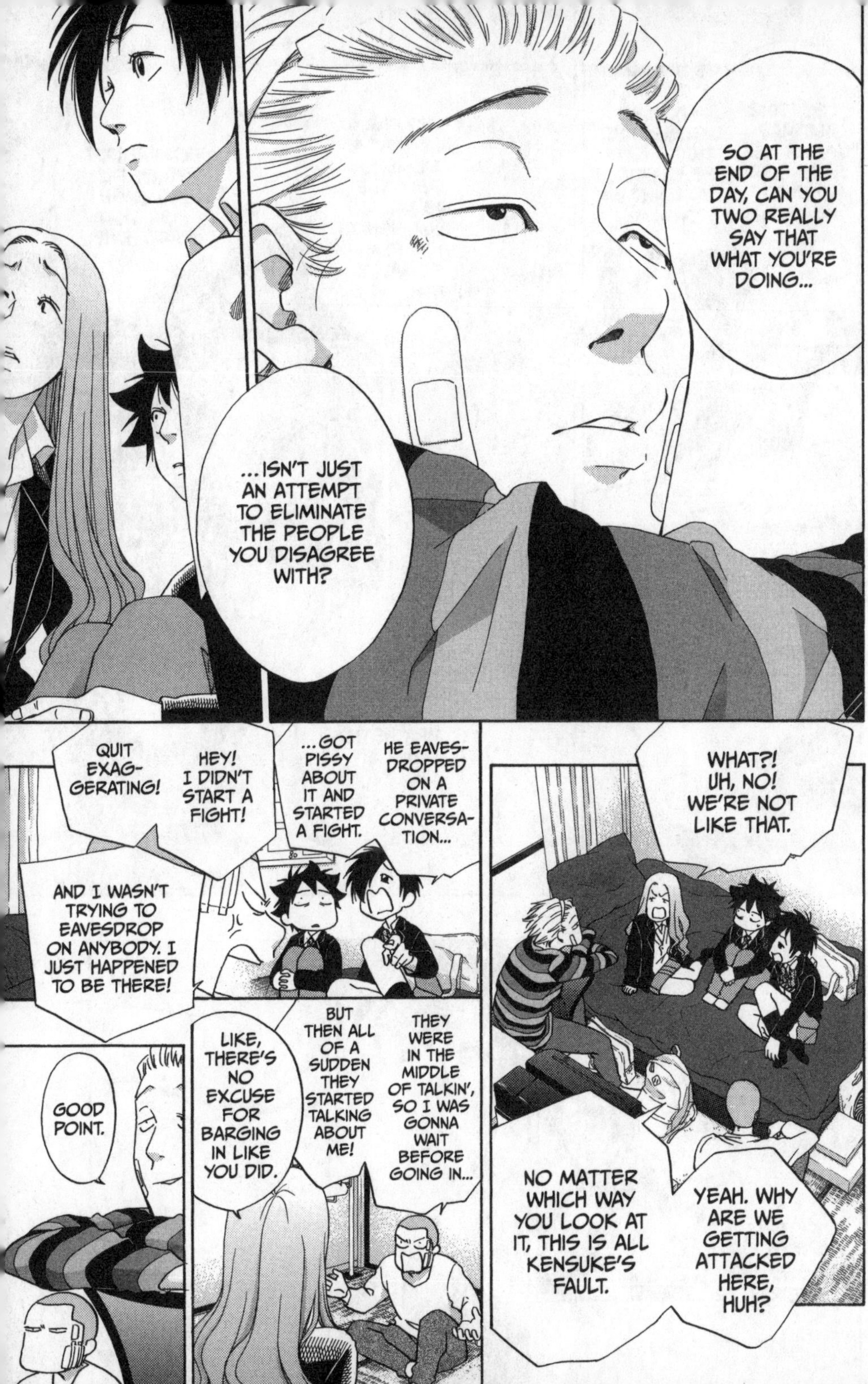
SO AT THE END OF THE DAY, CAN YOU TWO REALLY SAY THAT WHAT YOU'RE DOING...
...ISN'T JUST AN ATTEMPT TO ELIMINATE THE PEOPLE YOU DISAGREE WITH?
WHAT?! UH, NO! WE'RE NOT LIKE THAT.
YEAH. WHY ARE WE GETTING ATTACKED HERE, HUH?
NO MATTER WHICH WAY YOU LOOK AT IT, THIS IS ALL KENSUKE'S FAULT.
HE EAVES-DROPPED ON A PRIVATE CONVERSA-TION...
...GOT PISSY ABOUT IT AND STARTED A FIGHT.
HEY! I DIDN'T START A FIGHT!
QUIT EXAG-GERATING!
AND I WASN'T TRYING TO EAVESDROP ON ANYBODY. I JUST HAPPENED TO BE THERE!
THEY WERE IN THE MIDDLE OF TALKIN', SO I WAS GONNA WAIT BEFORE GOING IN...
BUT THEN ALL OF A SUDDEN THEY STARTED TALKING ABOUT ME!
LIKE, THERE'S NO EXCUSE FOR BARGING IN LIKE YOU DID.
GOOD POINT.

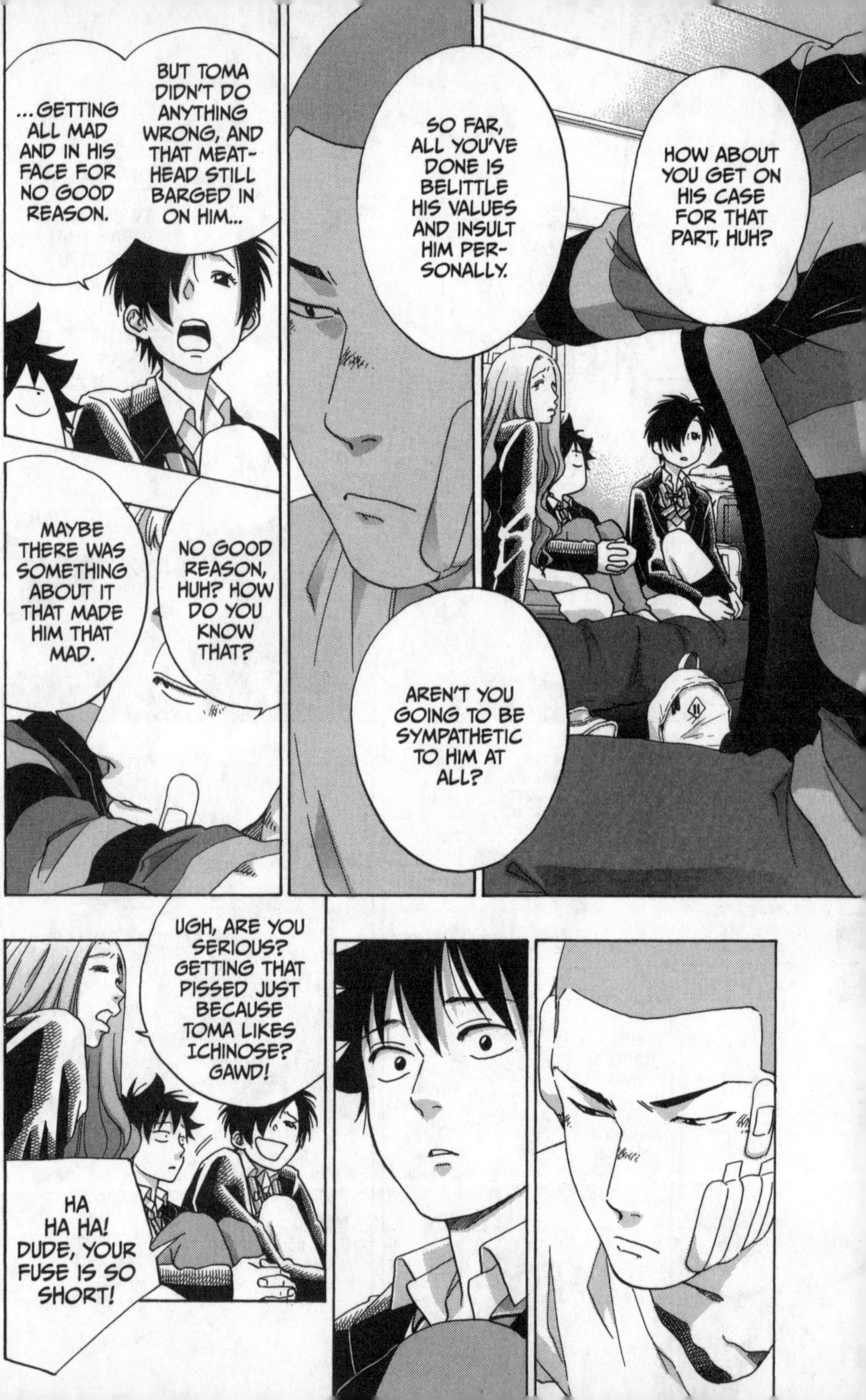
HOW ABOUT YOU GET ON HIS CASE FOR THAT PART, HUH?
AREN'T YOU GOING TO BE SYMPATHETIC TO HIM AT ALL?
SO FAR, ALL YOU'VE DONE IS BELITTLE HIS VALUES AND INSULT HIM PERSONALLY.
BUT TOMA DIDN'T DO ANYTHING WRONG, AND THAT MEATHEAD STILL BARGED IN ON HIM...
...GETTING ALL MAD AND IN HIS FACE FOR NO GOOD REASON.
NO GOOD REASON, HUH? HOW DO YOU KNOW THAT?
MAYBE THERE WAS SOMETHING ABOUT IT THAT MADE HIM THAT MAD.
UGH, ARE YOU SERIOUS? GETTING THAT PISSED JUST BECAUSE TOMA LIKES ICHINOSE? GAWD!
HA HA HA! DUDE, YOUR FUSE IS SO SHORT!

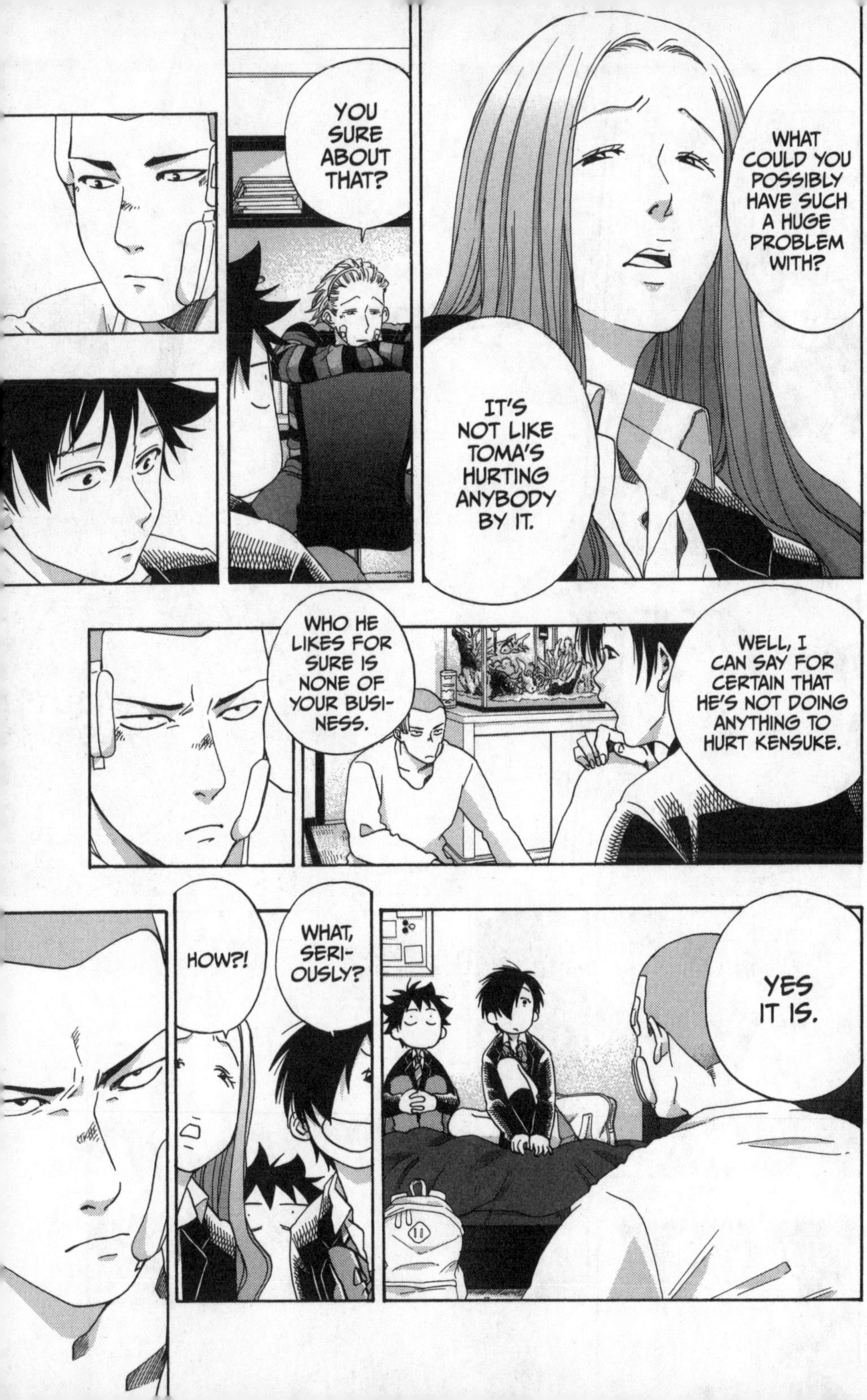
WHAT COULD YOU POSSIBLY HAVE SUCH A HUGE PROBLEM WITH?
IT'S NOT LIKE TOMA'S HURTING ANYBODY BY IT.
YOU SURE ABOUT THAT?
WELL, I CAN SAY FOR CERTAIN THAT HE'S NOT DOING ANYTHING TO HURT KENSUKE.
WHO HE LIKES FOR SURE IS NONE OF YOUR BUSI-NESS.
YES IT IS.
WHAT, SERI-OUSLY?
HOW?!

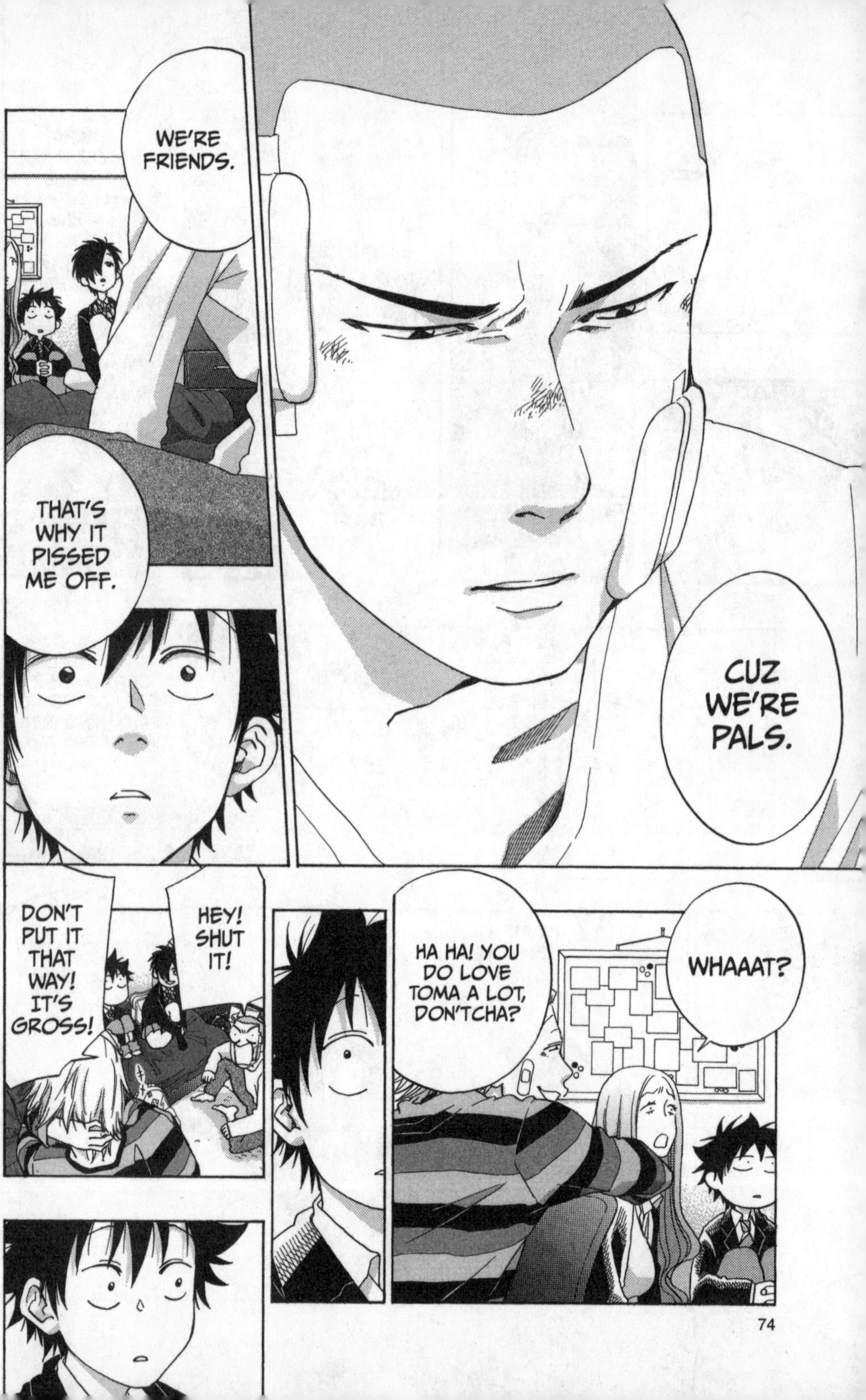
WE'RE FRIENDS.
THAT'S WHY IT PISSED ME OFF.
CUZ WE'RE PALS.
HA HA! YOU DO LOVE TOMA A LOT, DON'TCHA?
WHAAAT?
HEY! SHUT IT!
DON'T PUT IT THAT WAY! IT'S GROSS!

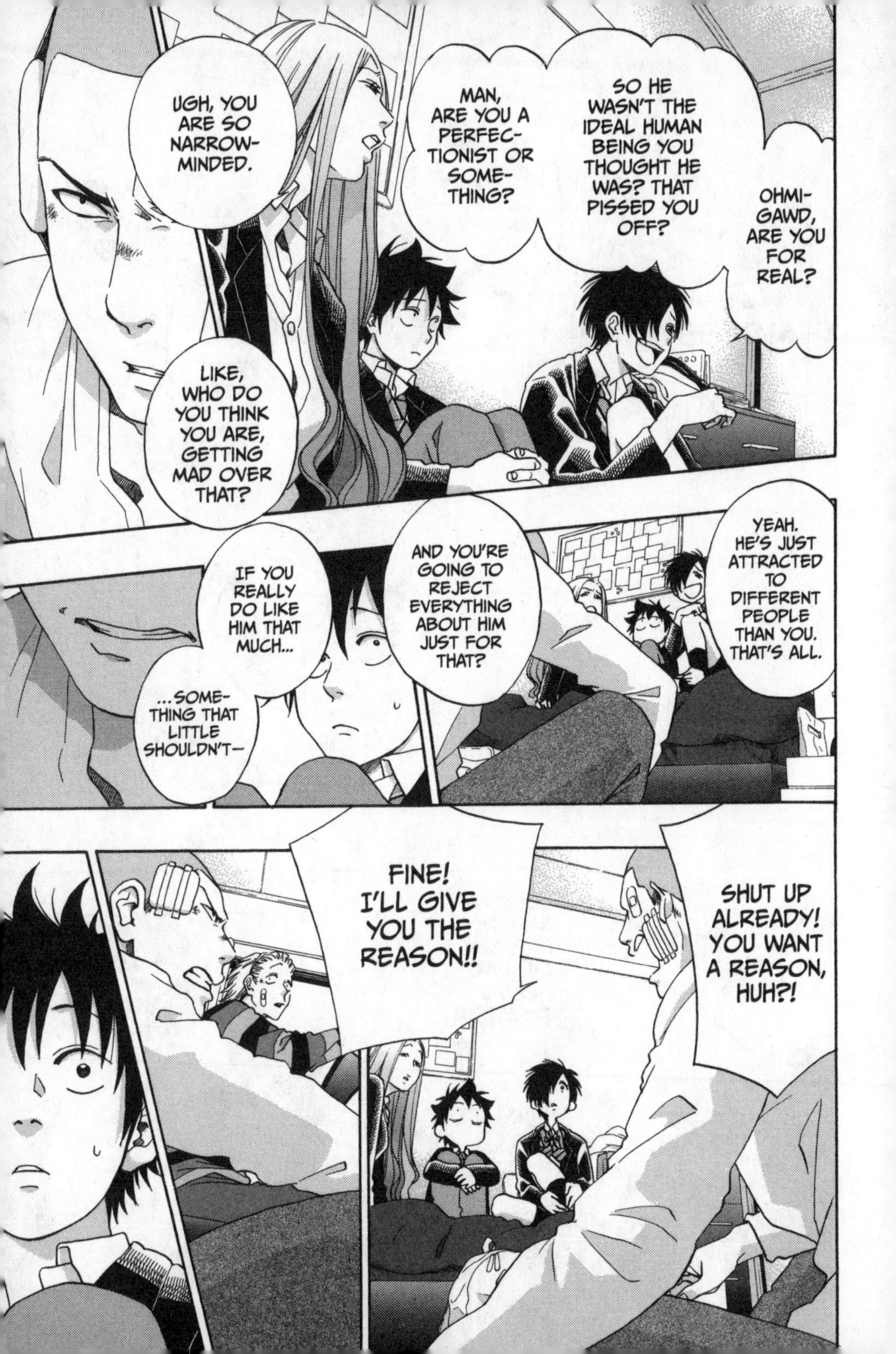
OHMI-GAWD, ARE YOU FOR REAL?
SO HE WASN'T THE IDEAL HUMAN BEING YOU THOUGHT HE WAS? THAT PISSED YOU OFF?
MAN, ARE YOU A PERFEC-TIONIST OR SOME-THING?
UGH, YOU ARE SO NARROW-MINDED.
LIKE, WHO DO YOU THINK YOU ARE, GETTING MAD OVER THAT?
YEAH. HE'S JUST ATTRACTED TO DIFFERENT PEOPLE THAN YOU. THAT'S ALL.
AND YOU'RE GOING TO REJECT EVERYTHING ABOUT HIM JUST FOR THAT?
IF YOU REALLY DO LIKE HIM THAT MUCH...
...SOME-THING THAT LITTLE SHOULDN'T—
SHUT UP ALREADY! YOU WANT A REASON, HUH?!
FINE! I'LL GIVE YOU THE REASON!!

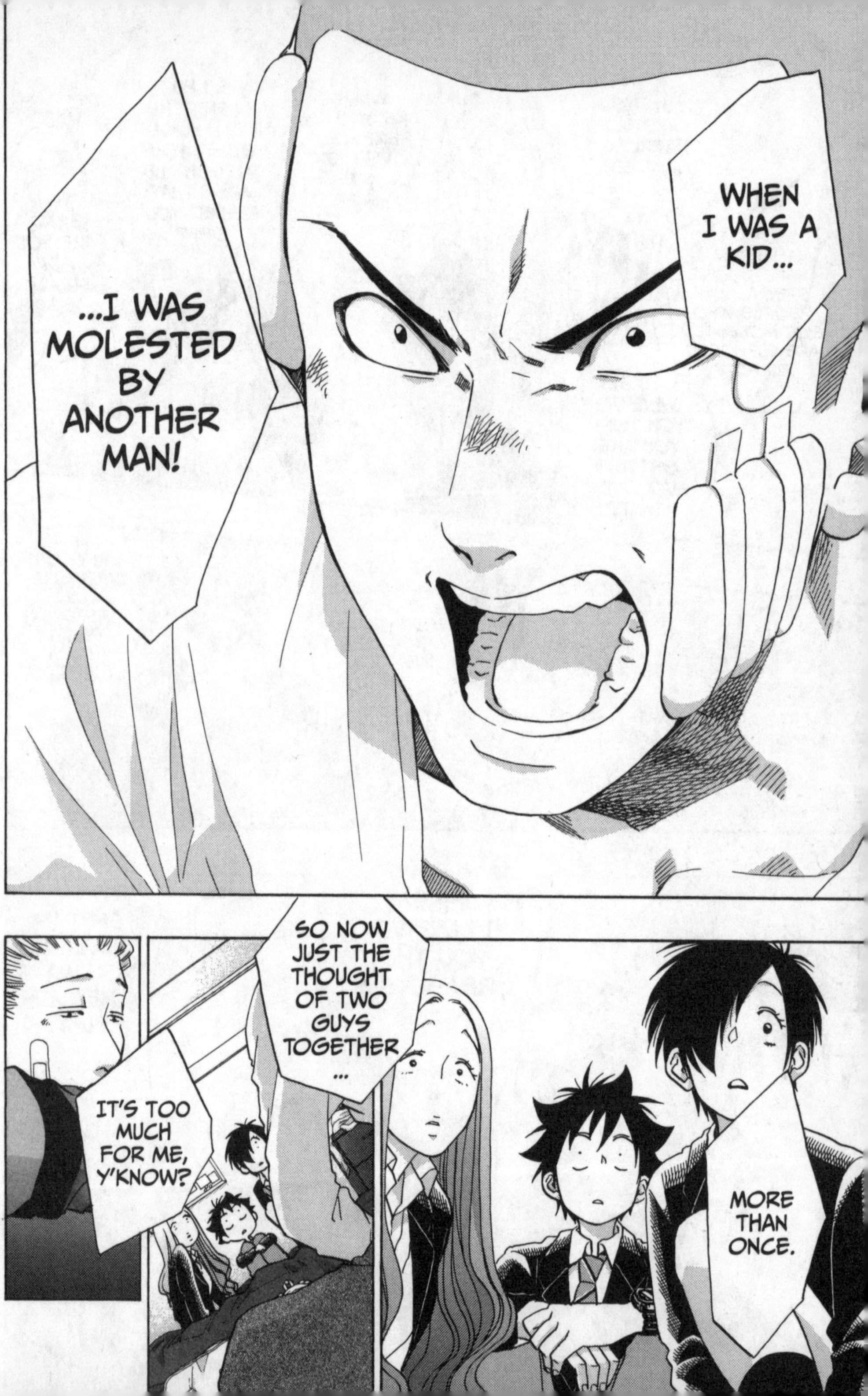
WHEN I WAS A KID...
...I WAS MOLESTED BY ANOTHER MAN!
MORE THAN ONCE.
SO NOW JUST THE THOUGHT OF TWO GUYS TOGETHER ...
IT'S TOO MUCH FOR ME, Y'KNOW?

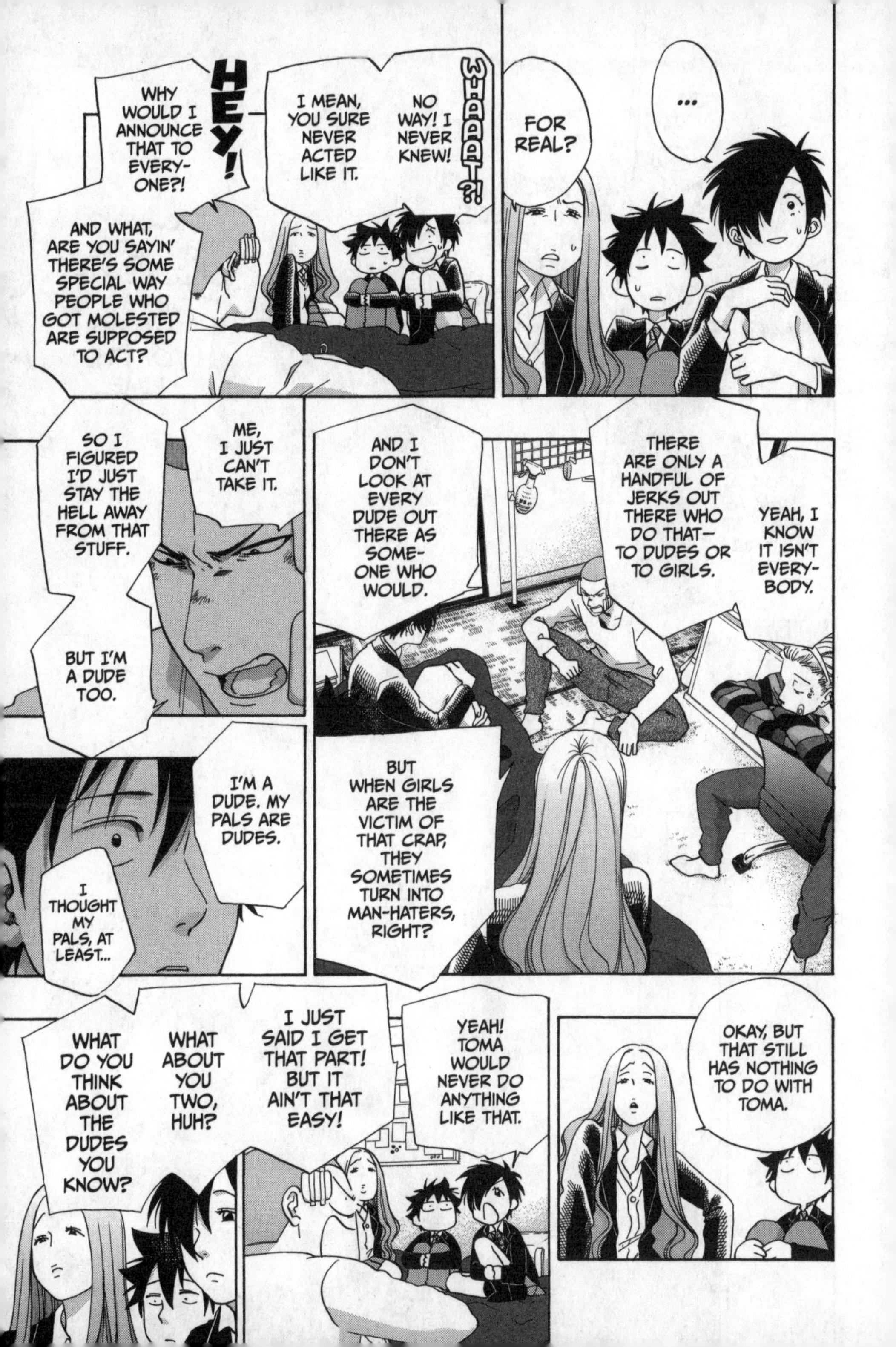
...
FOR REAL?
WHADDAT?!
NO WAY! I NEVER KNEW!
I MEAN, YOU SURE NEVER ACTED LIKE IT.
HEY!
WHY WOULD I ANNOUNCE THAT TO EVERY-ONE?!
AND WHAT, ARE YOU SAYIN' THERE'S SOME SPECIAL WAY PEOPLE WHO GOT MOLESTED ARE SUPPOSED TO ACT?
YEAH, I KNOW IT ISN'T EVERY-BODY.
THERE ARE ONLY A HANDFUL OF JERKS OUT THERE WHO DO THAT— TO DUDES OR TO GIRLS.
AND I DON'T LOOK AT EVERY DUDE OUT THERE AS SOME-ONE WHO WOULD.
BUT WHEN GIRLS ARE THE VICTIM OF THAT CRAP, THEY SOMETIMES TURN INTO MAN-HATERS, RIGHT?
ME, I JUST CAN'T TAKE IT.
SO I FIGURED I'D JUST STAY THE HELL AWAY FROM THAT STUFF.
BUT I'M A DUDE TOO.
I'M A DUDE. MY PALS ARE DUDES.
I THOUGHT MY PALS, AT LEAST...
OKAY, BUT THAT STILL HAS NOTHING TO DO WITH TOMA.
YEAH! TOMA WOULD NEVER DO ANYTHING LIKE THAT.
I JUST SAID I GET THAT PART! BUT IT AIN'T THAT EASY!
WHAT ABOUT YOU TWO, HUH?
WHAT DO YOU THINK ABOUT THE DUDES YOU KNOW?

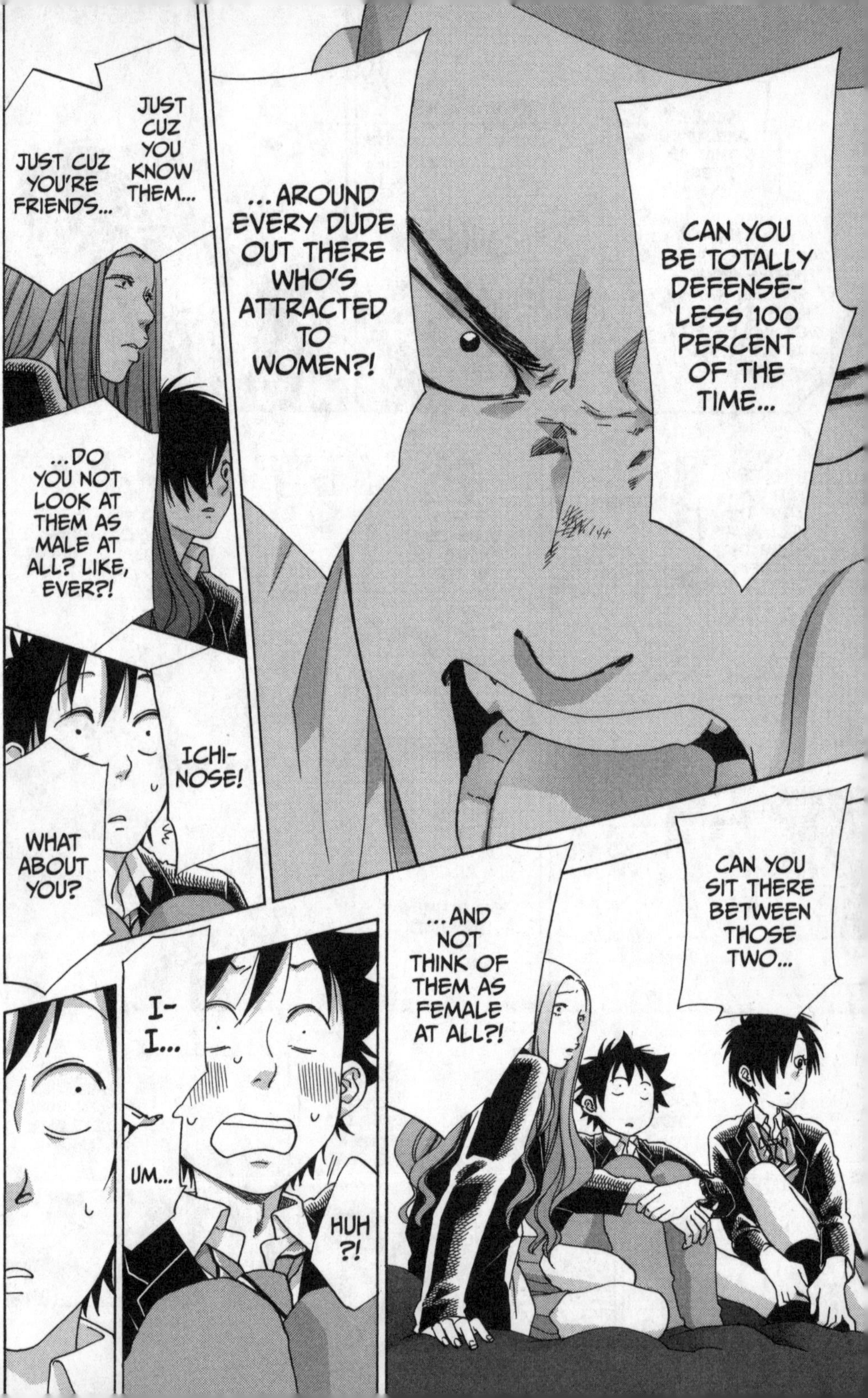
CAN YOU BE TOTALLY DEFENSE-LESS 100 PERCENT OF THE TIME...
...AROUND EVERY DUDE OUT THERE WHO'S ATTRACTED TO WOMEN?!
JUST CUZ YOU KNOW THEM...
JUST CUZ YOU'RE FRIENDS...
...DO YOU NOT LOOK AT THEM AS MALE AT ALL? LIKE, EVER?!
ICHI-NOSE!
WHAT ABOUT YOU?
CAN YOU SIT THERE BETWEEN THOSE TWO...
...AND NOT THINK OF THEM AS FEMALE AT ALL?!
I- I...
HUH ?!
UM...

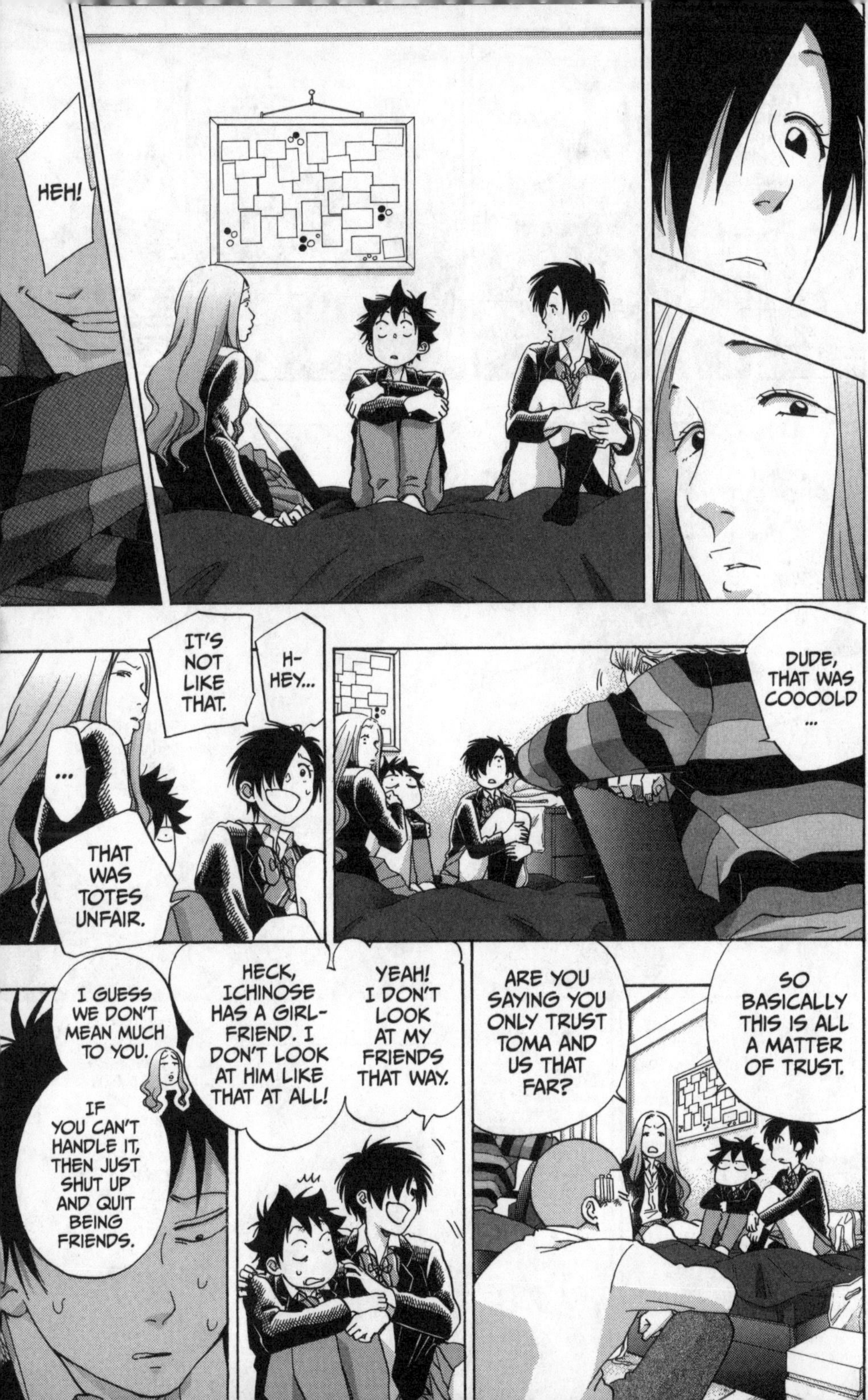
HEH!
DUDE, THAT WAS COOOOLD ...
H-HEY...
IT'S NOT LIKE THAT.
...
THAT WAS TOTES UNFAIR.
SO BASICALLY THIS IS ALL A MATTER OF TRUST.
ARE YOU SAYING YOU ONLY TRUST TOMA AND US THAT FAR?
YEAH! I DON'T LOOK AT MY FRIENDS THAT WAY.
HECK, ICHINOSE HAS A GIRL-FRIEND. I DON'T LOOK AT HIM LIKE THAT AT ALL!
I GUESS WE DON'T MEAN MUCH TO YOU.
IF YOU CAN'T HANDLE IT, THEN JUST SHUT UP AND QUIT BEING FRIENDS.

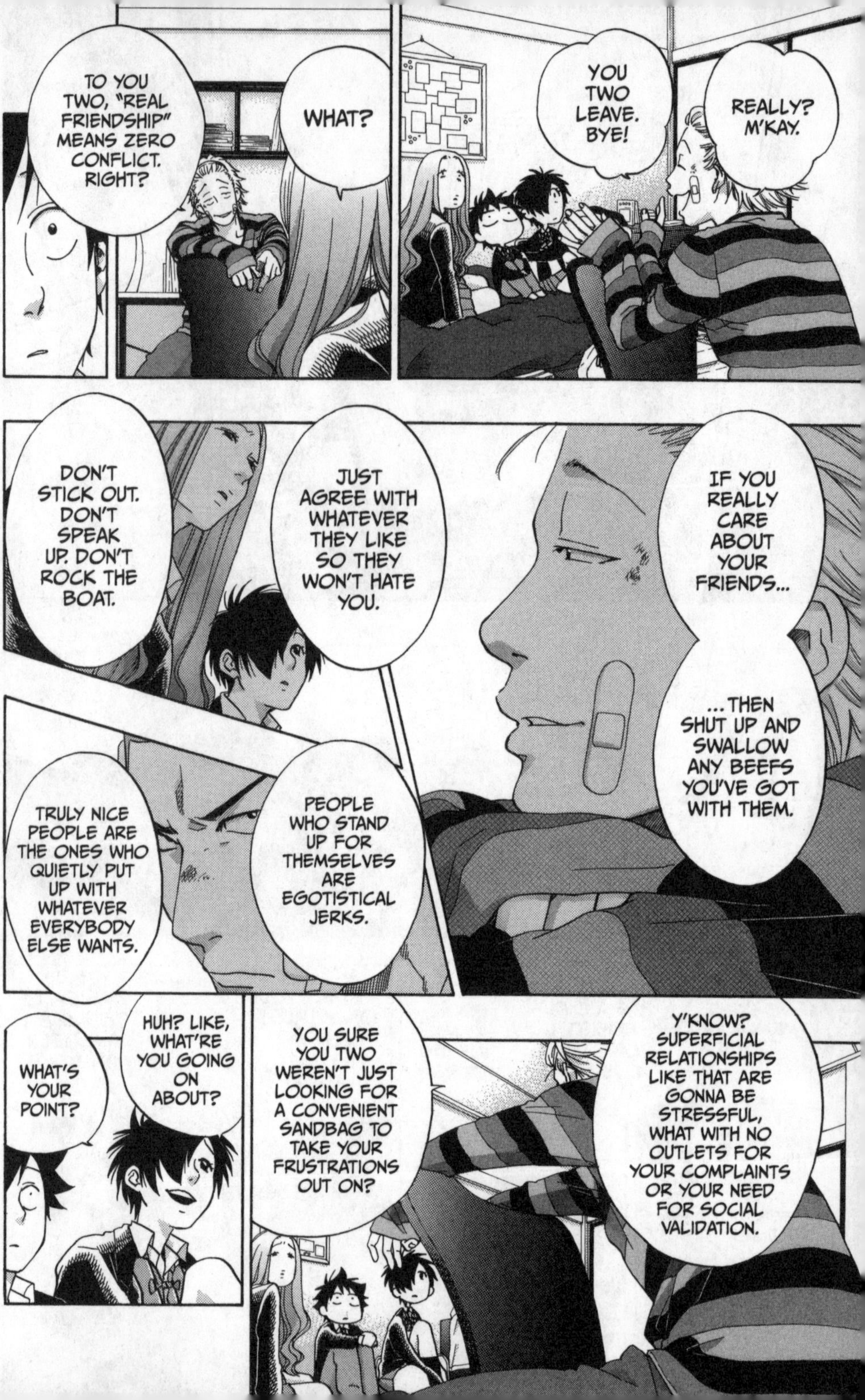
REALLY? M'KAY.
YOU TWO LEAVE. BYE!
TO YOU TWO, "REAL FRIENDSHIP" MEANS ZERO CONFLICT. RIGHT?
WHAT?
IF YOU REALLY CARE ABOUT YOUR FRIENDS...
...THEN SHUT UP AND SWALLOW ANY BEEFS YOU'VE GOT WITH THEM.
JUST AGREE WITH WHATEVER THEY LIKE SO THEY WON'T HATE YOU.
DON'T STICK OUT. DON'T SPEAK UP. DON'T ROCK THE BOAT.
PEOPLE WHO STAND UP FOR THEMSELVES ARE EGOTISTICAL JERKS.
TRULY NICE PEOPLE ARE THE ONES WHO QUIETLY PUT UP WITH WHATEVER EVERYBODY ELSE WANTS.
Y'KNOW? SUPERFICIAL RELATIONSHIPS LIKE THAT ARE GONNA BE STRESSFUL, WHAT WITH NO OUTLETS FOR YOUR COMPLAINTS OR YOUR NEED FOR SOCIAL VALIDATION.
YOU SURE YOU TWO WEREN'T JUST LOOKING FOR A CONVENIENT SANDBAG TO TAKE YOUR FRUSTRATIONS OUT ON?
HUH? LIKE, WHAT'RE YOU GOING ON ABOUT?
WHAT'S YOUR POINT?

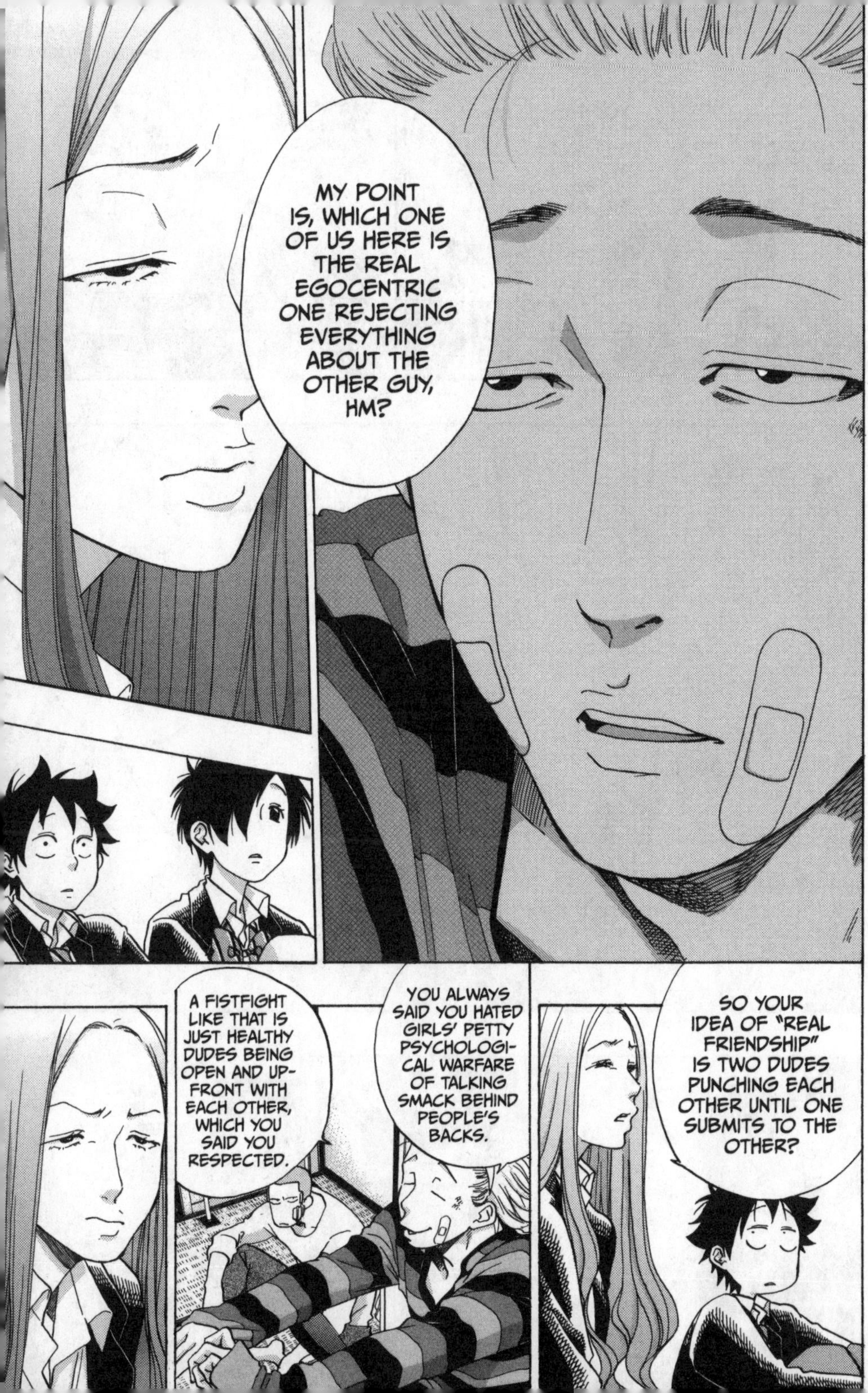

MY POINT IS, WHICH ONE OF US HERE IS THE REAL EGOCENTRIC ONE REJECTING EVERYTHING ABOUT THE OTHER GUY, HM?
SO YOUR IDEA OF "REAL FRIENDSHIP" IS TWO DUDES PUNCHING EACH OTHER UNTIL ONE SUBMITS TO THE OTHER?
YOU ALWAYS SAID YOU HATED GIRLS' PETTY PSYCHOLOGICAL WARFARE OF TALKING SMACK BEHIND PEOPLE'S BACKS.
A FISTFIGHT LIKE THAT IS JUST HEALTHY DUDES BEING OPEN AND UP-FRONT WITH EACH OTHER, WHICH YOU SAID YOU RESPECTED.

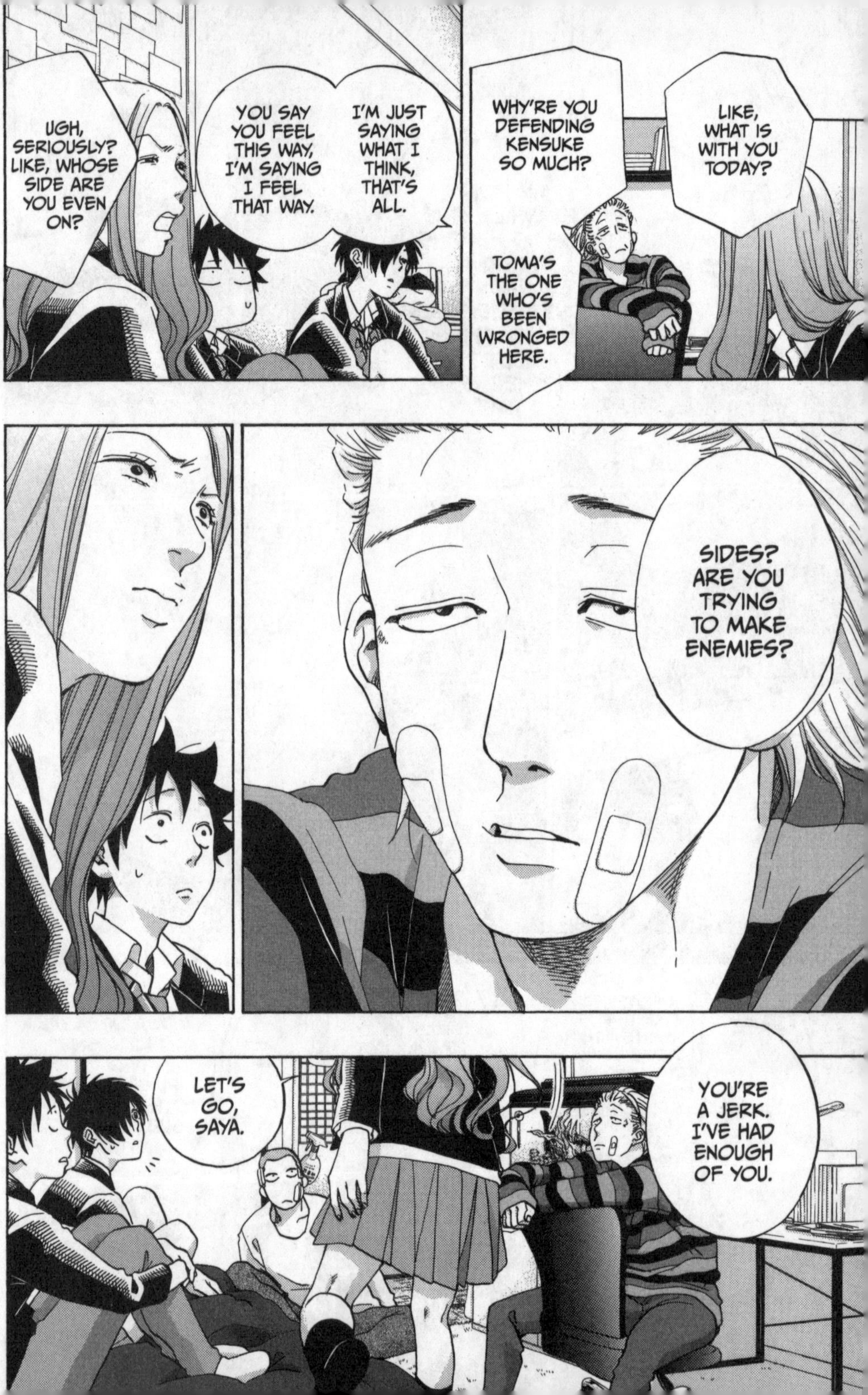

LIKE, WHAT IS WITH YOU TODAY?
WHY'RE YOU DEFENDING KENSUKE SO MUCH?
TOMA'S THE ONE WHO'S BEEN WRONGED HERE.
I'M JUST SAYING WHAT I THINK, THAT'S ALL.
YOU SAY YOU FEEL THIS WAY, I'M SAYING I FEEL THAT WAY.
UGH, SERIOUSLY? LIKE, WHOSE SIDE ARE YOU EVEN ON?
SIDES? ARE YOU TRYING TO MAKE ENEMIES?
YOU'RE A JERK. I'VE HAD ENOUGH OF YOU.
LET'S GO, SAYA.

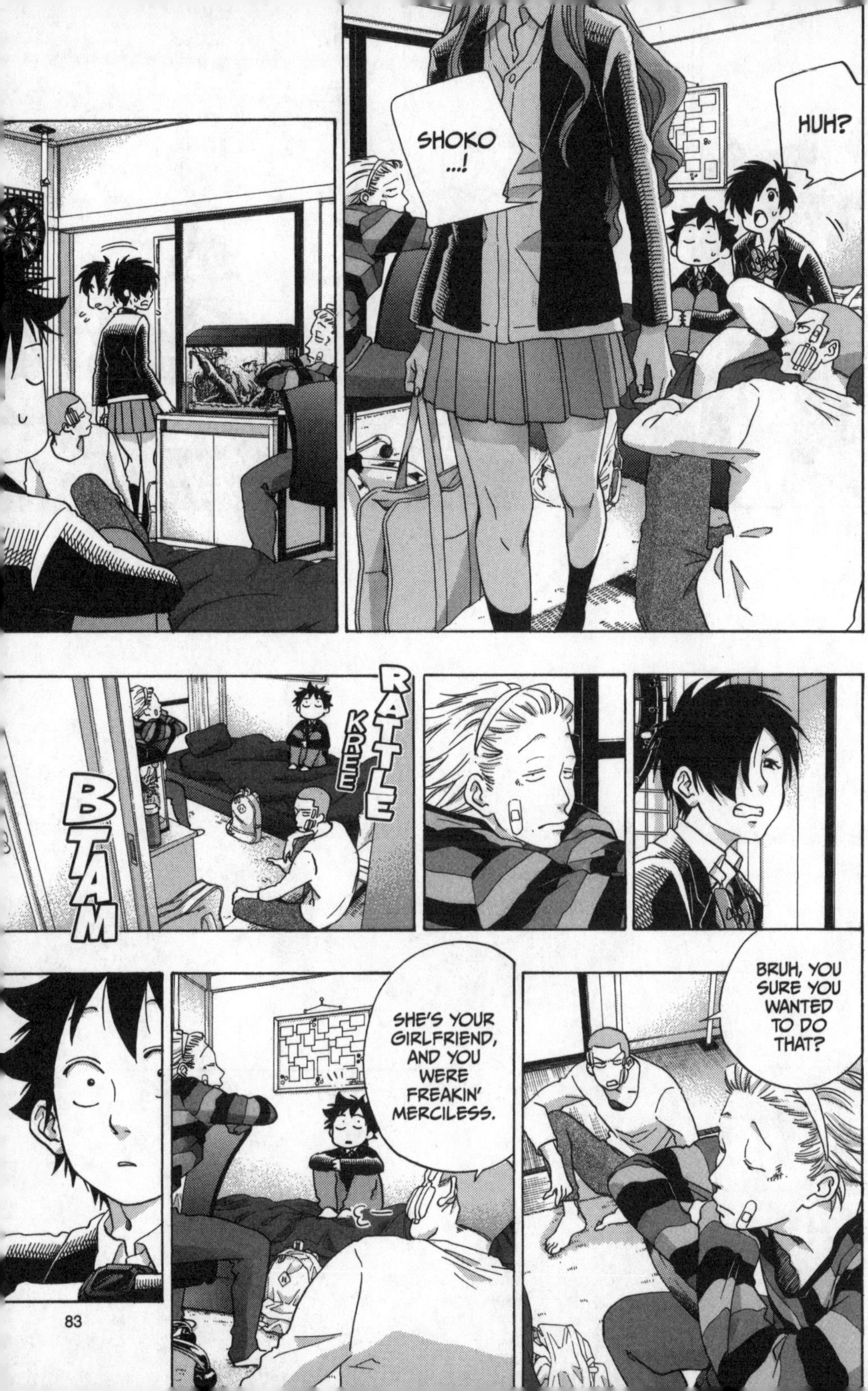

HUH?
SHOKO ...!
RATTLE
KREE
BTAM
BRUH, YOU SURE YOU WANTED TO DO THAT?
SHE'S YOUR GIRLFRIEND, AND YOU WERE FREAKIN' MERCILESS.

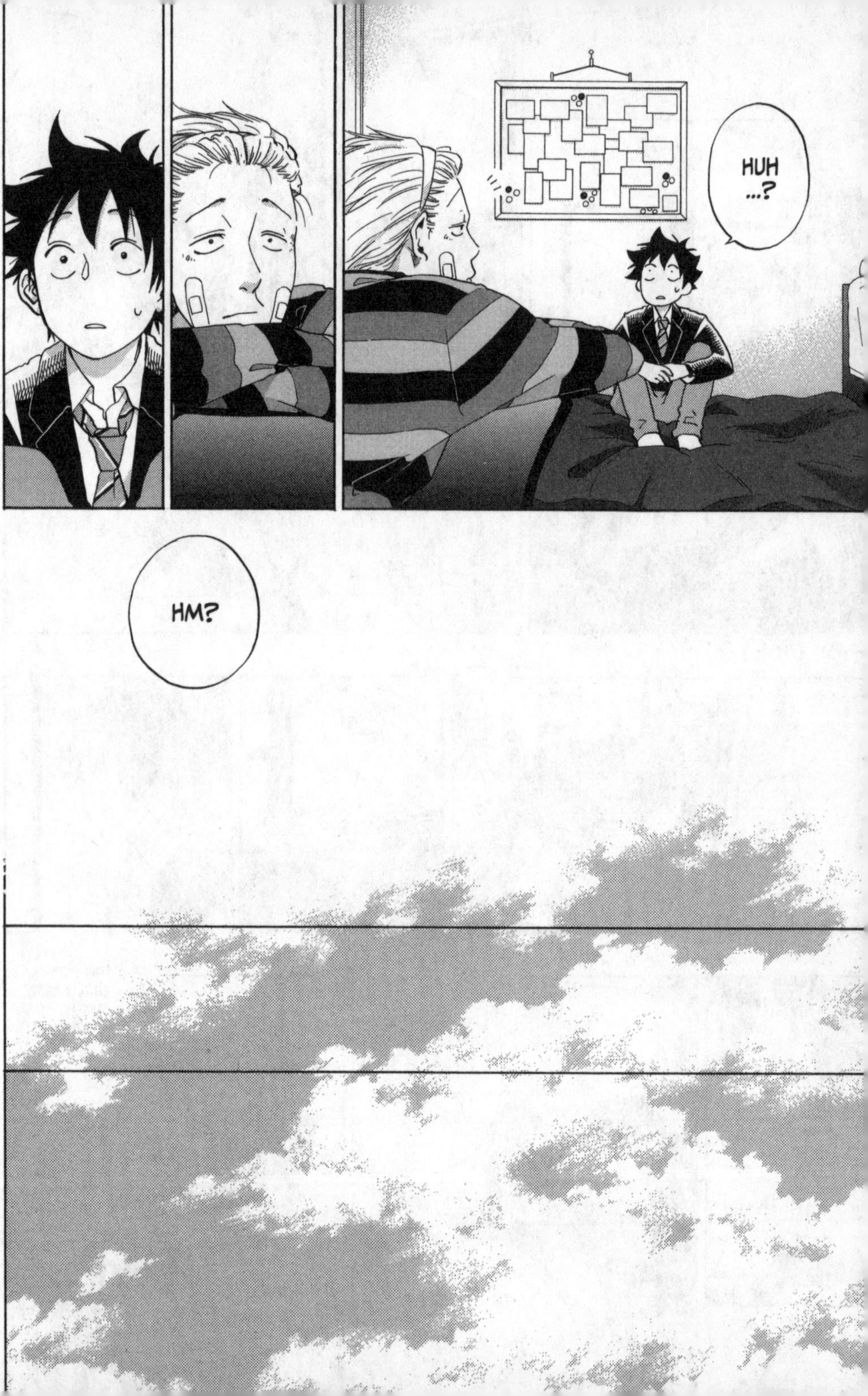
HUH ...?
HM?

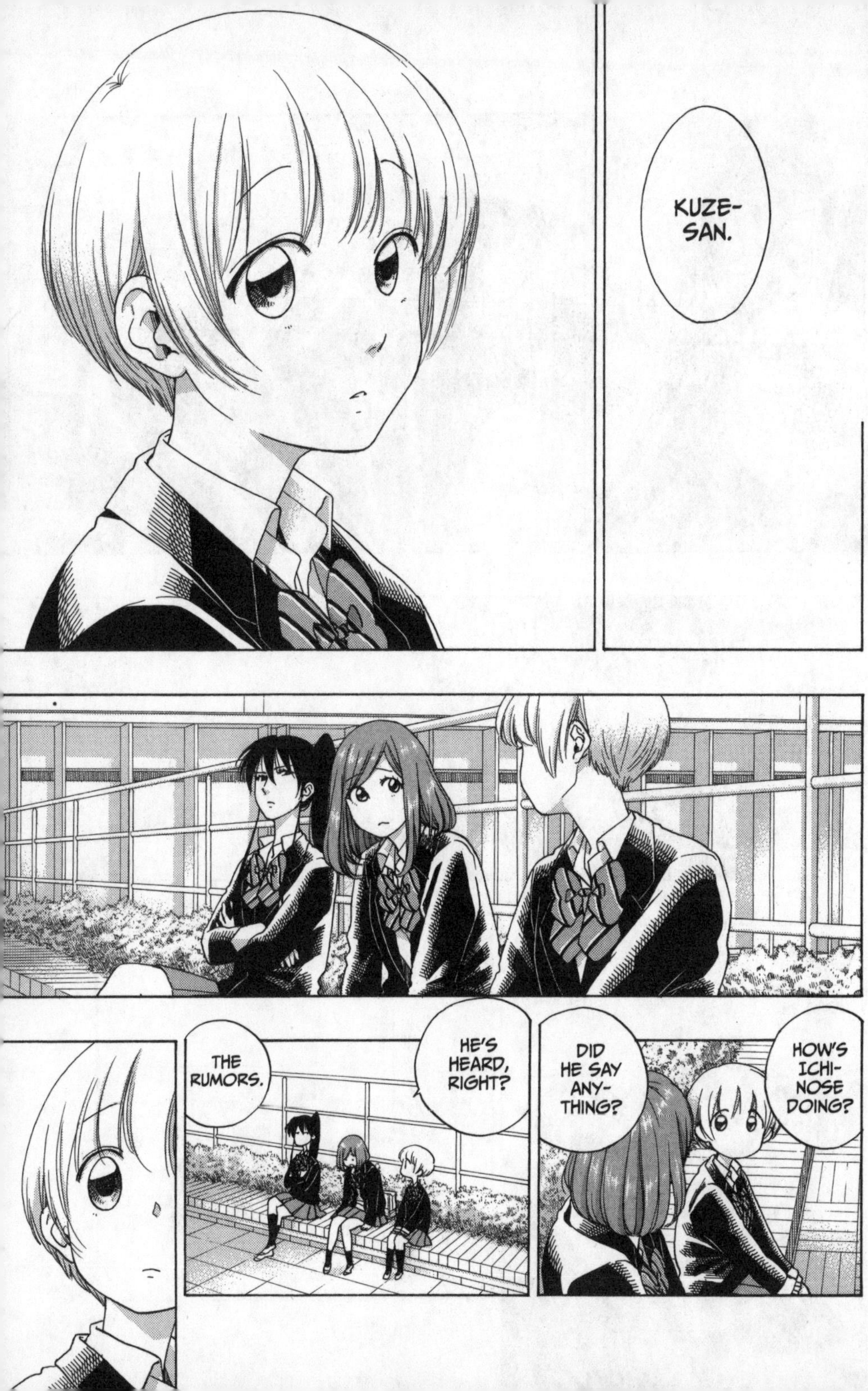
KUZE-SAN.
HOW'S ICHINOSE DOING?
DID HE SAY ANYTHING?
HE'S HEARD, RIGHT?
THE RUMORS.

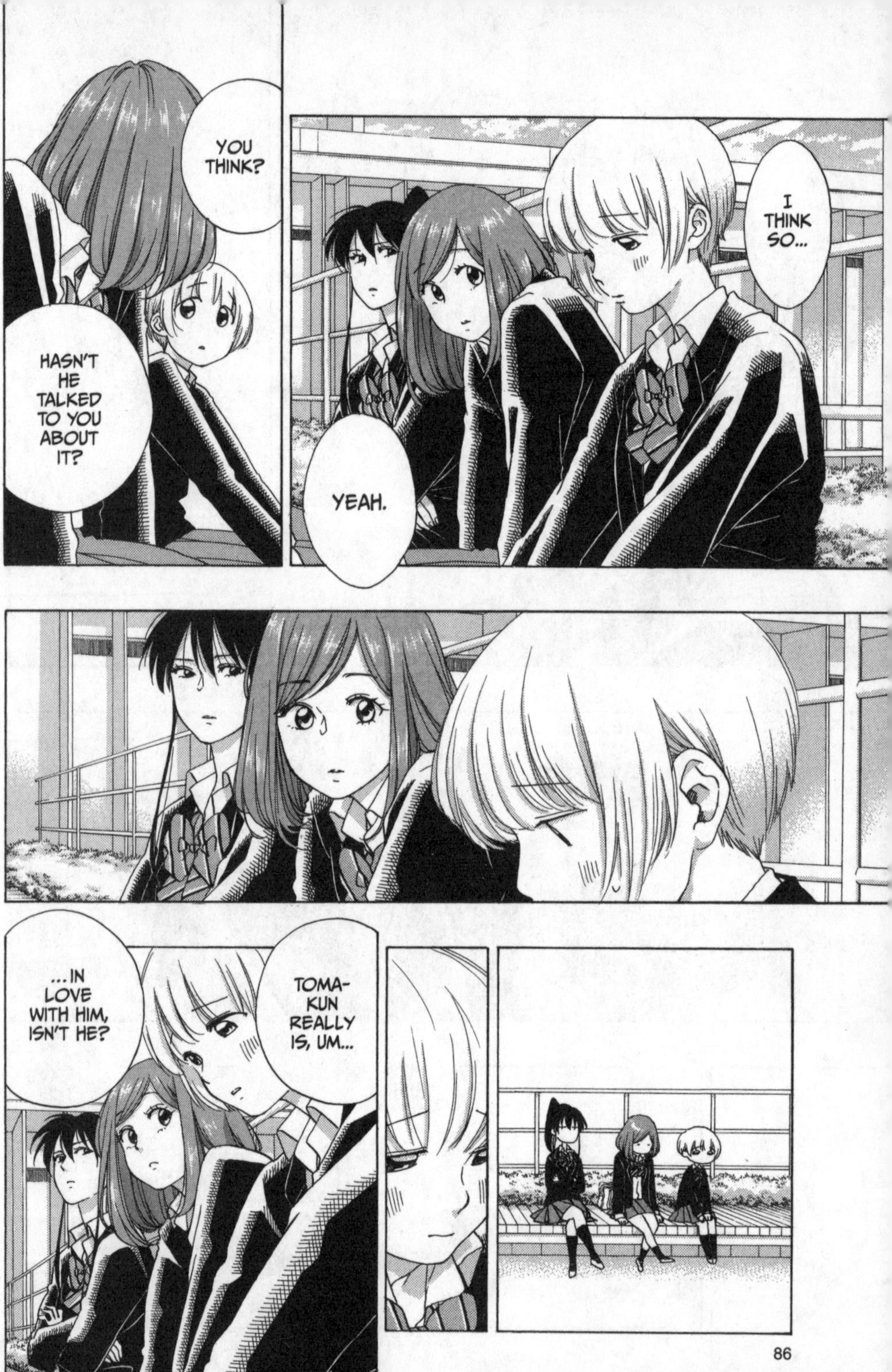
I THINK SO...
YEAH.
YOU THINK?
HASN'T HE TALKED TO YOU ABOUT IT?
TOMA-KUN REALLY IS, UM...
...IN LOVE WITH HIM, ISN'T HE?

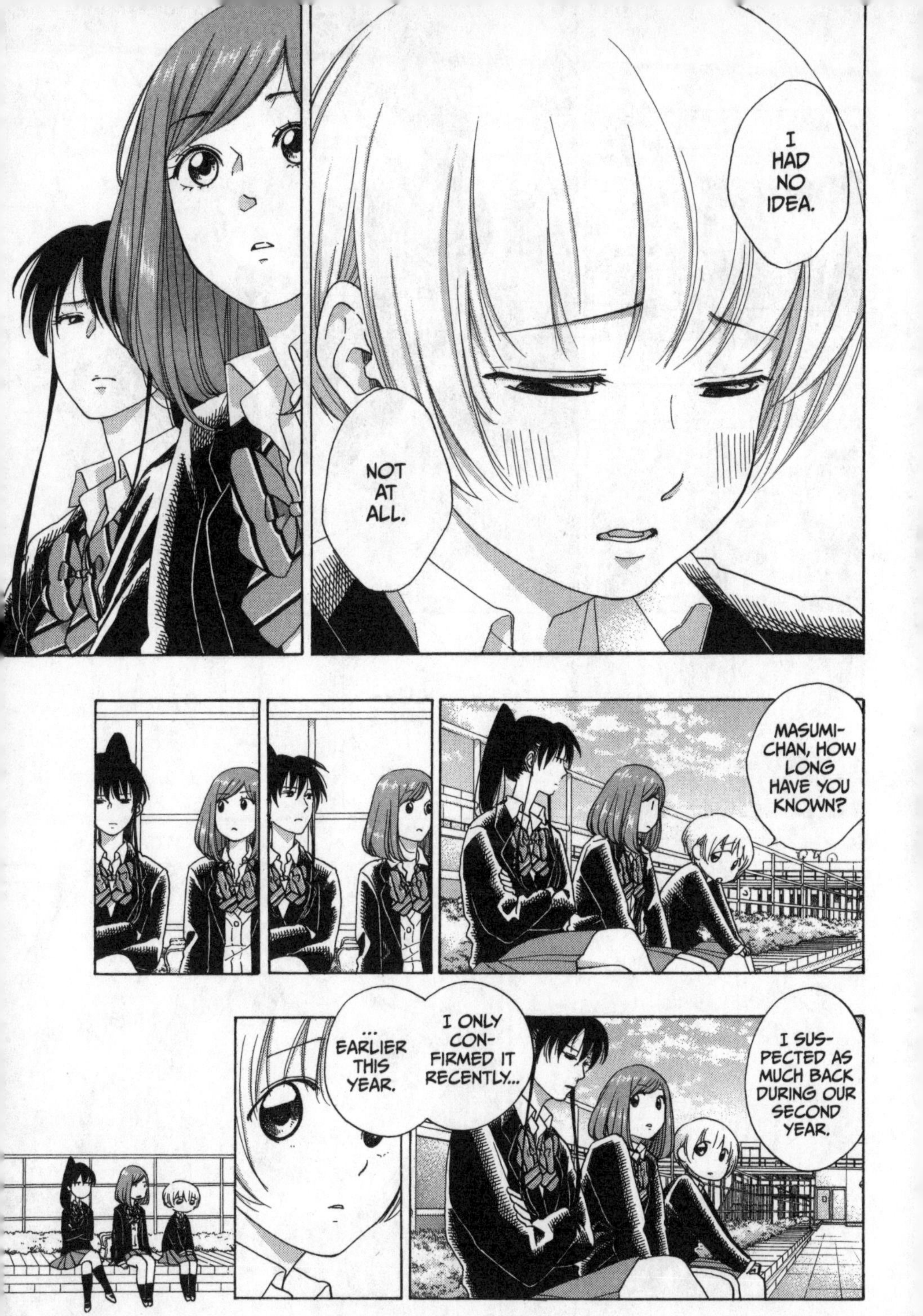
I HAD NO IDEA.
NOT AT ALL.
MASUMI-CHAN, HOW LONG HAVE YOU KNOWN?
I SUSPECTED AS MUCH BACK DURING OUR SECOND YEAR.
I ONLY CONFIRMED IT RECENTLY...
... EARLIER THIS YEAR.

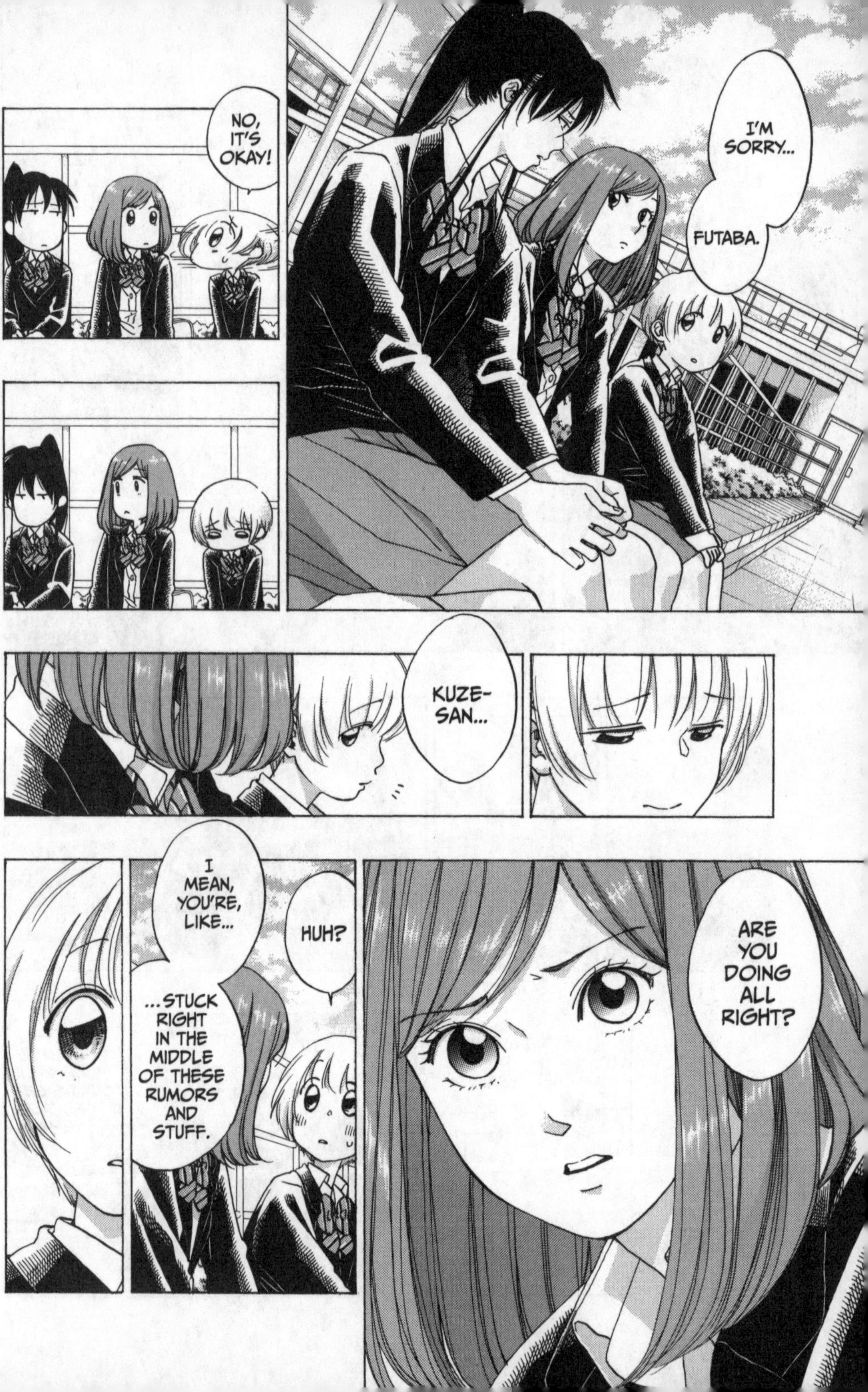
I'M SORRY...
FUTABA.
NO, IT'S OKAY!
KUZE-SAN...
ARE YOU DOING ALL RIGHT?
HUH?
I MEAN, YOU'RE, LIKE...
...STUCK RIGHT IN THE MIDDLE OF THESE RUMORS AND STUFF.

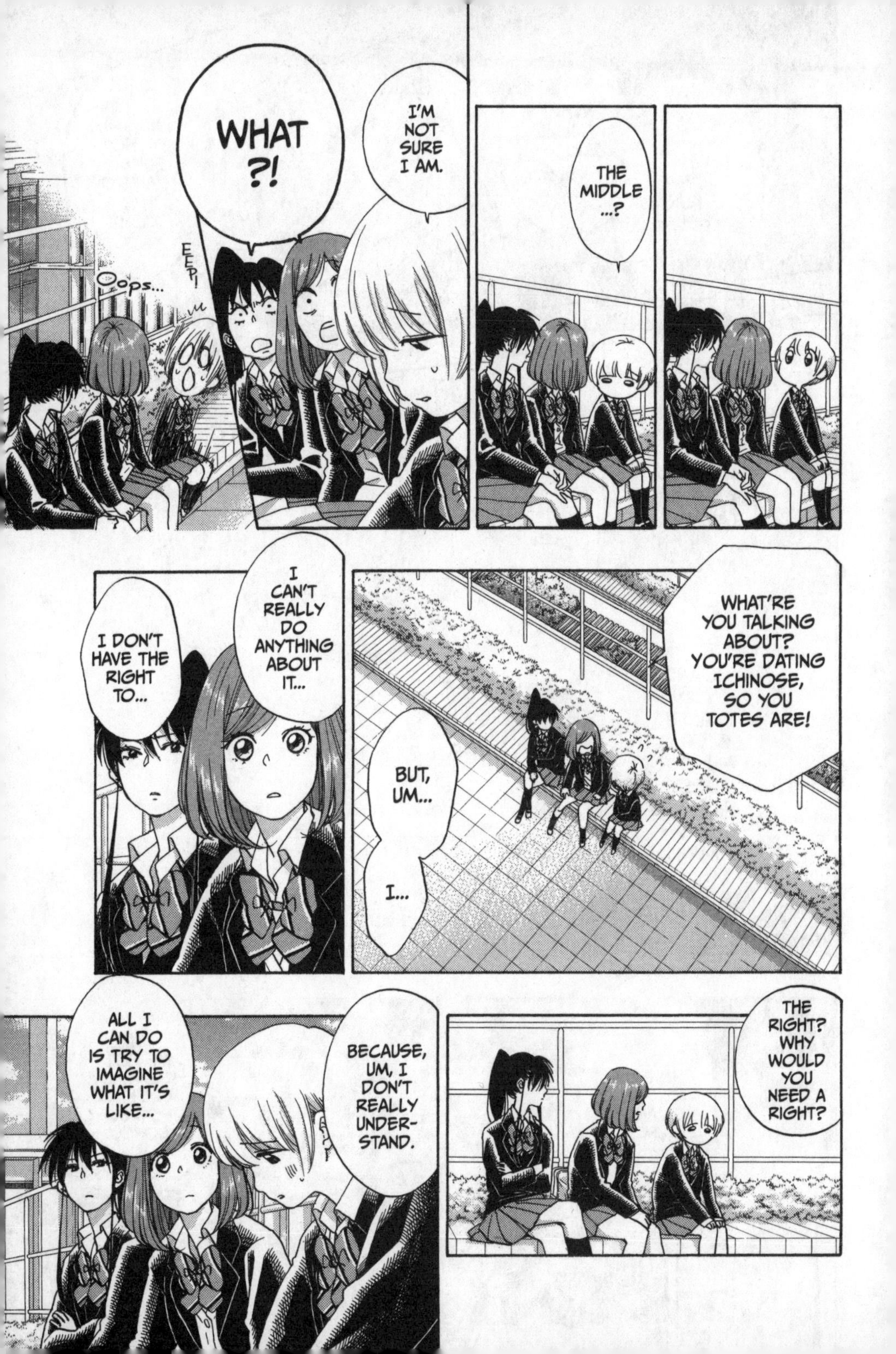
THE MIDDLE ...?
I'M NOT SURE I AM.
WHAT ?!
EEP!
Oops...
WHAT'RE YOU TALKING ABOUT? YOU'RE DATING ICHINOSE, SO YOU TOTES ARE!
BUT, UM...
I...
I CAN'T REALLY DO ANYTHING ABOUT IT...
I DON'T HAVE THE RIGHT TO...
THE RIGHT? WHY WOULD YOU NEED A RIGHT?
BECAUSE, UM, I DON'T REALLY UNDER-STAND.
ALL I CAN DO IS TRY TO IMAGINE WHAT IT'S LIKE...

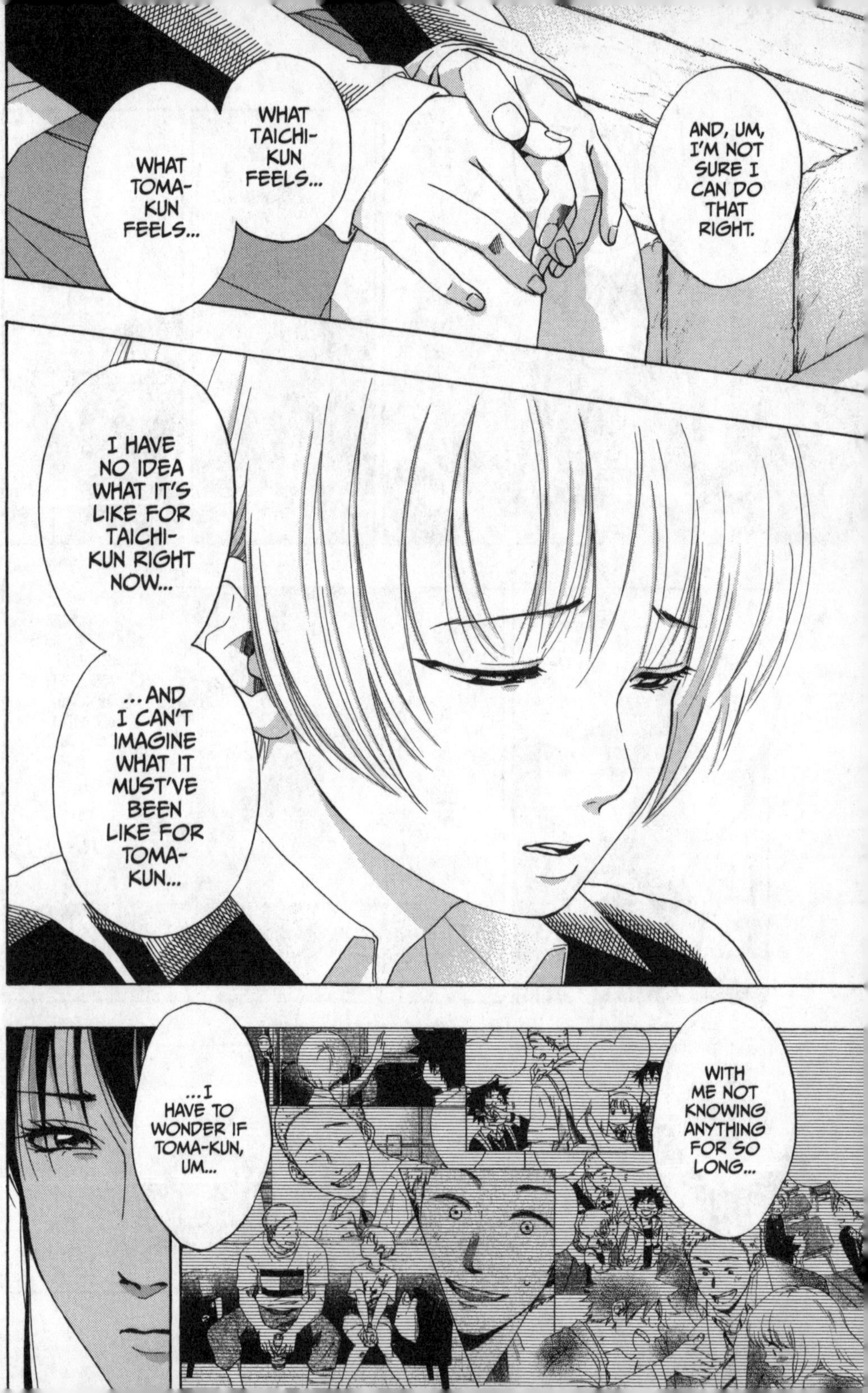
AND, UM, I'M NOT SURE I CAN DO THAT RIGHT.
WHAT TAICHI-KUN FEELS...
WHAT TOMA-KUN FEELS...
I HAVE NO IDEA WHAT IT'S LIKE FOR TAICHI-KUN RIGHT NOW...
...AND I CAN'T IMAGINE WHAT IT MUST'VE BEEN LIKE FOR TOMA-KUN...
WITH ME NOT KNOWING ANYTHING FOR SO LONG...
...I HAVE TO WONDER IF TOMA-KUN, UM...

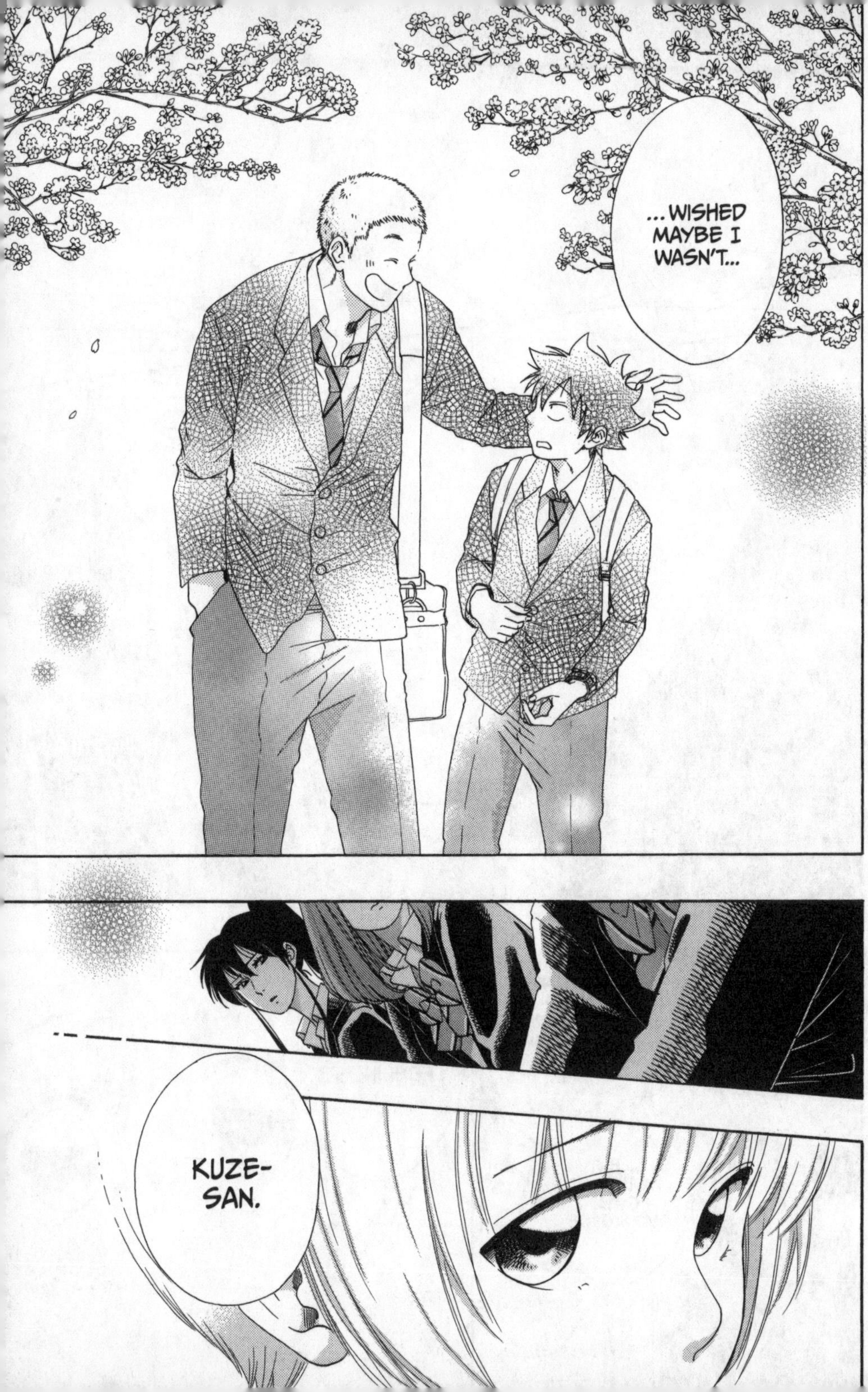
...WISHED MAYBE I WASN'T...
KUZE-SAN.

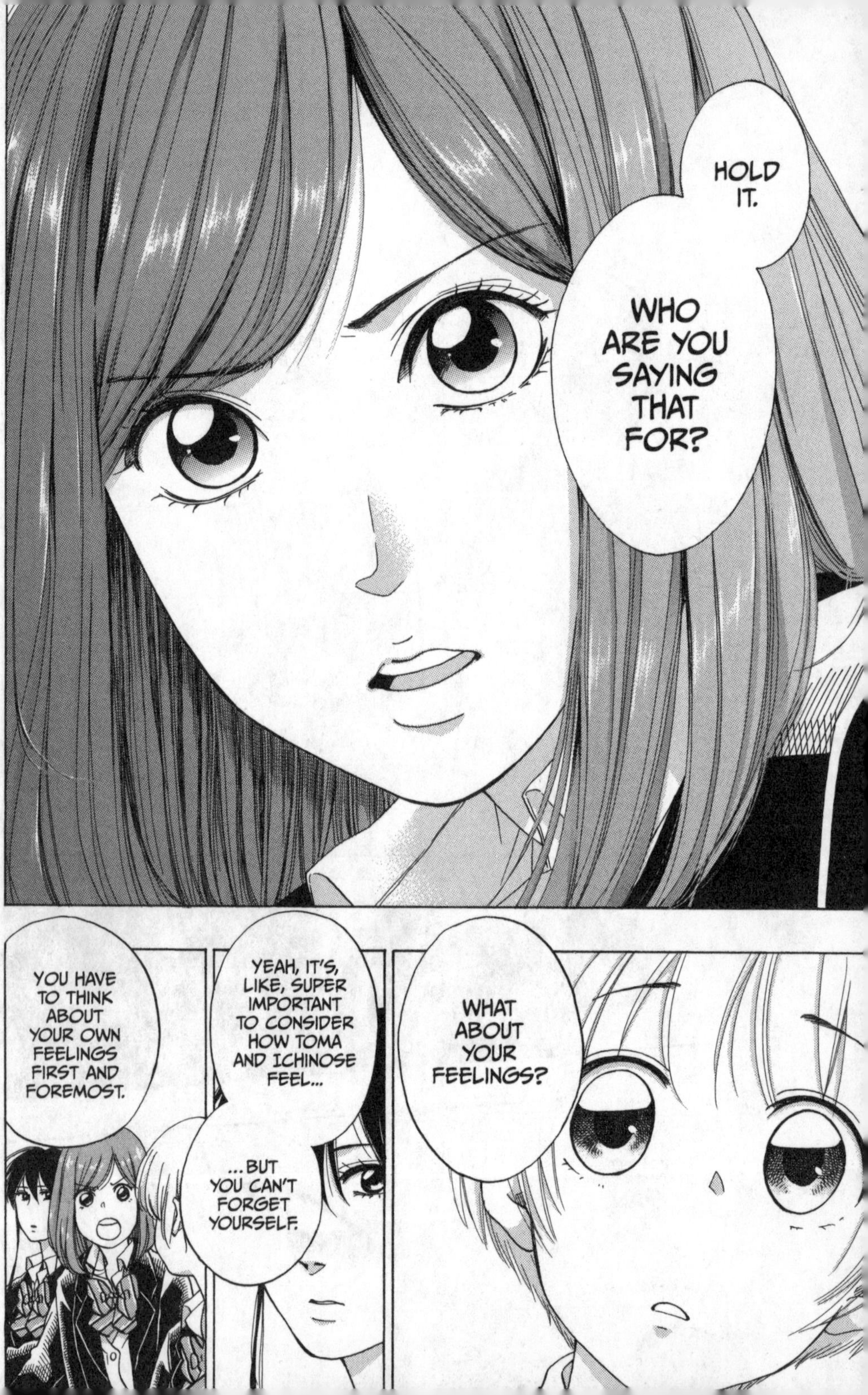
HOLD IT.
WHO ARE YOU SAYING THAT FOR?
WHAT ABOUT YOUR FEELINGS?
YEAH, IT'S, LIKE, SUPER IMPORTANT TO CONSIDER HOW TOMA AND ICHINOSE FEEL...
...BUT YOU CAN'T FORGET YOURSELF.
YOU HAVE TO THINK ABOUT YOUR OWN FEELINGS FIRST AND FOREMOST.

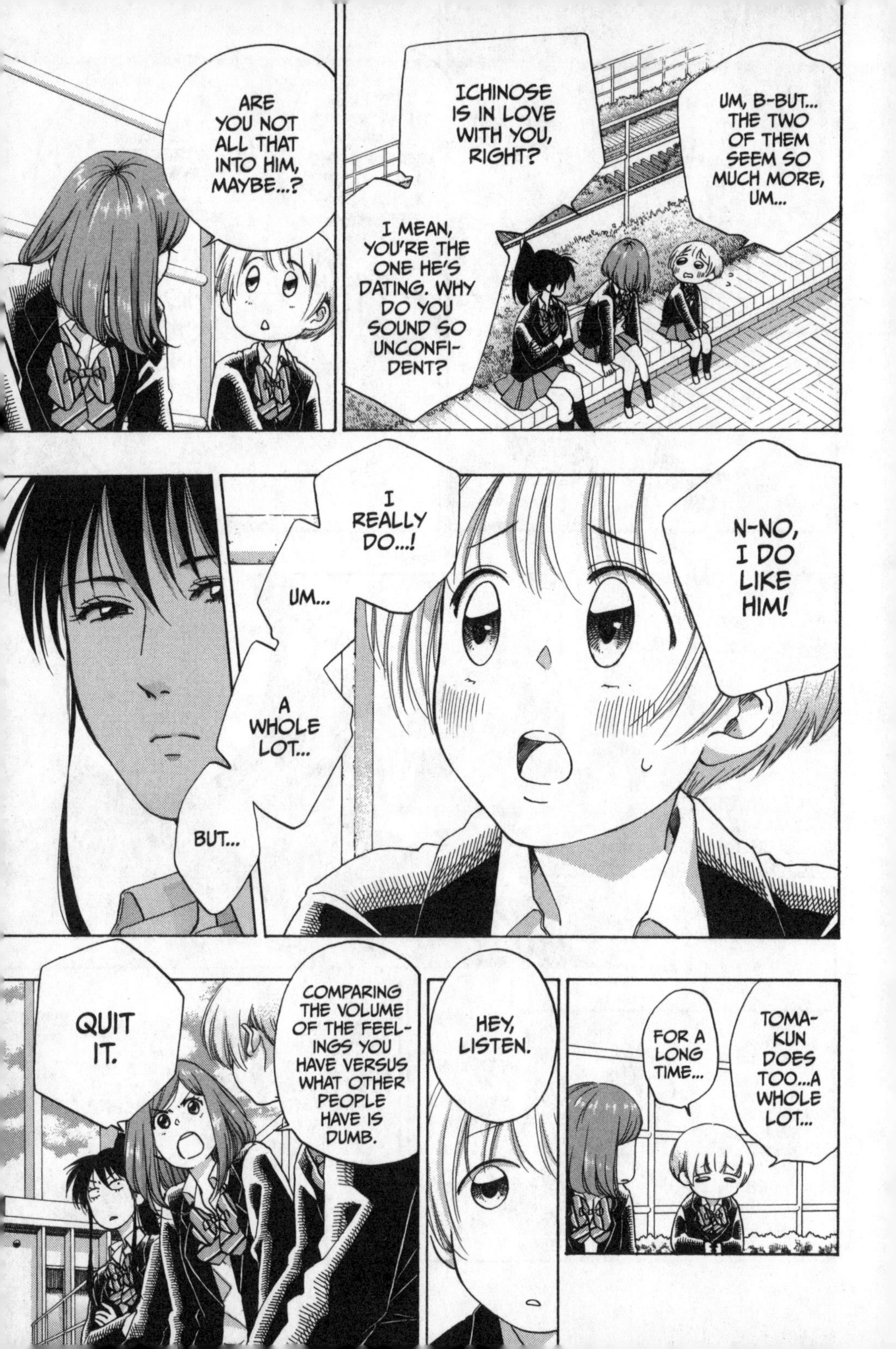
UM, B-BUT... THE TWO OF THEM SEEM SO MUCH MORE, UM...
ICHINOSE IS IN LOVE WITH YOU, RIGHT?
I MEAN, YOU'RE THE ONE HE'S DATING. WHY DO YOU SOUND SO UNCONFI-DENT?
ARE YOU NOT ALL THAT INTO HIM, MAYBE...?
N-NO, I DO LIKE HIM!
I REALLY DO...!
UM...
A WHOLE LOT...
BUT...
TOMA-KUN DOES TOO...A WHOLE LOT...
FOR A LONG TIME...
HEY, LISTEN.
COMPARING THE VOLUME OF THE FEEL-INGS YOU HAVE VERSUS WHAT OTHER PEOPLE HAVE IS DUMB.
QUIT IT.

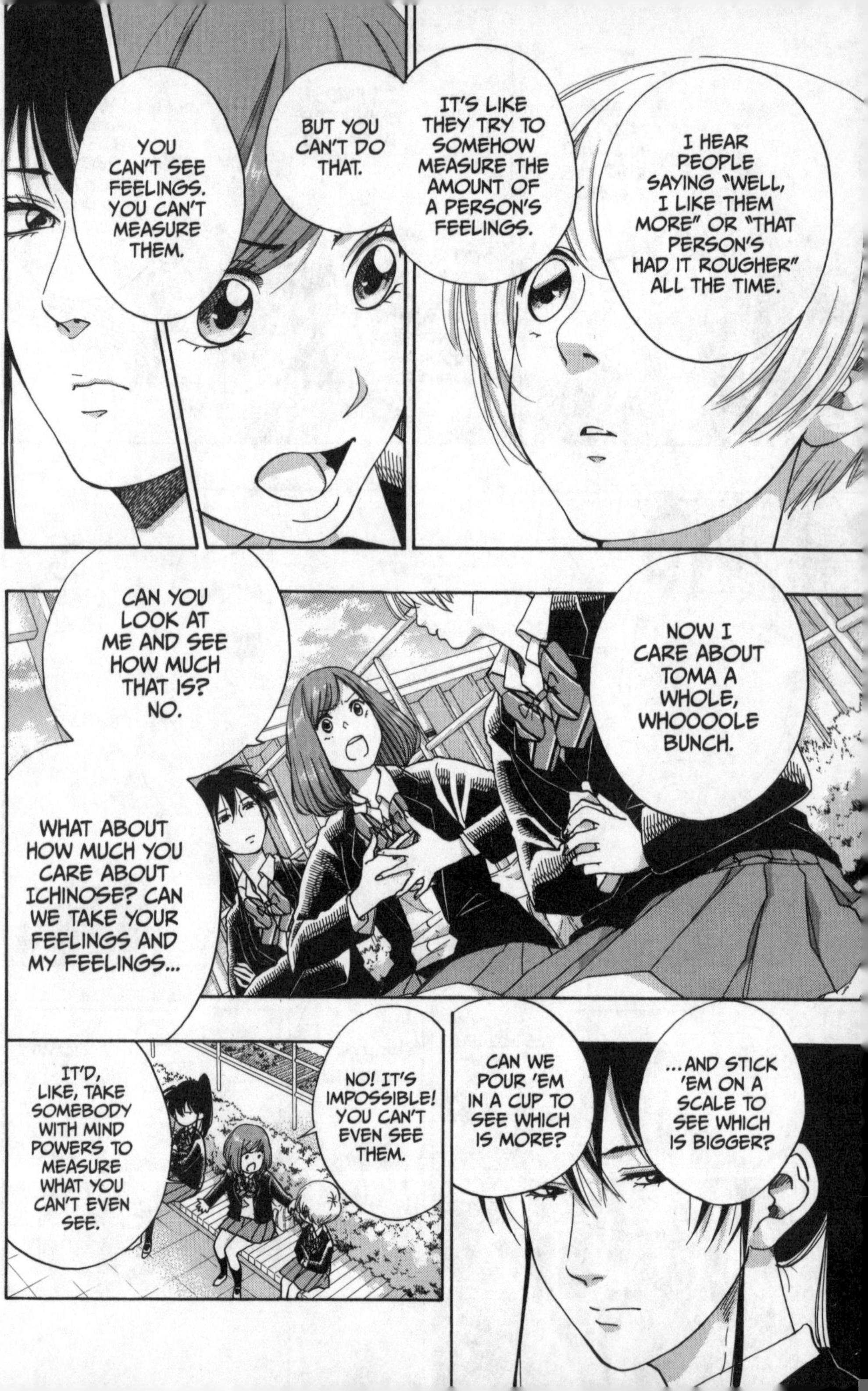
I HEAR PEOPLE SAYING "WELL, I LIKE THEM MORE" OR "THAT PERSON'S HAD IT ROUGHER" ALL THE TIME.
IT'S LIKE THEY TRY TO SOMEHOW MEASURE THE AMOUNT OF A PERSON'S FEELINGS.
BUT YOU CAN'T DO THAT.
YOU CAN'T SEE FEELINGS. YOU CAN'T MEASURE THEM.
NOW I CARE ABOUT TOMA A WHOLE, WHOOOOLE BUNCH.
CAN YOU LOOK AT ME AND SEE HOW MUCH THAT IS? NO.
WHAT ABOUT HOW MUCH YOU CARE ABOUT ICHINOSE? CAN WE TAKE YOUR FEELINGS AND MY FEELINGS...
...AND STICK 'EM ON A SCALE TO SEE WHICH IS BIGGER?
CAN WE POUR 'EM IN A CUP TO SEE WHICH IS MORE?
NO! IT'S IMPOSSIBLE! YOU CAN'T EVEN SEE THEM.
IT'D, LIKE, TAKE SOMEBODY WITH MIND POWERS TO MEASURE WHAT YOU CAN'T EVEN SEE.

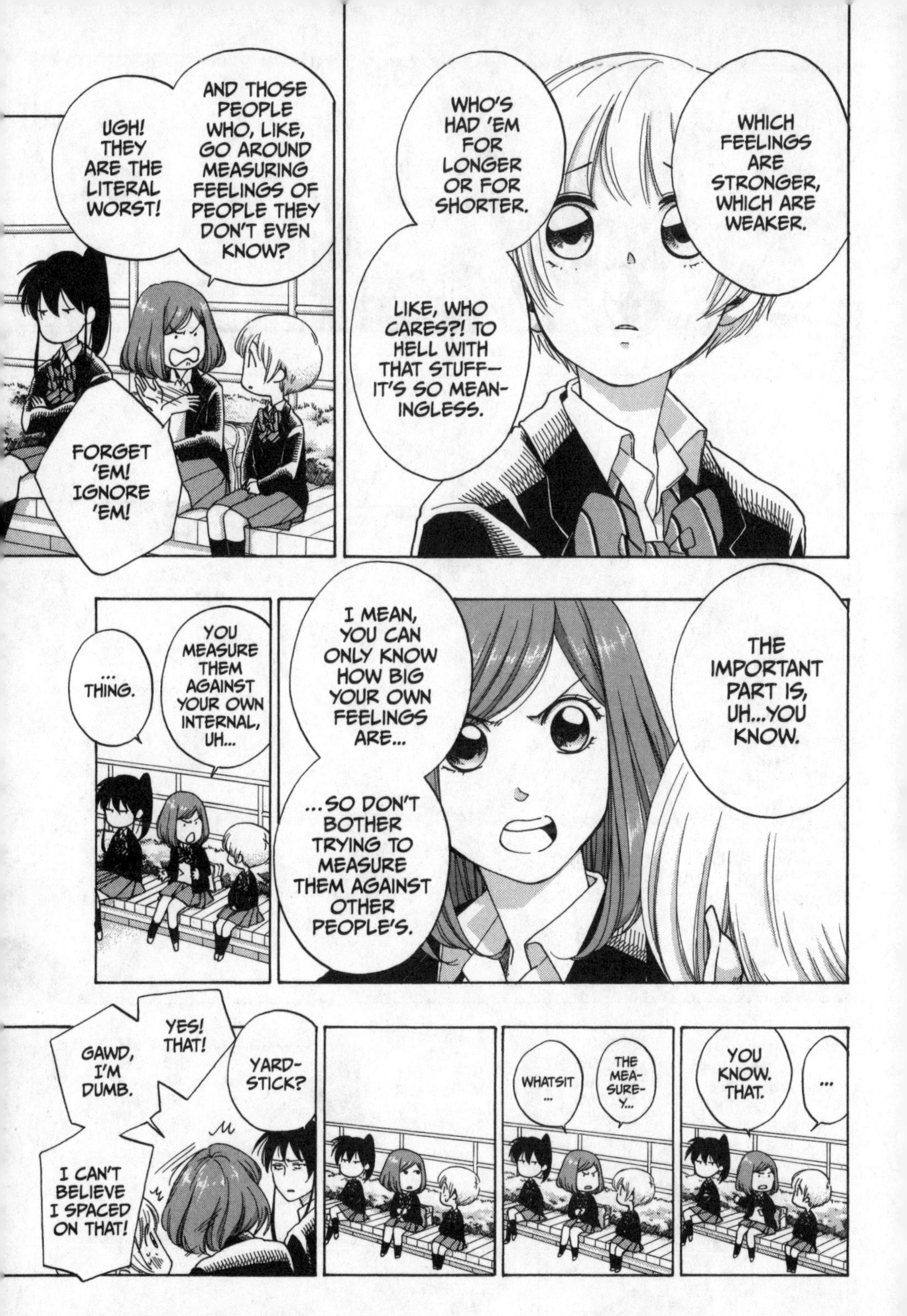
WHICH FEELINGS ARE STRONGER, WHICH ARE WEAKER.
WHO'S HAD 'EM FOR LONGER OR FOR SHORTER.
LIKE, WHO CARES?! TO HELL WITH THAT STUFF—IT'S SO MEANINGLESS.
AND THOSE PEOPLE WHO, LIKE, GO AROUND MEASURING FEELINGS OF PEOPLE THEY DON'T EVEN KNOW?
UGH! THEY ARE THE LITERAL WORST!
FORGET 'EM! IGNORE 'EM!
THE IMPORTANT PART IS, UH...YOU KNOW.
I MEAN, YOU CAN ONLY KNOW HOW BIG YOUR OWN FEELINGS ARE...
...SO DON'T BOTHER TRYING TO MEASURE THEM AGAINST OTHER PEOPLE'S.
YOU MEASURE THEM AGAINST YOUR OWN INTERNAL, UH...
...THING.
...
YOU KNOW. THAT.
THE MEASUREY...
WHATSIT...
YARDSTICK?
YES! THAT!
GAWD, I'M DUMB.
I CAN'T BELIEVE I SPACED ON THAT!

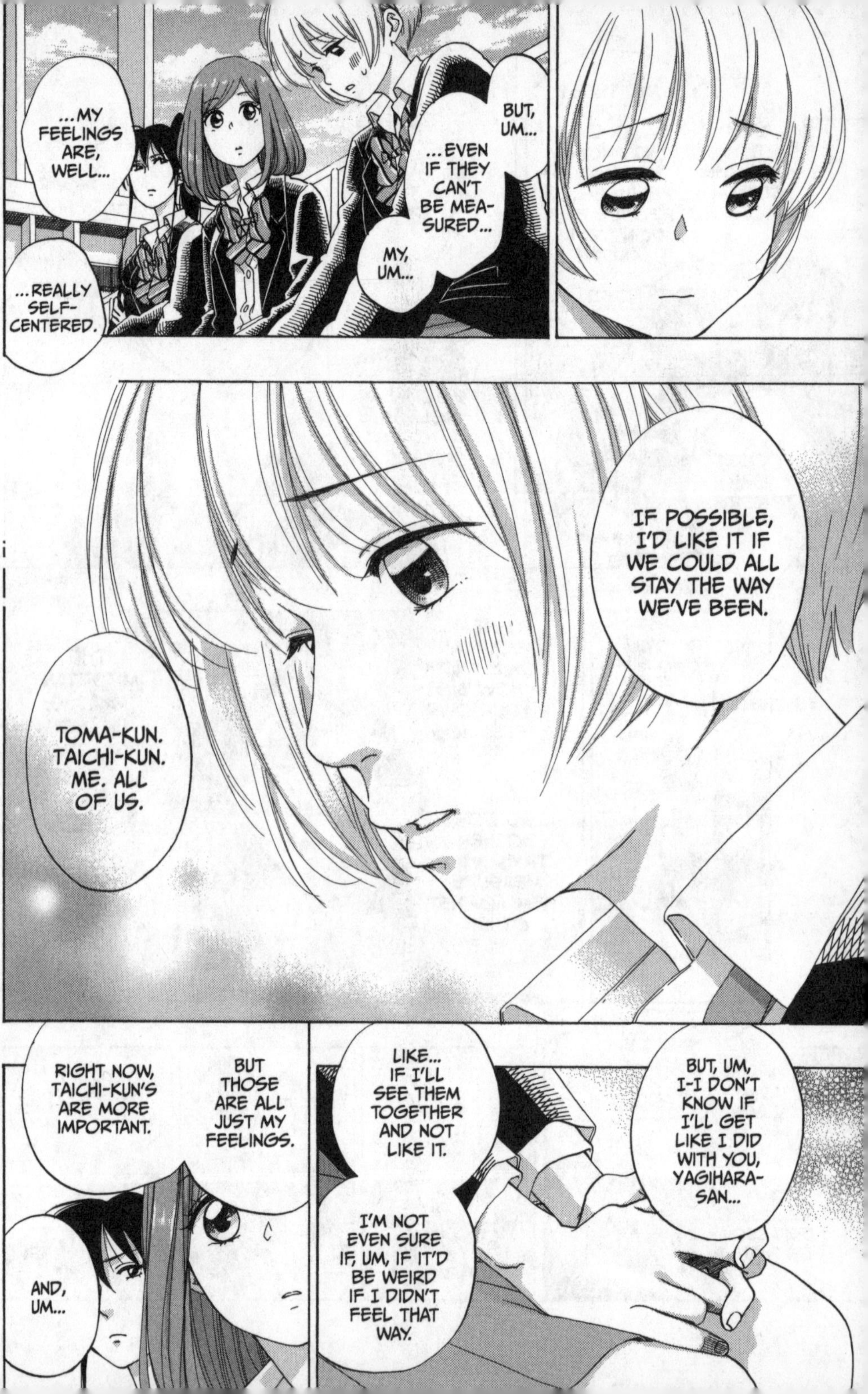
BUT, UM...
...EVEN IF THEY CAN'T BE MEA-SURED...
MY, UM...
...MY FEELINGS ARE, WELL...
...REALLY SELF-CENTERED.
IF POSSIBLE, I'D LIKE IT IF WE COULD ALL STAY THE WAY WE'VE BEEN.
TOMA-KUN. TAICHI-KUN. ME. ALL OF US.
BUT, UM, I-I DON'T KNOW IF I'LL GET LIKE I DID WITH YOU, YAGIHARA-SAN...
LIKE... IF I'LL SEE THEM TOGETHER AND NOT LIKE IT.
I'M NOT EVEN SURE IF, UM, IF IT'D BE WEIRD IF I DIDN'T FEEL THAT WAY.
BUT THOSE ARE ALL JUST MY FEELINGS.
RIGHT NOW, TAICHI-KUN'S ARE MORE IMPORTANT.
AND, UM...

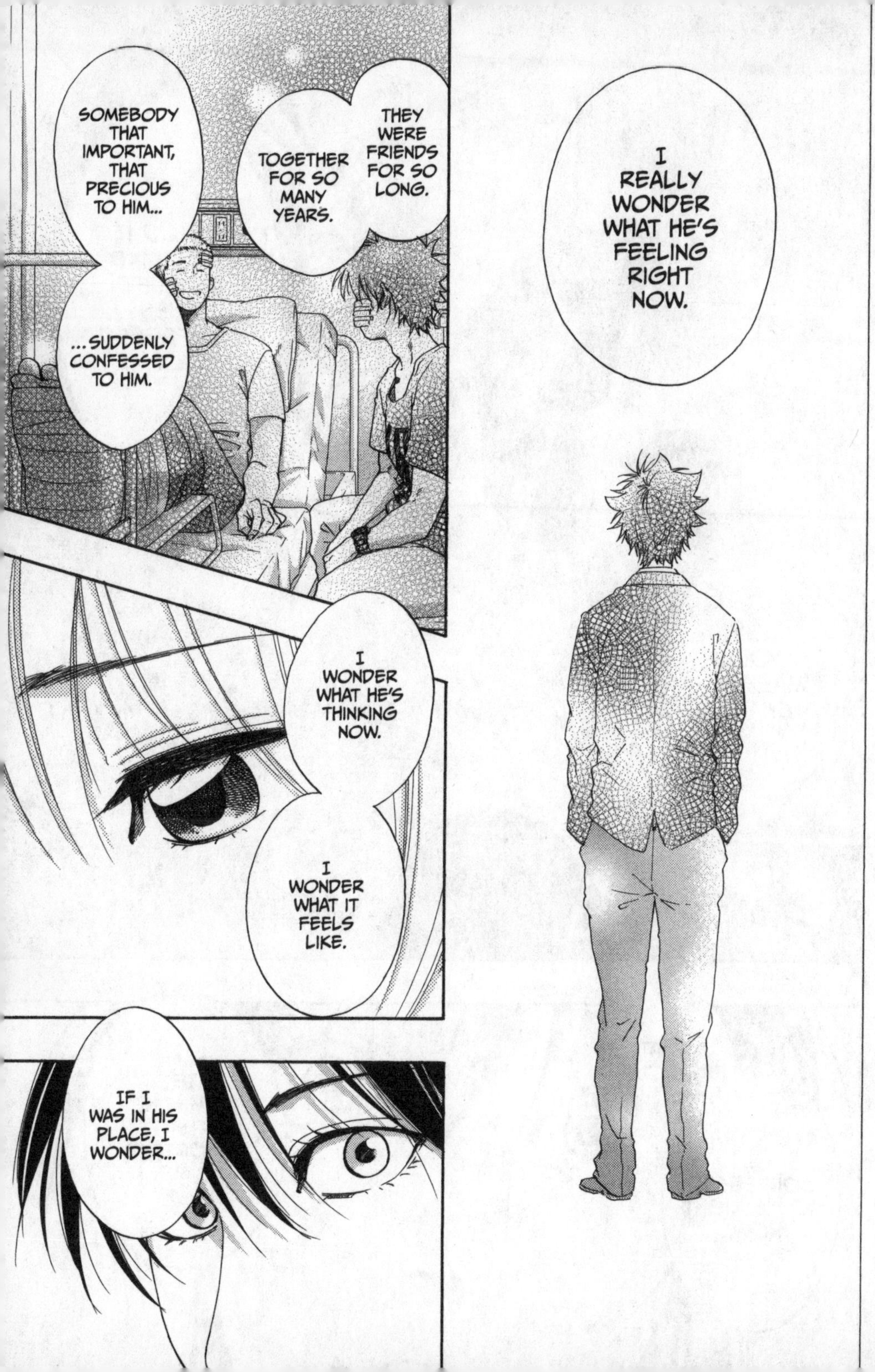
I REALLY WONDER WHAT HE'S FEELING RIGHT NOW.
THEY WERE FRIENDS FOR SO LONG.
TOGETHER FOR SO MANY YEARS.
SOMEBODY THAT IMPORTANT, THAT PRECIOUS TO HIM...
...SUDDENLY CONFESSED TO HIM.
I WONDER WHAT HE'S THINKING NOW.
I WONDER WHAT IT FEELS LIKE.
IF I WAS IN HIS PLACE, I WONDER...

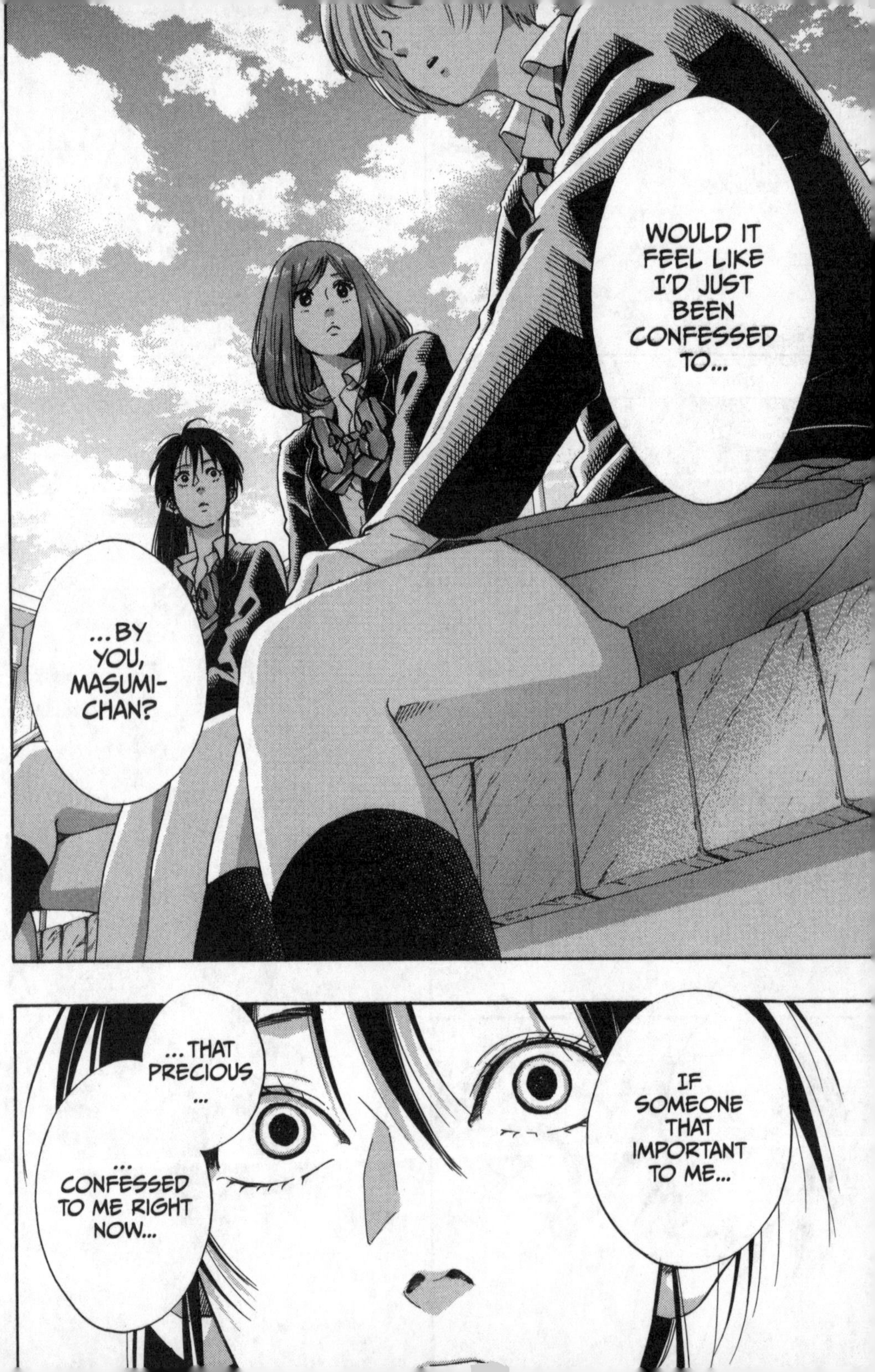
WOULD IT FEEL LIKE I'D JUST BEEN CONFESSED TO...
...BY YOU, MASUMI-CHAN?
IF SOMEONE THAT IMPORTANT TO ME...
...THAT PRECIOUS...
...CONFESSED TO ME RIGHT NOW...

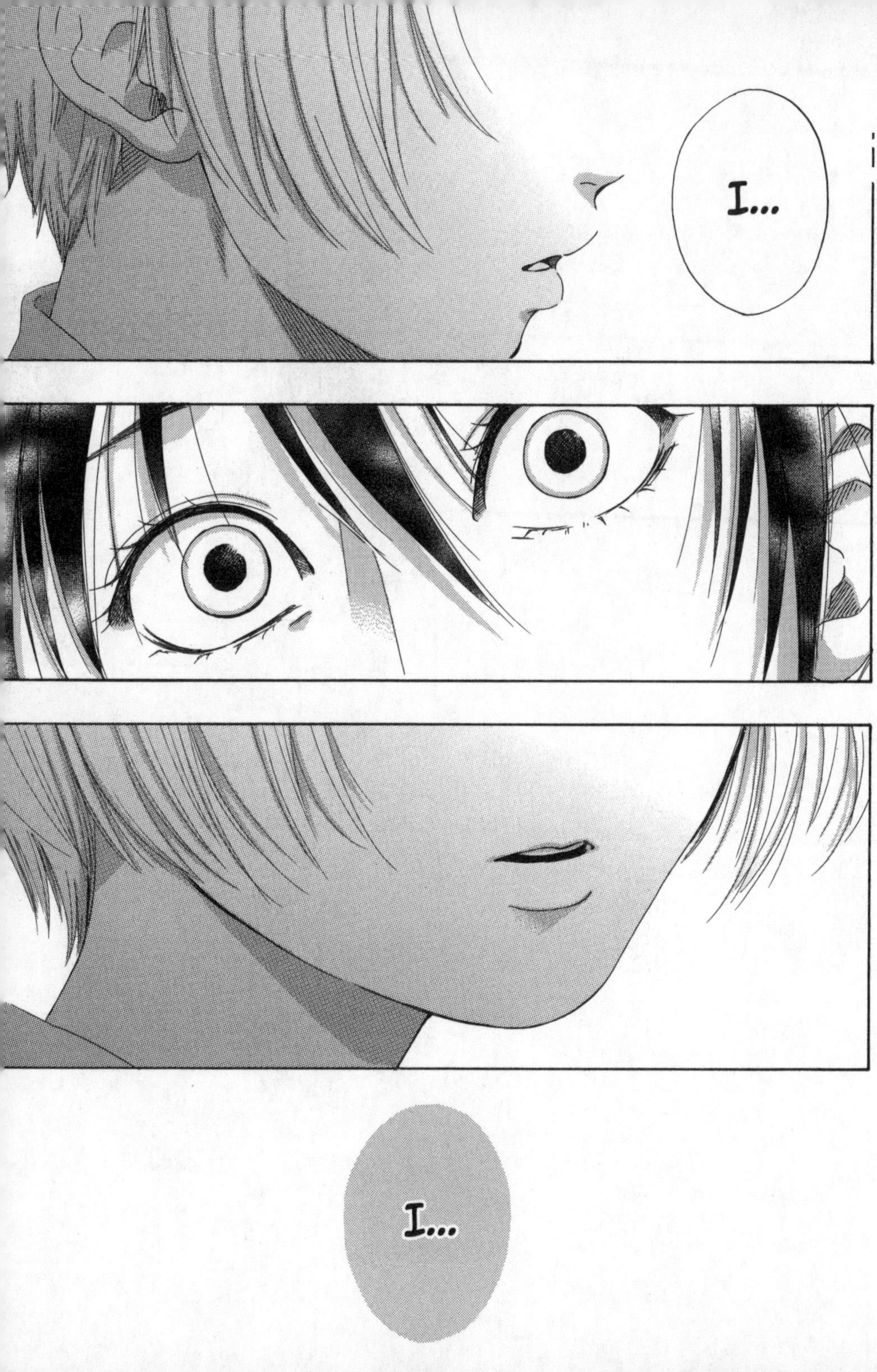
I...
I...

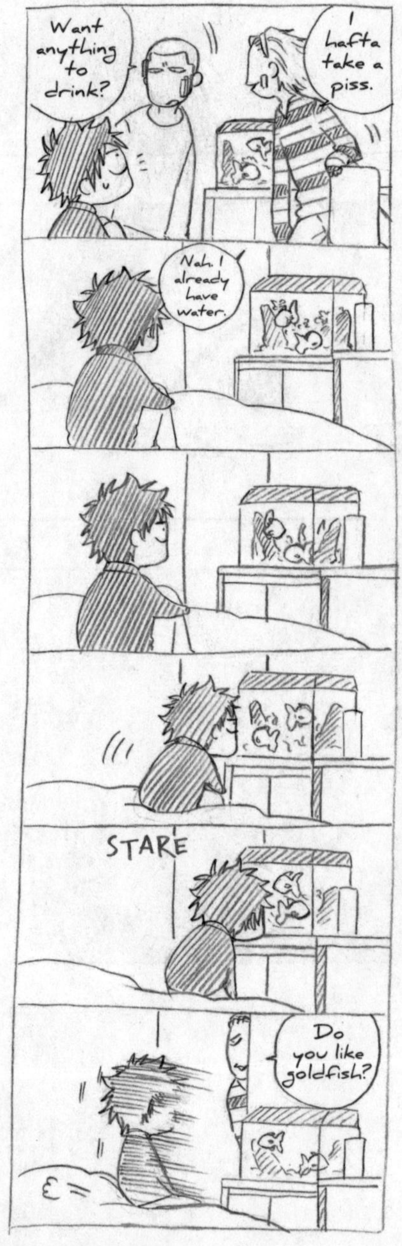
I hafta take a piss.
Want anything to drink?
Nah. I already have water.
STARE
Do you like goldfish?

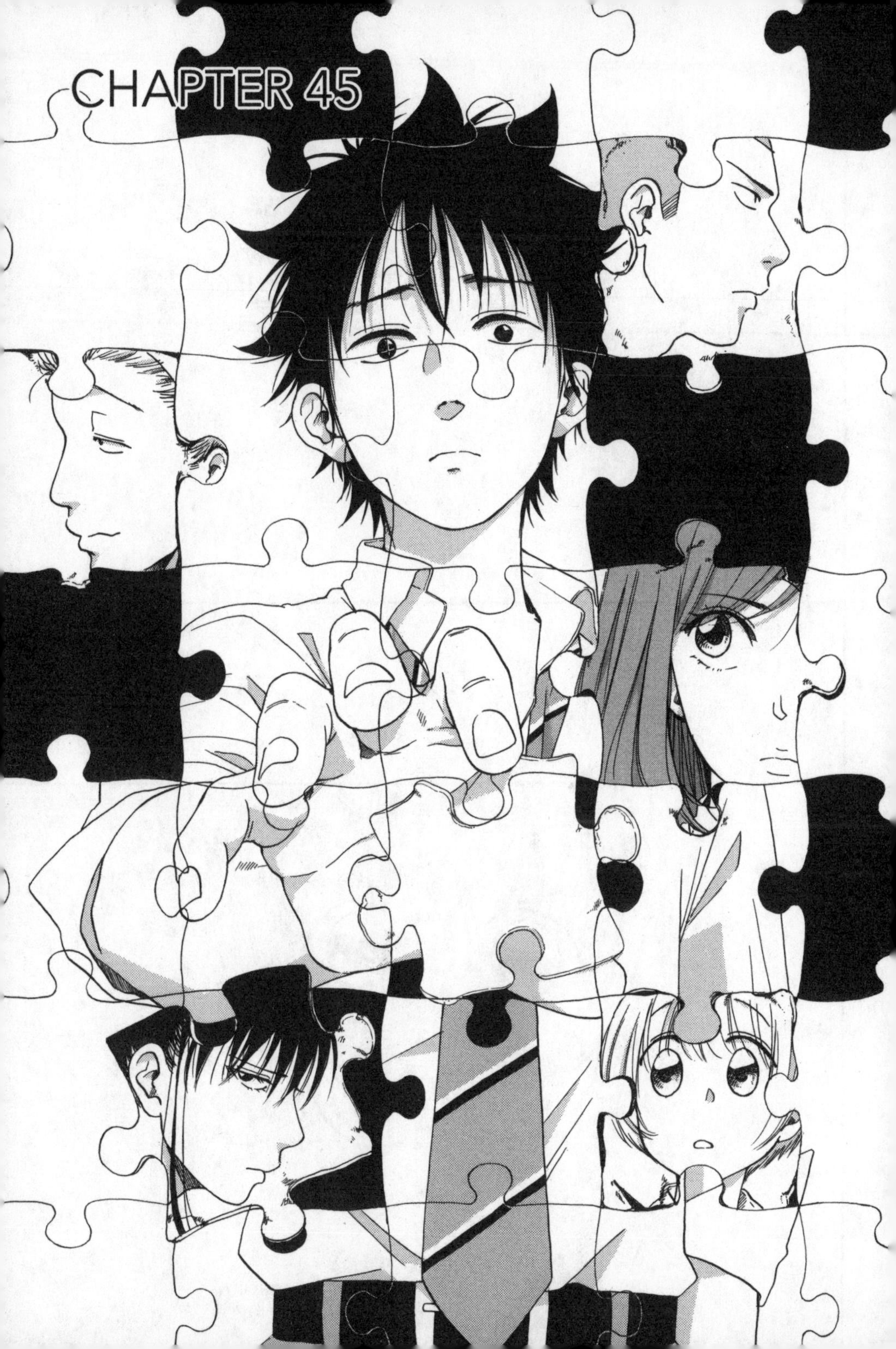
CHAPTER 45

...CONFESSED TO ME RIGHT NOW...

IF SOMEONE THAT IMPORTANT TO ME, THAT PRECIOUS...

I...

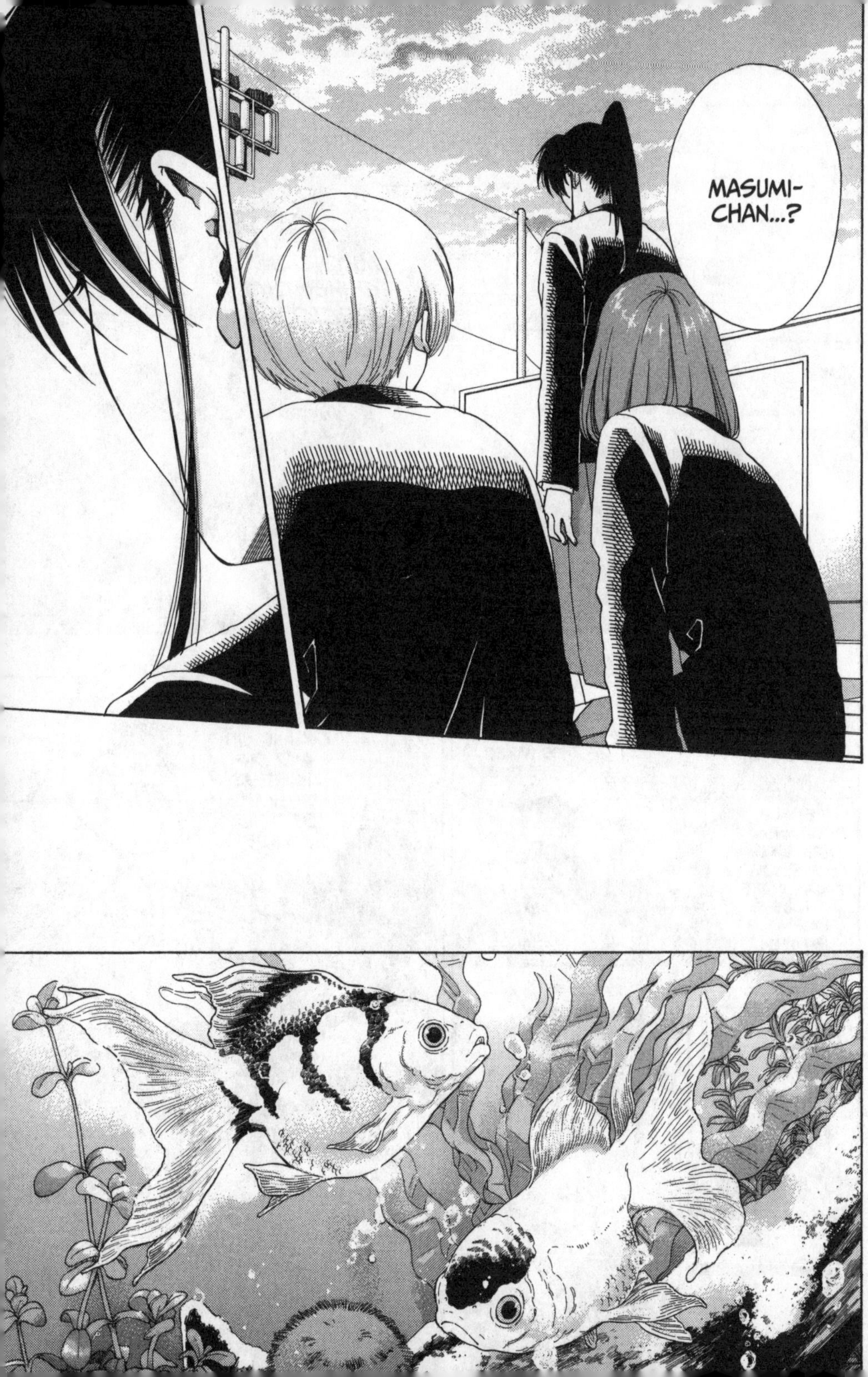
MASUMI-
CHAN...?

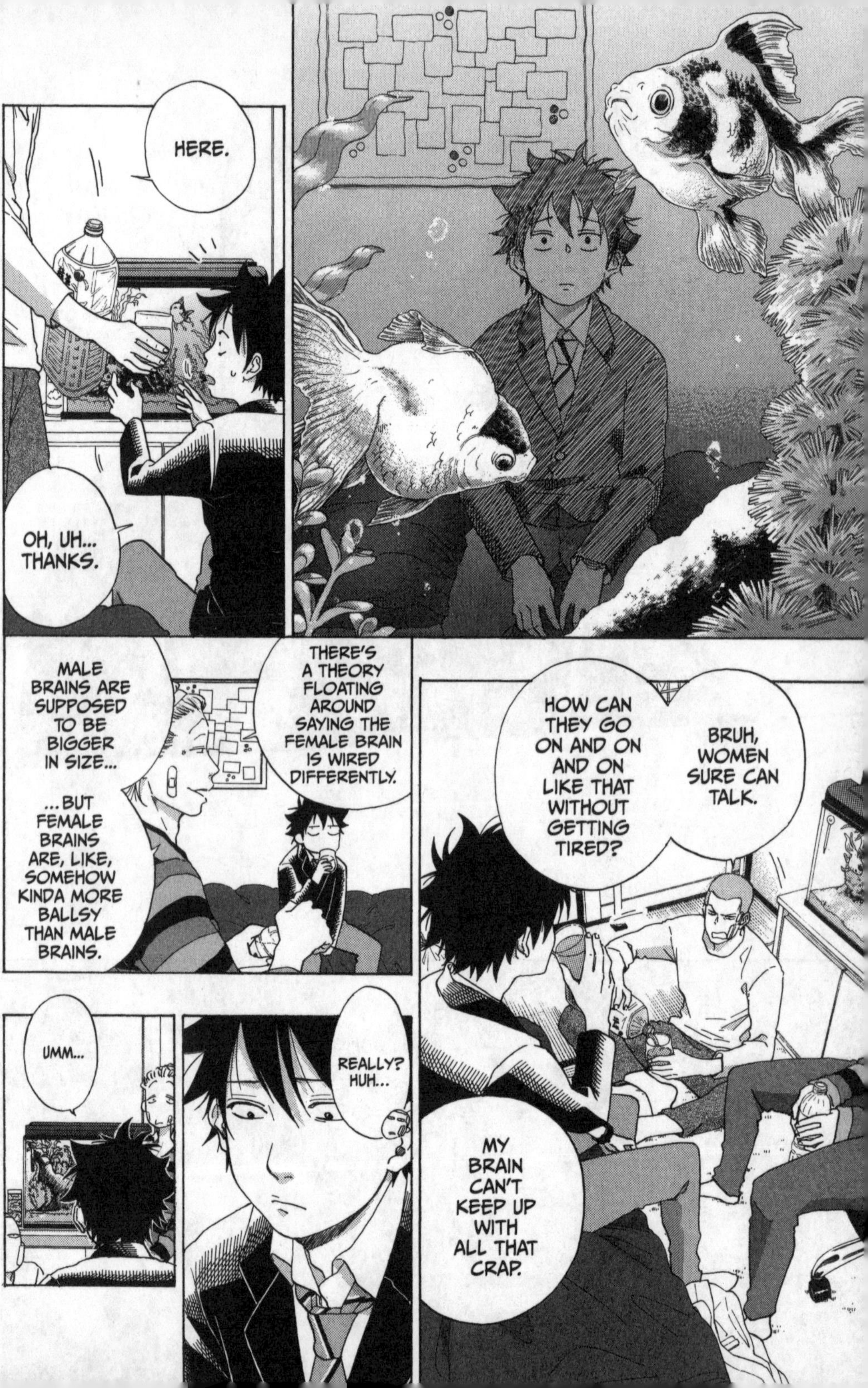
HERE.
OH, UH... THANKS.
BRUH, WOMEN SURE CAN TALK.
HOW CAN THEY GO ON AND ON AND ON LIKE THAT WITHOUT GETTING TIRED?
MY BRAIN CAN'T KEEP UP WITH ALL THAT CRAP.
THERE'S A THEORY FLOATING AROUND SAYING THE FEMALE BRAIN IS WIRED DIFFERENTLY.
MALE BRAINS ARE SUPPOSED TO BE BIGGER IN SIZE...
...BUT FEMALE BRAINS ARE, LIKE, SOMEHOW KINDA MORE BALLSY THAN MALE BRAINS.
REALLY? HUH...
UMM...

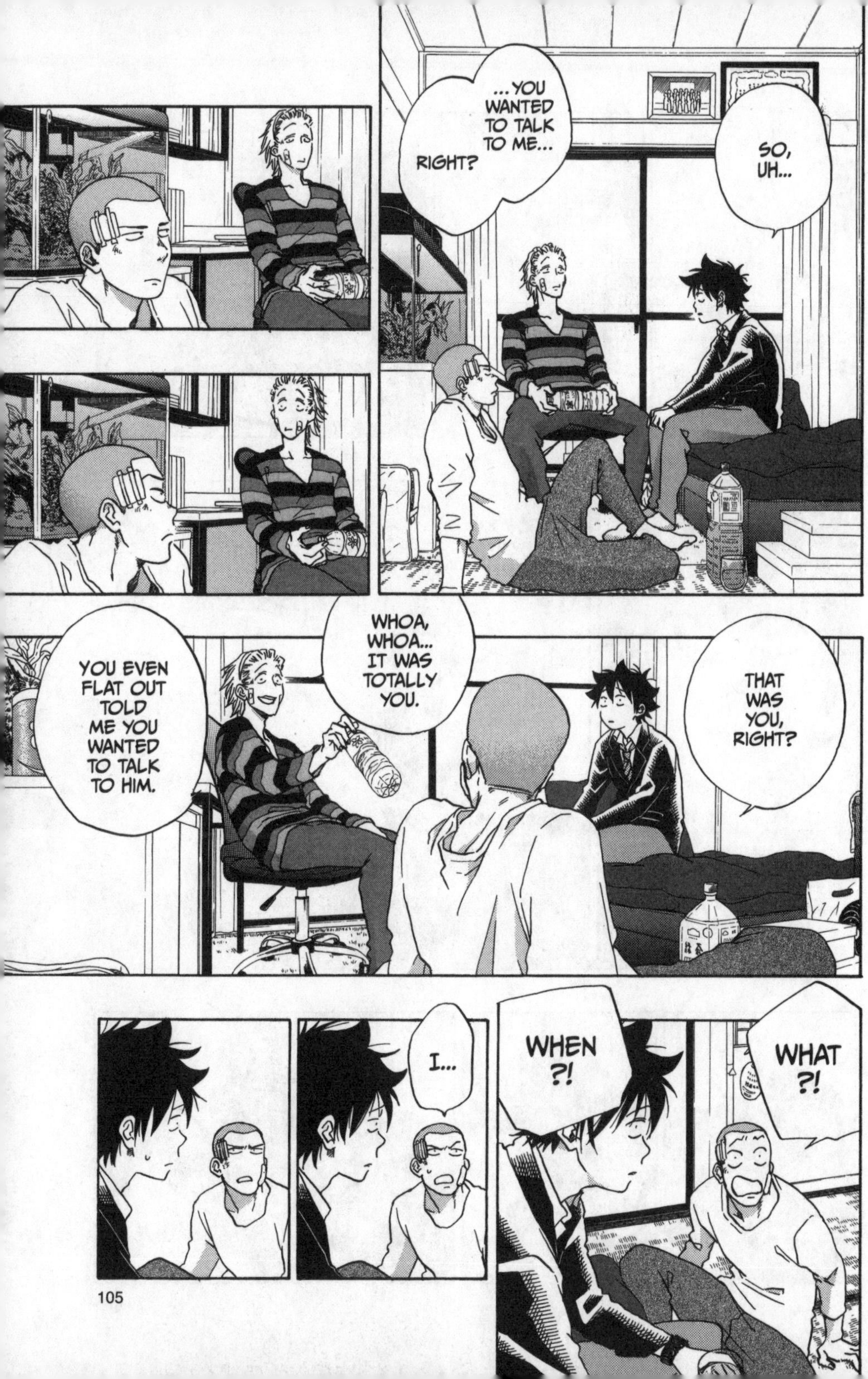
SO, UH...
...YOU WANTED TO TALK TO ME... RIGHT?
THAT WAS YOU, RIGHT?
WHOA, WHOA... IT WAS TOTALLY YOU.
YOU EVEN FLAT OUT TOLD ME YOU WANTED TO TALK TO HIM.
WHAT?!
WHEN?!
I...

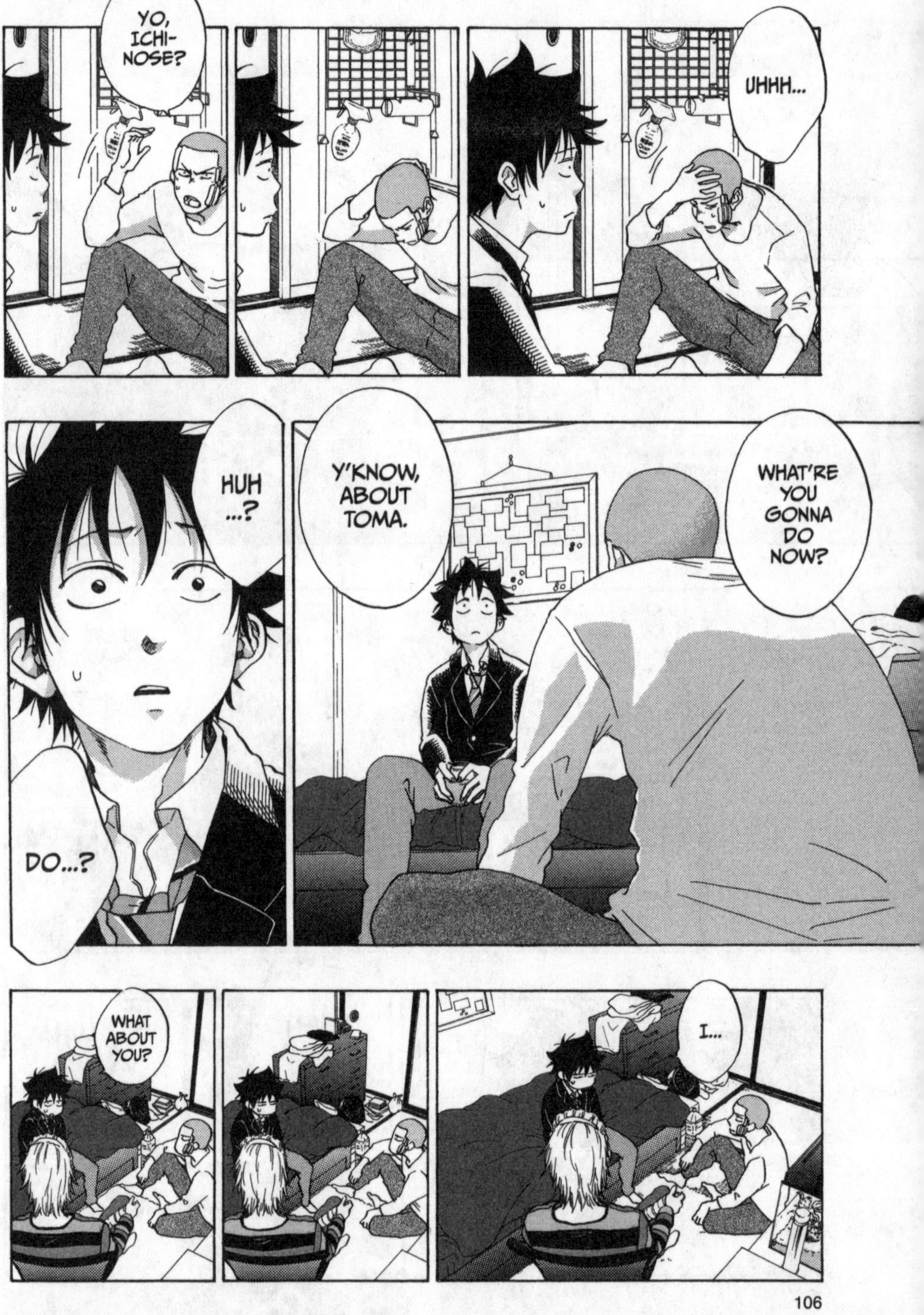
UHHH...
YO, ICHI-NOSE?
WHAT'RE YOU GONNA DO NOW?
Y'KNOW, ABOUT TOMA.
HUH ...?
DO...?
I...
WHAT ABOUT YOU?

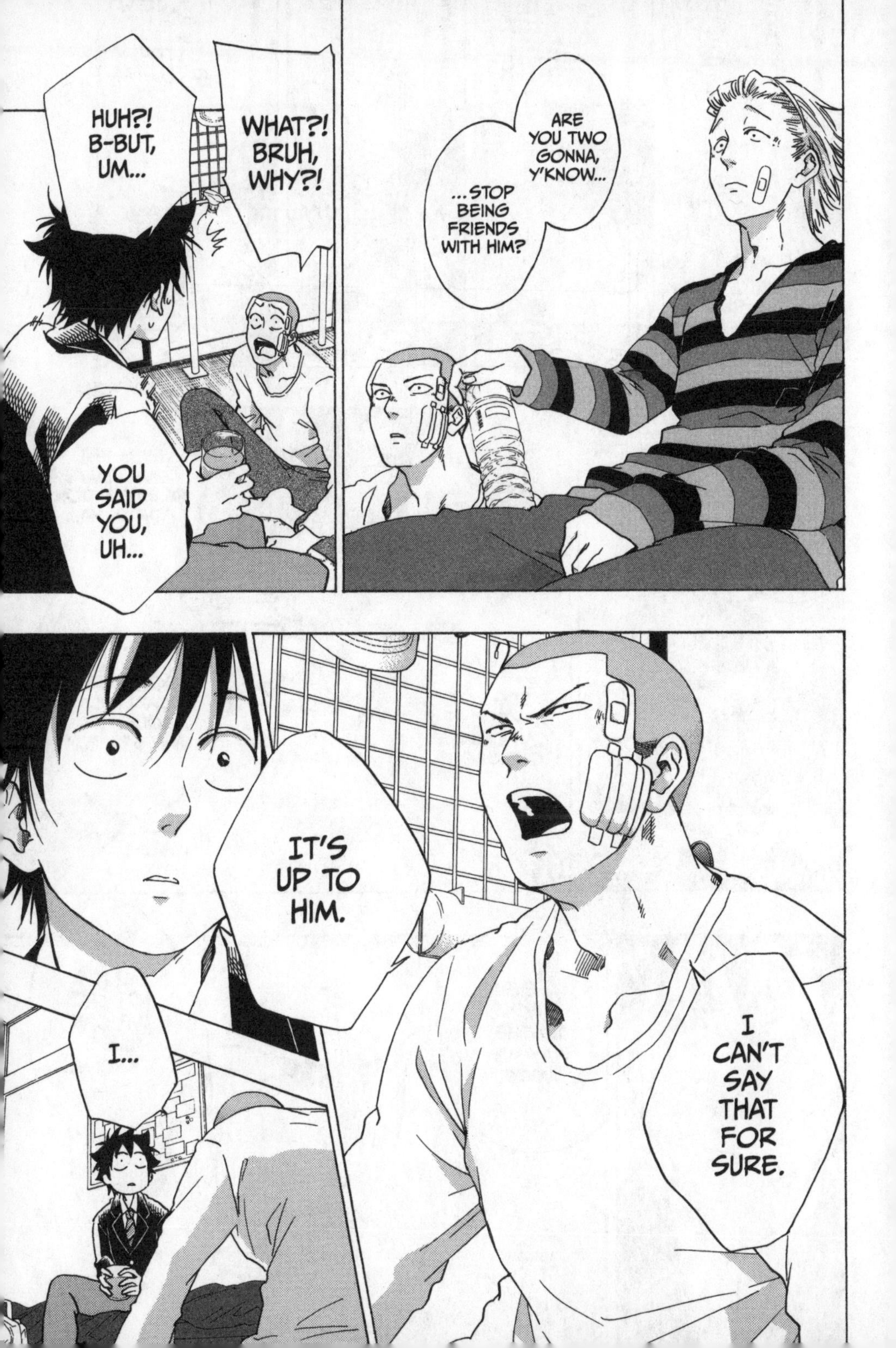
ARE YOU TWO GONNA, Y'KNOW...
...STOP BEING FRIENDS WITH HIM?
WHAT?! BRUH, WHY?!
HUH?! B-BUT, UM...
YOU SAID YOU, UH...
IT'S UP TO HIM.
I CAN'T SAY THAT FOR SURE.
I...

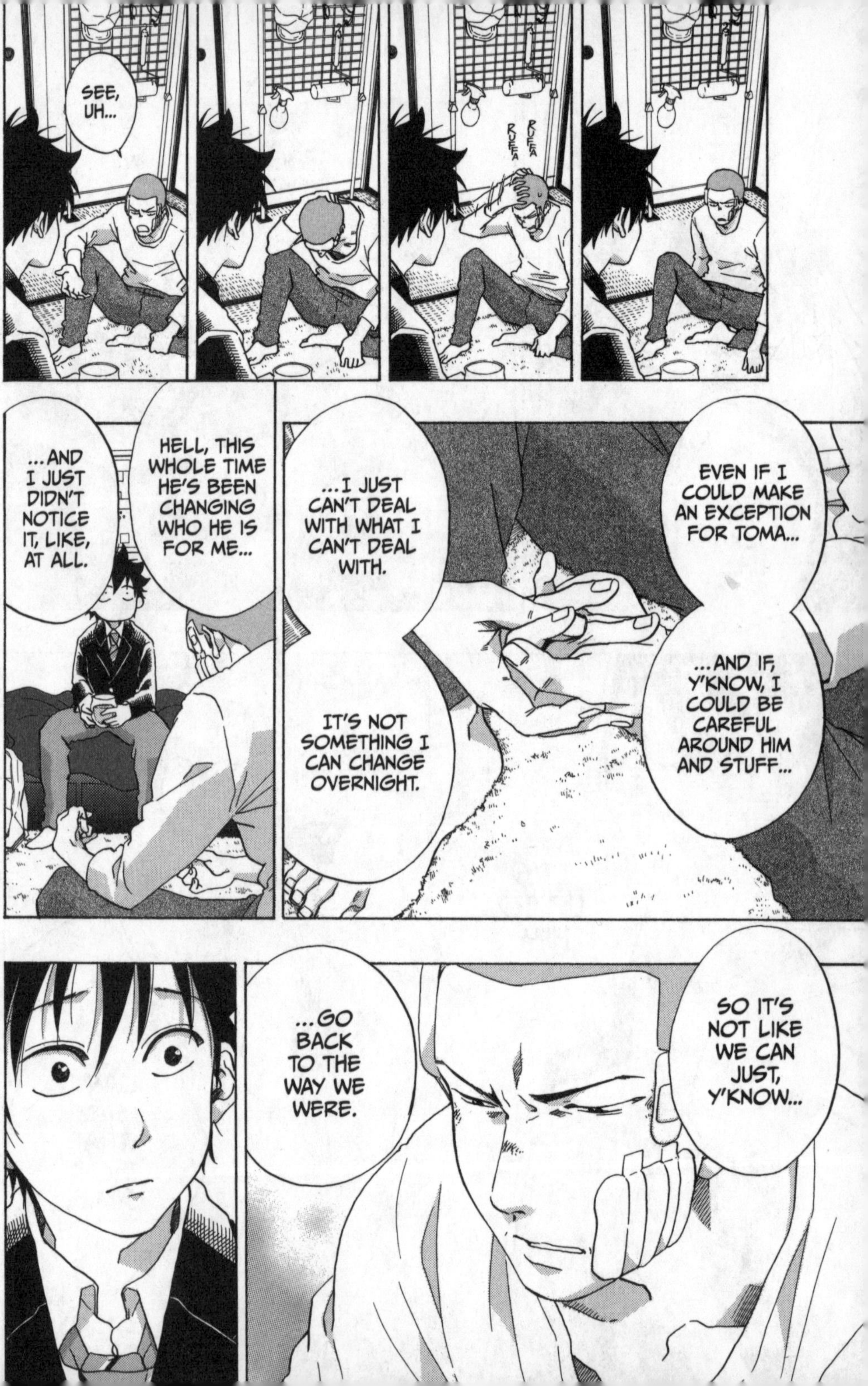
RUFFA RUFFA
SEE, UH...
EVEN IF I COULD MAKE AN EXCEPTION FOR TOMA...
...AND IF, Y'KNOW, I COULD BE CAREFUL AROUND HIM AND STUFF...
...I JUST CAN'T DEAL WITH WHAT I CAN'T DEAL WITH.
IT'S NOT SOMETHING I CAN CHANGE OVERNIGHT.
HELL, THIS WHOLE TIME HE'S BEEN CHANGING WHO HE IS FOR ME...
...AND I JUST DIDN'T NOTICE IT, LIKE, AT ALL.
SO IT'S NOT LIKE WE CAN JUST, Y'KNOW...
...GO BACK TO THE WAY WE WERE.

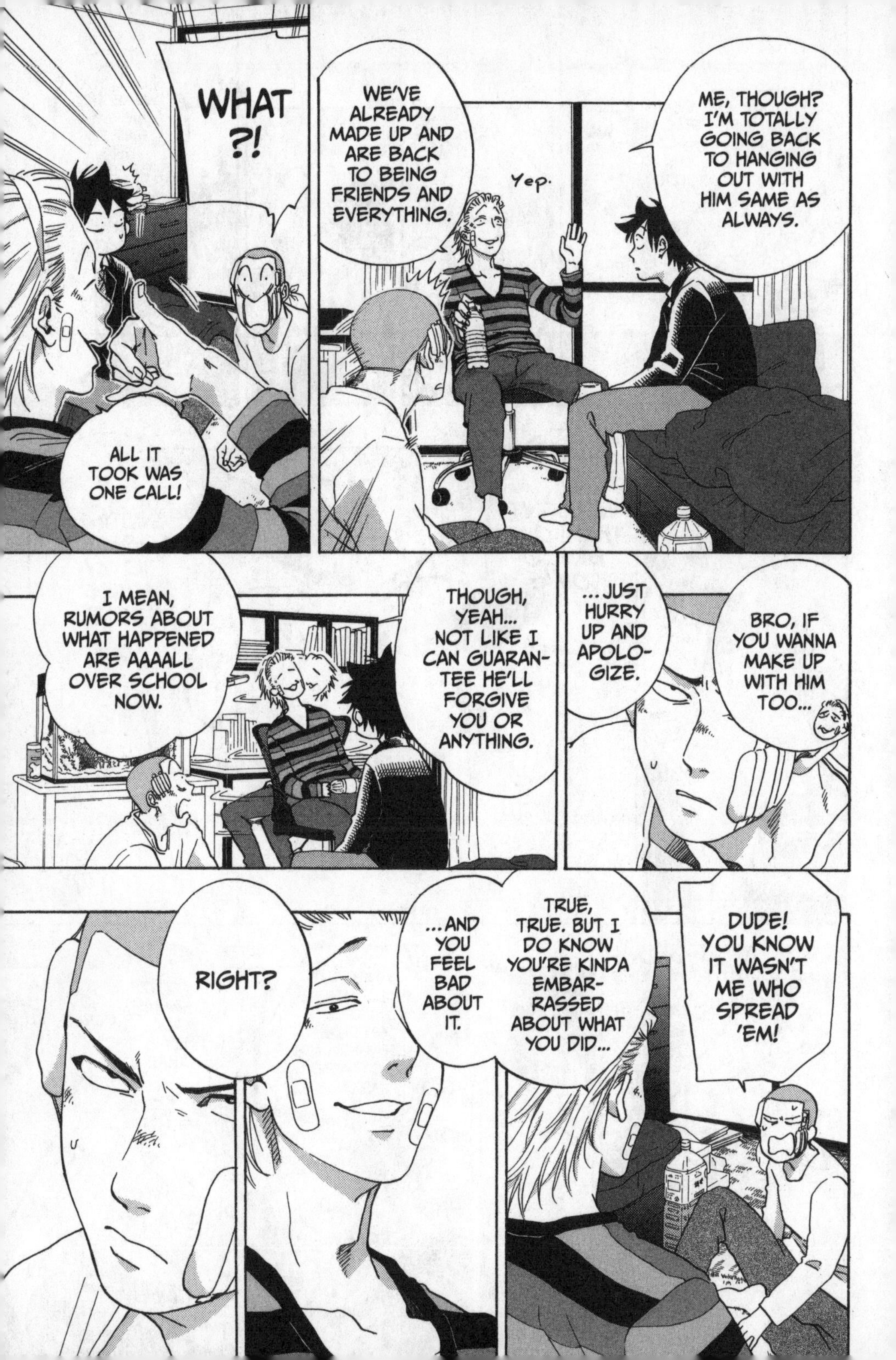
ME, THOUGH? I'M TOTALLY GOING BACK TO HANGING OUT WITH HIM SAME AS ALWAYS.
Yep.
WE'VE ALREADY MADE UP AND ARE BACK TO BEING FRIENDS AND EVERYTHING.
WHAT ?!
ALL IT TOOK WAS ONE CALL!
BRO, IF YOU WANNA MAKE UP WITH HIM TOO...
...JUST HURRY UP AND APOLOGIZE.
THOUGH, YEAH... NOT LIKE I CAN GUARANTEE HE'LL FORGIVE YOU OR ANYTHING.
I MEAN, RUMORS ABOUT WHAT HAPPENED ARE AAAALL OVER SCHOOL NOW.
DUDE! YOU KNOW IT WASN'T ME WHO SPREAD 'EM!
TRUE, TRUE. BUT I DO KNOW YOU'RE KINDA EMBARRASSED ABOUT WHAT YOU DID...
...AND YOU FEEL BAD ABOUT IT.
RIGHT?

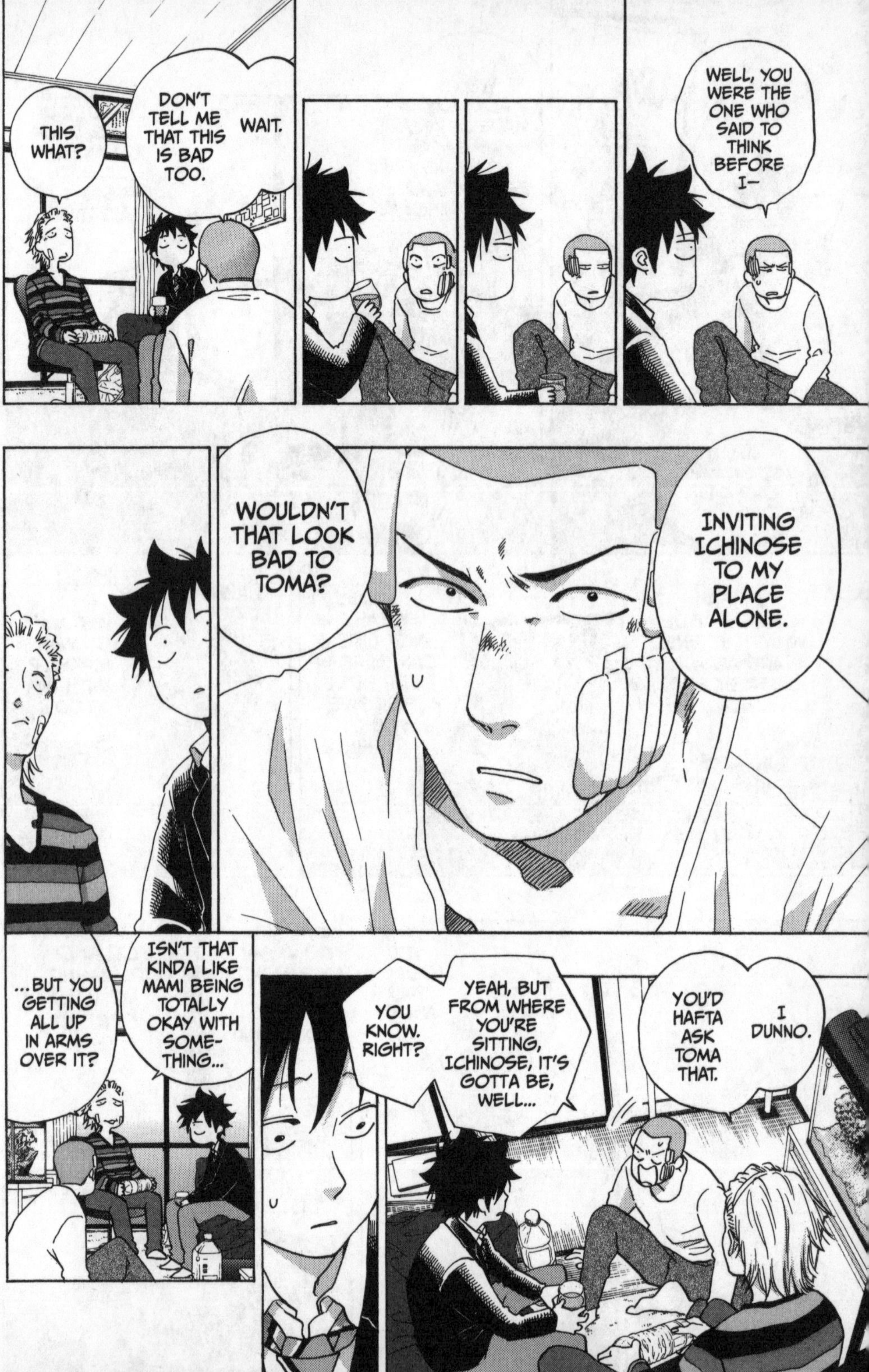
WELL, YOU WERE THE ONE WHO SAID TO THINK BEFORE I—
WAIT.
DON'T TELL ME THAT THIS IS BAD TOO.
THIS WHAT?
INVITING ICHINOSE TO MY PLACE ALONE.
WOULDN'T THAT LOOK BAD TO TOMA?
I DUNNO.
YOU'D HAFTA ASK TOMA THAT.
YEAH, BUT FROM WHERE YOU'RE SITTING, ICHINOSE, IT'S GOTTA BE, WELL...
YOU KNOW. RIGHT?
ISN'T THAT KINDA LIKE MAMI BEING TOTALLY OKAY WITH SOME-THING...
...BUT YOU GETTING ALL UP IN ARMS OVER IT?

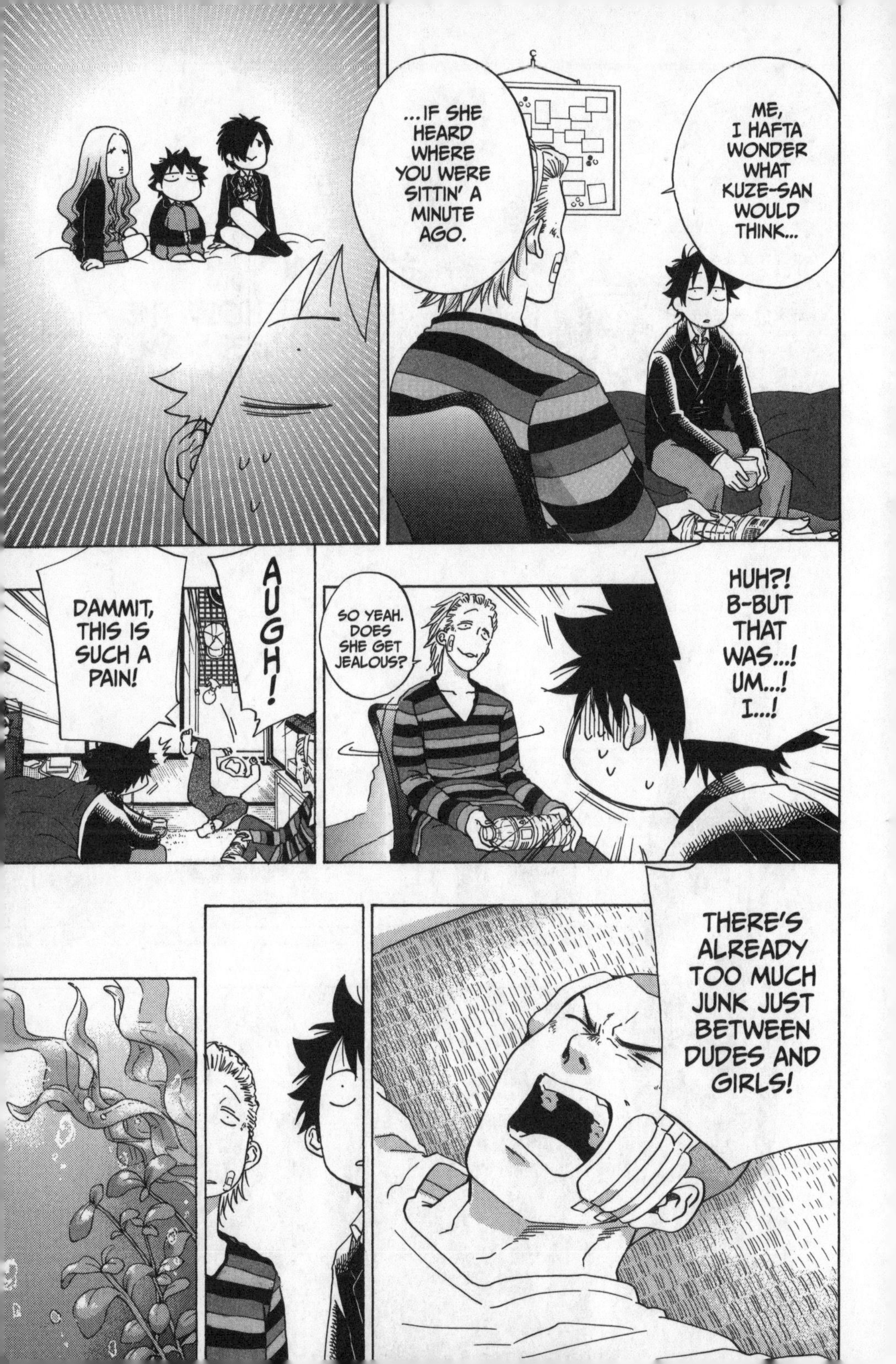
ME, I HAFTA WONDER WHAT KUZE-SAN WOULD THINK...
...IF SHE HEARD WHERE YOU WERE SITTIN' A MINUTE AGO.
HUH?! B-BUT THAT WAS...! UM...! I...!
SO YEAH. DOES SHE GET JEALOUS?
AUGH!
DAMMIT, THIS IS SUCH A PAIN!
THERE'S ALREADY TOO MUCH JUNK JUST BETWEEN DUDES AND GIRLS!

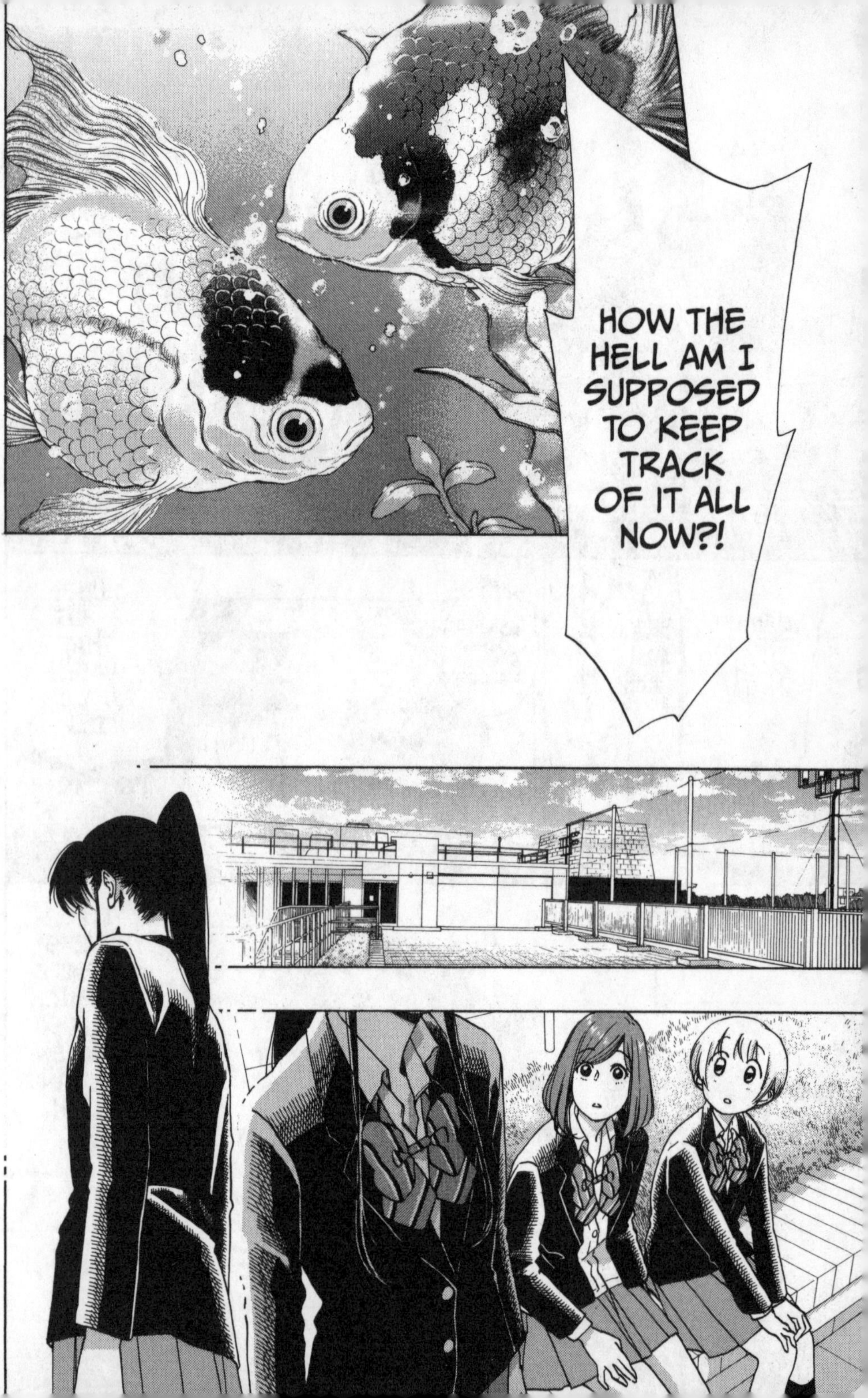
HOW THE HELL AM I SUPPOSED TO KEEP TRACK OF IT ALL NOW?!

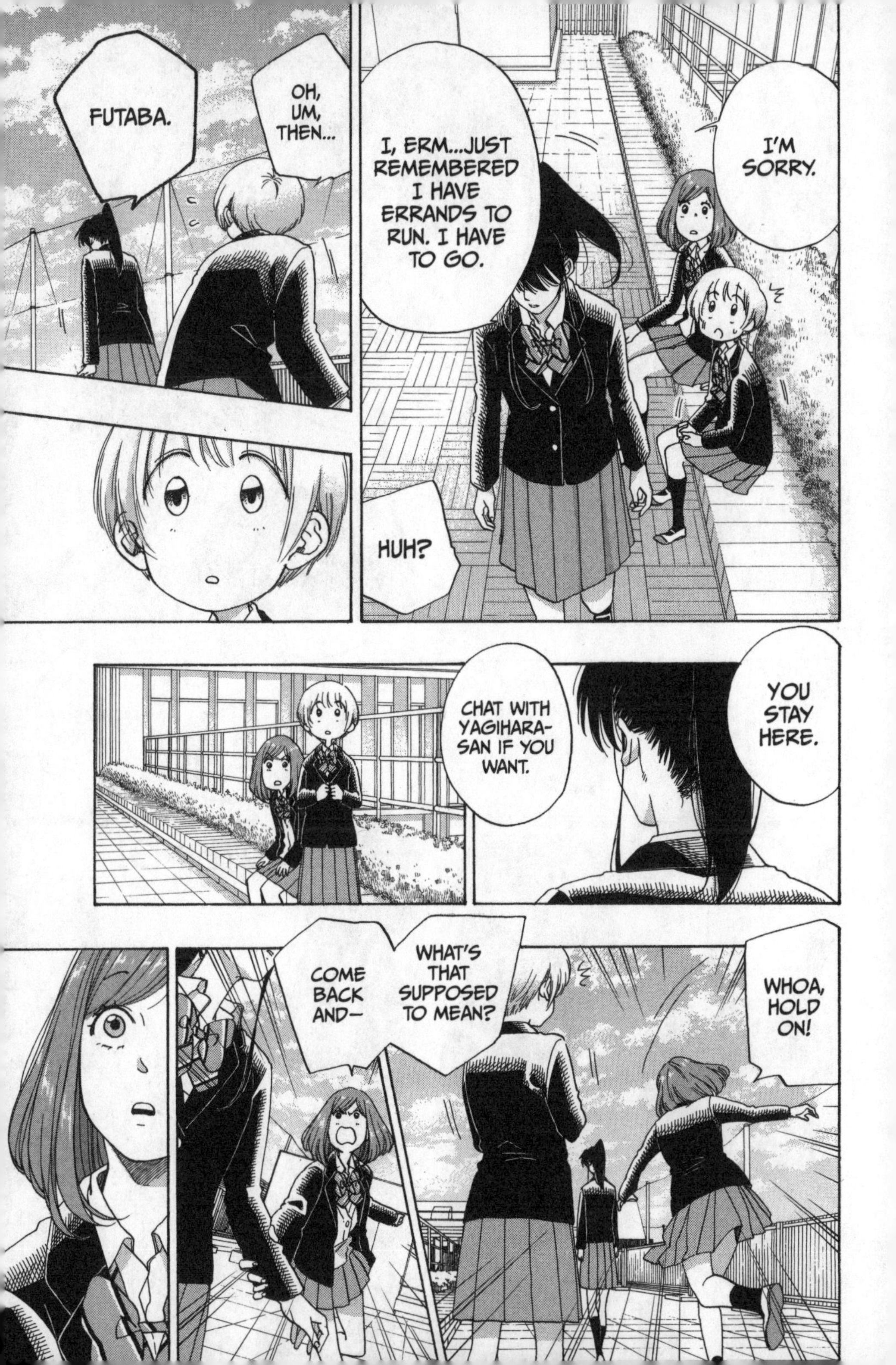

I'M SORRY.
I, ERM...JUST REMEMBERED I HAVE ERRANDS TO RUN. I HAVE TO GO.
HUH?
OH, UM, THEN...
FUTABA.
YOU STAY HERE.
CHAT WITH YAGIHARA-SAN IF YOU WANT.
WHOA, HOLD ON!
WHAT'S THAT SUPPOSED TO MEAN? COME BACK AND—

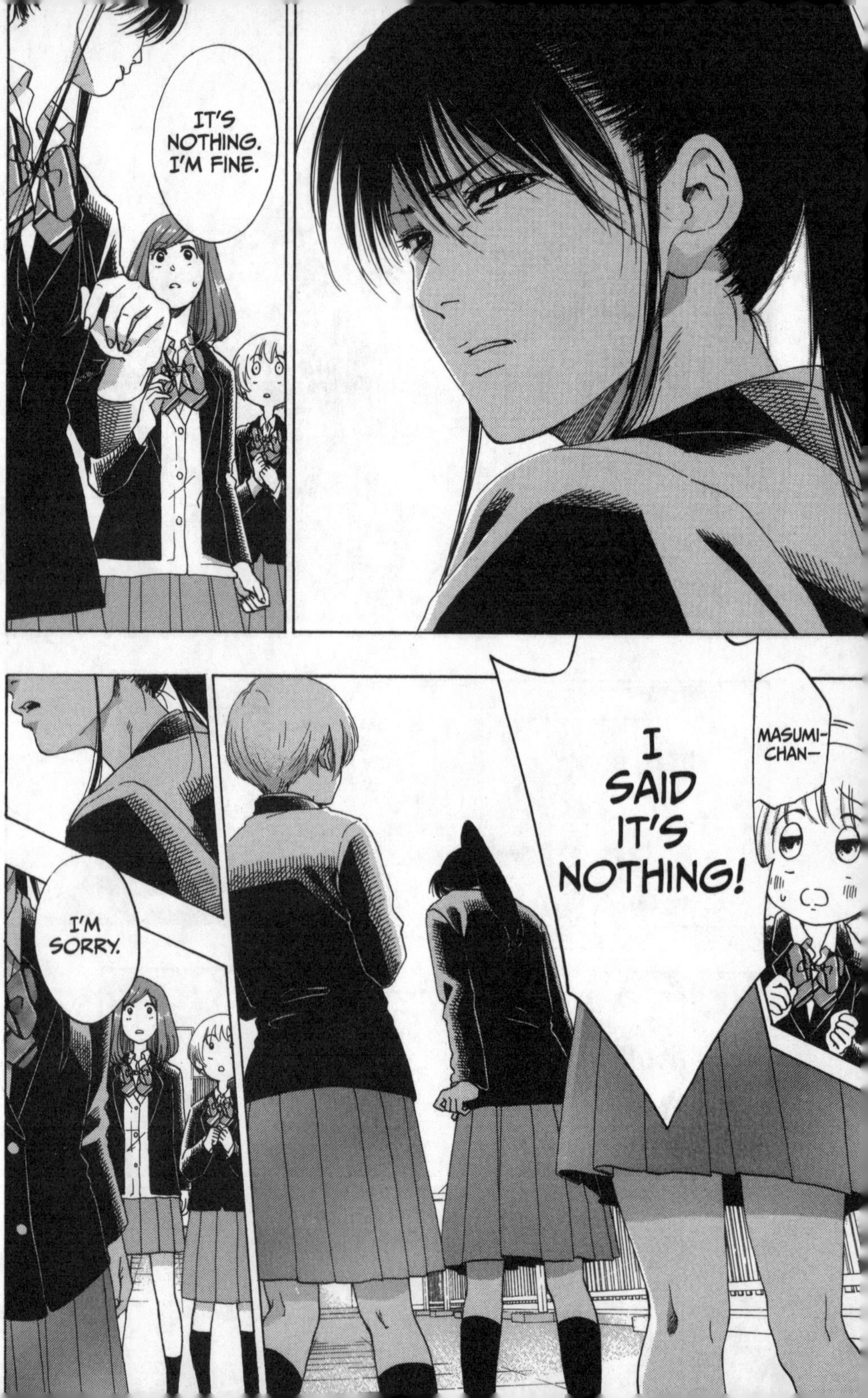
IT'S NOTHING. I'M FINE.
MASUMI-CHAN—
I SAID IT'S NOTHING!
I'M SORRY.

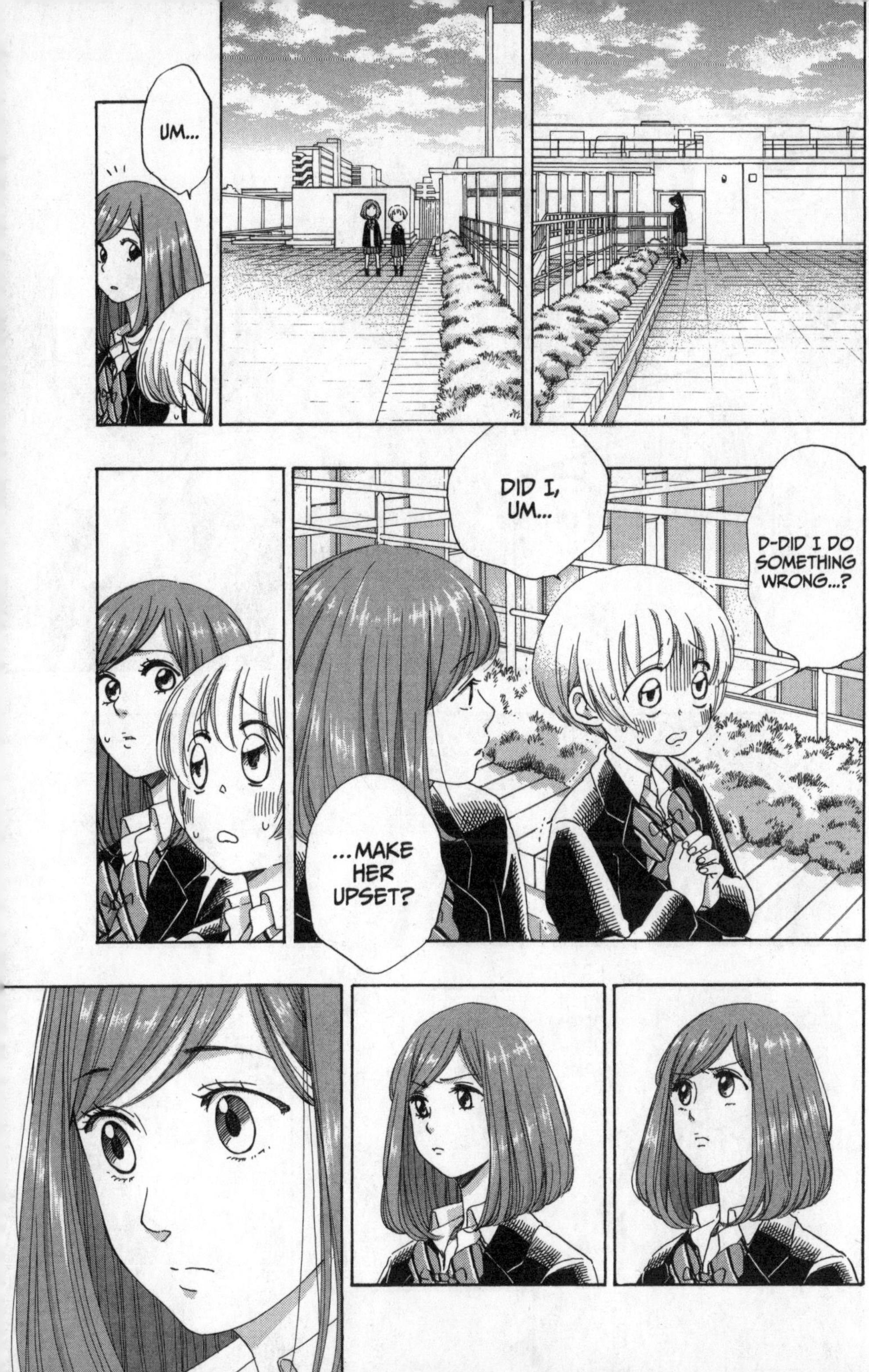
UM...
D-DID I DO SOMETHING WRONG...?
DID I, UM...
...MAKE HER UPSET?

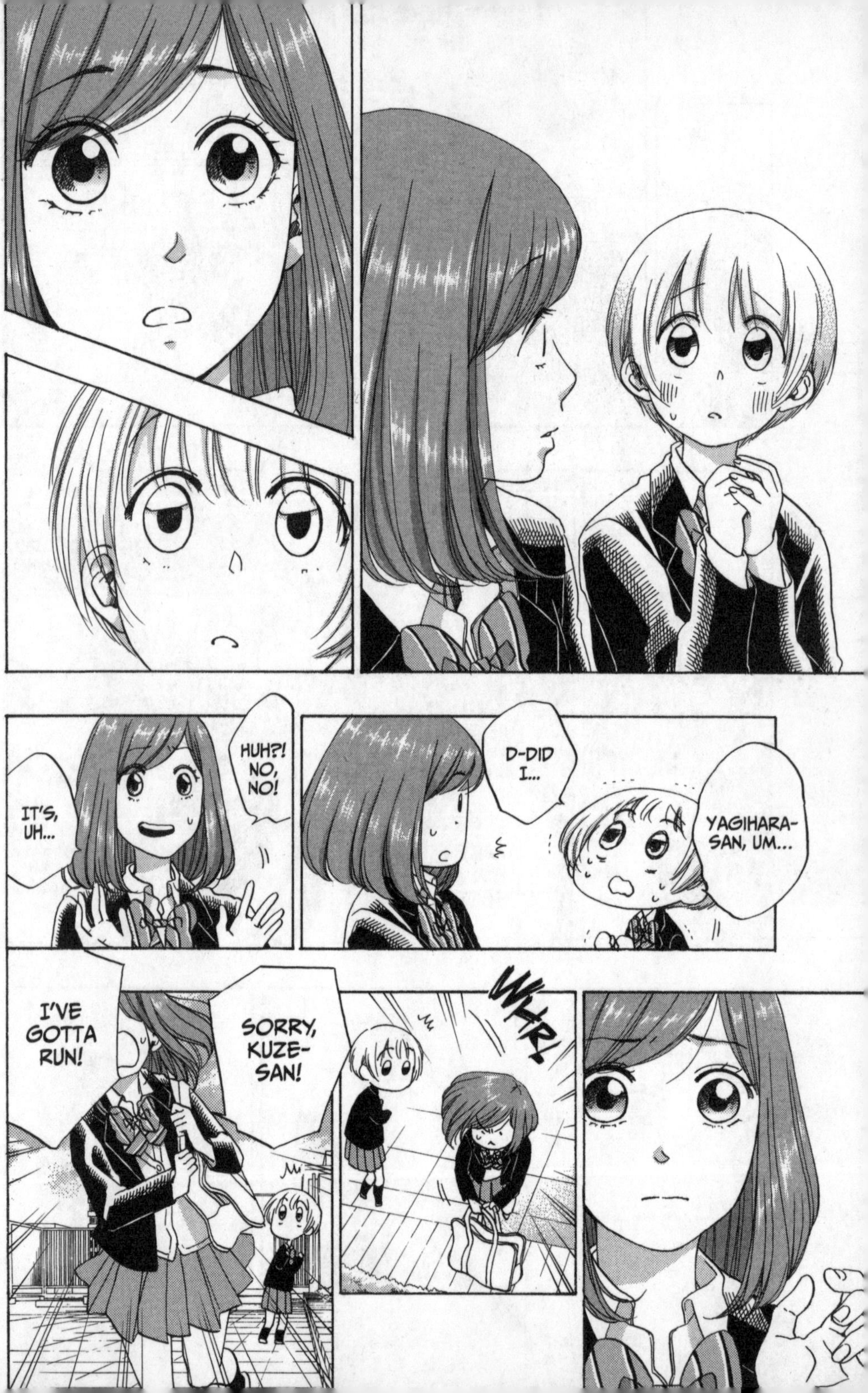
YAGIHARA-SAN, UM...
D-DID I...
HUH?! NO, NO!
IT'S, UH...
WHR!
SORRY, KUZE-SAN!
I'VE GOTTA RUN!

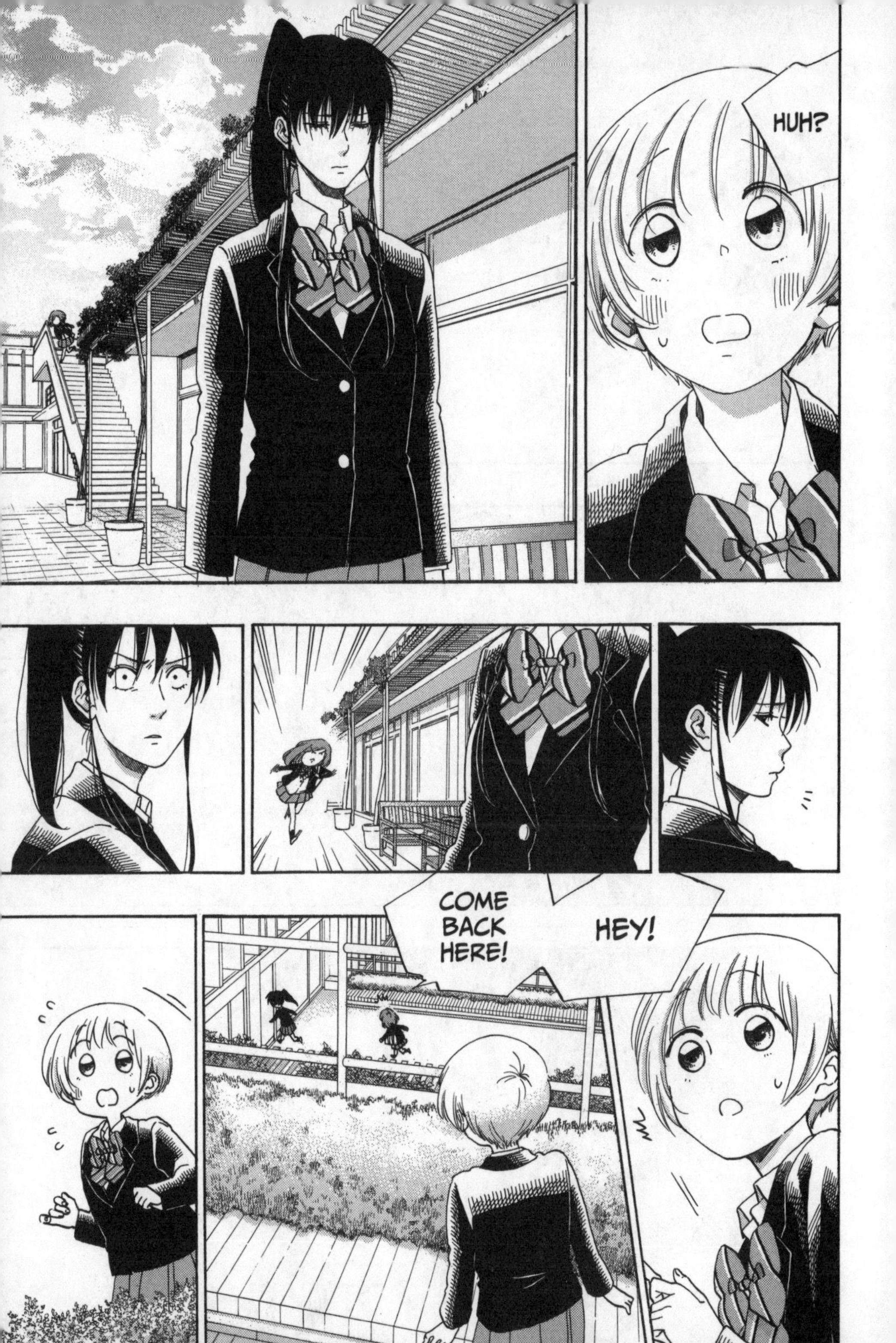
HUH?
HEY!
COME BACK HERE!

MAN, POOR TOMA. HE'S GOT A REAL PAIR OF HEADACHES SUPER ATTACHED TO HIM.

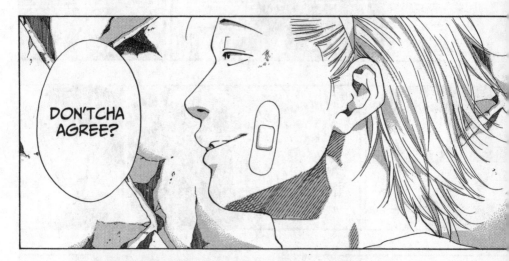

DON'TCHA AGREE?

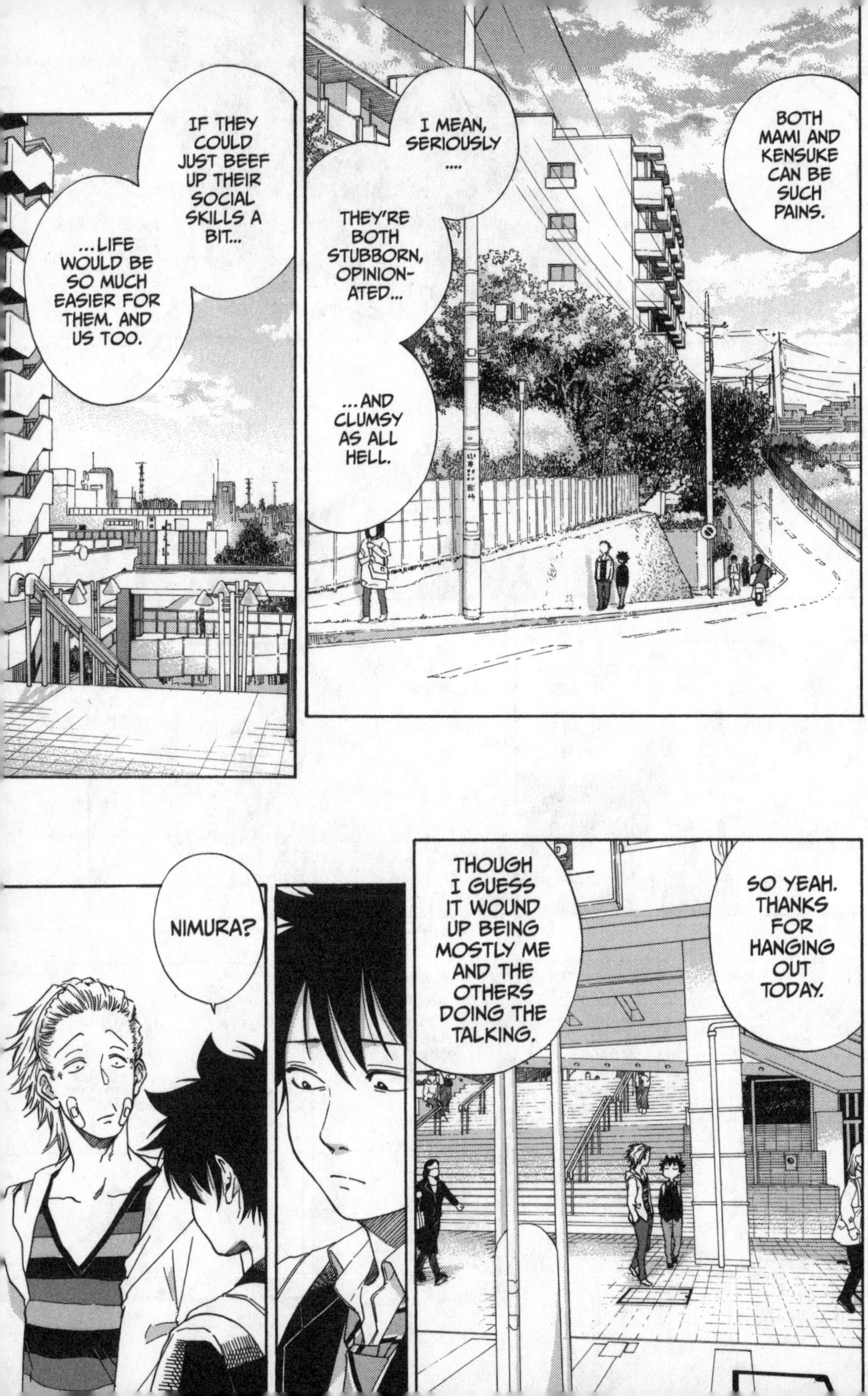
BOTH MAMI AND KENSUKE CAN BE SUCH PAINS.
I MEAN, SERIOUSLY ....
THEY'RE BOTH STUBBORN, OPINION-ATED...
...AND CLUMSY AS ALL HELL.
IF THEY COULD JUST BEEF UP THEIR SOCIAL SKILLS A BIT...
...LIFE WOULD BE SO MUCH EASIER FOR THEM. AND US TOO.
SO YEAH. THANKS FOR HANGING OUT TODAY.
THOUGH I GUESS IT WOUND UP BEING MOSTLY ME AND THE OTHERS DOING THE TALKING.
NIMURA?

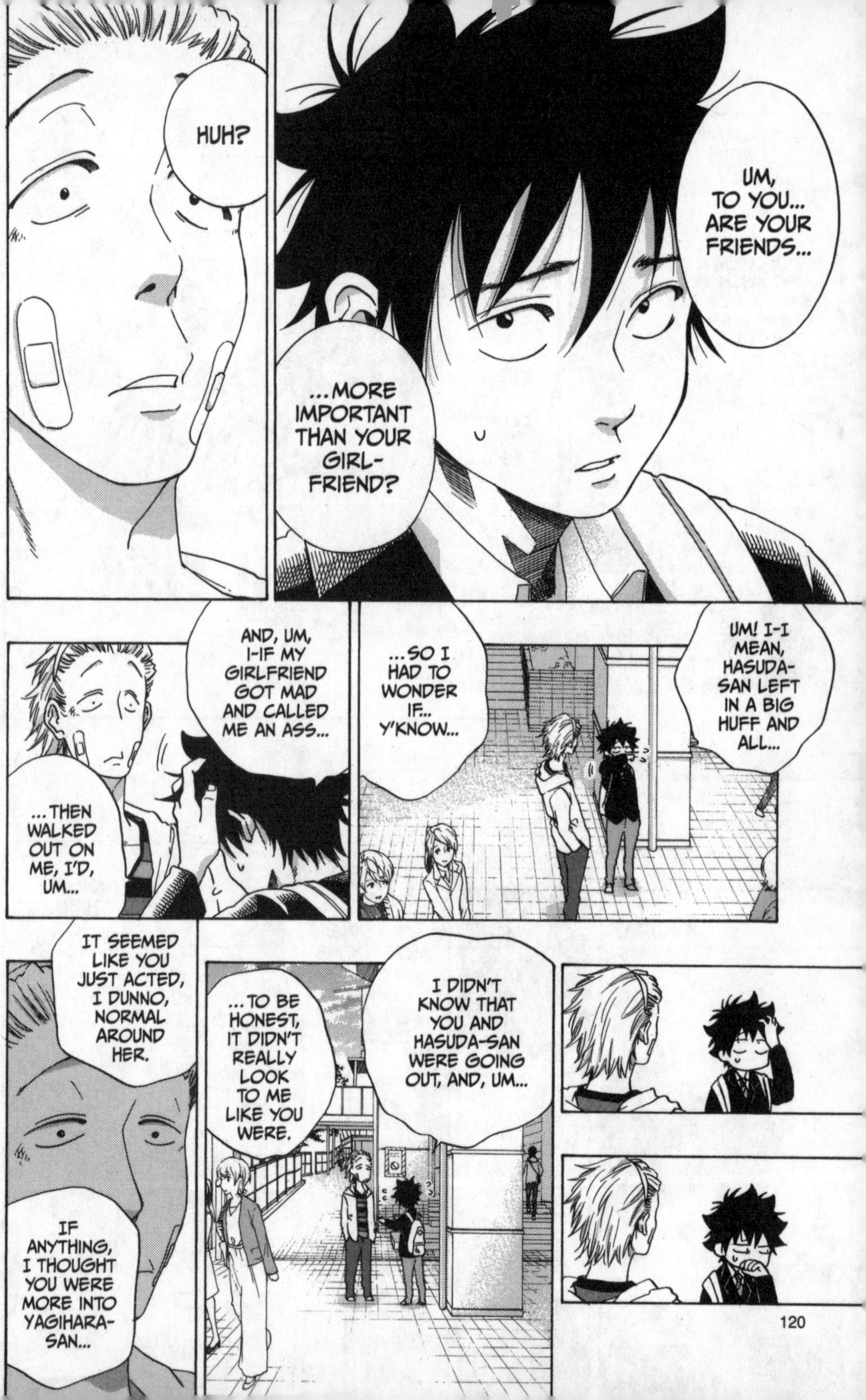
UM, TO YOU... ARE YOUR FRIENDS...
...MORE IMPORTANT THAN YOUR GIRL-FRIEND?
HUH?
UM! I-I MEAN, HASUDA-SAN LEFT IN A BIG HUFF AND ALL...
...SO I HAD TO WONDER IF... Y'KNOW...
AND, UM, I-IF MY GIRLFRIEND GOT MAD AND CALLED ME AN ASS...
...THEN WALKED OUT ON ME, I'D, UM...
I DIDN'T KNOW THAT YOU AND HASUDA-SAN WERE GOING OUT, AND, UM...
...TO BE HONEST, IT DIDN'T REALLY LOOK TO ME LIKE YOU WERE.
IT SEEMED LIKE YOU JUST ACTED, I DUNNO, NORMAL AROUND HER.
IF ANYTHING, I THOUGHT YOU WERE MORE INTO YAGIHARA-SAN...

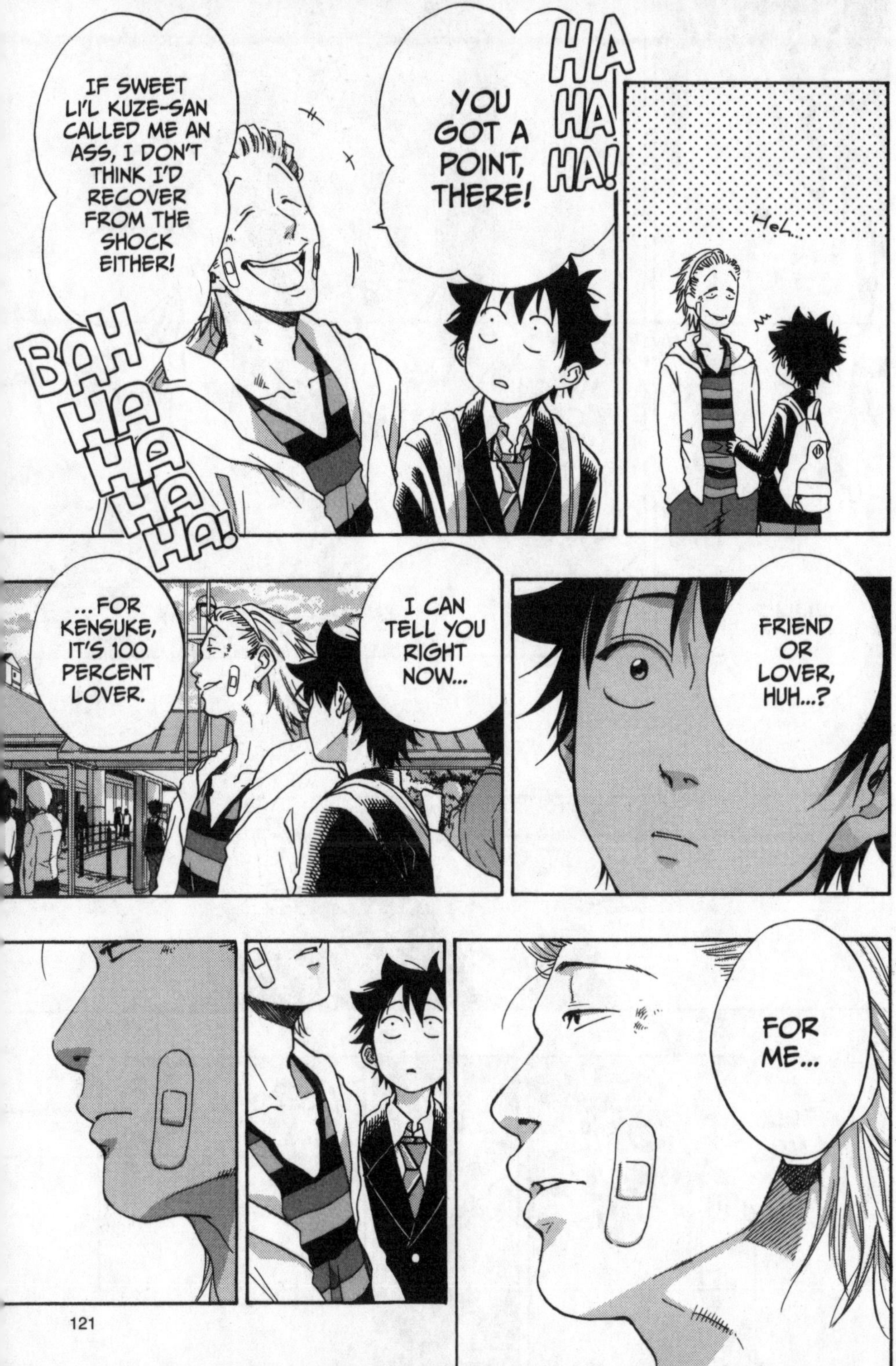

Heh...
HA HA HA!
YOU GOT A POINT, THERE!
IF SWEET LI'L KUZE-SAN CALLED ME AN ASS, I DON'T THINK I'D RECOVER FROM THE SHOCK EITHER!
BAH HA HA HA HA HA!
FRIEND OR LOVER, HUH...?
I CAN TELL YOU RIGHT NOW...
...FOR KENSUKE, IT'S 100 PERCENT LOVER.
FOR ME...

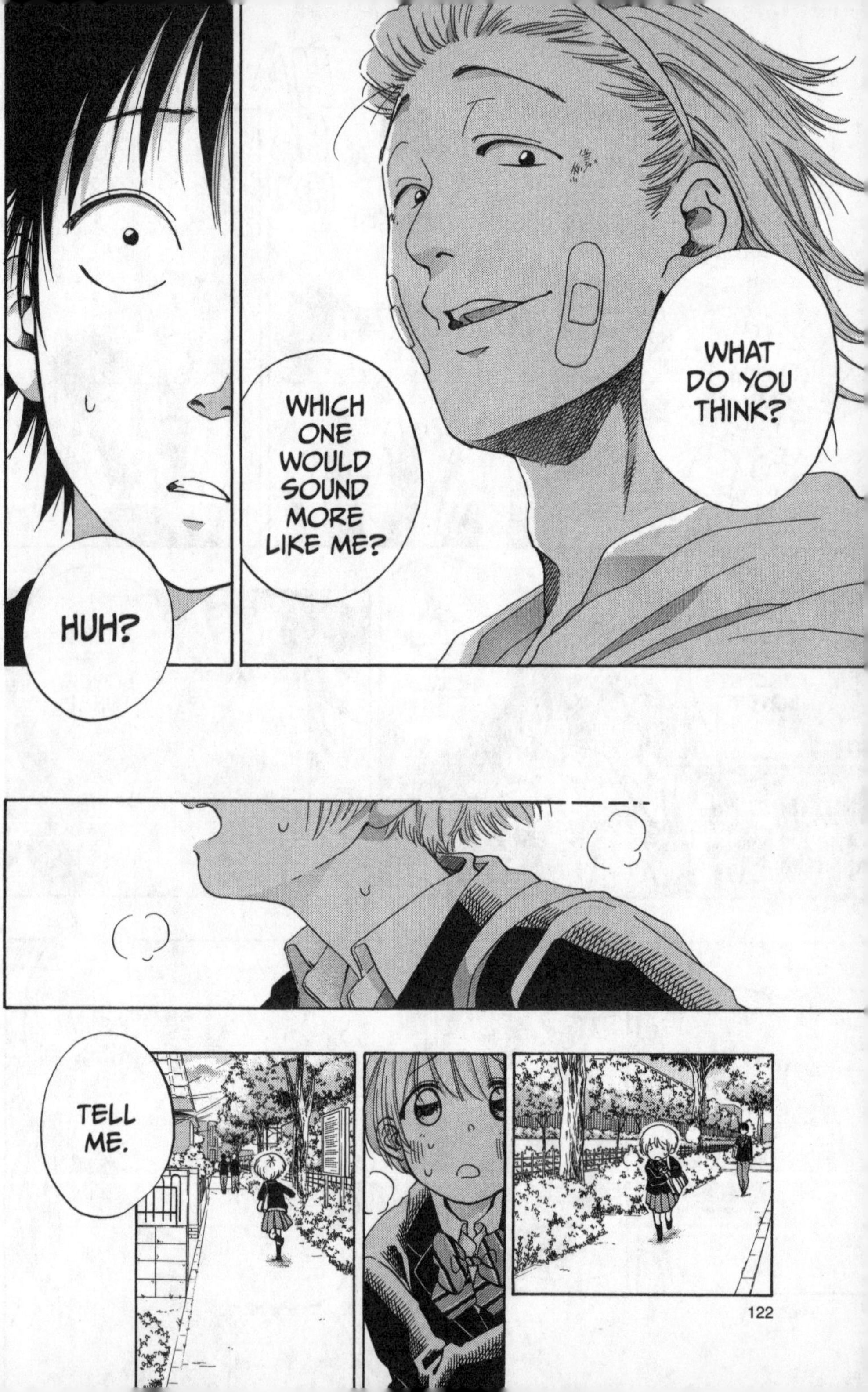
WHAT DO YOU THINK?
WHICH ONE WOULD SOUND MORE LIKE ME?
HUH?
TELL ME.

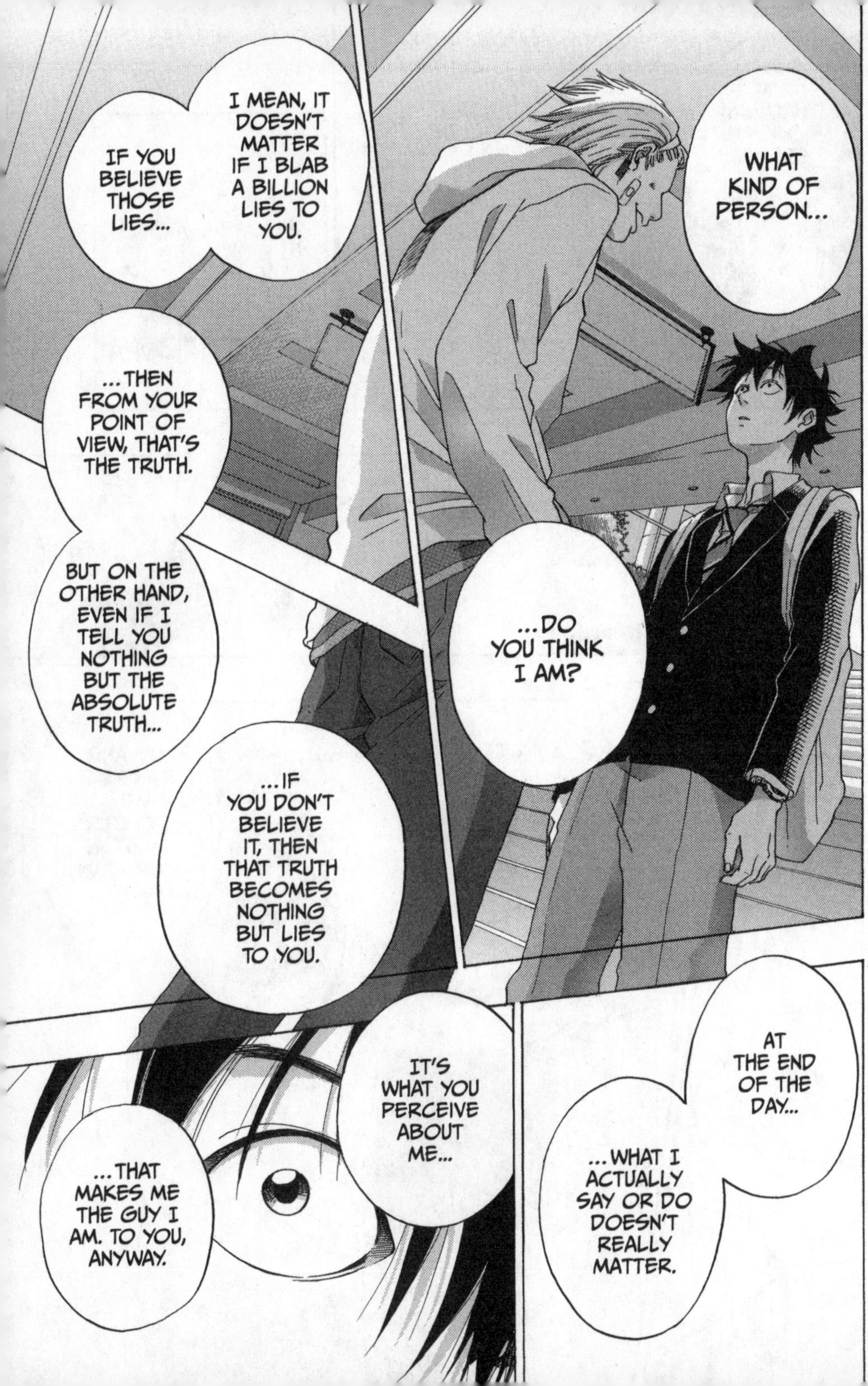
WHAT KIND OF PERSON...
...DO YOU THINK I AM?
I MEAN, IT DOESN'T MATTER IF I BLAB A BILLION LIES TO YOU.
IF YOU BELIEVE THOSE LIES...
...THEN FROM YOUR POINT OF VIEW, THAT'S THE TRUTH.
BUT ON THE OTHER HAND, EVEN IF I TELL YOU NOTHING BUT THE ABSOLUTE TRUTH...
...IF YOU DON'T BELIEVE IT, THEN THAT TRUTH BECOMES NOTHING BUT LIES TO YOU.
AT THE END OF THE DAY...
...WHAT I ACTUALLY SAY OR DO DOESN'T REALLY MATTER.
IT'S WHAT YOU PERCEIVE ABOUT ME...
...THAT MAKES ME THE GUY I AM. TO YOU, ANYWAY.

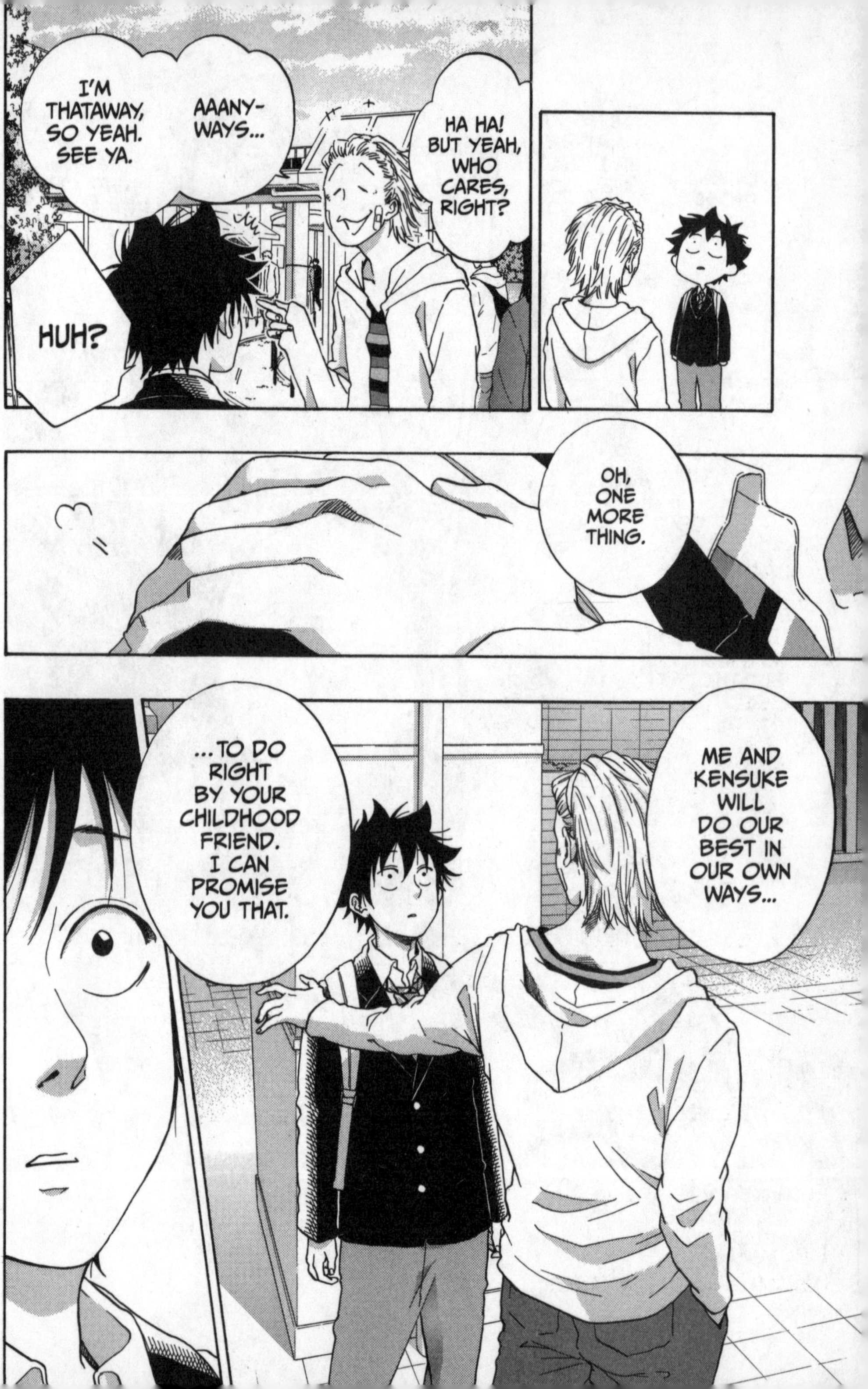
HA HA! BUT YEAH, WHO CARES, RIGHT?
AAANY-WAYS...
I'M THATAWAY, SO YEAH. SEE YA.
HUH?
OH, ONE MORE THING.
ME AND KENSUKE WILL DO OUR BEST IN OUR OWN WAYS...
...TO DO RIGHT BY YOUR CHILDHOOD FRIEND. I CAN PROMISE YOU THAT.

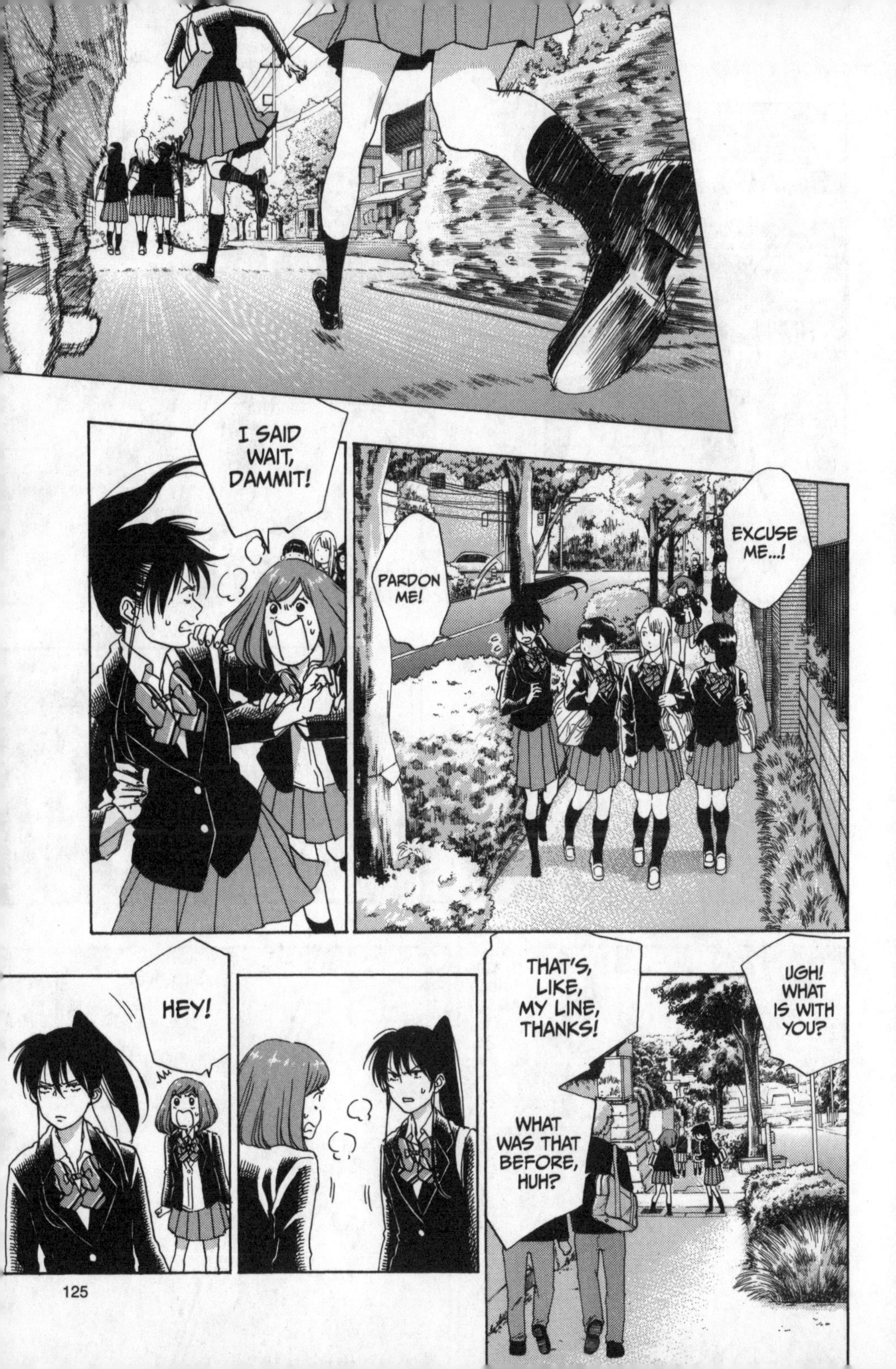
EXCUSE ME...!
PARDON ME!
I SAID WAIT, DAMMIT!
UGH! WHAT IS WITH YOU?
THAT'S, LIKE, MY LINE, THANKS!
WHAT WAS THAT BEFORE, HUH?
HEY!

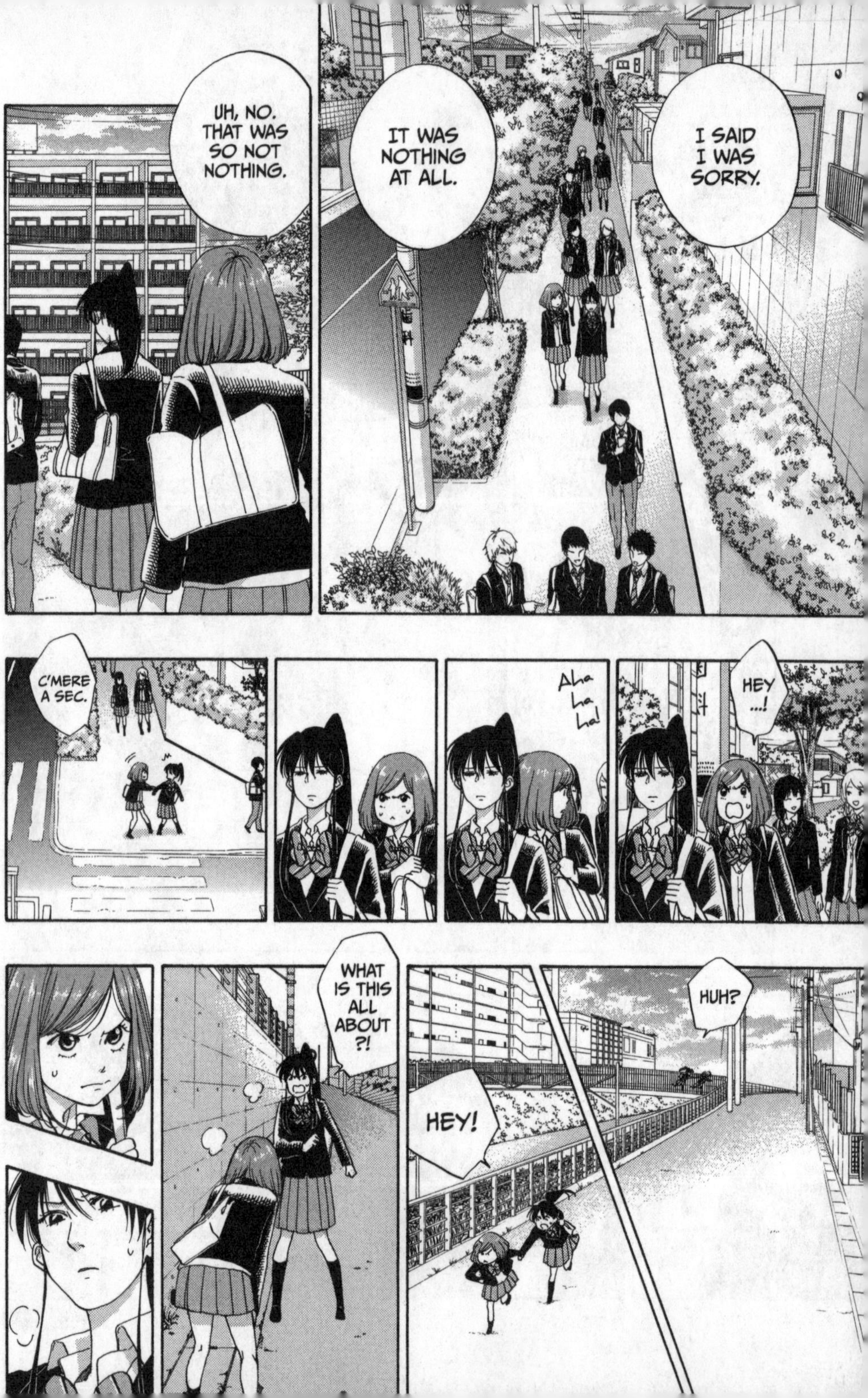

I SAID I WAS SORRY.
IT WAS NOTHING AT ALL.
UH, NO. THAT WAS SO NOT NOTHING.
HEY ...!
Aha ha ha!
C'MERE A SEC.
HUH?
HEY!
WHAT IS THIS ALL ABOUT ?!

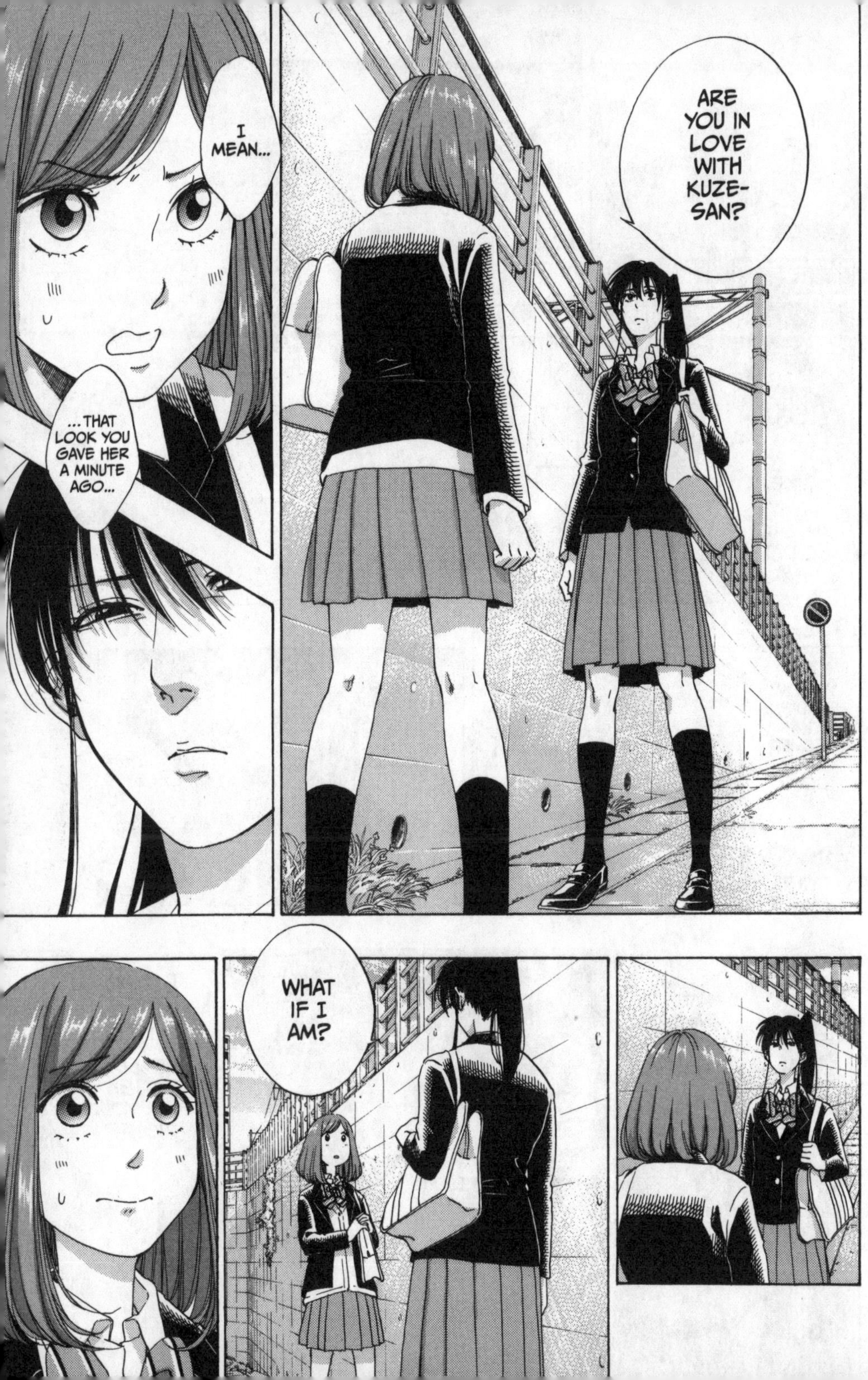
ARE YOU IN LOVE WITH KUZE-SAN?
I MEAN...
...THAT LOOK YOU GAVE HER A MINUTE AGO...
WHAT IF I AM?

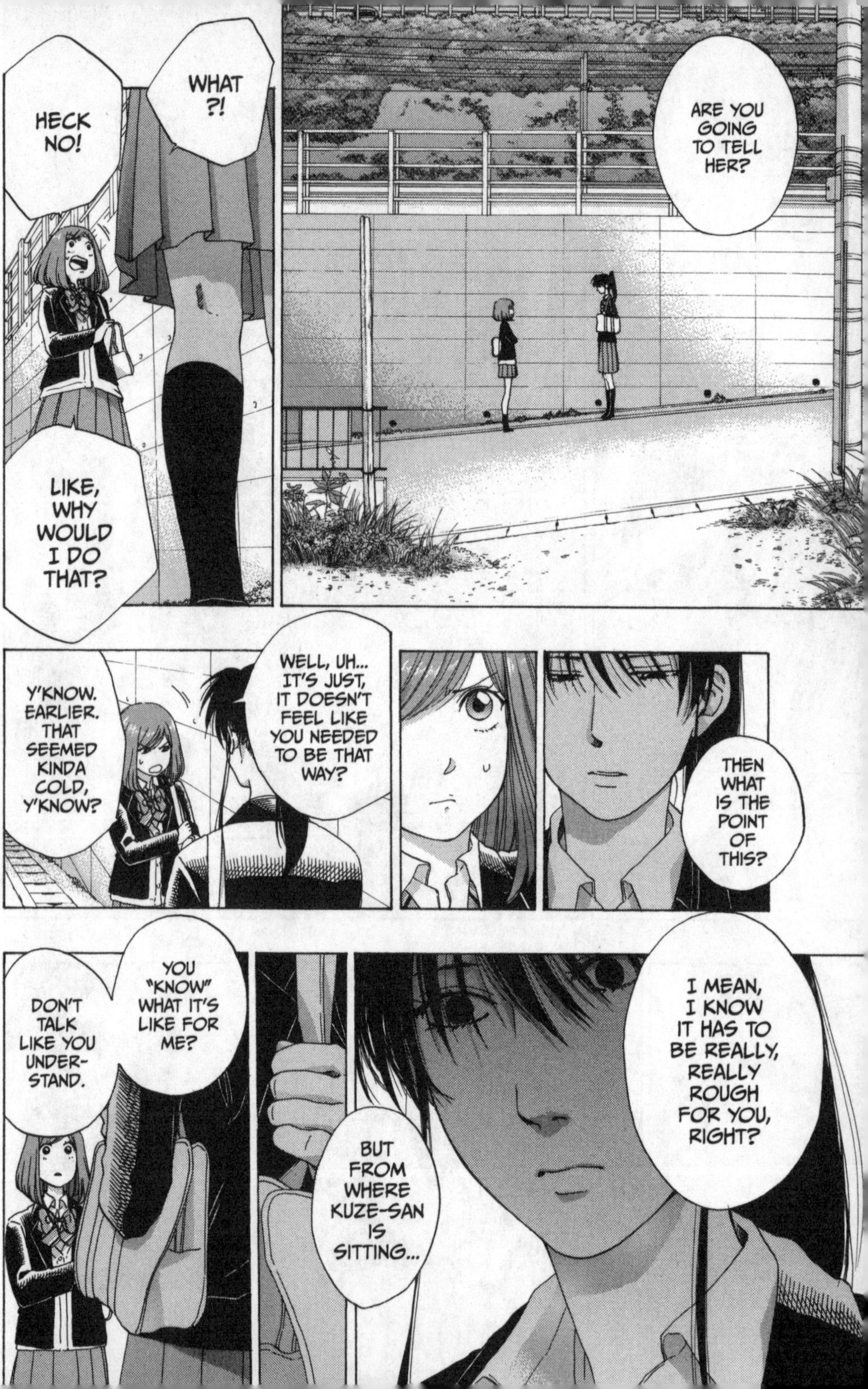
ARE YOU GOING TO TELL HER?
WHAT?!
HECK NO!
LIKE, WHY WOULD I DO THAT?
THEN WHAT IS THE POINT OF THIS?
WELL, UH... IT'S JUST, IT DOESN'T FEEL LIKE YOU NEEDED TO BE THAT WAY?
Y'KNOW. EARLIER. THAT SEEMED KINDA COLD, Y'KNOW?
I MEAN, I KNOW IT HAS TO BE REALLY, REALLY ROUGH FOR YOU, RIGHT?
BUT FROM WHERE KUZE-SAN IS SITTING...
YOU "KNOW" WHAT IT'S LIKE FOR ME?
DON'T TALK LIKE YOU UNDERSTAND.

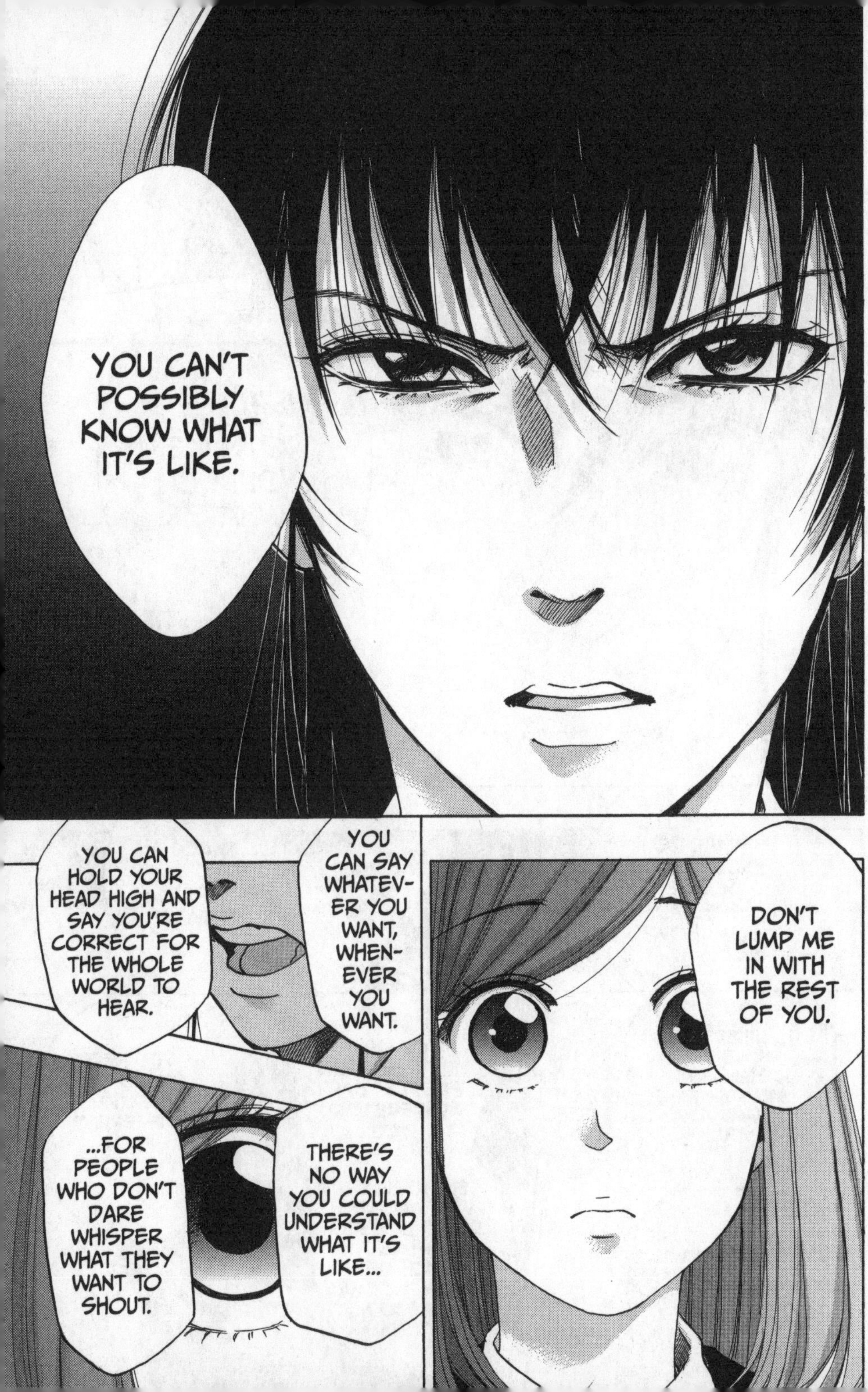
YOU CAN'T POSSIBLY KNOW WHAT IT'S LIKE.
DON'T LUMP ME IN WITH THE REST OF YOU.
YOU CAN SAY WHATEV-ER YOU WANT, WHEN-EVER YOU WANT.
YOU CAN HOLD YOUR HEAD HIGH AND SAY YOU'RE CORRECT FOR THE WHOLE WORLD TO HEAR.
THERE'S NO WAY YOU COULD UNDERSTAND WHAT IT'S LIKE...
...FOR PEOPLE WHO DON'T DARE WHISPER WHAT THEY WANT TO SHOUT.

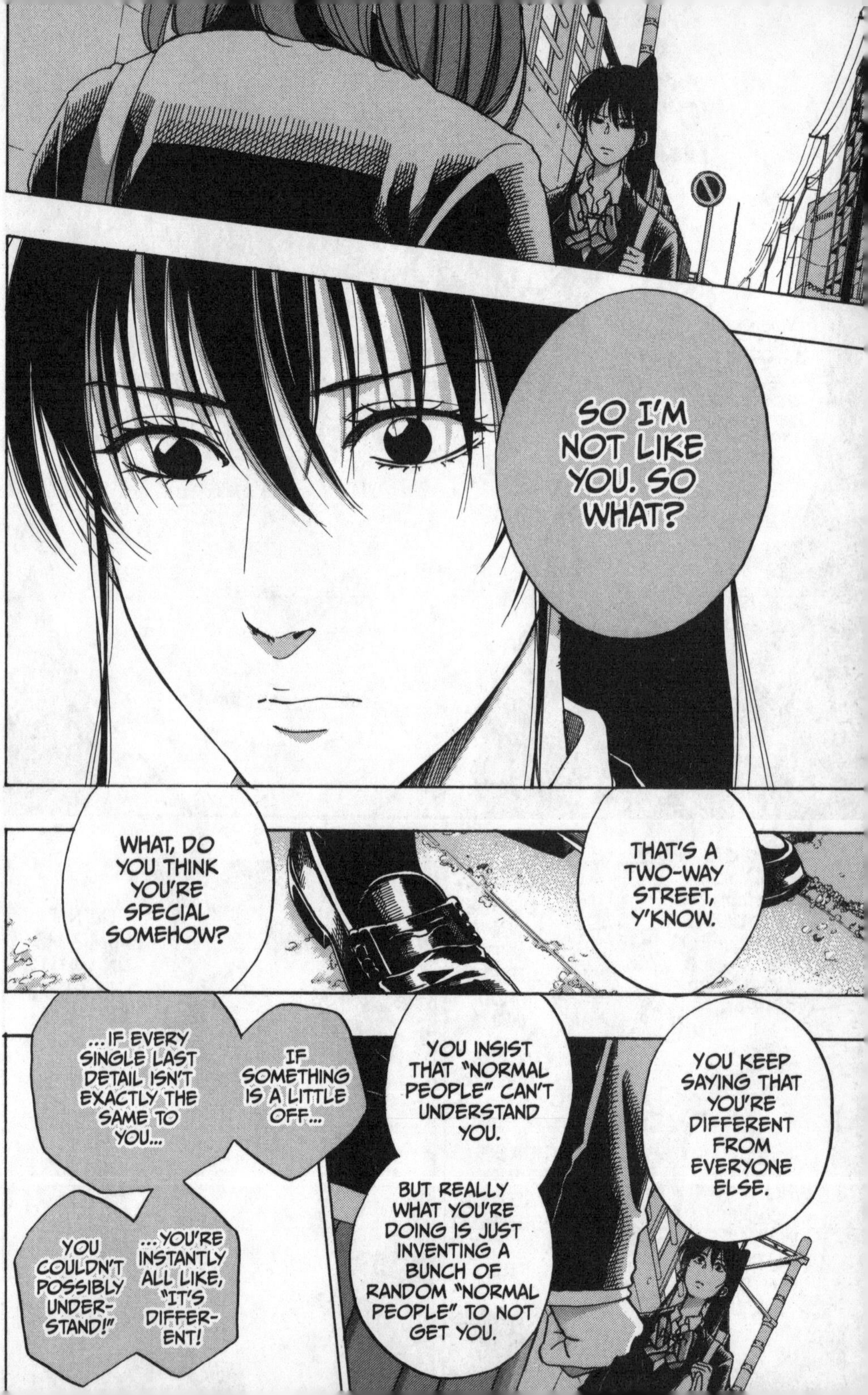
SO I'M NOT LIKE YOU. SO WHAT?
THAT'S A TWO-WAY STREET, Y'KNOW.
WHAT, DO YOU THINK YOU'RE SPECIAL SOMEHOW?
YOU KEEP SAYING THAT YOU'RE DIFFERENT FROM EVERYONE ELSE.
YOU INSIST THAT "NORMAL PEOPLE" CAN'T UNDERSTAND YOU.
BUT REALLY WHAT YOU'RE DOING IS JUST INVENTING A BUNCH OF RANDOM "NORMAL PEOPLE" TO NOT GET YOU.
IF SOMETHING IS A LITTLE OFF...
...IF EVERY SINGLE LAST DETAIL ISN'T EXACTLY THE SAME TO YOU...
...YOU'RE INSTANTLY ALL LIKE, "IT'S DIFFER-ENT!
YOU COULDN'T POSSIBLY UNDER-STAND!"

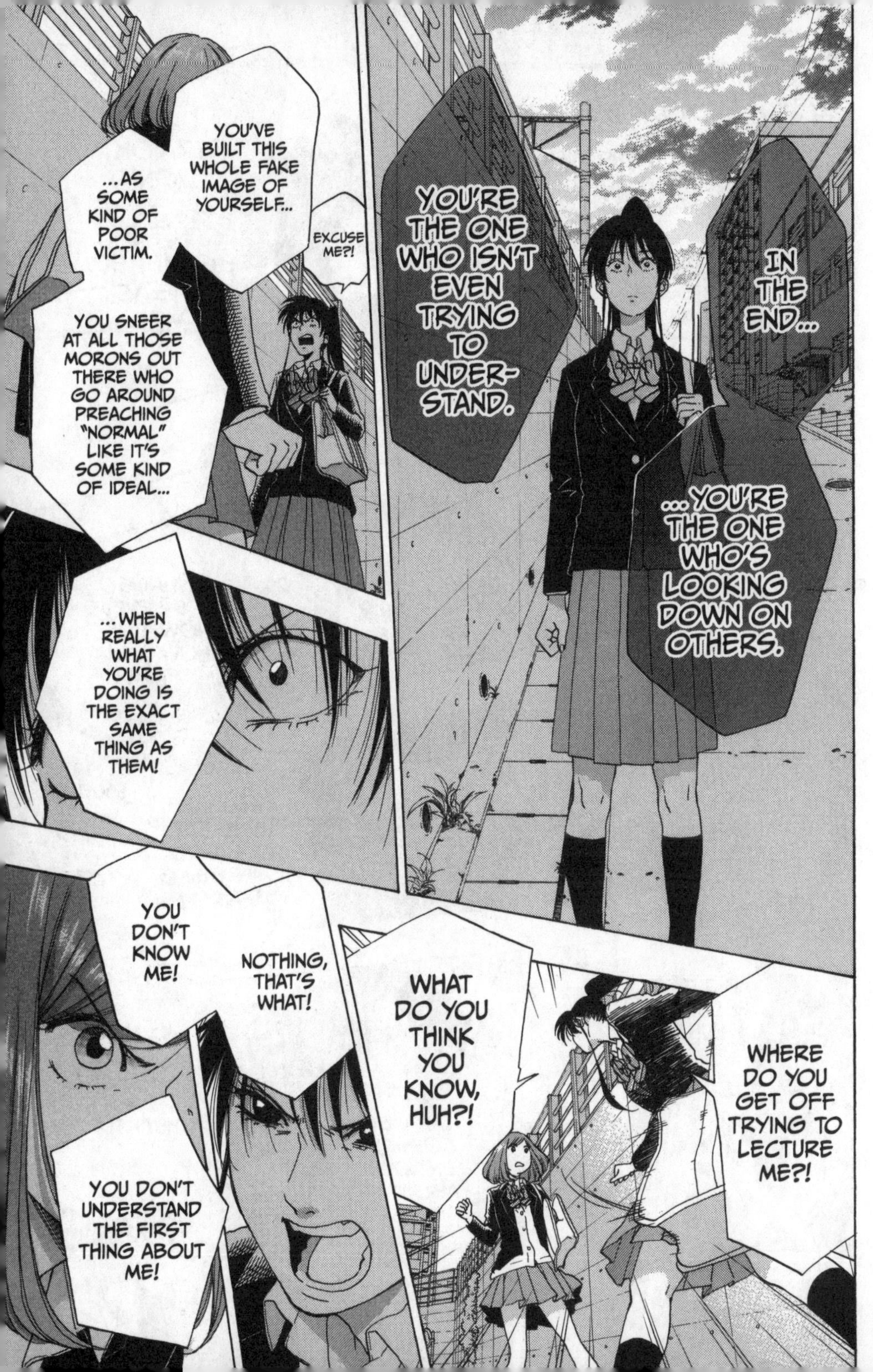
IN THE END...
...YOU'RE THE ONE WHO'S LOOKING DOWN ON OTHERS.
YOU'RE THE ONE WHO ISN'T EVEN TRYING TO UNDER-STAND.
EXCUSE ME?!
YOU'VE BUILT THIS WHOLE FAKE IMAGE OF YOURSELF...
...AS SOME KIND OF POOR VICTIM.
YOU SNEER AT ALL THOSE MORONS OUT THERE WHO GO AROUND PREACHING "NORMAL" LIKE IT'S SOME KIND OF IDEAL...
...WHEN REALLY WHAT YOU'RE DOING IS THE EXACT SAME THING AS THEM!
WHERE DO YOU GET OFF TRYING TO LECTURE ME?!
WHAT DO YOU THINK YOU KNOW, HUH?!
NOTHING, THAT'S WHAT!
YOU DON'T KNOW ME!
YOU DON'T UNDERSTAND THE FIRST THING ABOUT ME!

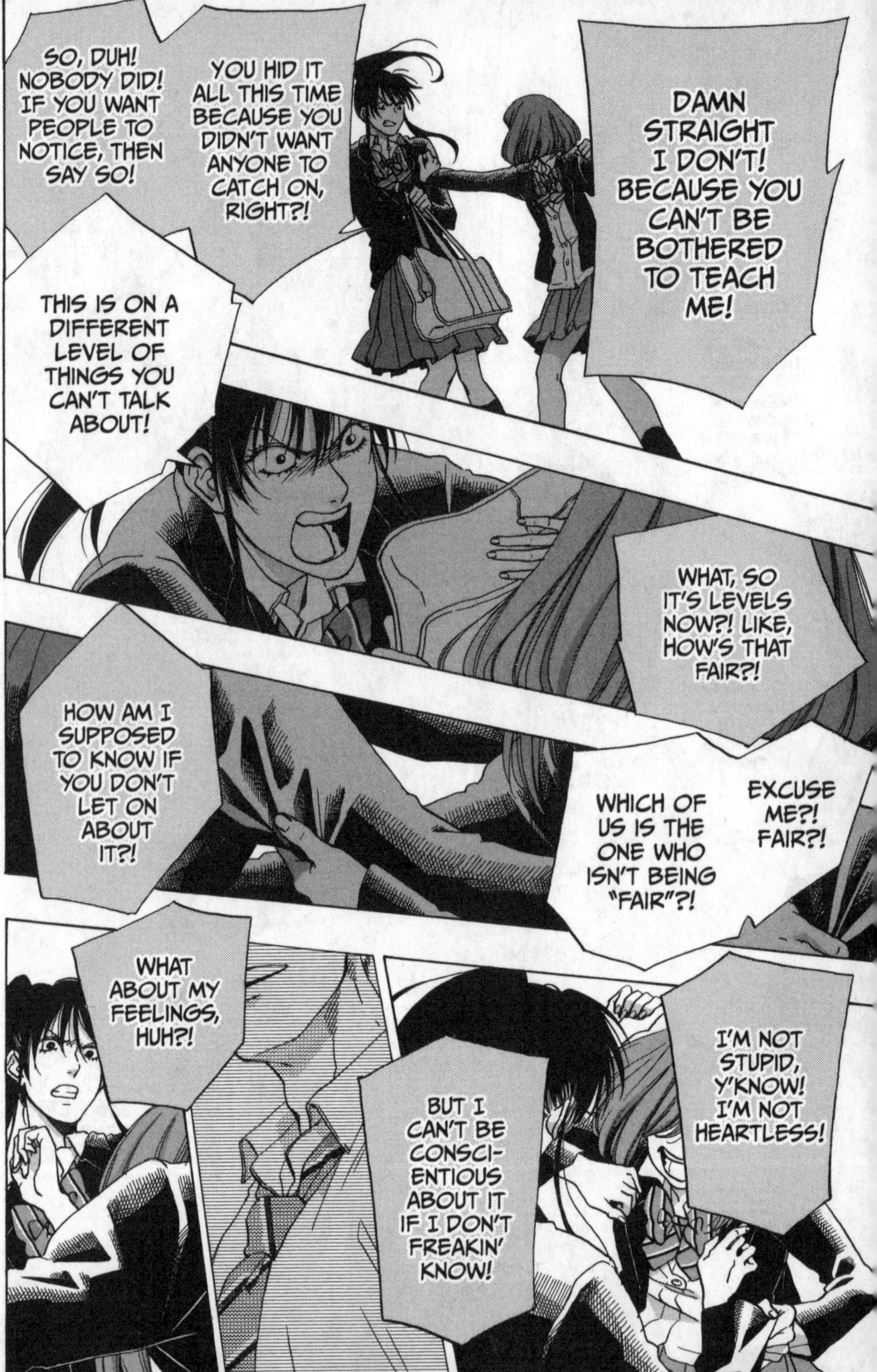
DAMN STRAIGHT I DON'T! BECAUSE YOU CAN'T BE BOTHERED TO TEACH ME!
YOU HID IT ALL THIS TIME BECAUSE YOU DIDN'T WANT ANYONE TO CATCH ON, RIGHT?!
SO, DUH! NOBODY DID! IF YOU WANT PEOPLE TO NOTICE, THEN SAY SO!
THIS IS ON A DIFFERENT LEVEL OF THINGS YOU CAN'T TALK ABOUT!
WHAT, SO IT'S LEVELS NOW?! LIKE, HOW'S THAT FAIR?!
EXCUSE ME?! FAIR?!
WHICH OF US IS THE ONE WHO ISN'T BEING "FAIR"?!
HOW AM I SUPPOSED TO KNOW IF YOU DON'T LET ON ABOUT IT?!
I'M NOT STUPID, Y'KNOW! I'M NOT HEARTLESS!
BUT I CAN'T BE CONSCI-ENTIOUS ABOUT IT IF I DON'T FREAKIN' KNOW!
WHAT ABOUT MY FEELINGS, HUH?!

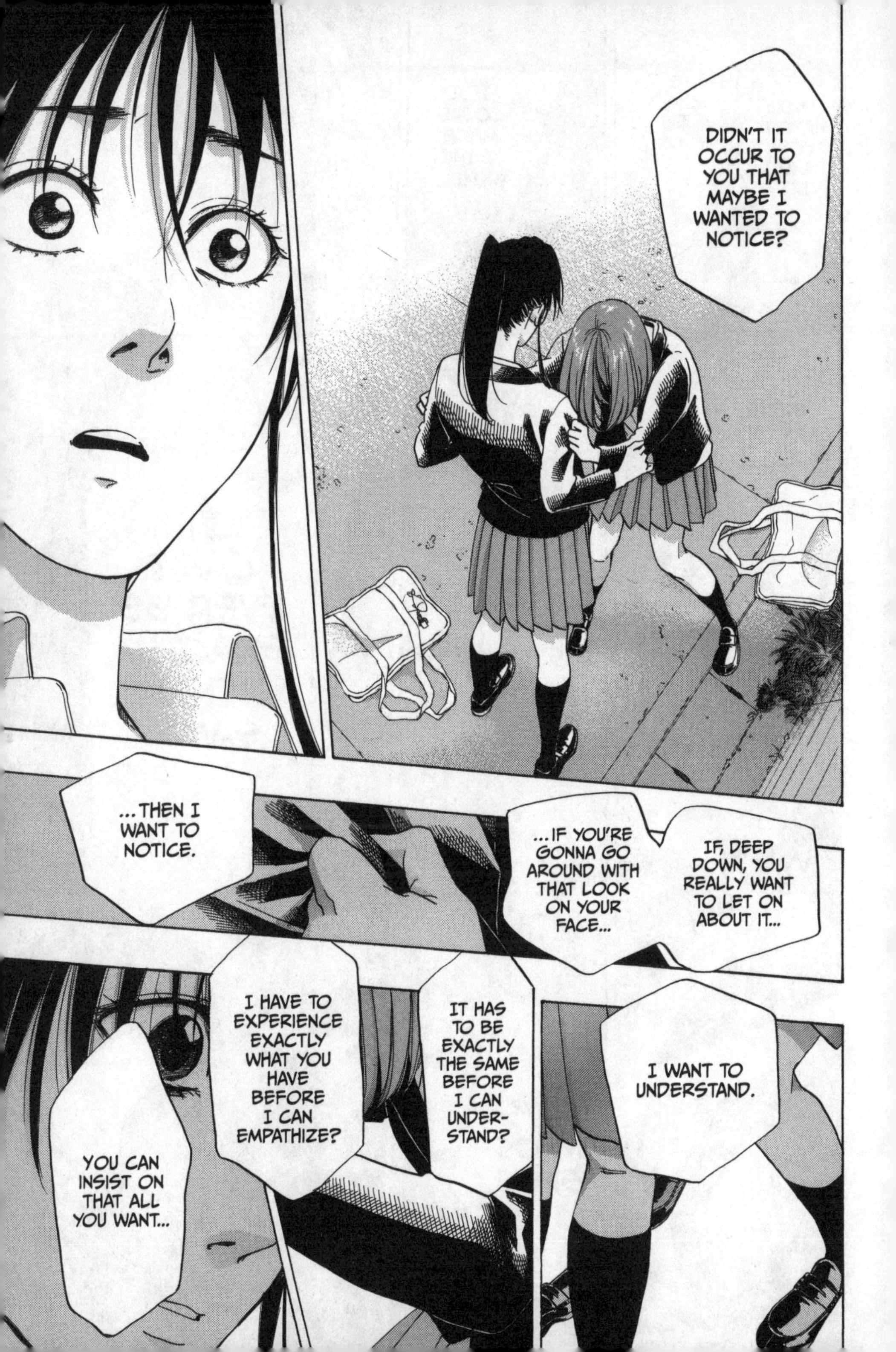
DIDN'T IT OCCUR TO YOU THAT MAYBE I WANTED TO NOTICE?
IF, DEEP DOWN, YOU REALLY WANT TO LET ON ABOUT IT...
...IF YOU'RE GONNA GO AROUND WITH THAT LOOK ON YOUR FACE...
...THEN I WANT TO NOTICE.
I WANT TO UNDERSTAND.
IT HAS TO BE EXACTLY THE SAME BEFORE I CAN UNDER-STAND?
I HAVE TO EXPERIENCE EXACTLY WHAT YOU HAVE BEFORE I CAN EMPATHIZE?
YOU CAN INSIST ON THAT ALL YOU WANT...

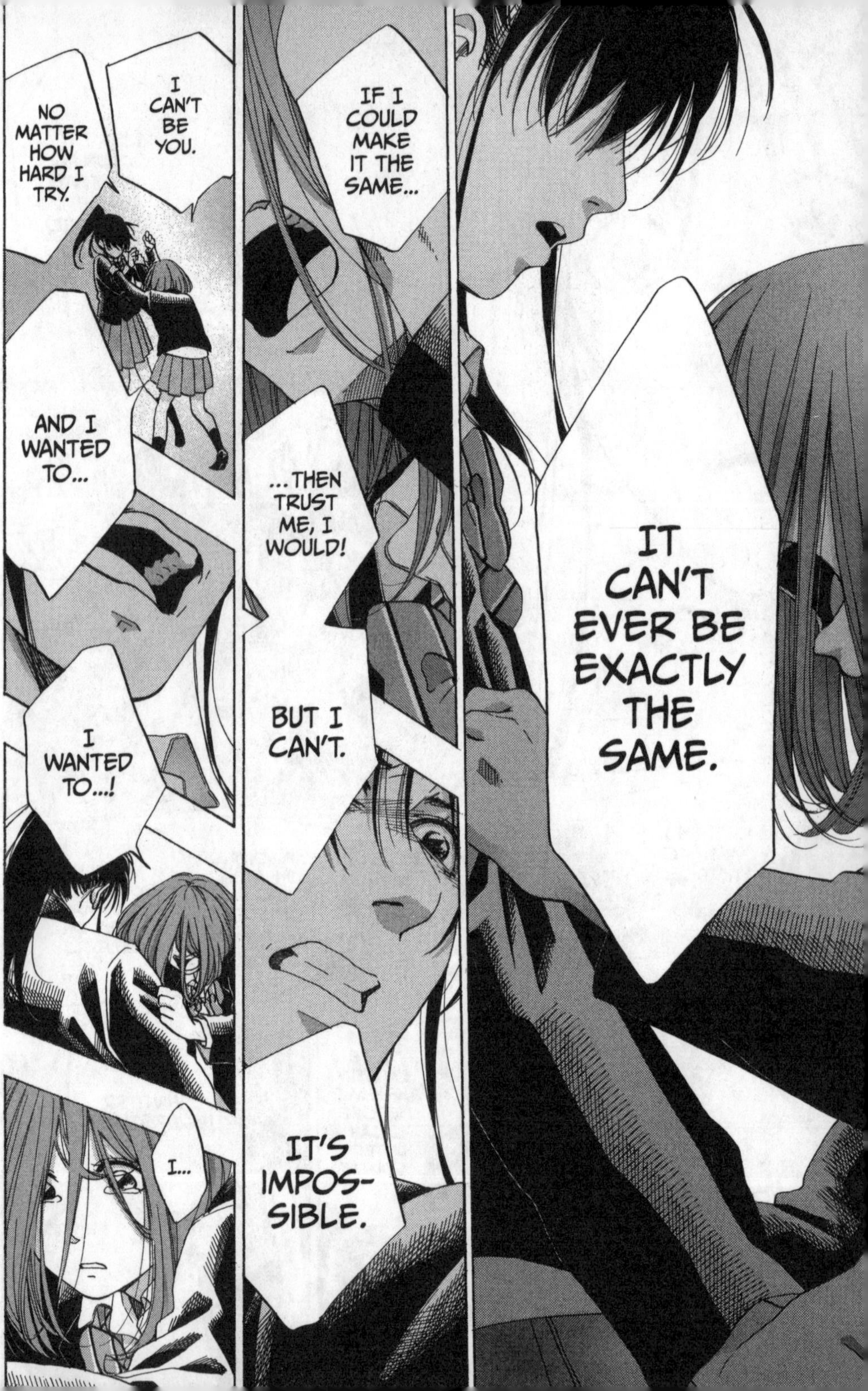
IT CAN'T EVER BE EXACTLY THE SAME.
IF I COULD MAKE IT THE SAME...
...THEN TRUST ME, I WOULD!
BUT I CAN'T.
IT'S IMPOS-SIBLE.
I CAN'T BE YOU.
NO MATTER HOW HARD I TRY.
AND I WANTED TO...
I WANTED TO...!
I...

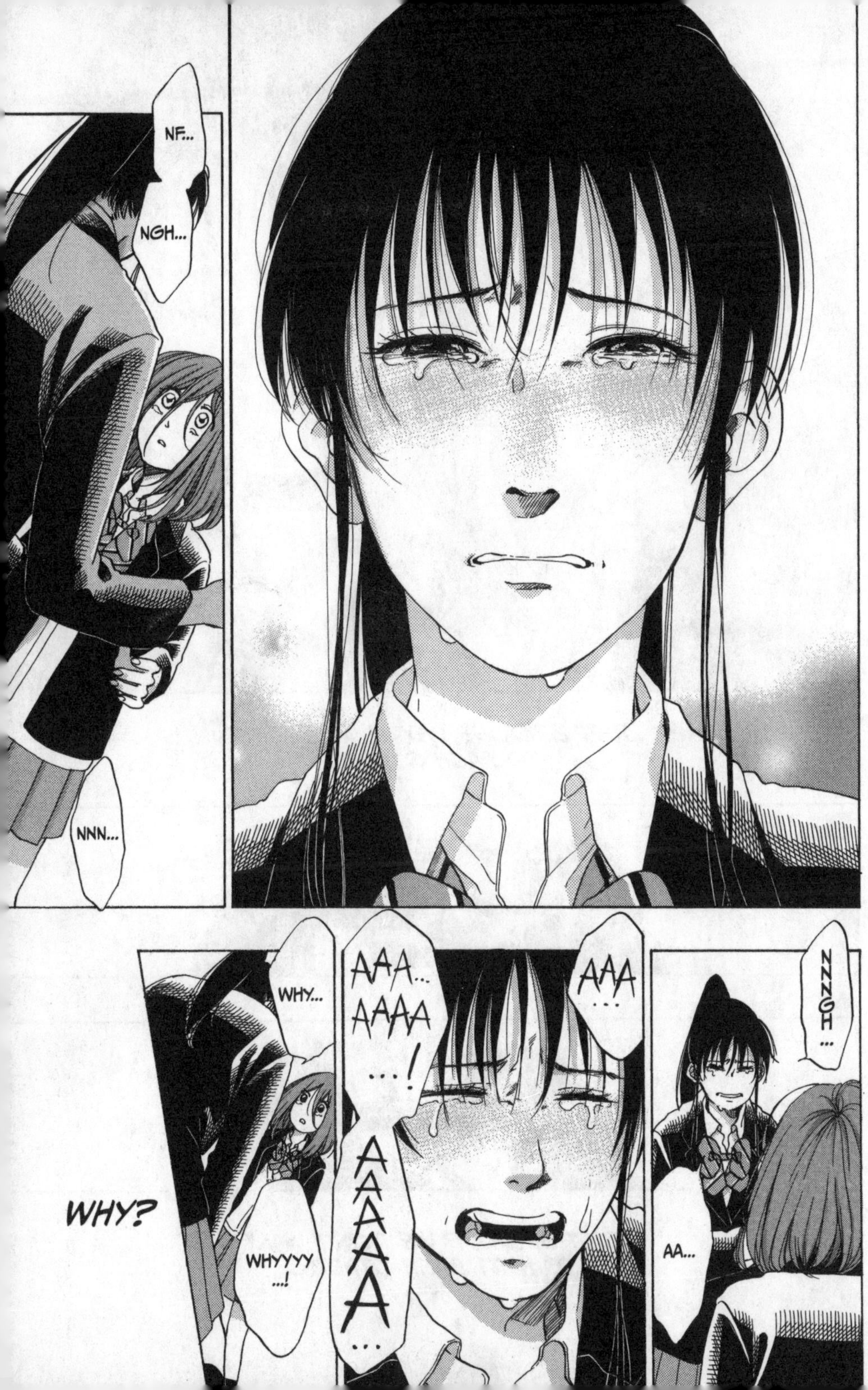
NF...
NGH...
NNN...
NNNGH...
AA...
AAA...
AAA... AAAA ...!
AAAAA...
WHY...
WHYYYY ...!
WHY?

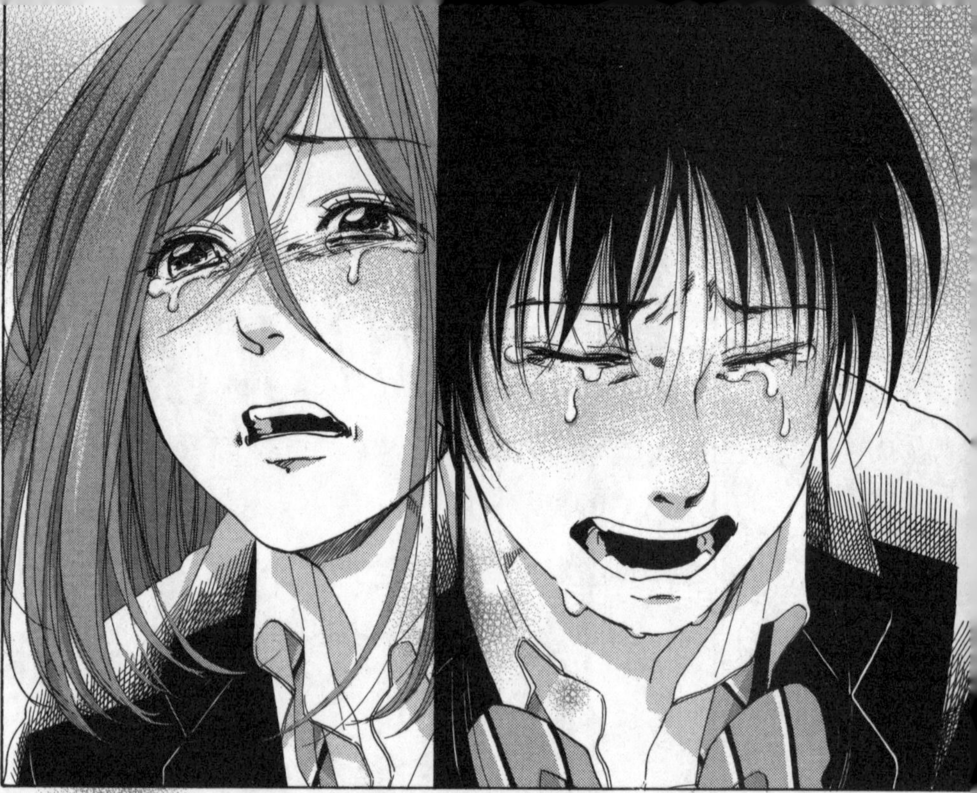

JUST BECAUSE WE'RE IMPORTANT
TO EACH OTHER...

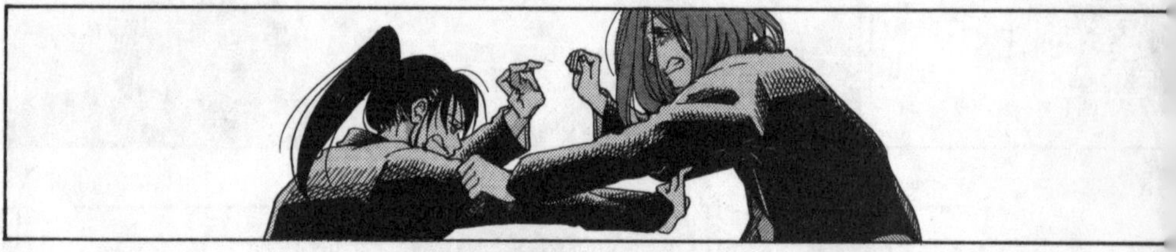

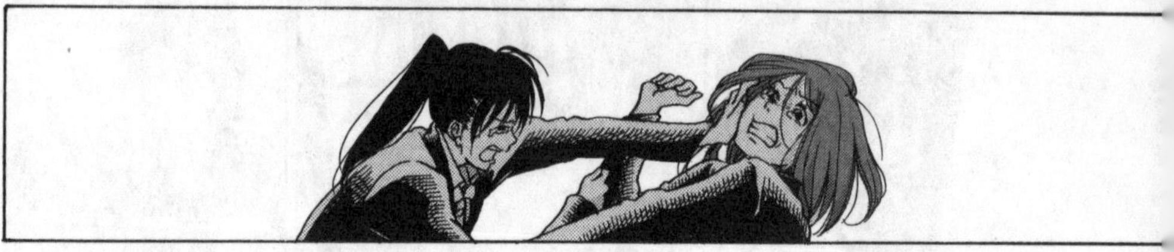

JUST BECAUSE WE DON'T WANT
TO HURT EACH OTHER...

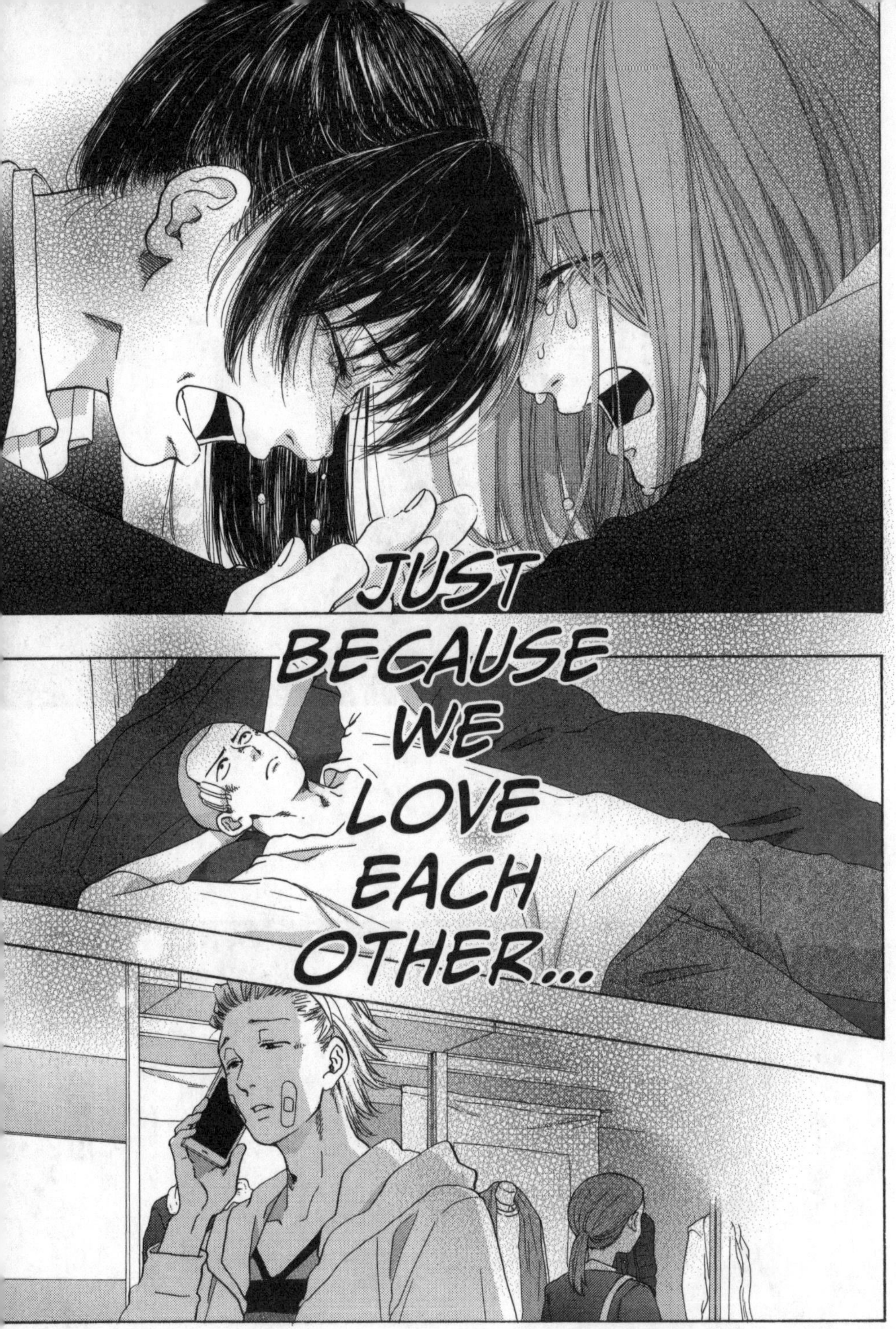
JUST BECAUSE WE LOVE EACH OTHER...

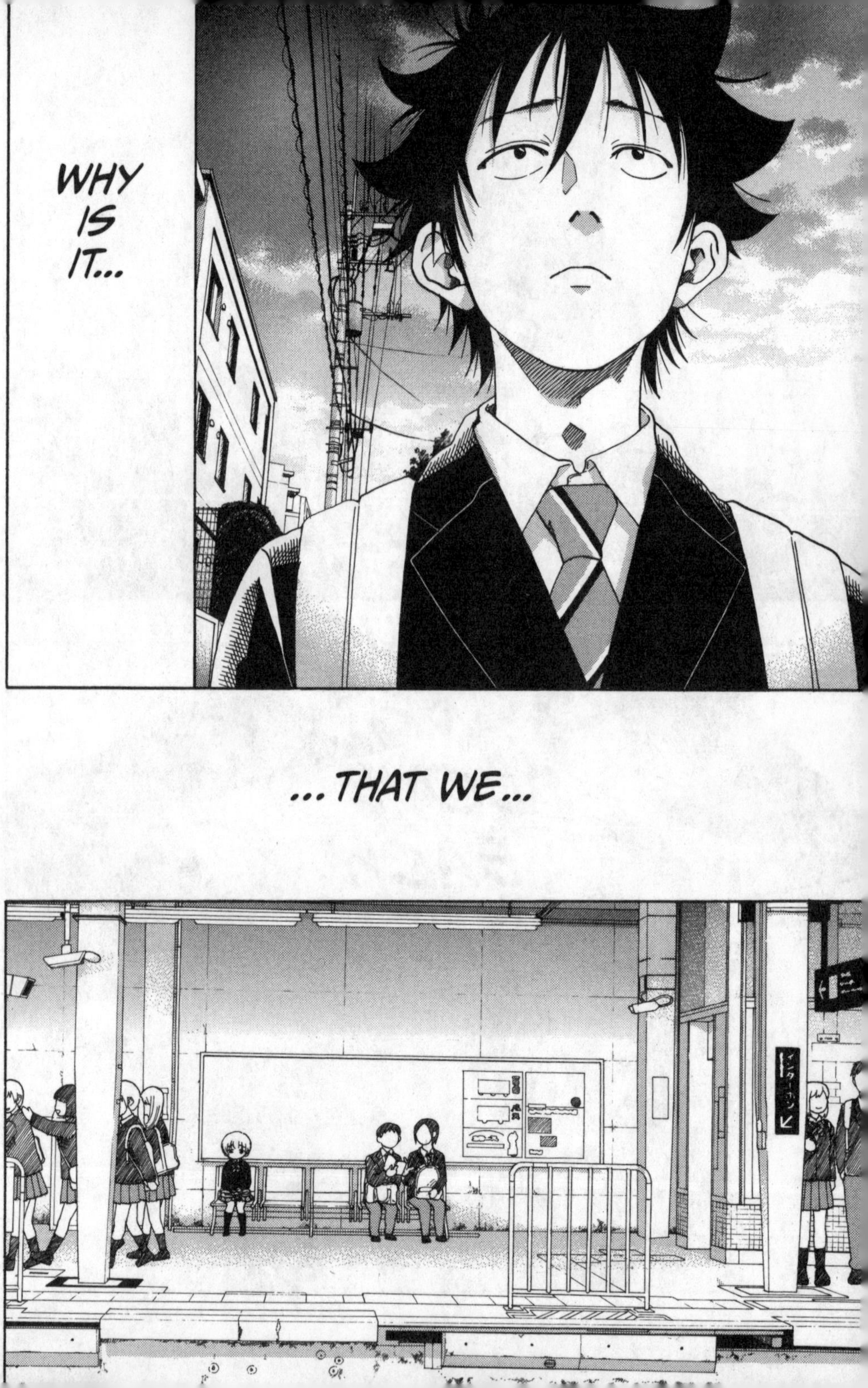
WHY IS IT...
...THAT WE...

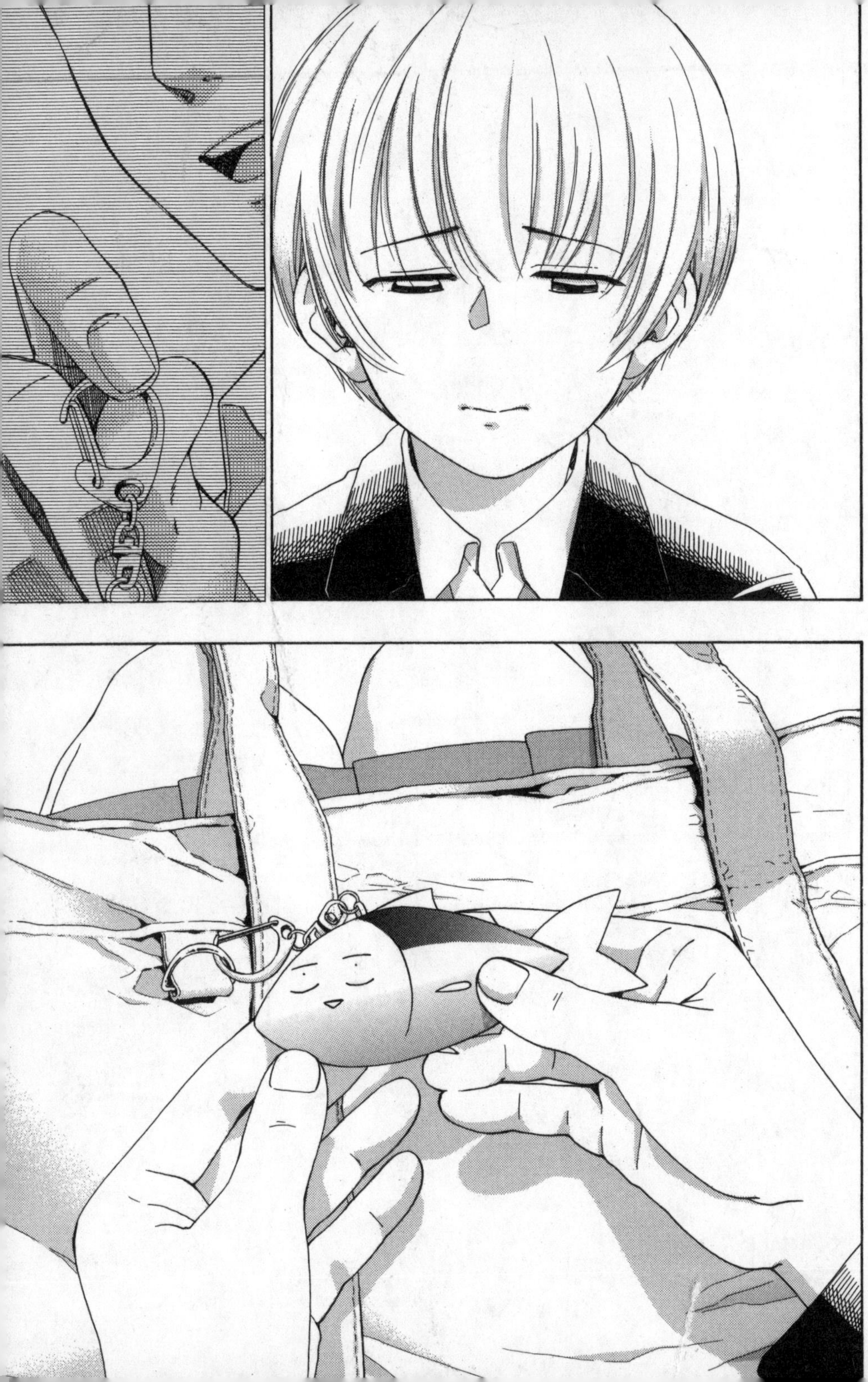

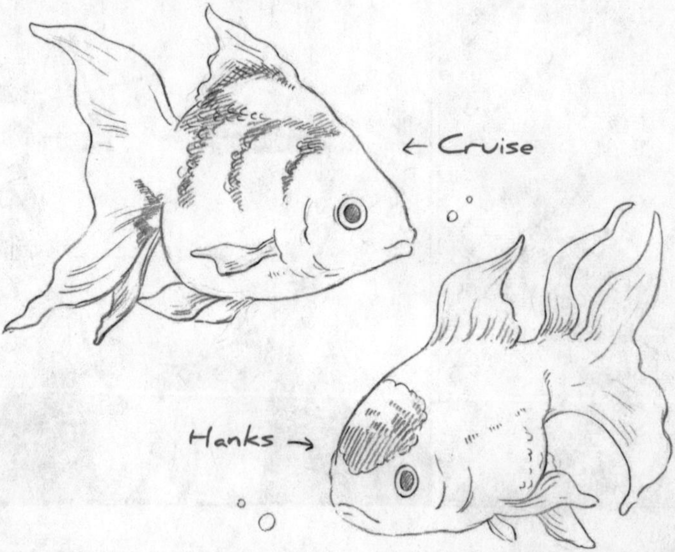
← Cruise
Hanks →

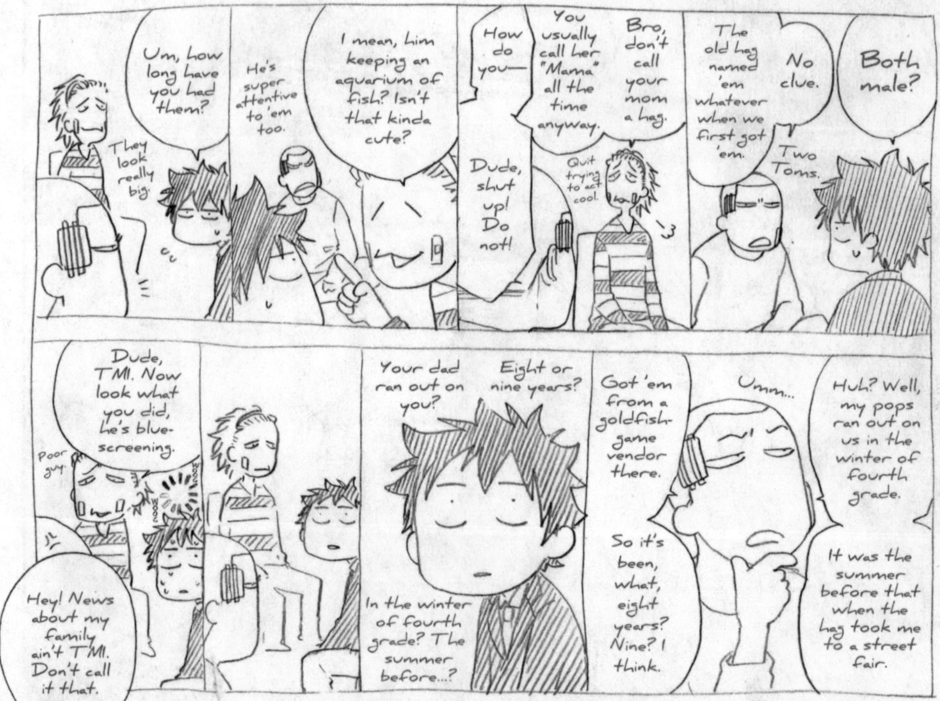
Both male?
No clue.
The old hag named 'em whatever when we first got 'em.
Two Toms.
Bro, don't call your mom a hag.
You usually call her "Mama" all the time anyway.
How do you—
Dude, shut up! Do not!
Quit trying to act cool.
I mean, him keeping an aquarium of fish? Isn't that kinda cute?
He's super attentive to 'em too.
Um, how long have you had them?
They look really big.
Huh? Well, my pops ran out on us in the winter of fourth grade.
Umm...
It was the summer before that when the hag took me to a street fair.
Got 'em from a goldfish-game vendor there.
So it's been, what, eight years? Nine? I think.
Eight or nine years?
Your dad ran out on you?
In the winter of fourth grade? The summer before...?
Dude, TMI. Now look what you did, he's blue-screening.
Poor guy.
Hey! News about my family ain't TMI. Don't call it that.

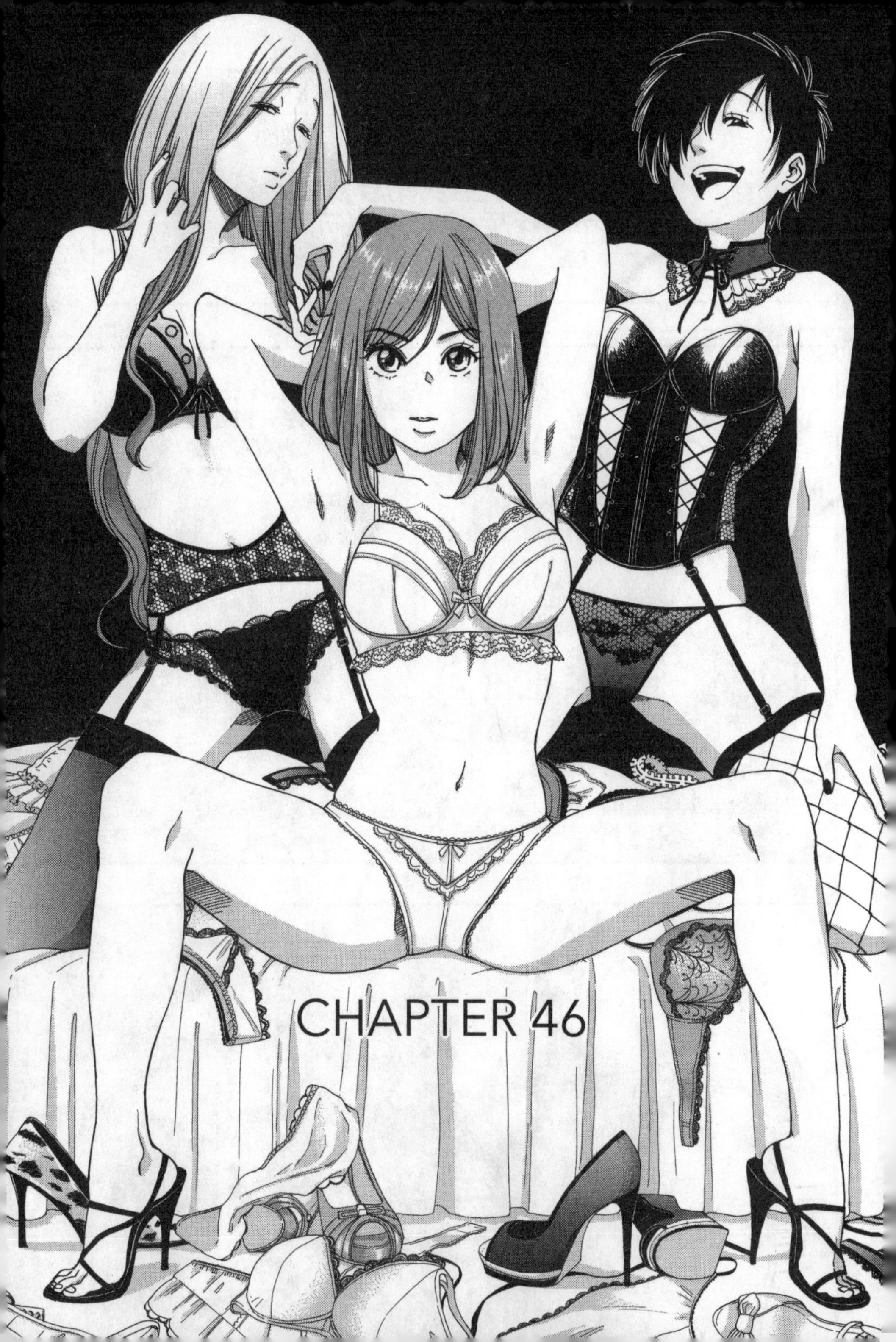
CHAPTER 46

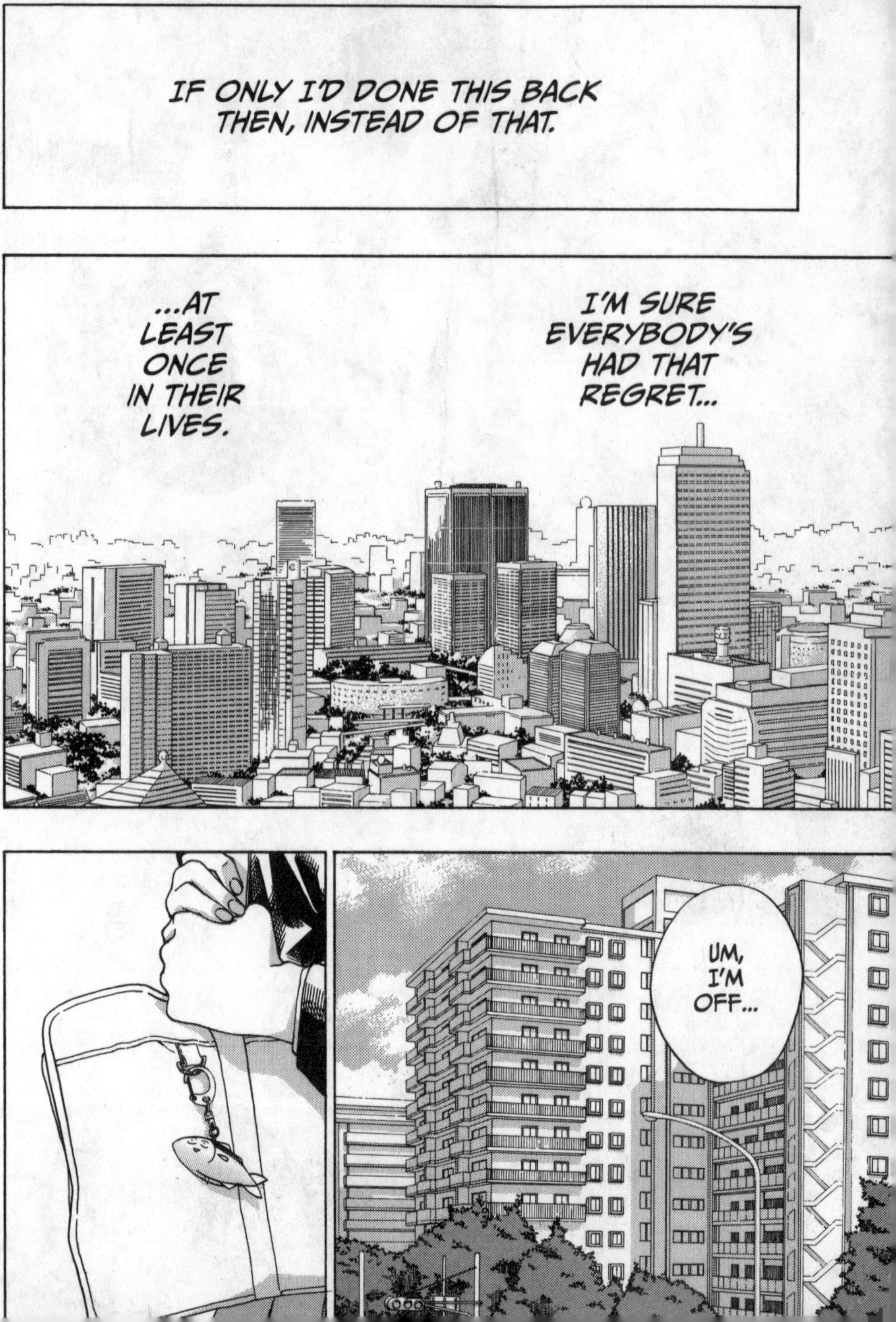
IF ONLY I'D DONE THIS BACK THEN, INSTEAD OF THAT.
I'M SURE EVERYBODY'S HAD THAT REGRET...
...AT LEAST ONCE IN THEIR LIVES.
UM, I'M OFF...

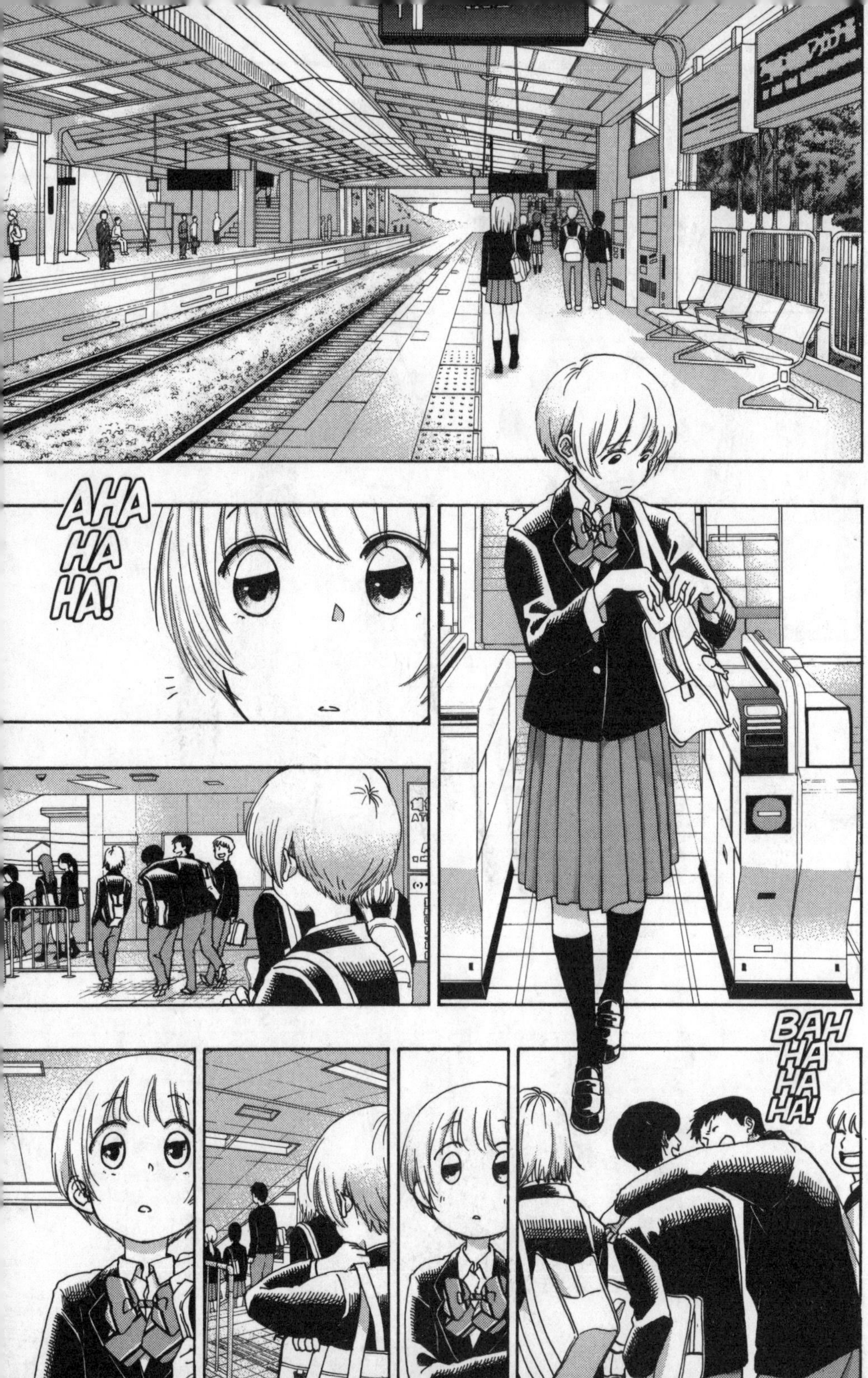
AHA HA HA!
BAH HA HA HA!

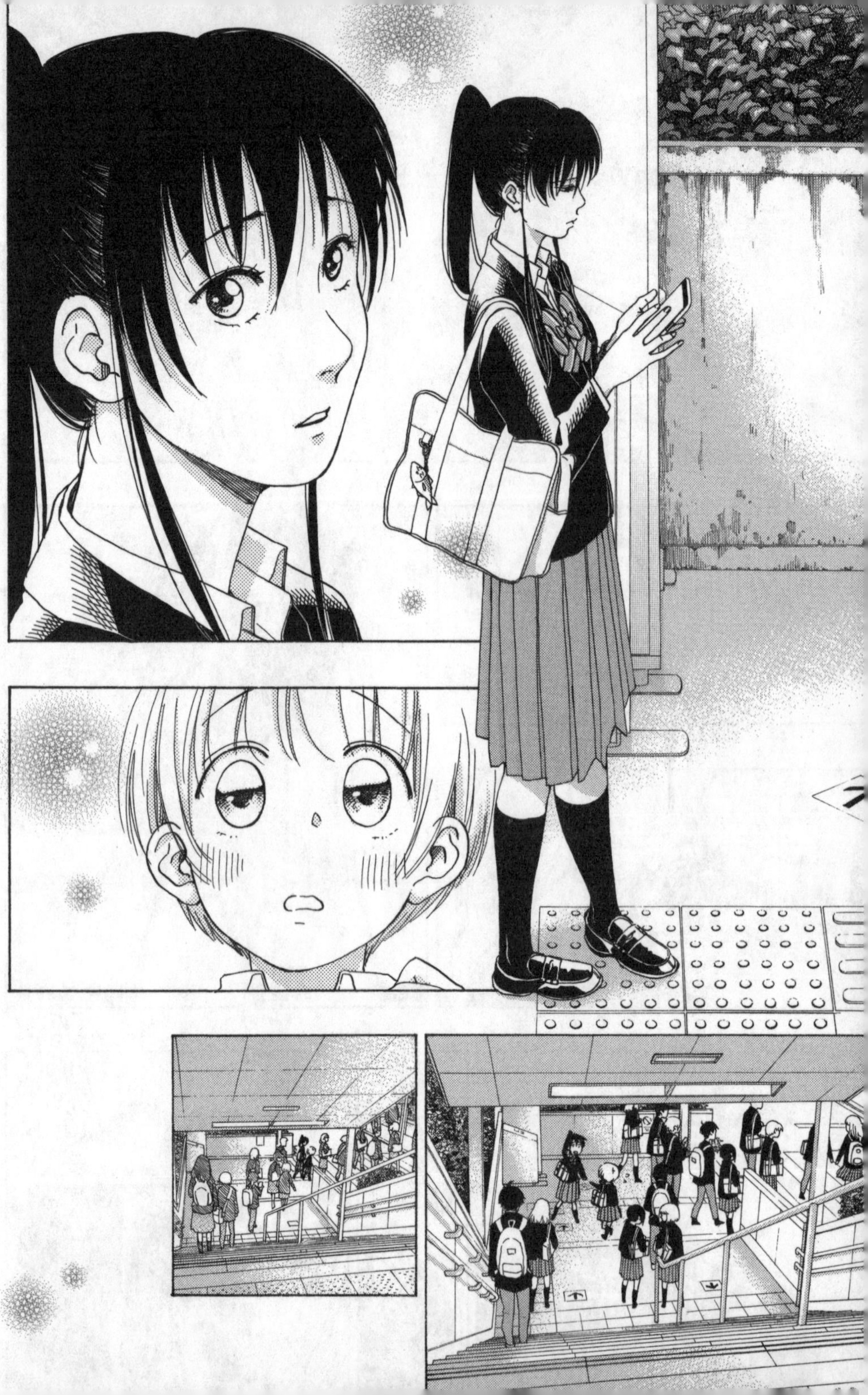

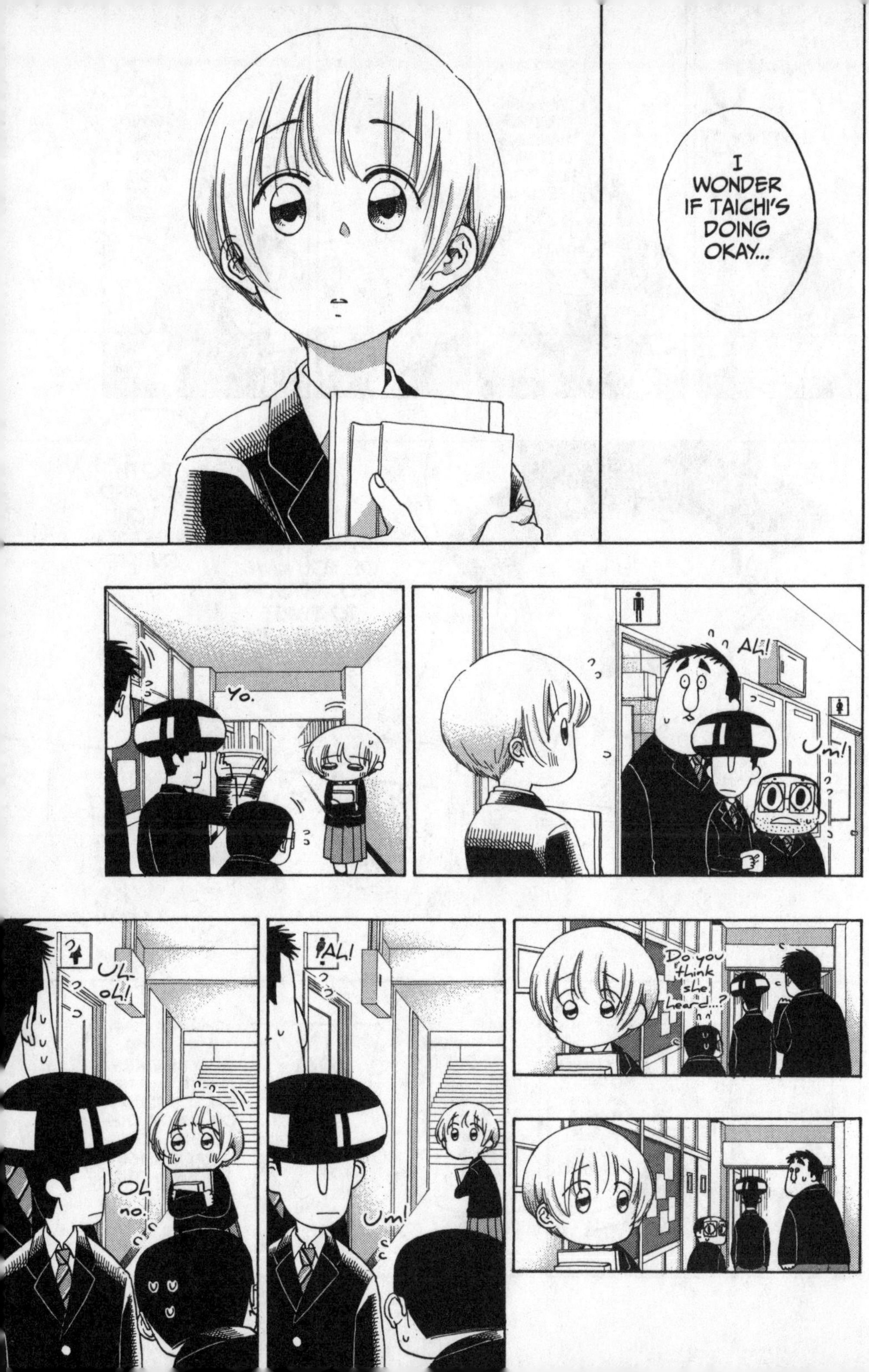
I WONDER IF TAICHI'S DOING OKAY...
Ah!
Um!
Yo.
Do you think she heard...?
Ah!
Um!
Uh-oh!
Oh no!

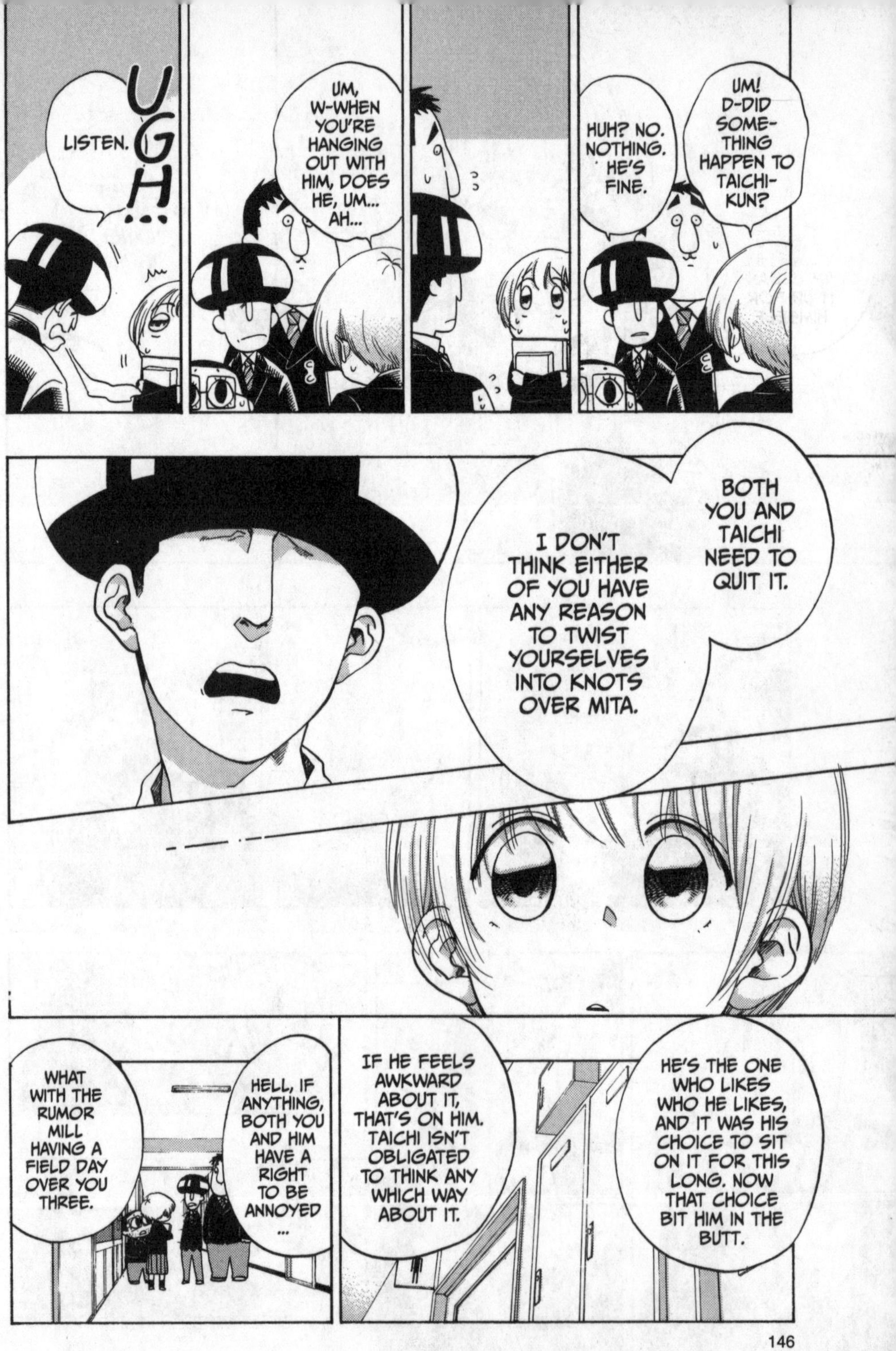
UM! D-DID SOMETHING HAPPEN TO TAICHI-KUN?
HUH? NO. NOTHING. HE'S FINE.
UM, W-WHEN YOU'RE HANGING OUT WITH HIM, DOES HE, UM... AH...
UGH!...
LISTEN.
BOTH YOU AND TAICHI NEED TO QUIT IT.
I DON'T THINK EITHER OF YOU HAVE ANY REASON TO TWIST YOURSELVES INTO KNOTS OVER MITA.
HE'S THE ONE WHO LIKES WHO HE LIKES, AND IT WAS HIS CHOICE TO SIT ON IT FOR THIS LONG. NOW THAT CHOICE BIT HIM IN THE BUTT.
IF HE FEELS AWKWARD ABOUT IT, THAT'S ON HIM. TAICHI ISN'T OBLIGATED TO THINK ANY WHICH WAY ABOUT IT.
HELL, IF ANYTHING, BOTH YOU AND HIM HAVE A RIGHT TO BE ANNOYED ...
WHAT WITH THE RUMOR MILL HAVING A FIELD DAY OVER YOU THREE.

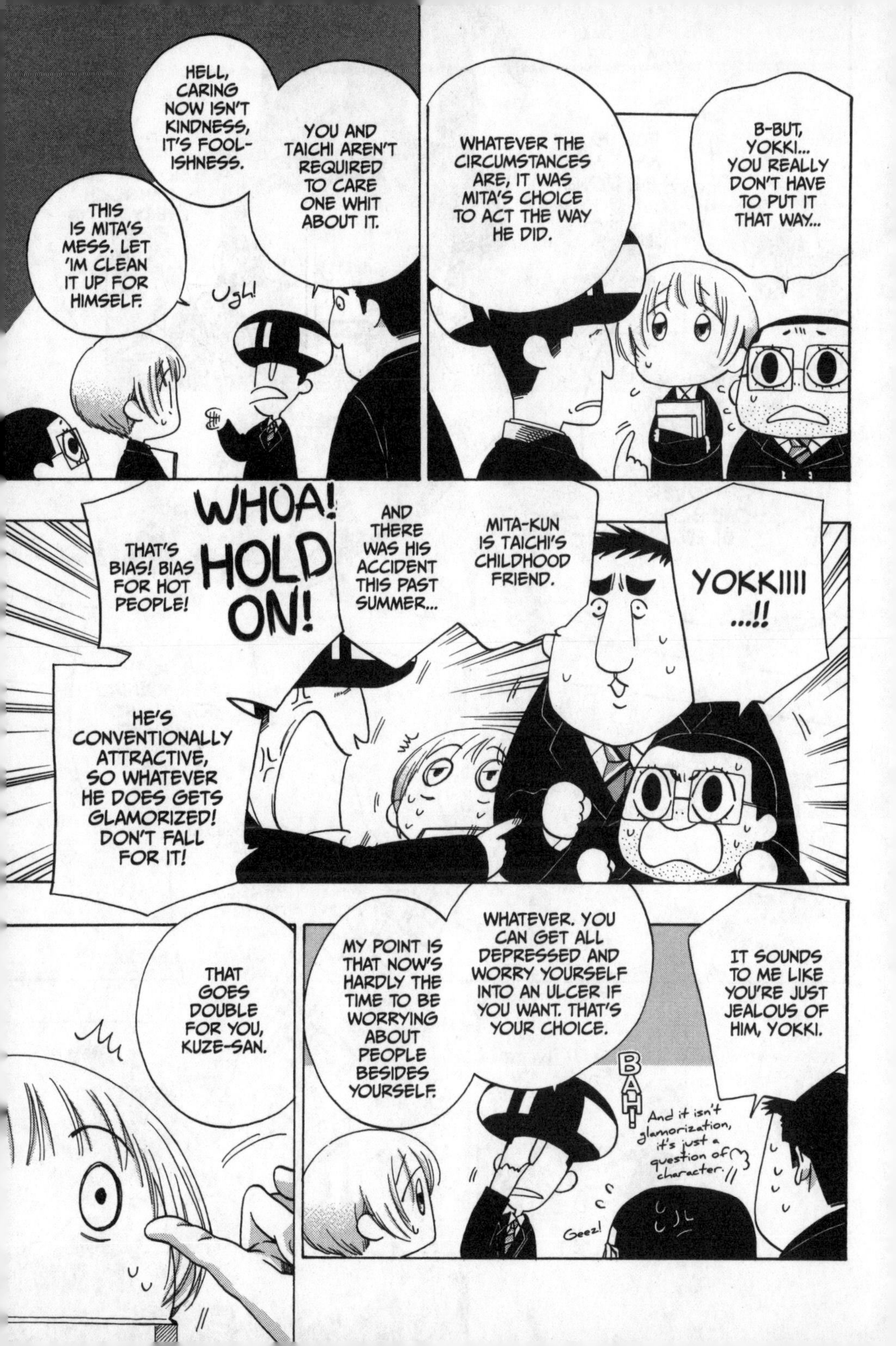

B-BUT, YOKKI... YOU REALLY DON'T HAVE TO PUT IT THAT WAY...
WHATEVER THE CIRCUMSTANCES ARE, IT WAS MITA'S CHOICE TO ACT THE WAY HE DID.
YOU AND TAICHI AREN'T REQUIRED TO CARE ONE WHIT ABOUT IT.
HELL, CARING NOW ISN'T KINDNESS, IT'S FOOLISHNESS.
THIS IS MITA'S MESS. LET 'IM CLEAN IT UP FOR HIMSELF.
Ugh!
YOKKIIII ...!!
MITA-KUN IS TAICHI'S CHILDHOOD FRIEND.
AND THERE WAS HIS ACCIDENT THIS PAST SUMMER...
WHOA! HOLD ON!
THAT'S BIAS! BIAS FOR HOT PEOPLE!
HE'S CONVENTIONALLY ATTRACTIVE, SO WHATEVER HE DOES GETS GLAMORIZED! DON'T FALL FOR IT!
IT SOUNDS TO ME LIKE YOU'RE JUST JEALOUS OF HIM, YOKKI.
WHATEVER. YOU CAN GET ALL DEPRESSED AND WORRY YOURSELF INTO AN ULCER IF YOU WANT. THAT'S YOUR CHOICE.
BAH!
And it isn't glamorization, it's just a question of character.
MY POINT IS THAT NOW'S HARDLY THE TIME TO BE WORRYING ABOUT PEOPLE BESIDES YOURSELF.
Geez!
THAT GOES DOUBLE FOR YOU, KUZE-SAN.

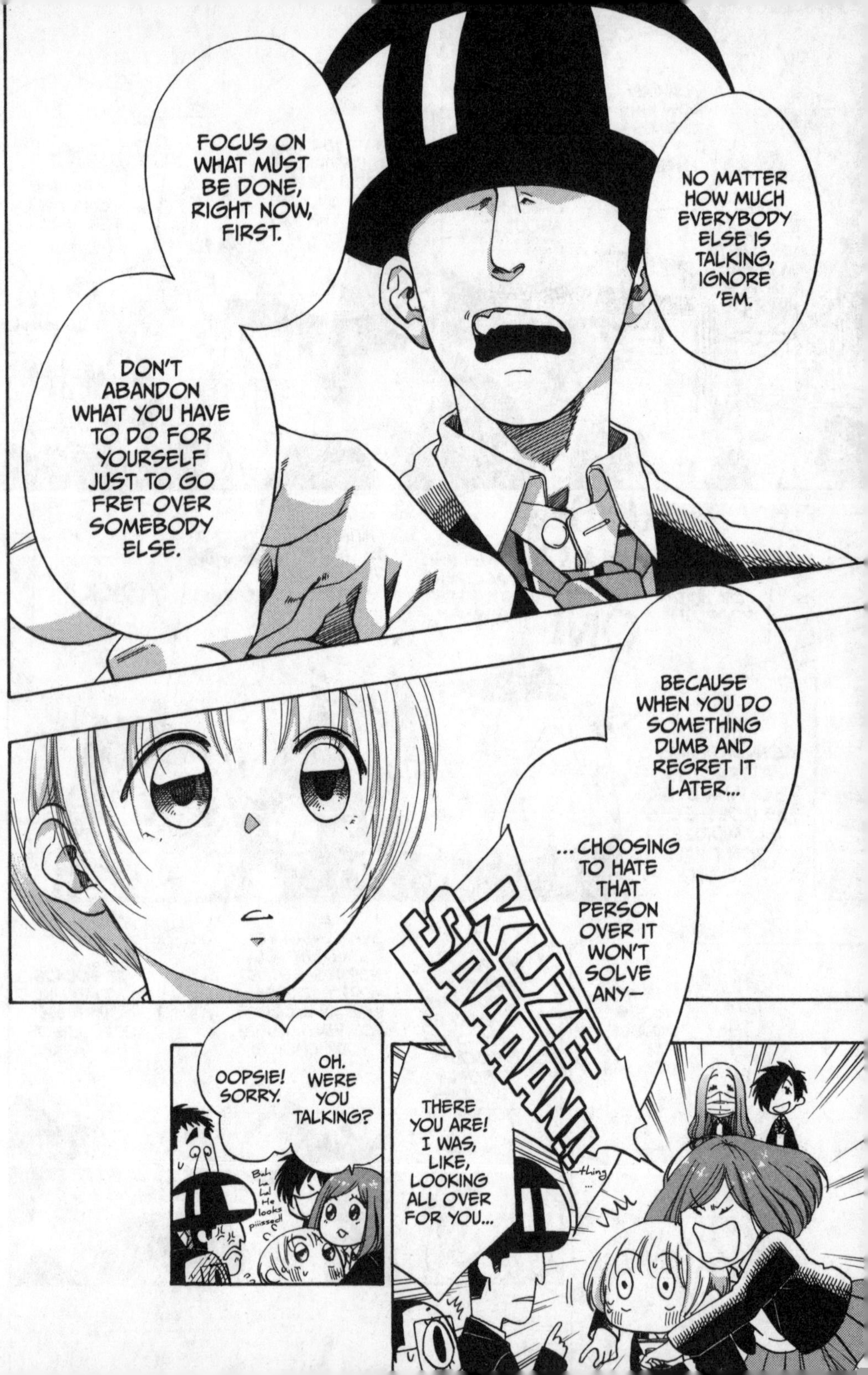
NO MATTER HOW MUCH EVERYBODY ELSE IS TALKING, IGNORE 'EM.
FOCUS ON WHAT MUST BE DONE, RIGHT NOW, FIRST.
DON'T ABANDON WHAT YOU HAVE TO DO FOR YOURSELF JUST TO GO FRET OVER SOMEBODY ELSE.
BECAUSE WHEN YOU DO SOMETHING DUMB AND REGRET IT LATER...
...CHOOSING TO HATE THAT PERSON OVER IT WON'T SOLVE ANY—
KUZE-SAAAAN!!
THERE YOU ARE! I WAS, LIKE, LOOKING ALL OVER FOR YOU...
—thing ...
OH. WERE YOU TALKING?
OOPSIE! SORRY.
Bah ha ha! He looks piiiissed!

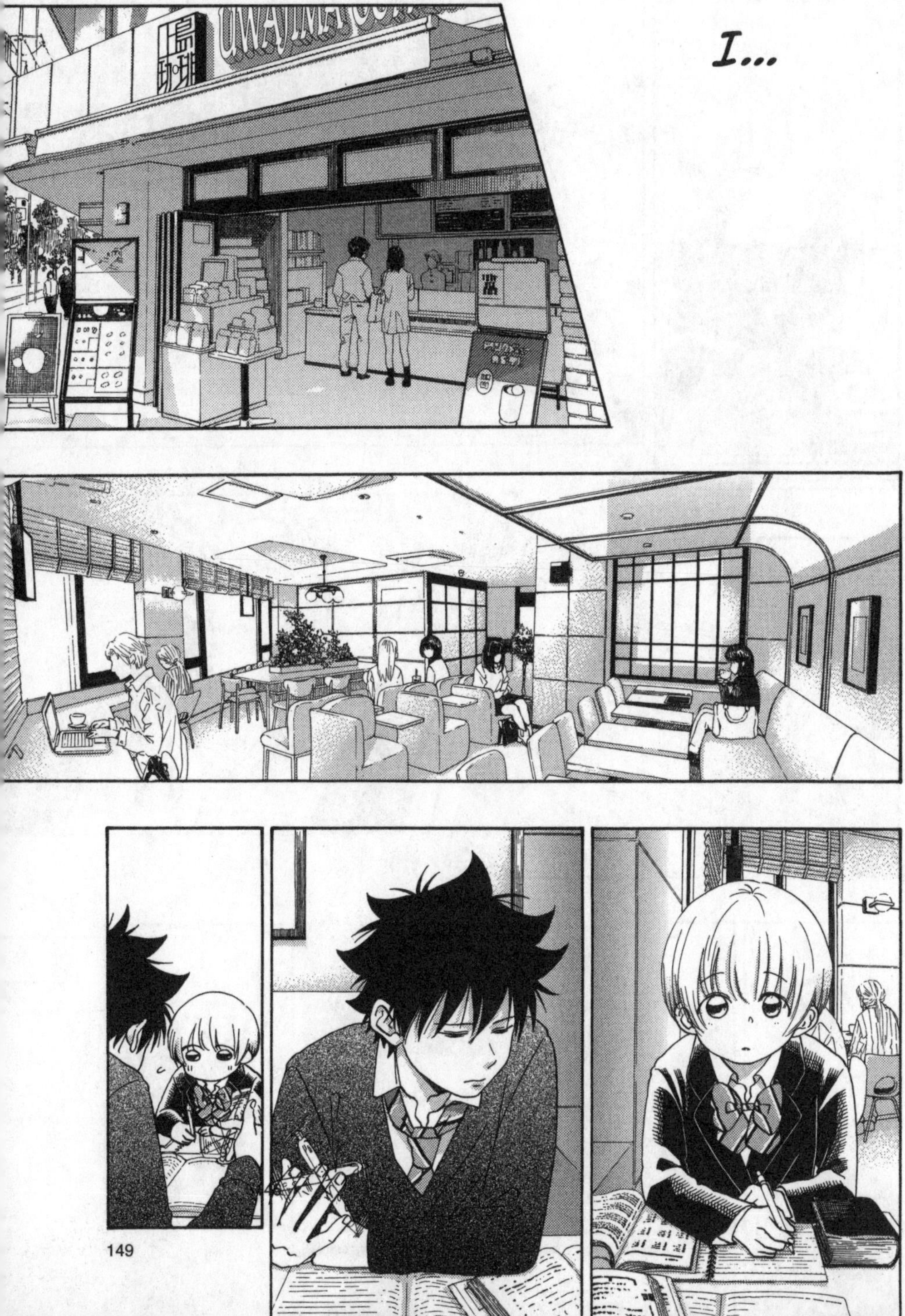
I...

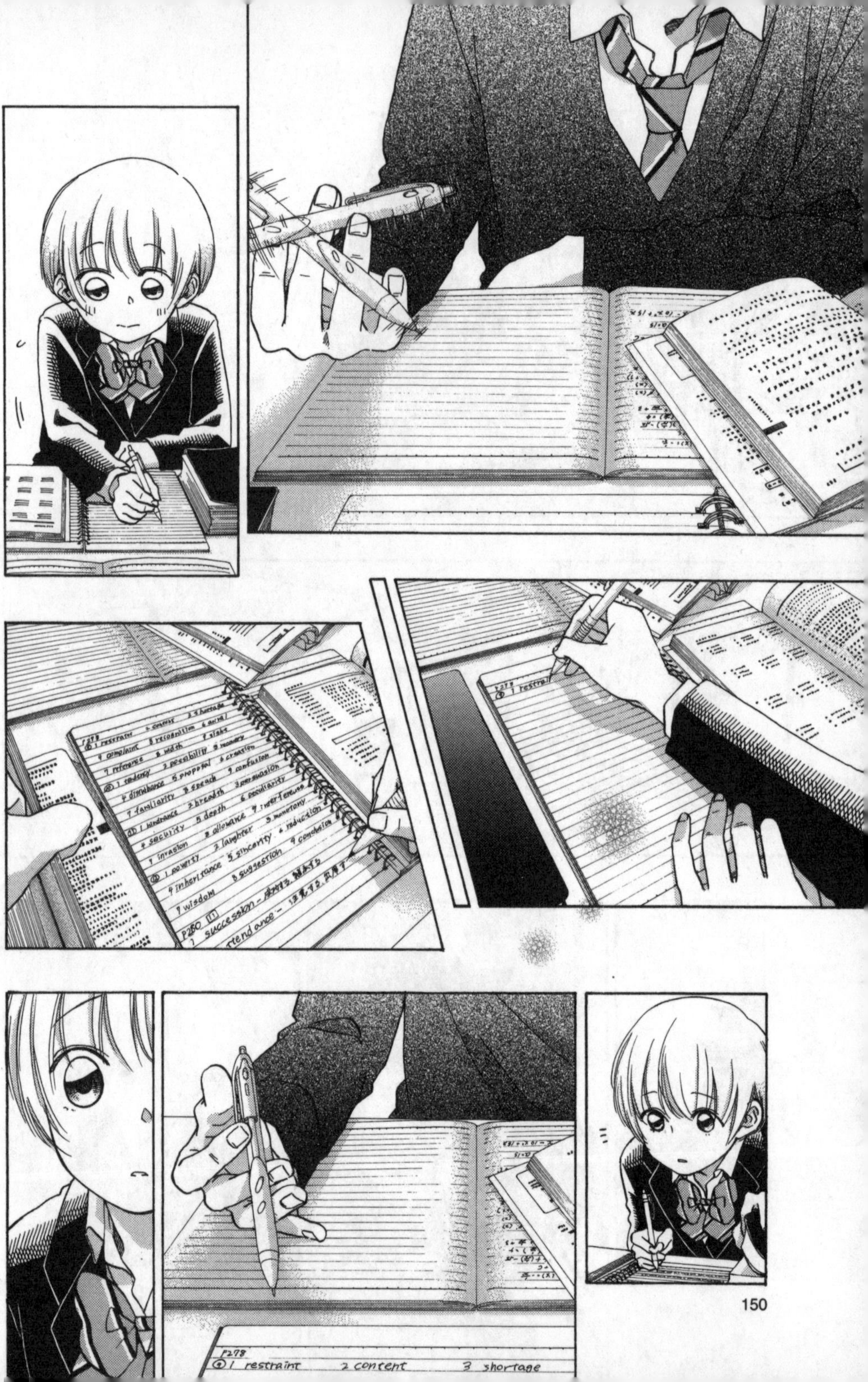
P278
① 1 restraint 2 content 3 shortage

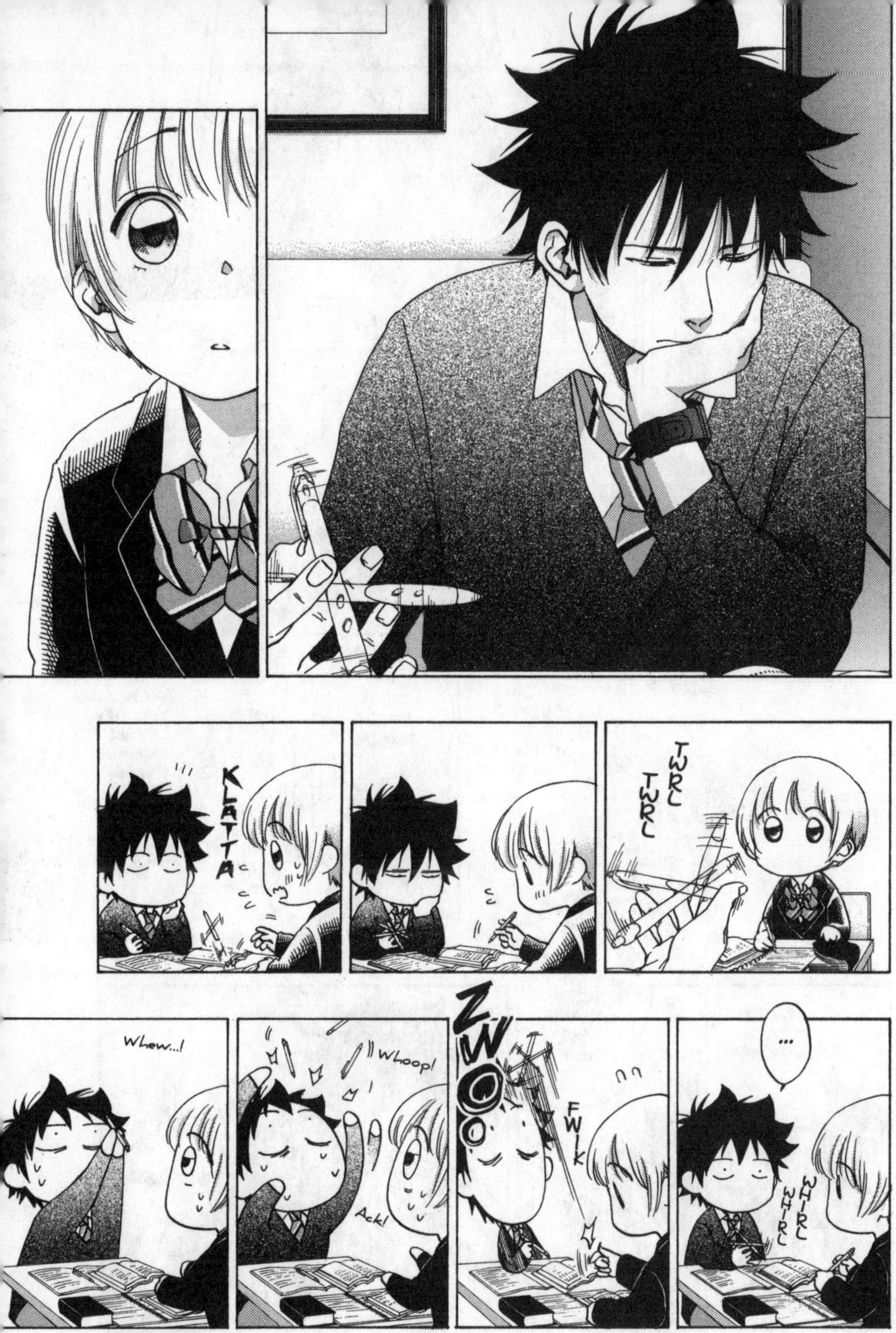
TWRL TWRL
KLATTA
...
WHIRL WHIRL
ZWOOO
FWIK
Whoop!
Ack!
Whew...!

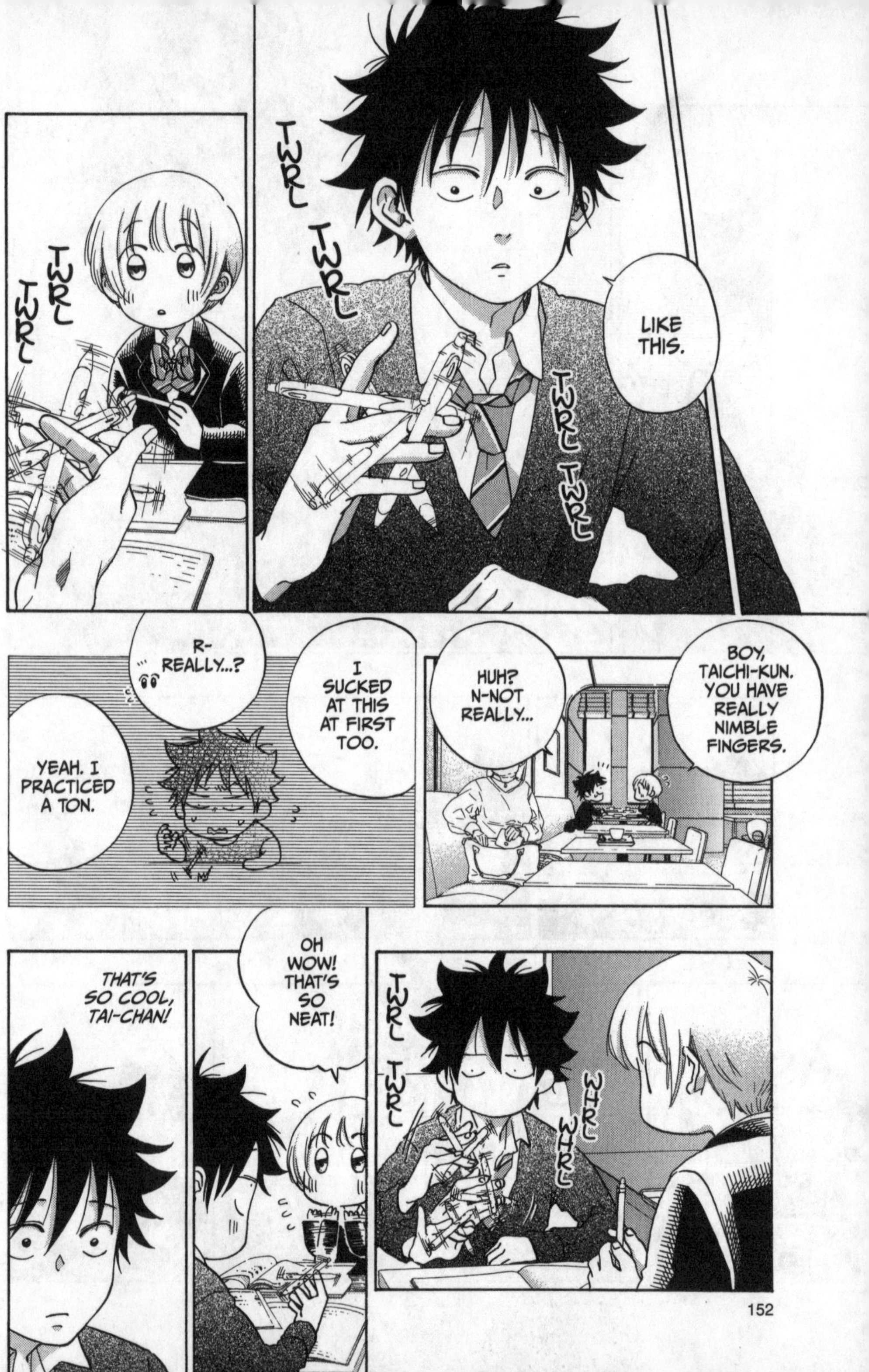
TWRL
TWRL
LIKE THIS.
TWRL TWRL
TWRL
TWRL
BOY, TAICHI-KUN. YOU HAVE REALLY NIMBLE FINGERS.
HUH? N-NOT REALLY...
I SUCKED AT THIS AT FIRST TOO.
R-REALLY...?
YEAH. I PRACTICED A TON.
WHRL
WHRL
TWRL TWRL
OH WOW! THAT'S SO NEAT!
THAT'S SO COOL, TAI-CHAN!

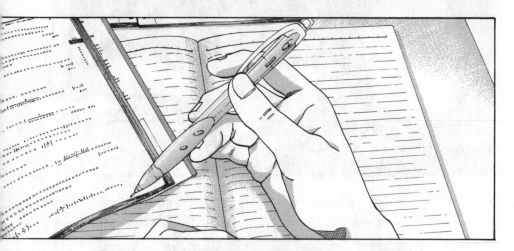

HEY, UM...

FUTABA?

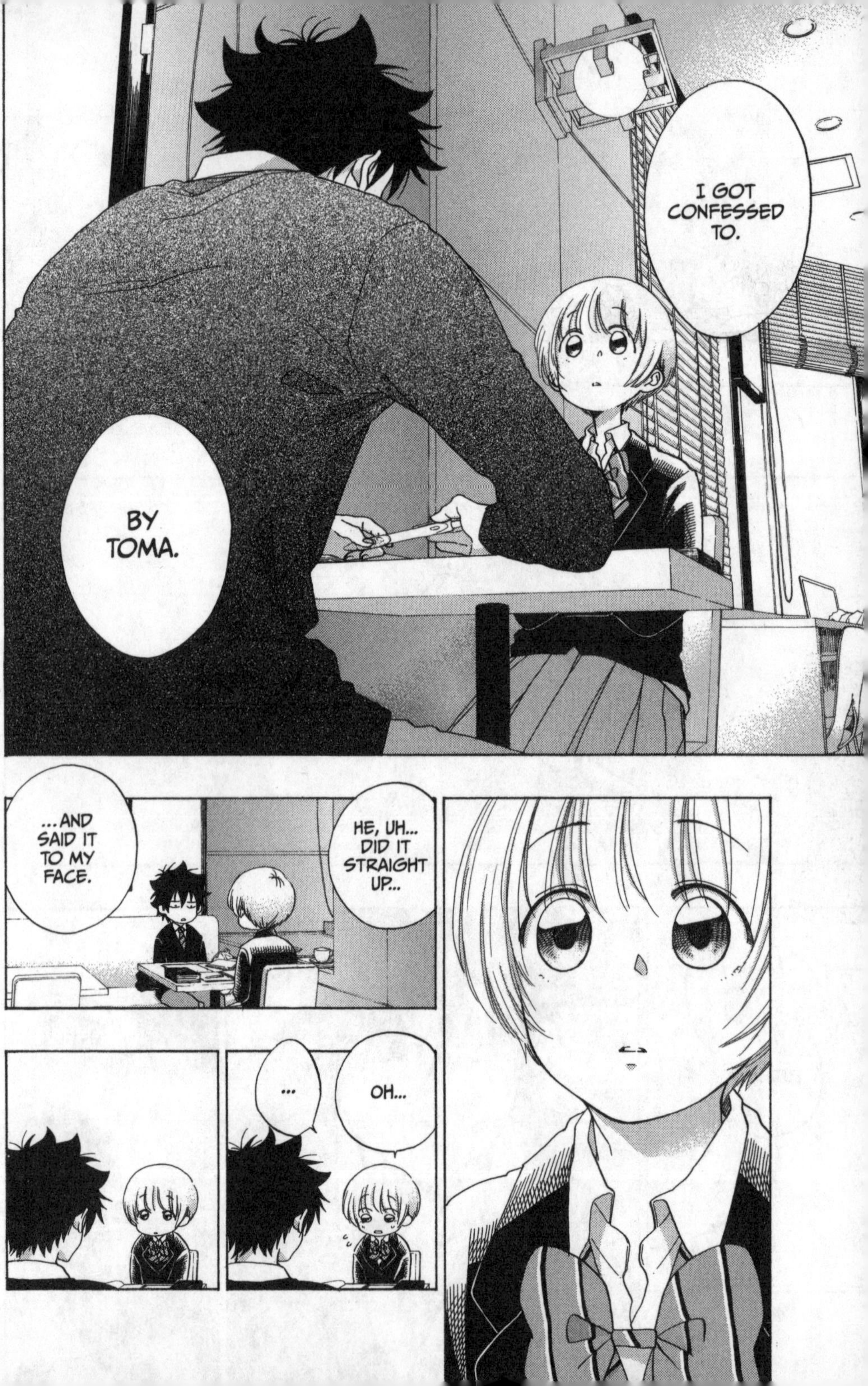
I GOT CONFESSED TO.
BY TOMA.
HE, UH... DID IT STRAIGHT UP...
...AND SAID IT TO MY FACE.
OH...
...

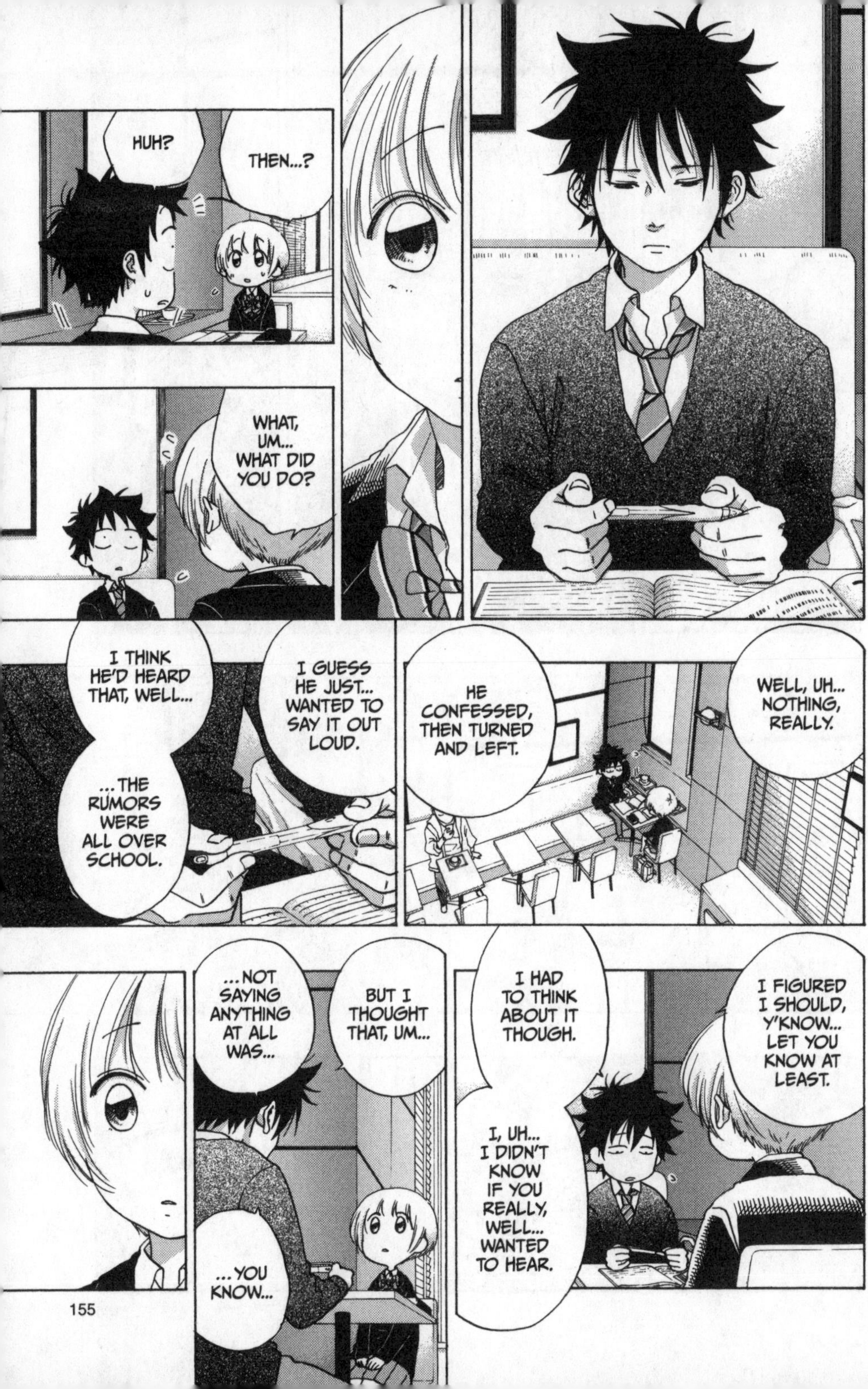
THEN...?
HUH?
WHAT, UM... WHAT DID YOU DO?
WELL, UH... NOTHING, REALLY.
HE CONFESSED, THEN TURNED AND LEFT.
I GUESS HE JUST... WANTED TO SAY IT OUT LOUD.
I THINK HE'D HEARD THAT, WELL...
...THE RUMORS WERE ALL OVER SCHOOL.
I FIGURED I SHOULD, Y'KNOW... LET YOU KNOW AT LEAST.
I HAD TO THINK ABOUT IT THOUGH.
I, UH... I DIDN'T KNOW IF YOU REALLY, WELL... WANTED TO HEAR.
BUT I THOUGHT THAT, UM...
...NOT SAYING ANYTHING AT ALL WAS...
...YOU KNOW...

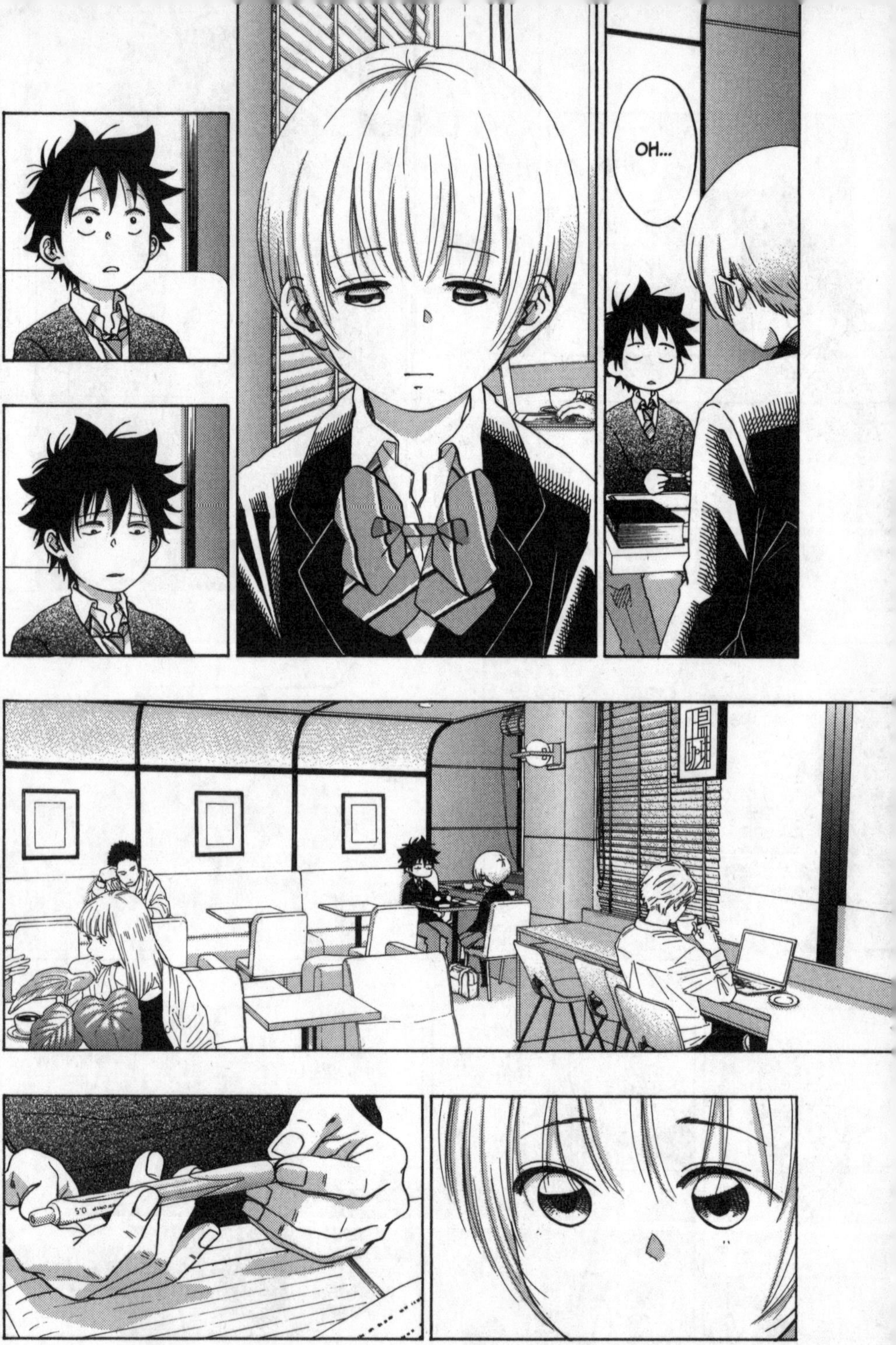
OH...

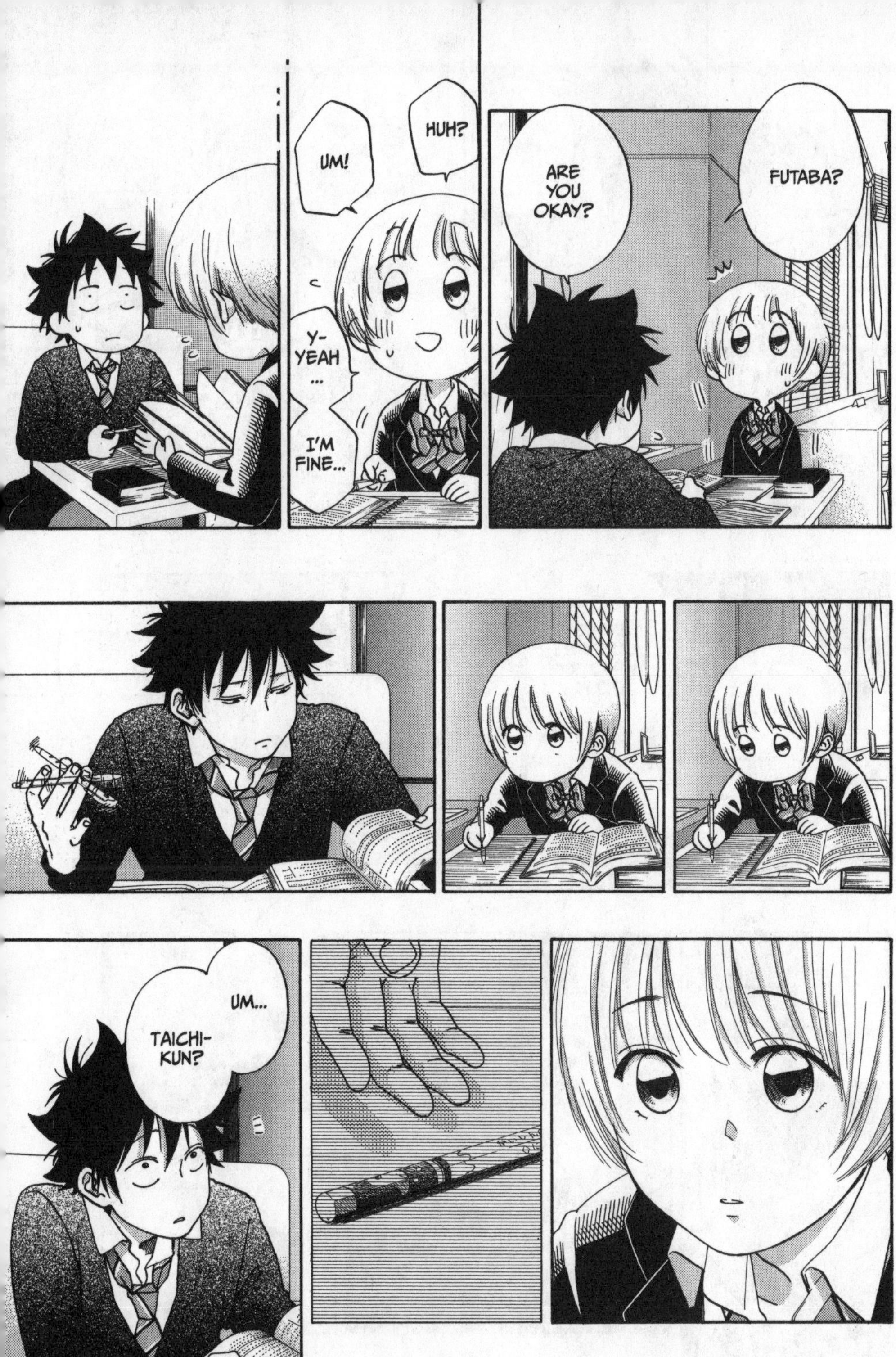
FUTABA?
ARE YOU OKAY?
HUH?
UM!
Y-YEAH ...
I'M FINE...
UM...
TAICHI-KUN?

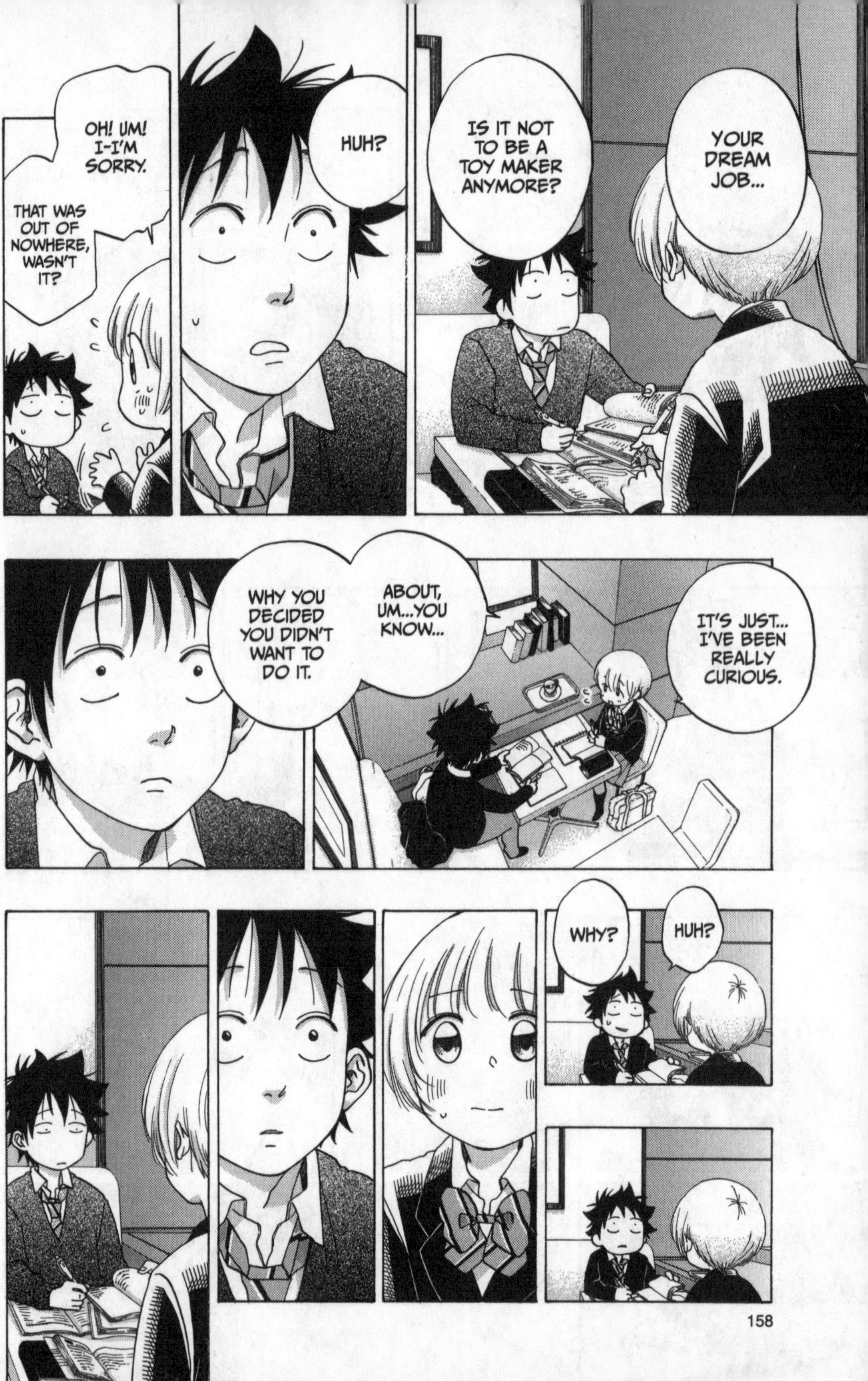
YOUR DREAM JOB...
IS IT NOT TO BE A TOY MAKER ANYMORE?
HUH?
OH! UM! I-I'M SORRY.
THAT WAS OUT OF NOWHERE, WASN'T IT?
IT'S JUST... I'VE BEEN REALLY CURIOUS.
ABOUT, UM...YOU KNOW...
WHY YOU DECIDED YOU DIDN'T WANT TO DO IT.
HUH?
WHY?

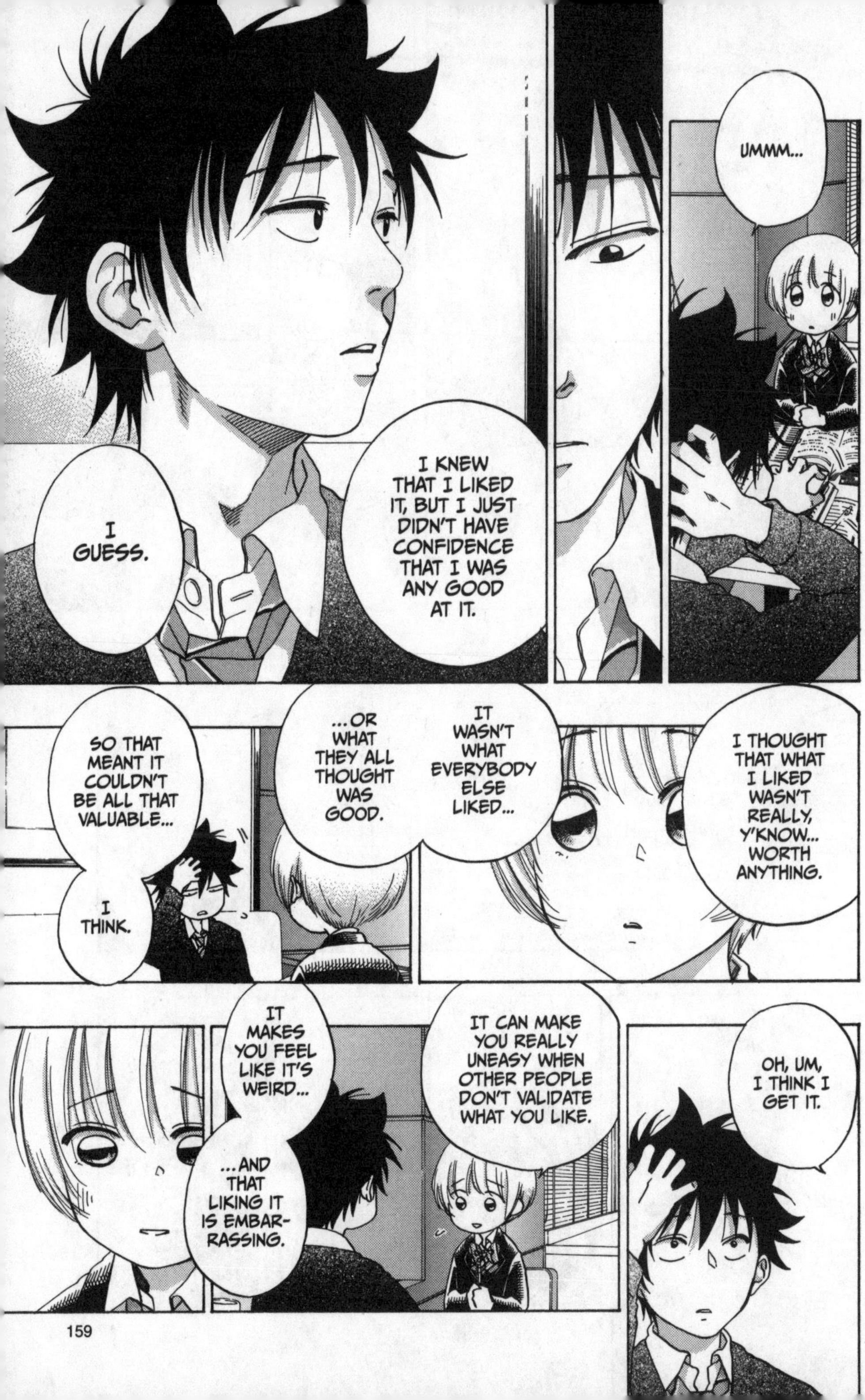
UMMM...
I KNEW THAT I LIKED IT, BUT I JUST DIDN'T HAVE CONFIDENCE THAT I WAS ANY GOOD AT IT.
I GUESS.
I THOUGHT THAT WHAT I LIKED WASN'T REALLY, Y'KNOW... WORTH ANYTHING.
IT WASN'T WHAT EVERYBODY ELSE LIKED...
...OR WHAT THEY ALL THOUGHT WAS GOOD.
SO THAT MEANT IT COULDN'T BE ALL THAT VALUABLE...
I THINK.
OH, UM, I THINK I GET IT.
IT CAN MAKE YOU REALLY UNEASY WHEN OTHER PEOPLE DON'T VALIDATE WHAT YOU LIKE.
IT MAKES YOU FEEL LIKE IT'S WEIRD...
...AND THAT LIKING IT IS EMBARRASSING.

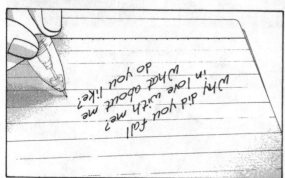

Why did you fall
in love with me?
What about me
do you like?

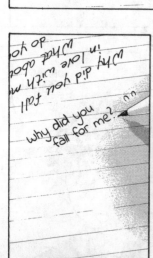

Why did you fall
in love with me
What about
do yo

Why did you
fall for me?

UM!

HUH
?!

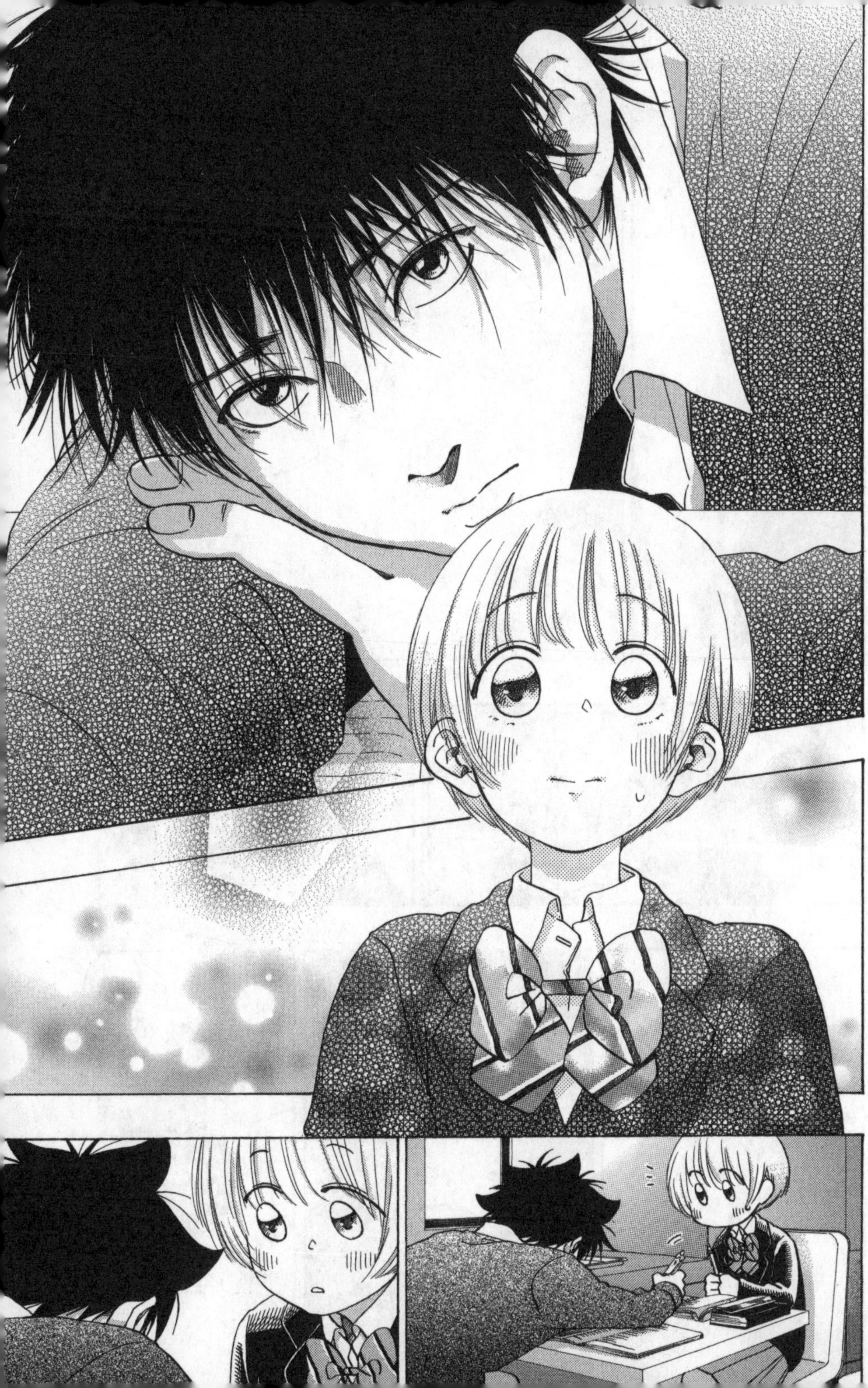

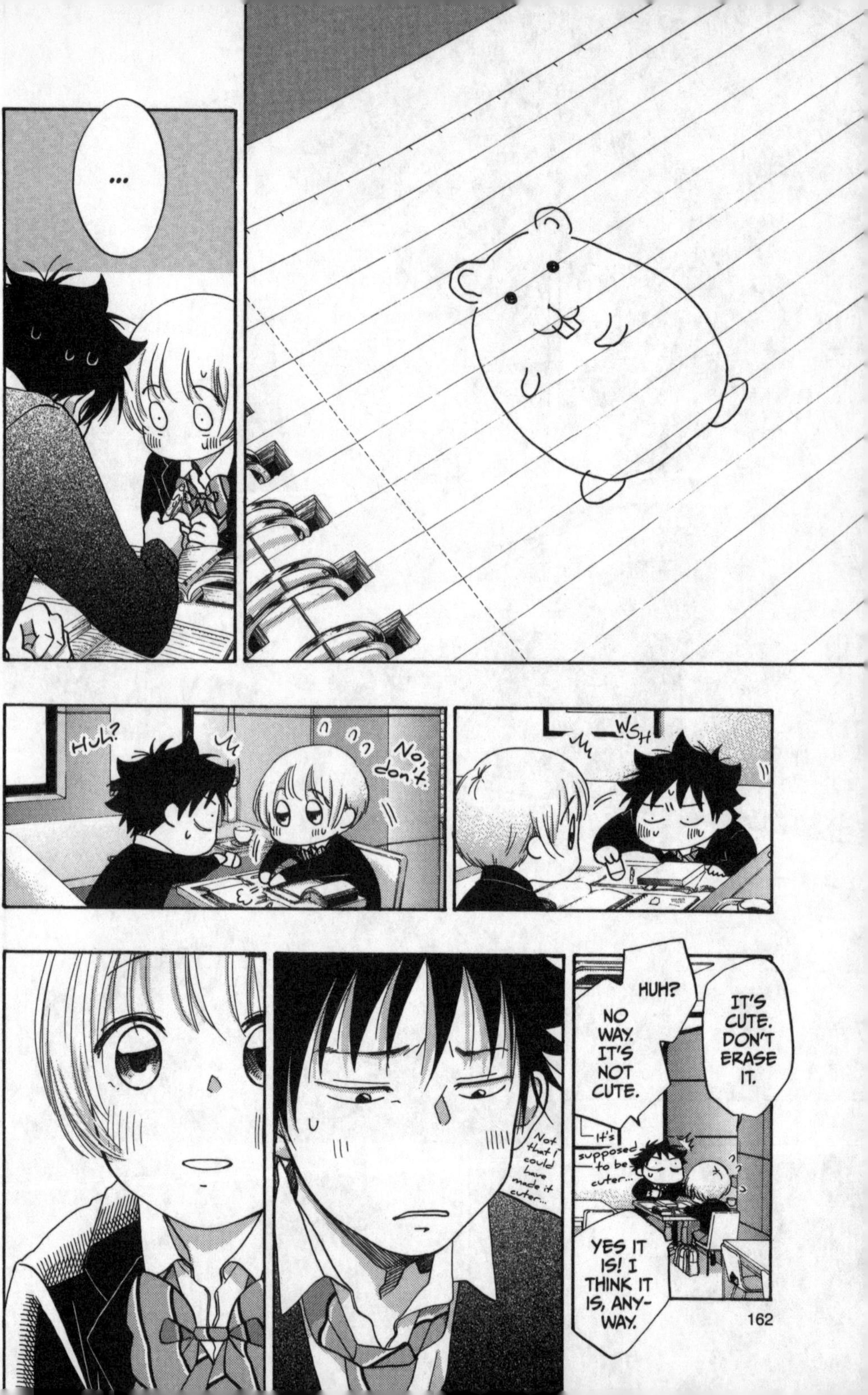
...
WSH
No, don't.
Huh?
IT'S CUTE. DON'T ERASE IT.
HUH?
NO WAY. IT'S NOT CUTE.
It's supposed to be cuter...
YES IT IS! I THINK IT IS, ANYWAY.
Not that I could have made it cuter...

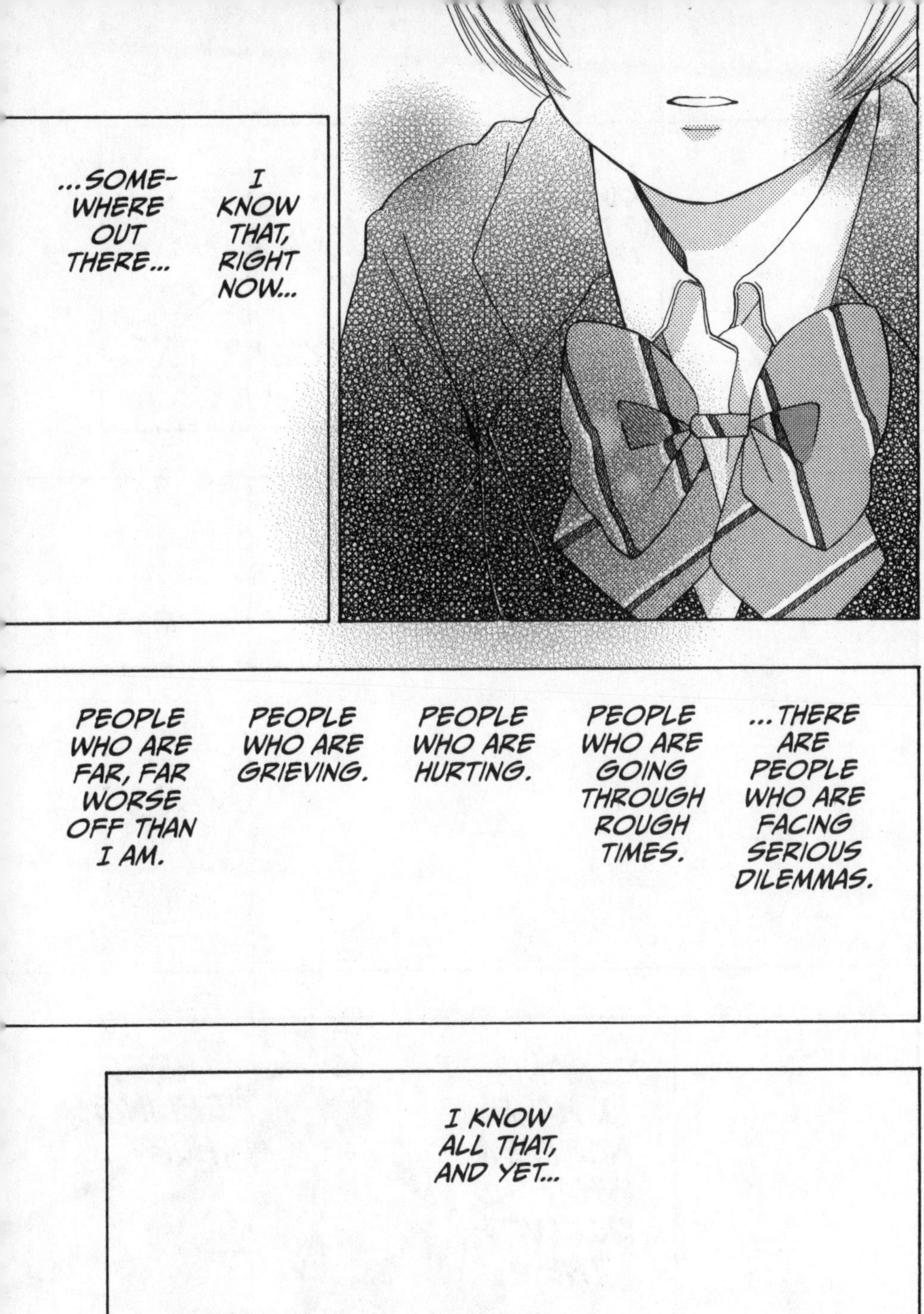
I KNOW THAT, RIGHT NOW...
...SOME-WHERE OUT THERE...
...THERE ARE PEOPLE WHO ARE FACING SERIOUS DILEMMAS.
PEOPLE WHO ARE GOING THROUGH ROUGH TIMES.
PEOPLE WHO ARE HURTING.
PEOPLE WHO ARE GRIEVING.
PEOPLE WHO ARE FAR, FAR WORSE OFF THAN I AM.
I KNOW ALL THAT, AND YET...

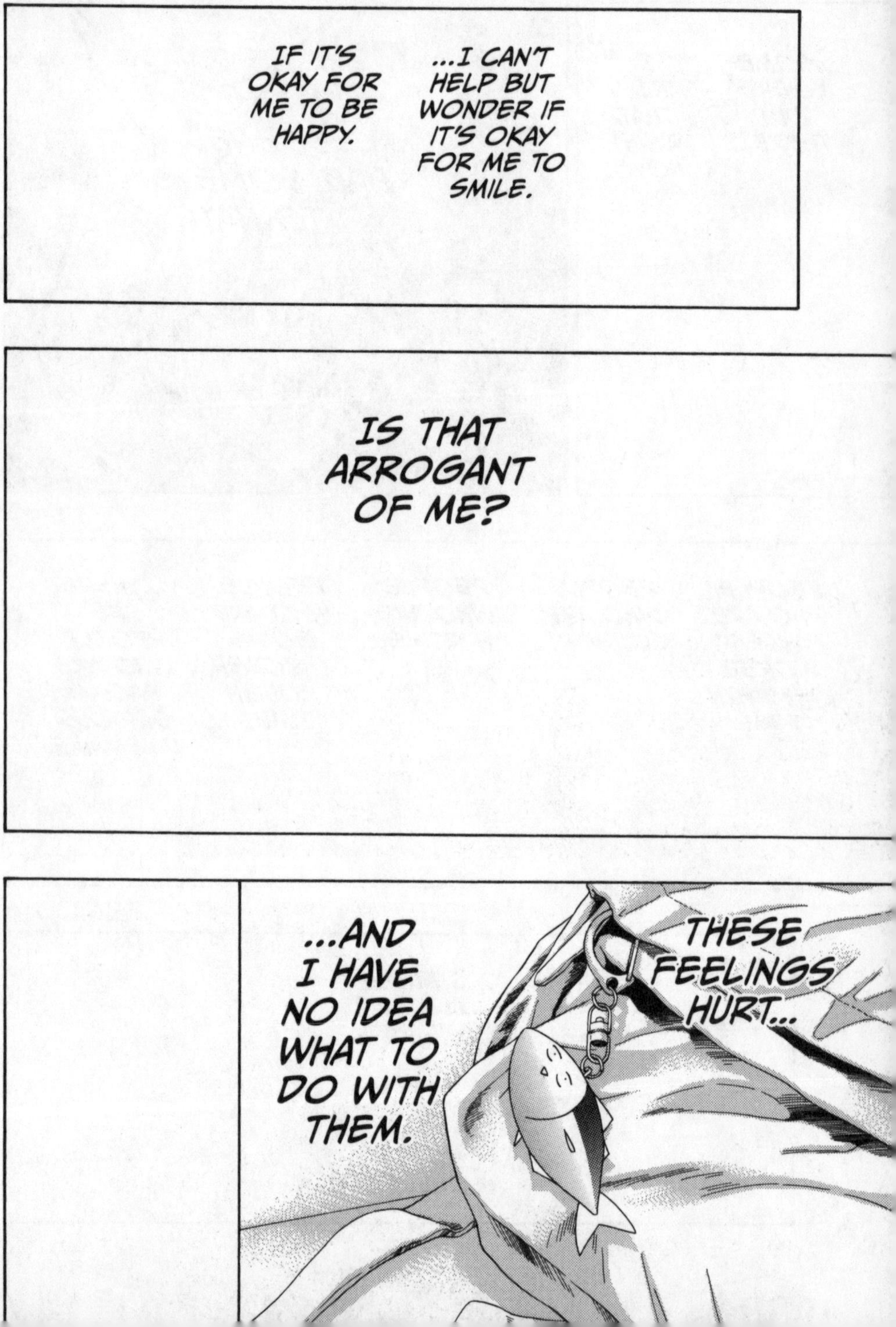
...I CAN'T HELP BUT WONDER IF IT'S OKAY FOR ME TO SMILE.
IF IT'S OKAY FOR ME TO BE HAPPY.
IS THAT ARROGANT OF ME?
THESE FEELINGS HURT...
...AND I HAVE NO IDEA WHAT TO DO WITH THEM.

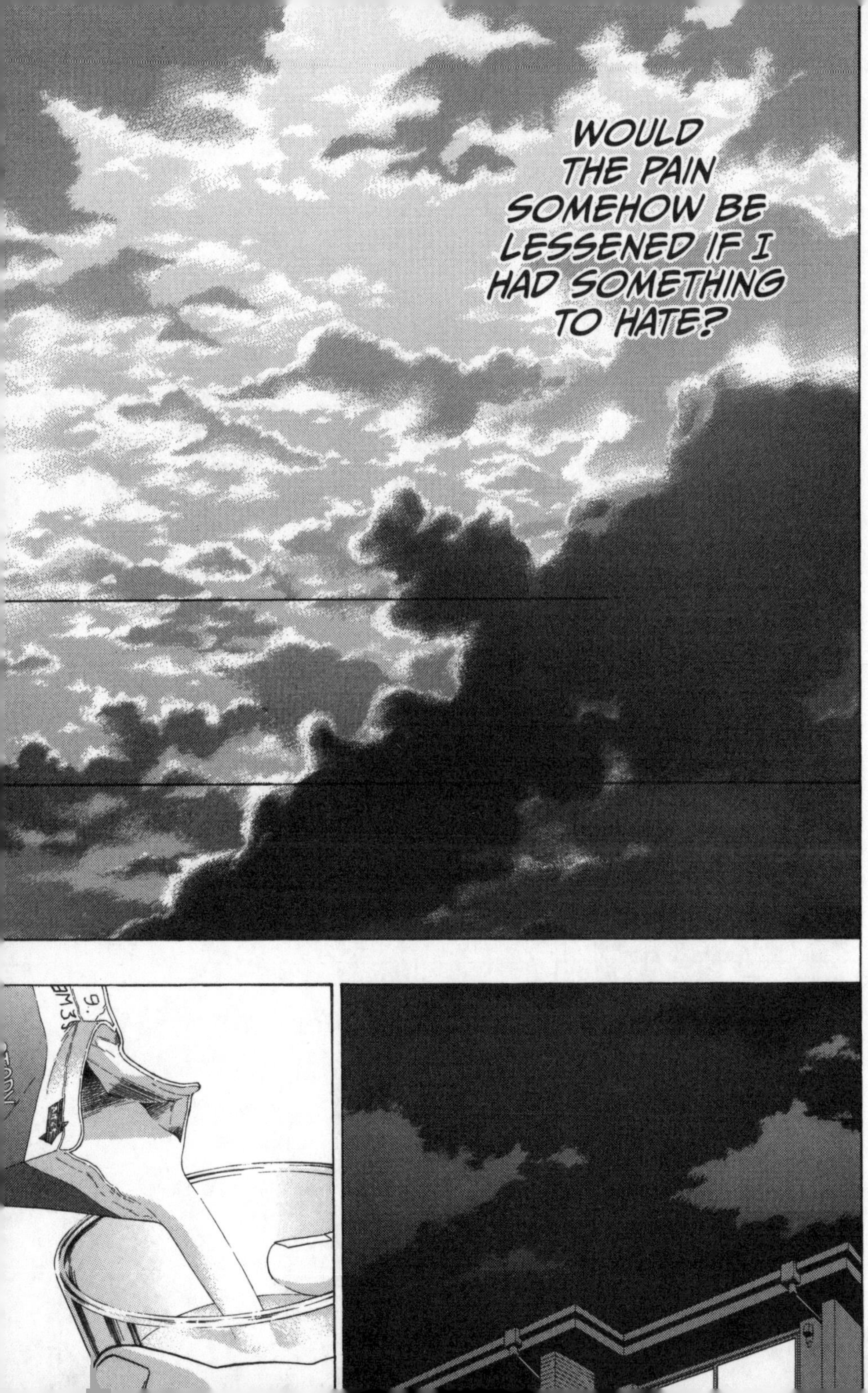
WOULD THE PAIN SOMEHOW BE LESSENED IF I HAD SOMETHING TO HATE?

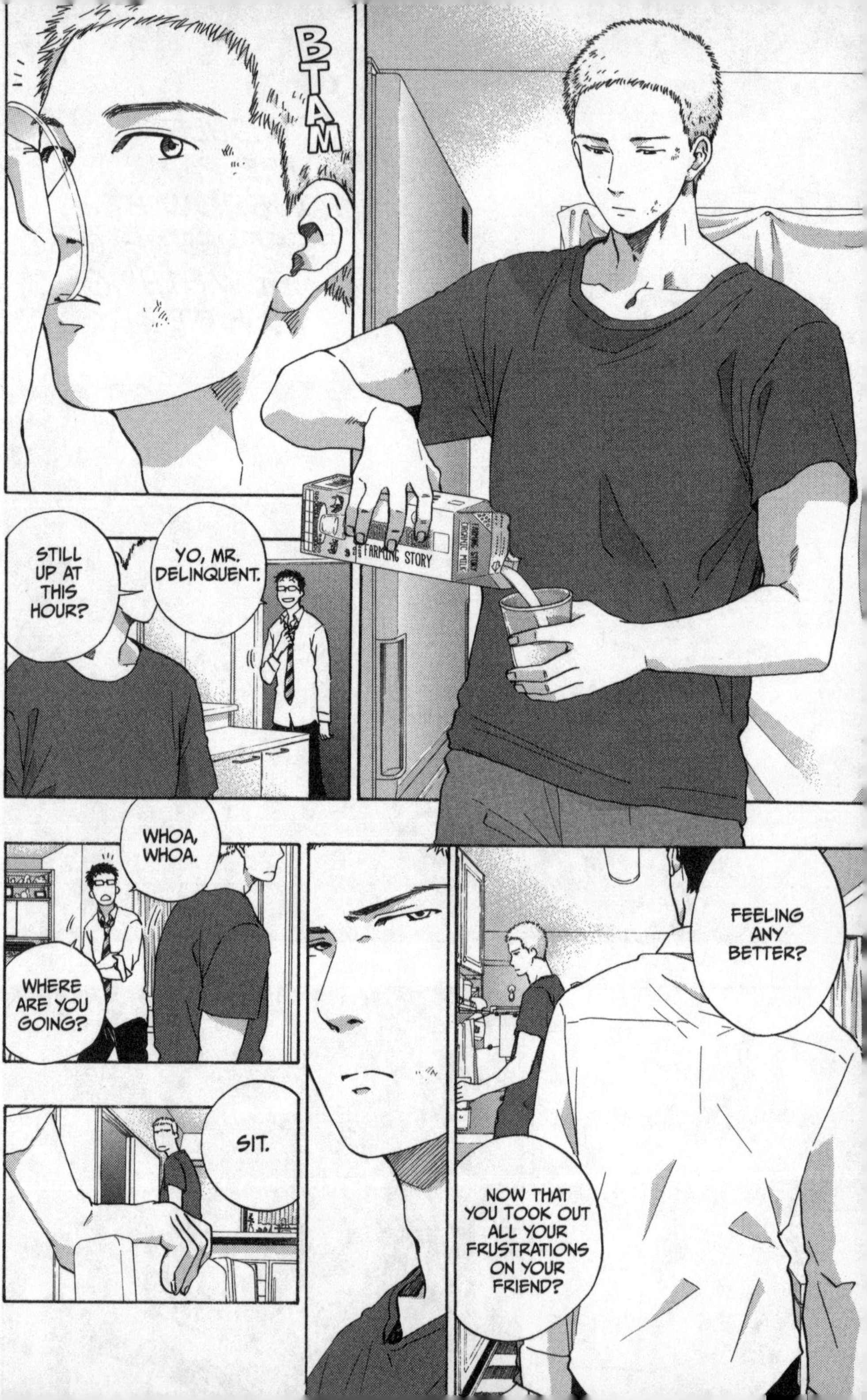
FARMING STORY
BTAM
YO, MR. DELINQUENT.
STILL UP AT THIS HOUR?
FEELING ANY BETTER?
NOW THAT YOU TOOK OUT ALL YOUR FRUSTRATIONS ON YOUR FRIEND?
WHOA, WHOA.
WHERE ARE YOU GOING?
SIT.

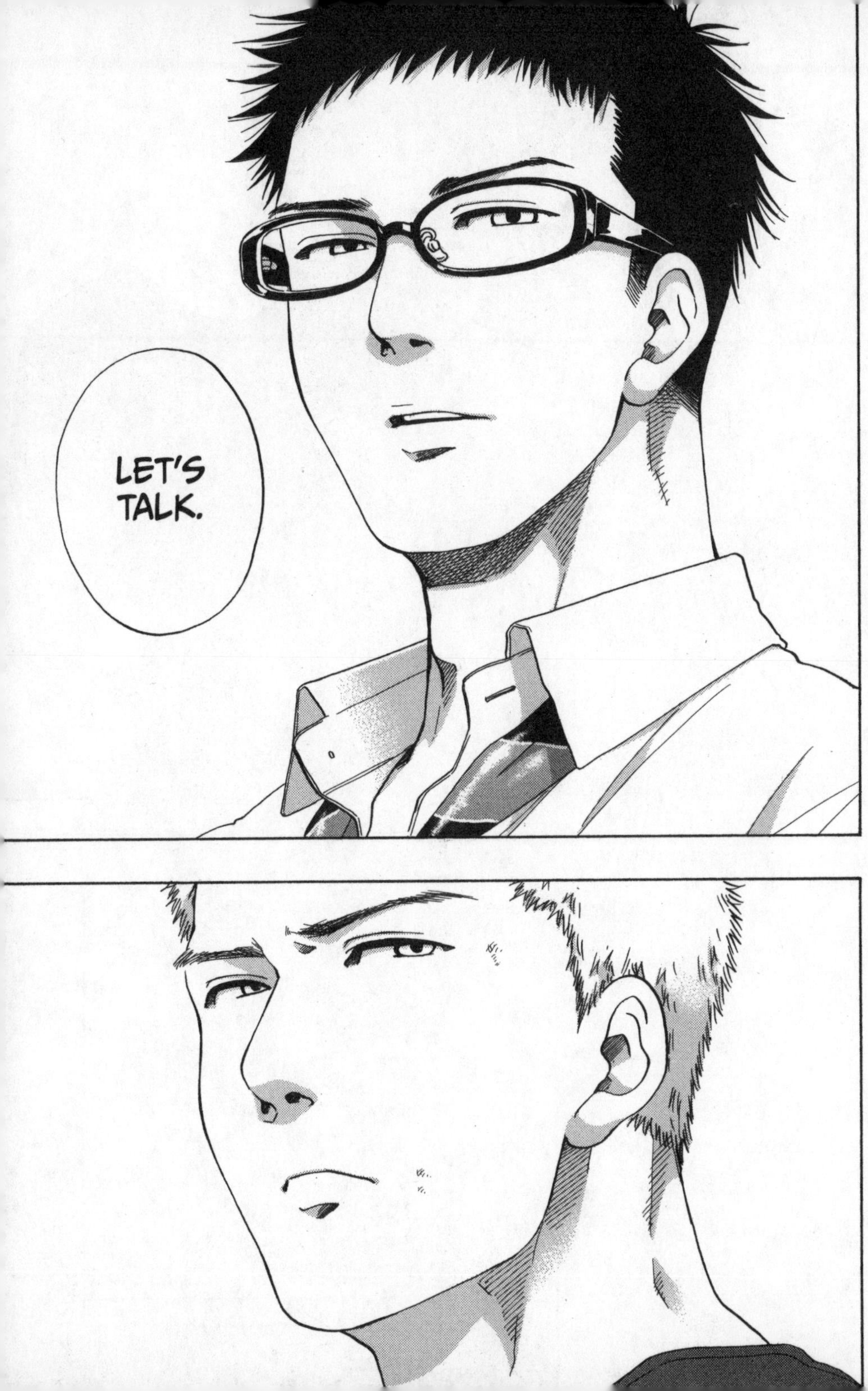
LET'S TALK.

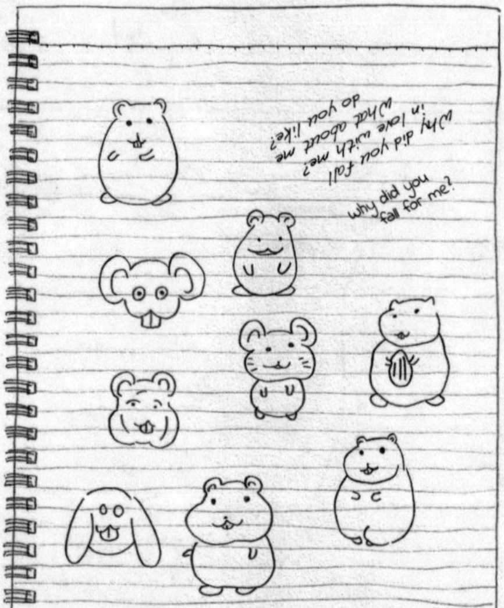
why did you fall
in love with me?
What about me
do you like?
why did you
fall for me?

CHAPTER 47

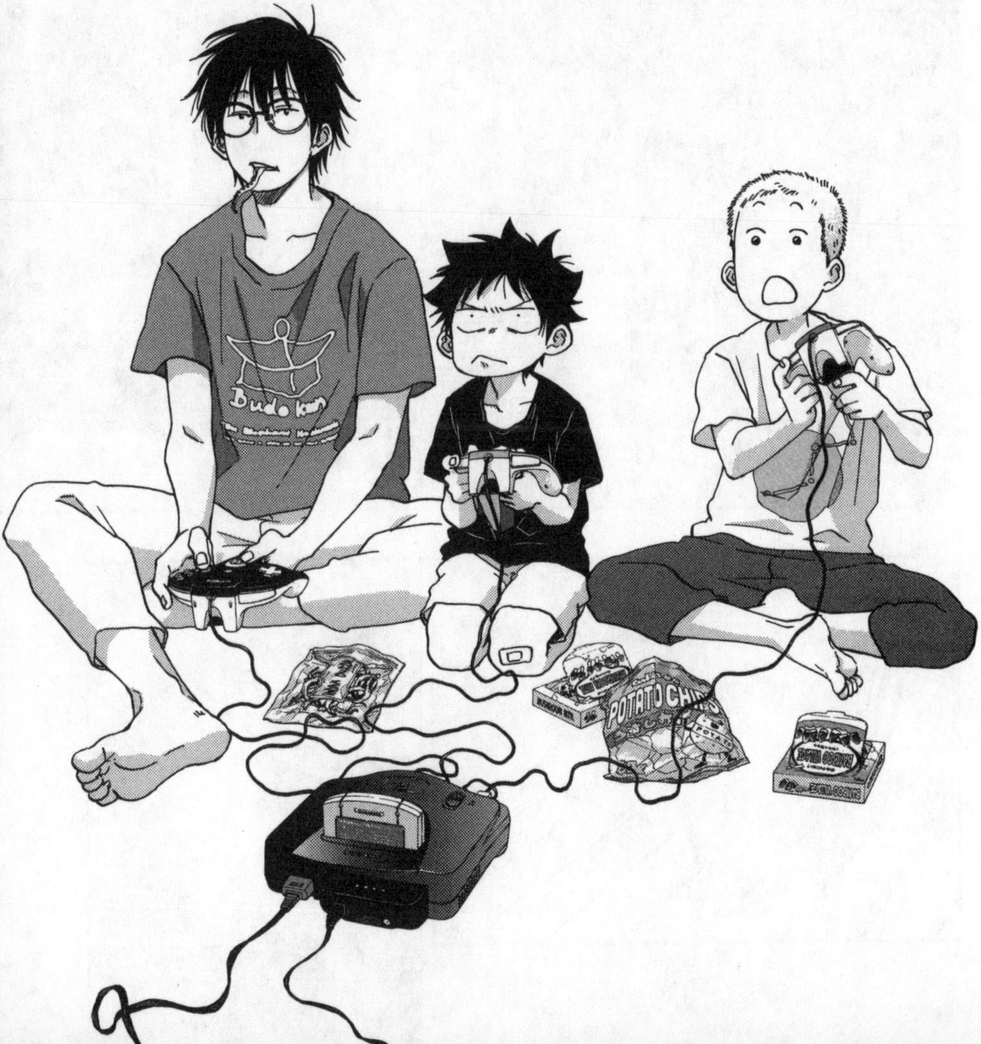
Budo kan
POTATO CHIP

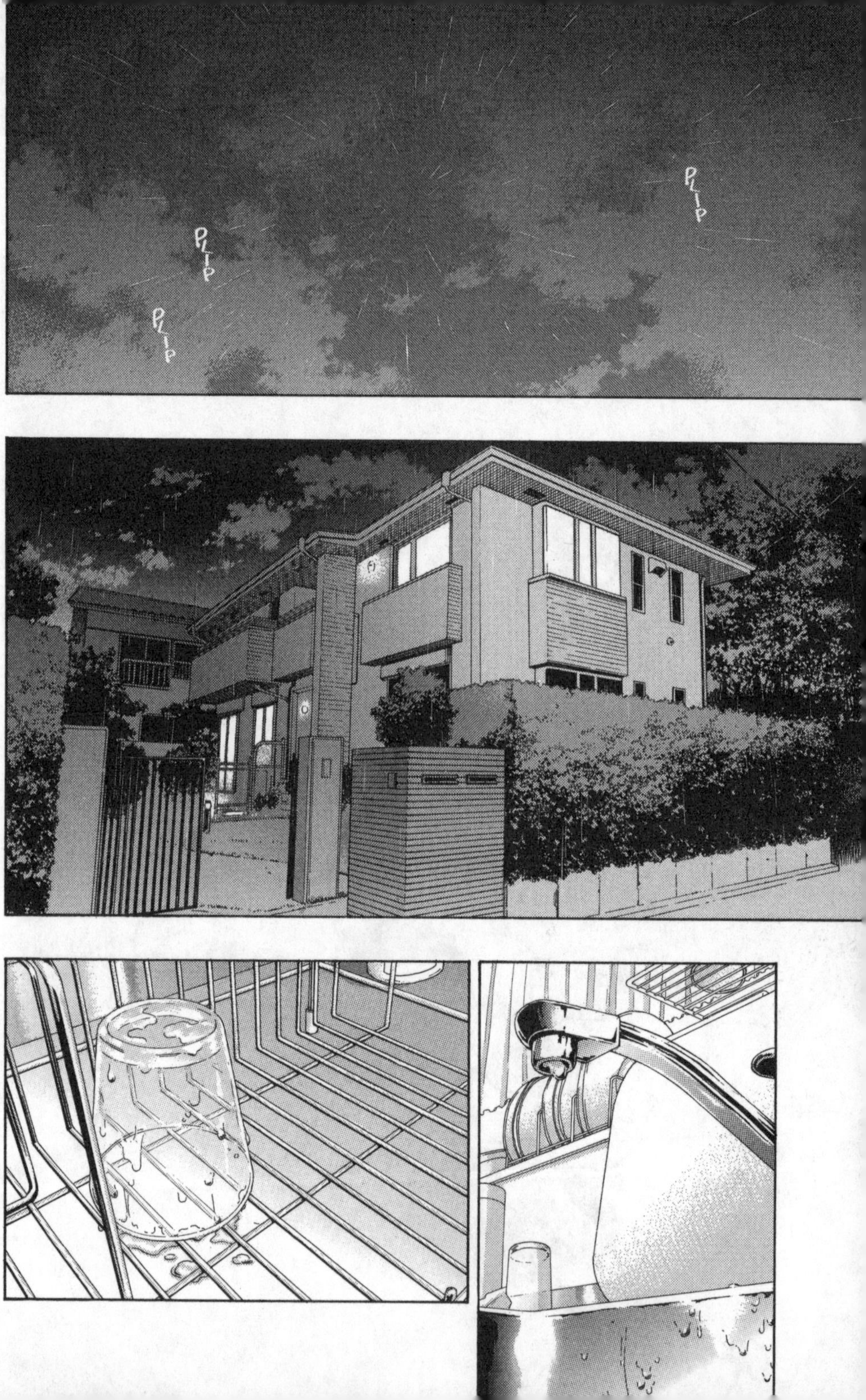
PLIP
PLIP
PLIP

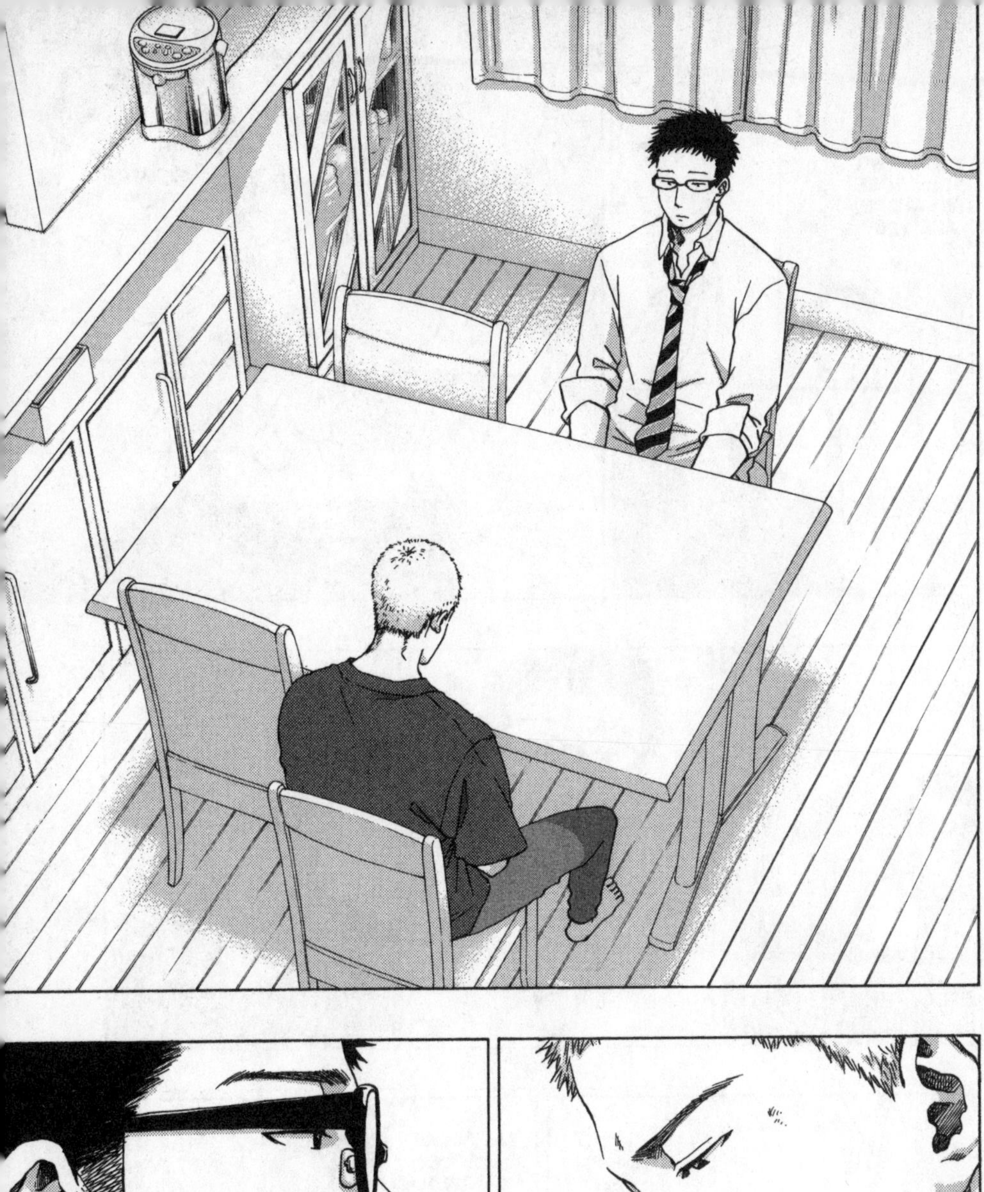
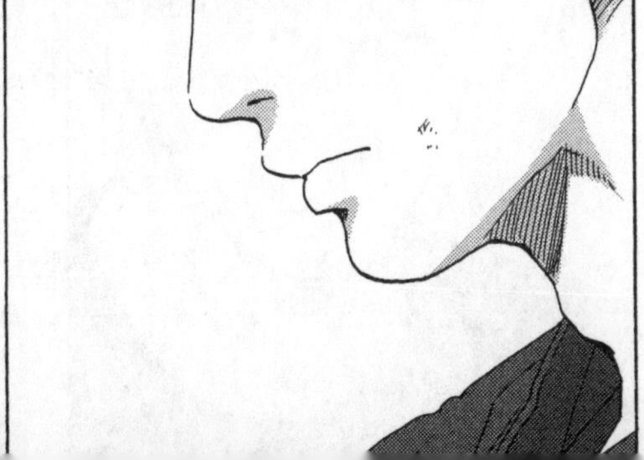
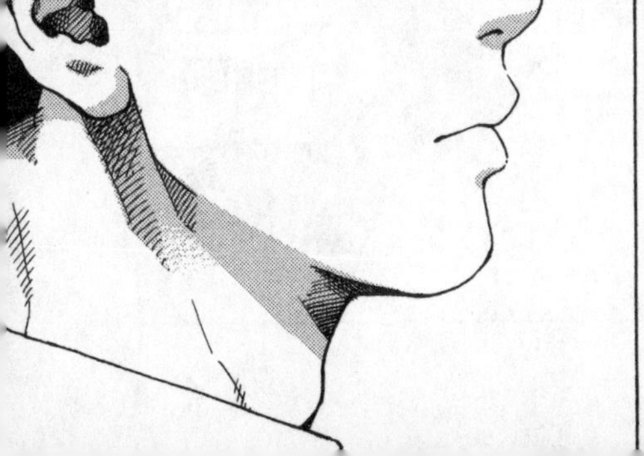

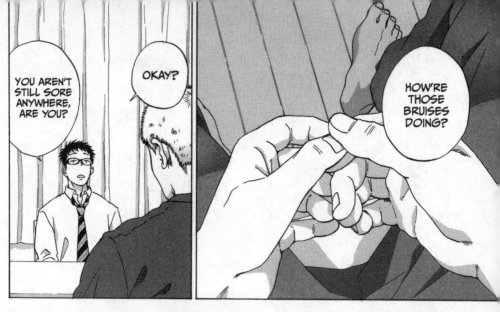

HOW'RE THOSE BRUISES DOING?
OKAY?
YOU AREN'T STILL SORE ANYWHERE, ARE YOU?
THIS, RIGHT AFTER YOU GET DONE HEALING FROM A BROKEN LEG.
ALL ABOUT THE ROUGH-AND-TUMBLE HORSEPLAY WITH YOU, ISN'T IT?
SO. WHY'D YOU GET IN A FIGHT?

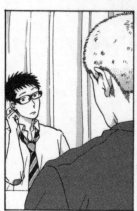

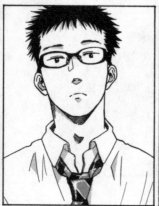

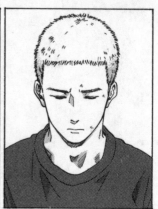

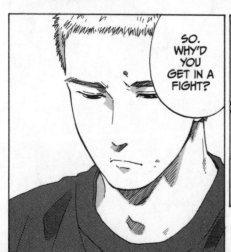

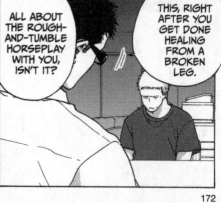

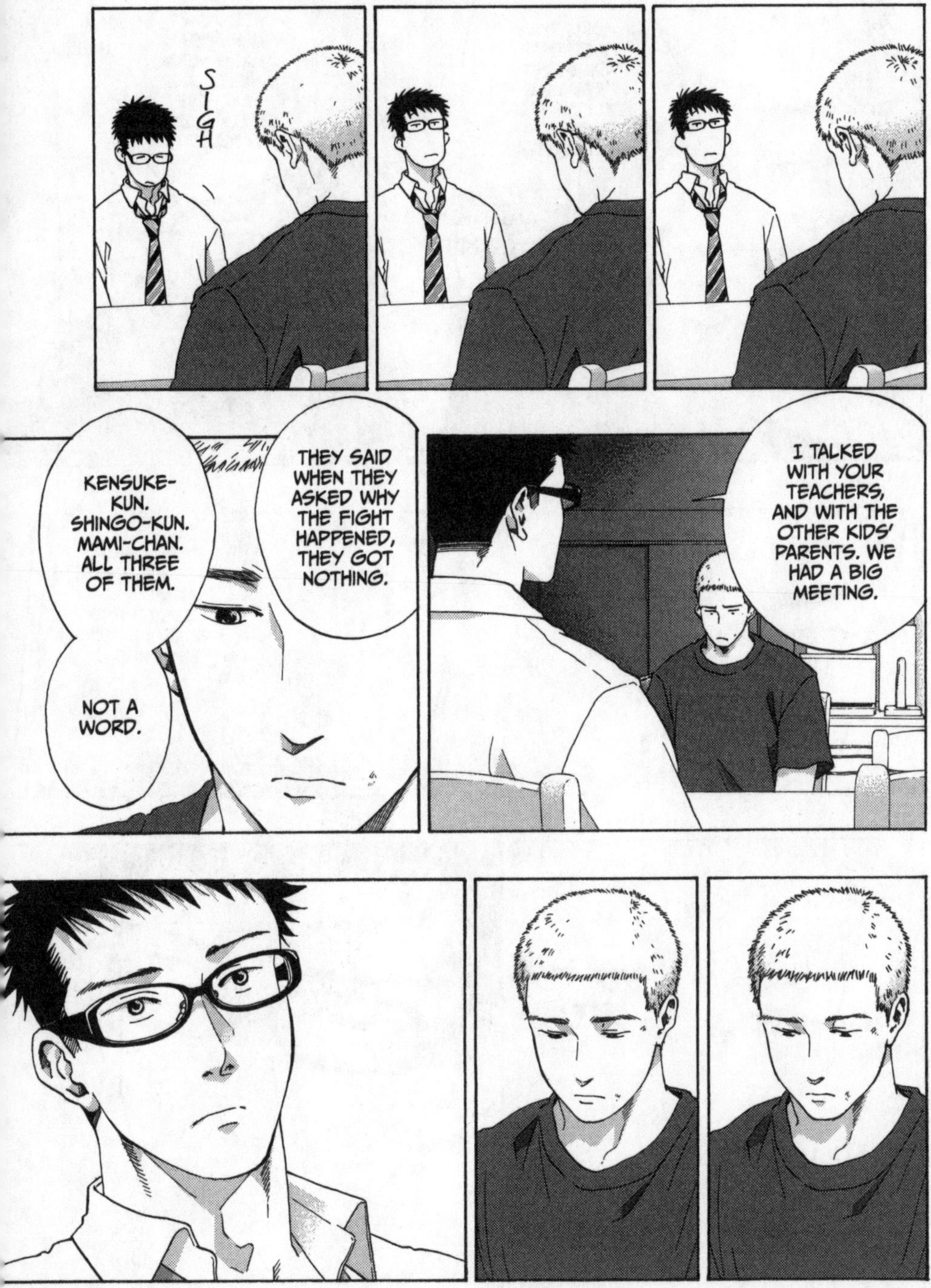
SIGH
I TALKED WITH YOUR TEACHERS, AND WITH THE OTHER KIDS' PARENTS. WE HAD A BIG MEETING.
THEY SAID WHEN THEY ASKED WHY THE FIGHT HAPPENED, THEY GOT NOTHING.
KENSUKE-KUN. SHINGO-KUN. MAMI-CHAN. ALL THREE OF THEM.
NOT A WORD.

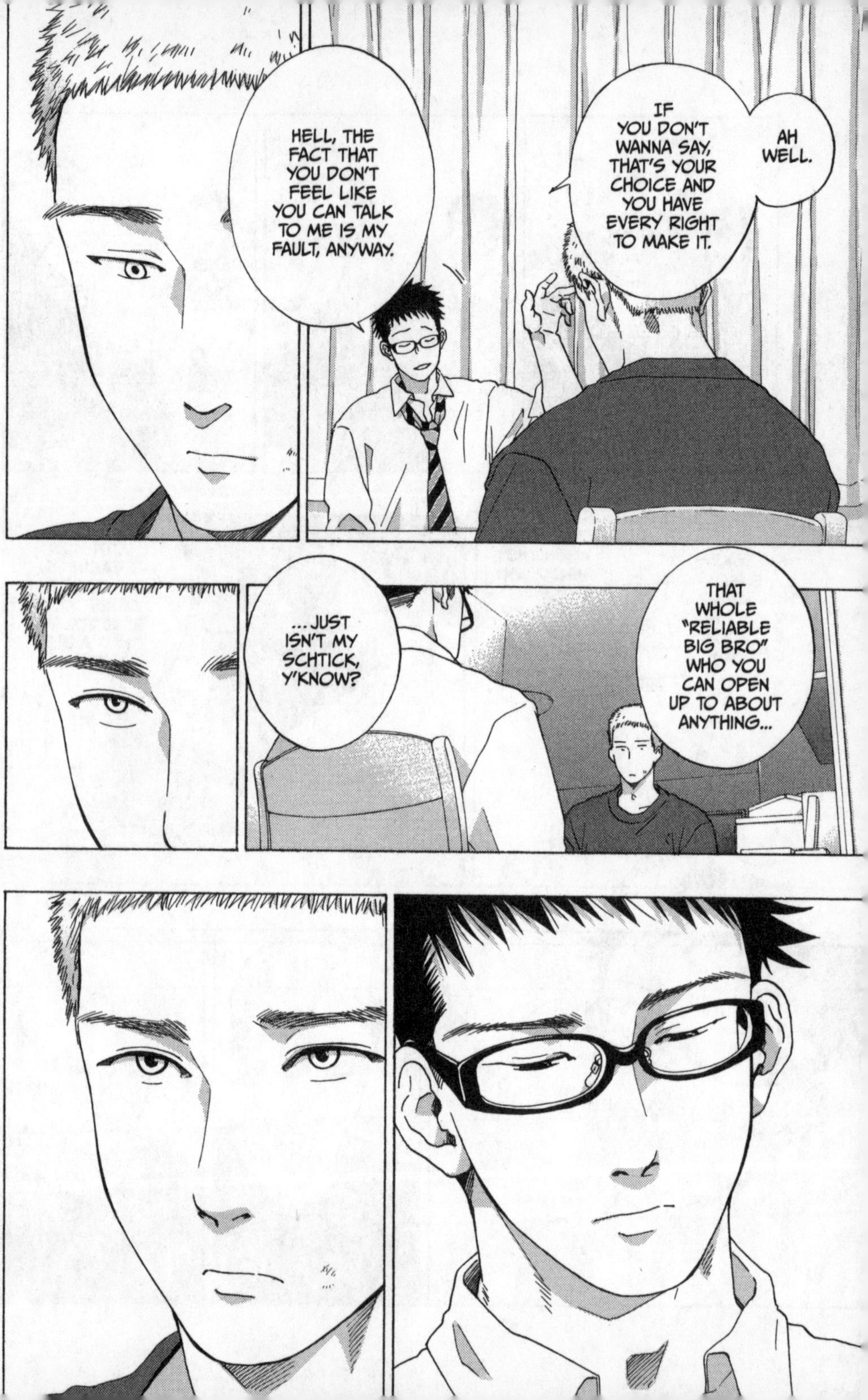
AH WELL.
IF YOU DON'T WANNA SAY, THAT'S YOUR CHOICE AND YOU HAVE EVERY RIGHT TO MAKE IT.
HELL, THE FACT THAT YOU DON'T FEEL LIKE YOU CAN TALK TO ME IS MY FAULT, ANYWAY.
THAT WHOLE "RELIABLE BIG BRO" WHO YOU CAN OPEN UP TO ABOUT ANYTHING...
...JUST ISN'T MY SCHTICK, Y'KNOW?

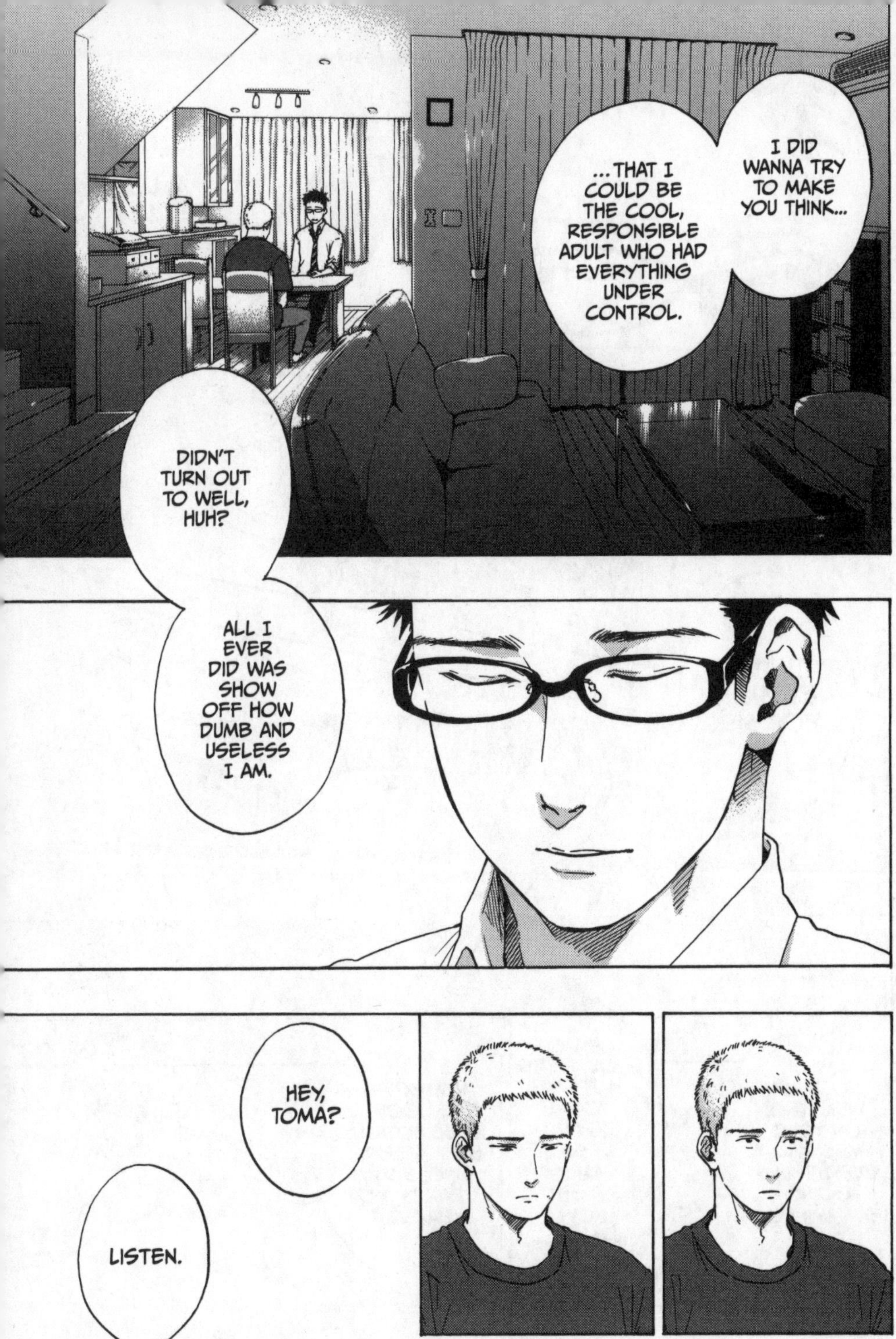
I DID WANNA TRY TO MAKE YOU THINK...
...THAT I COULD BE THE COOL, RESPONSIBLE ADULT WHO HAD EVERYTHING UNDER CONTROL.
DIDN'T TURN OUT TO WELL, HUH?
ALL I EVER DID WAS SHOW OFF HOW DUMB AND USELESS I AM.
HEY, TOMA?
LISTEN.

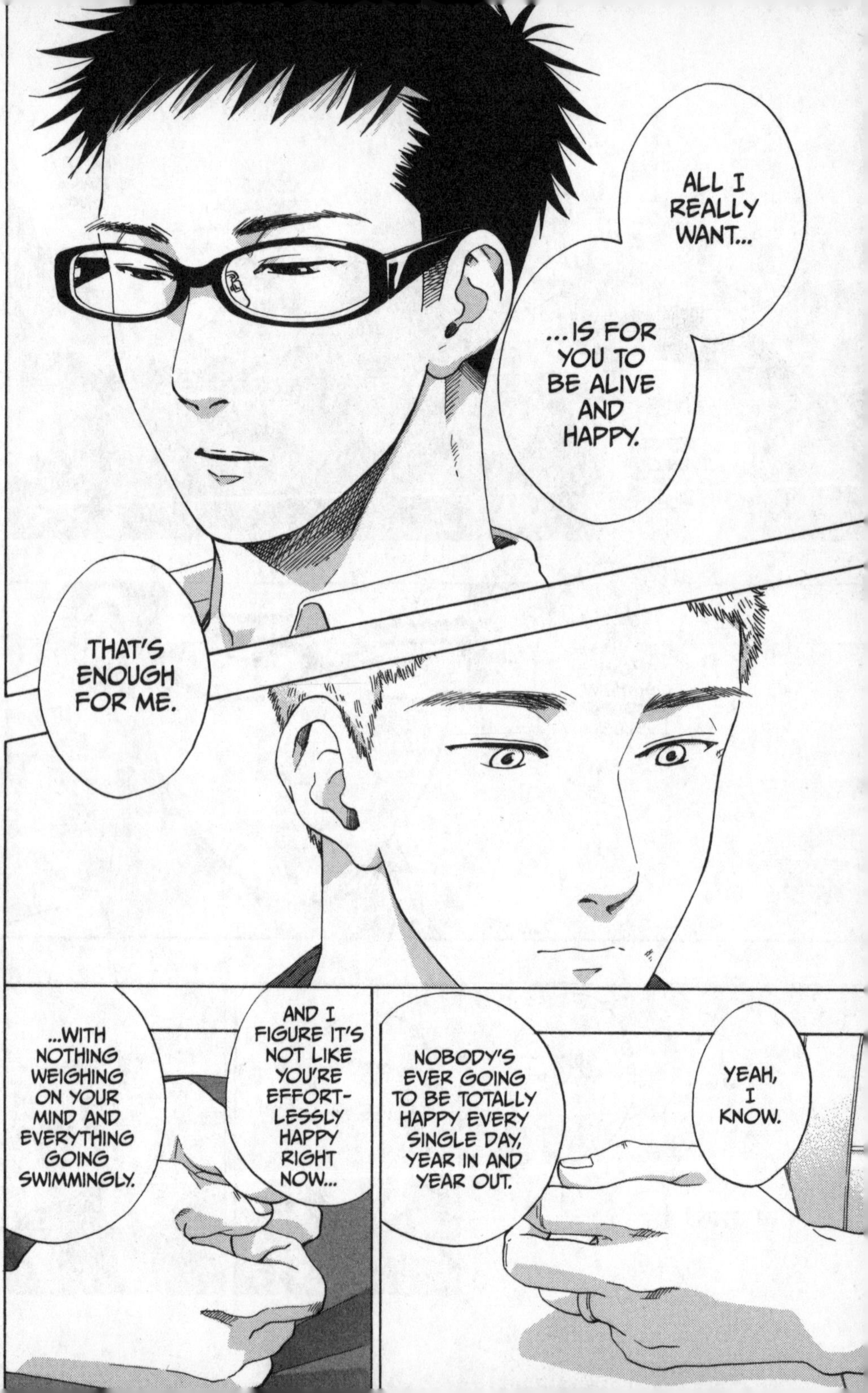
ALL I REALLY WANT...
...IS FOR YOU TO BE ALIVE AND HAPPY.
THAT'S ENOUGH FOR ME.
YEAH, I KNOW.
NOBODY'S EVER GOING TO BE TOTALLY HAPPY EVERY SINGLE DAY, YEAR IN AND YEAR OUT.
AND I FIGURE IT'S NOT LIKE YOU'RE EFFORT-LESSLY HAPPY RIGHT NOW...
...WITH NOTHING WEIGHING ON YOUR MIND AND EVERYTHING GOING SWIMMINGLY.

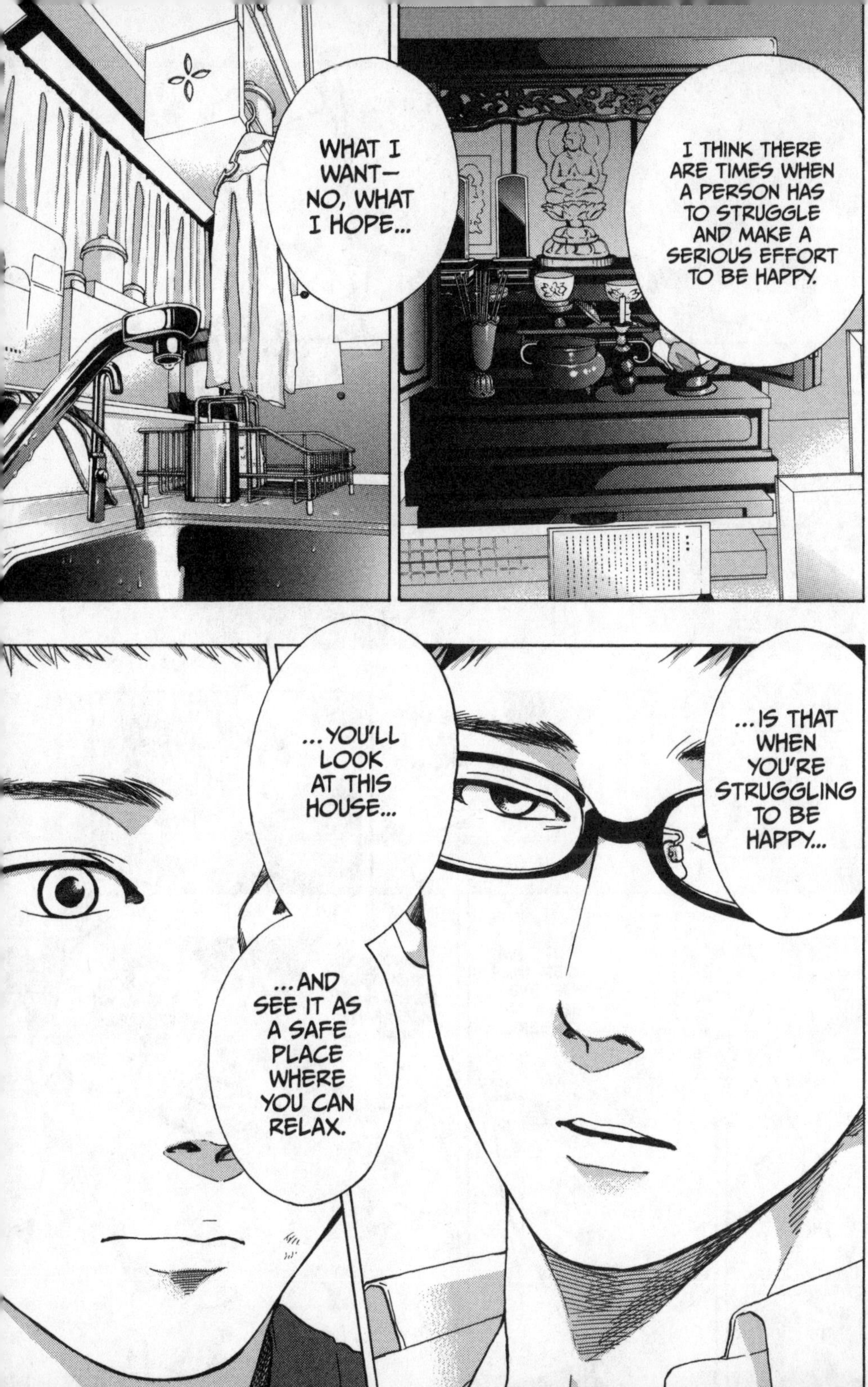
I THINK THERE ARE TIMES WHEN A PERSON HAS TO STRUGGLE AND MAKE A SERIOUS EFFORT TO BE HAPPY.
WHAT I WANT— NO, WHAT I HOPE...
...IS THAT WHEN YOU'RE STRUGGLING TO BE HAPPY...
...YOU'LL LOOK AT THIS HOUSE...
...AND SEE IT AS A SAFE PLACE WHERE YOU CAN RELAX.

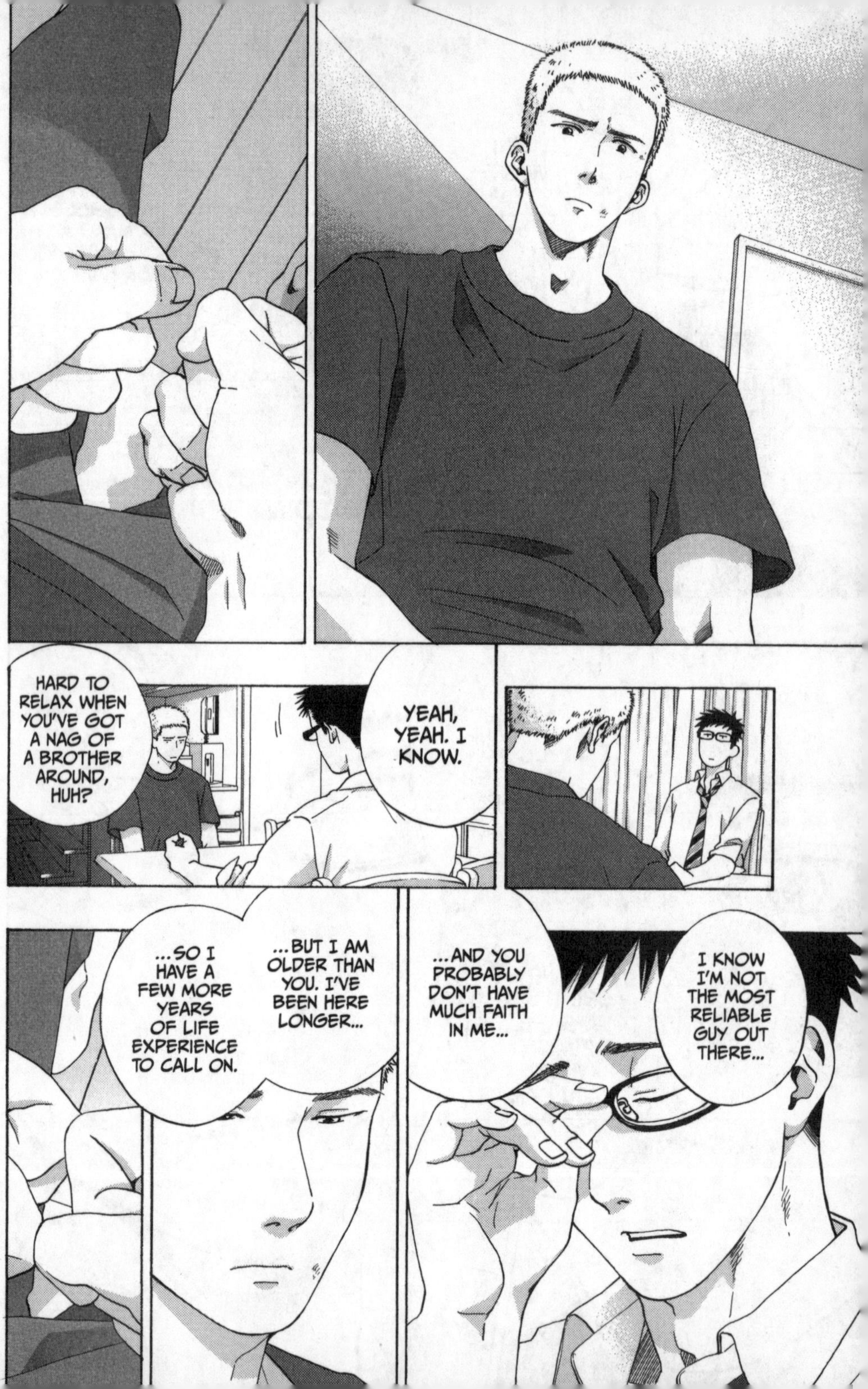
YEAH, YEAH. I KNOW.
HARD TO RELAX WHEN YOU'VE GOT A NAG OF A BROTHER AROUND, HUH?
I KNOW I'M NOT THE MOST RELIABLE GUY OUT THERE...
...AND YOU PROBABLY DON'T HAVE MUCH FAITH IN ME...
...BUT I AM OLDER THAN YOU. I'VE BEEN HERE LONGER...
...SO I HAVE A FEW MORE YEARS OF LIFE EXPERIENCE TO CALL ON.

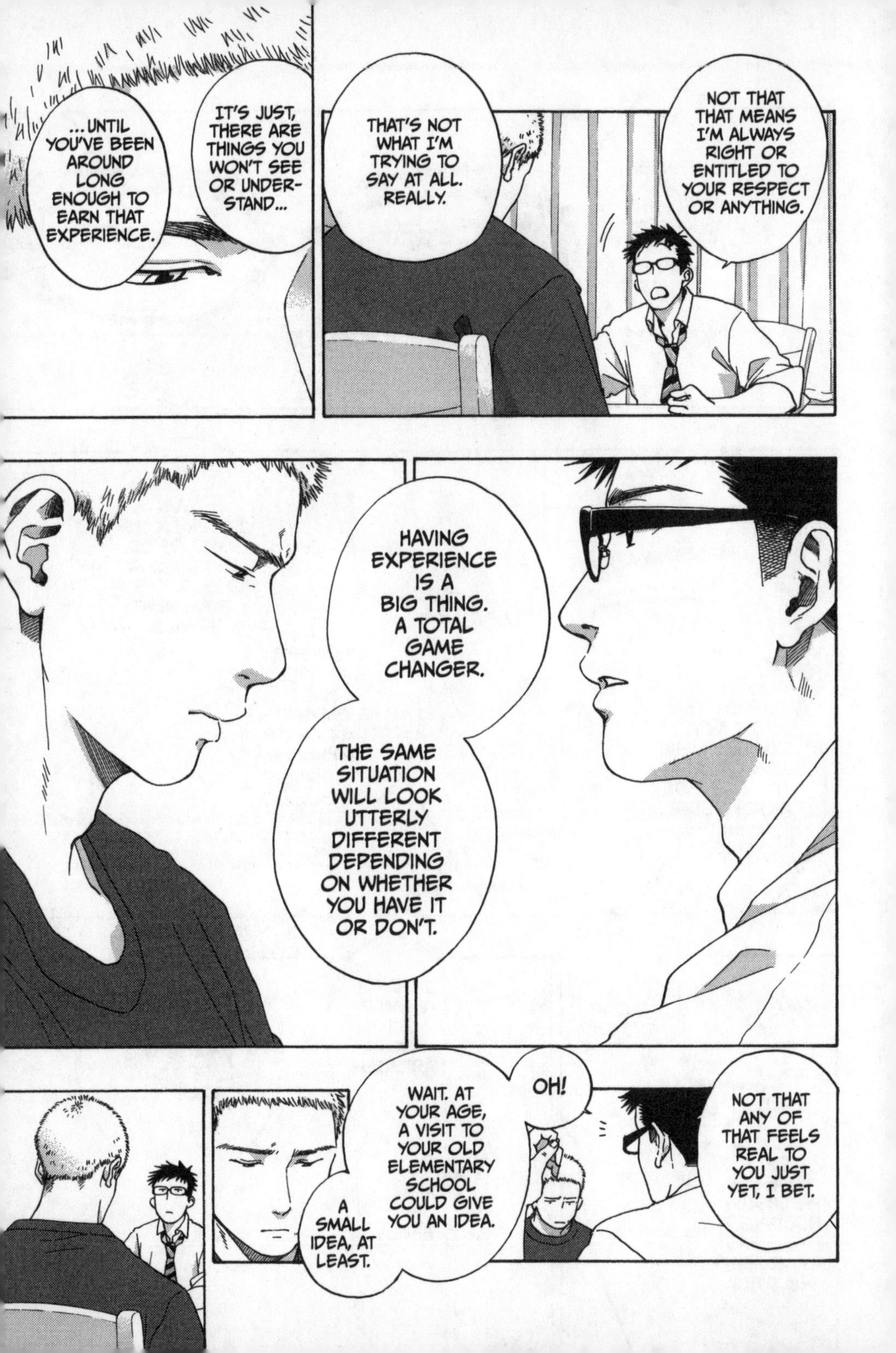
NOT THAT THAT MEANS I'M ALWAYS RIGHT OR ENTITLED TO YOUR RESPECT OR ANYTHING.
THAT'S NOT WHAT I'M TRYING TO SAY AT ALL. REALLY.
IT'S JUST, THERE ARE THINGS YOU WON'T SEE OR UNDER-STAND...
...UNTIL YOU'VE BEEN AROUND LONG ENOUGH TO EARN THAT EXPERIENCE.
HAVING EXPERIENCE IS A BIG THING. A TOTAL GAME CHANGER.
THE SAME SITUATION WILL LOOK UTTERLY DIFFERENT DEPENDING ON WHETHER YOU HAVE IT OR DON'T.
NOT THAT ANY OF THAT FEELS REAL TO YOU JUST YET, I BET.
OH!
WAIT. AT YOUR AGE, A VISIT TO YOUR OLD ELEMENTARY SCHOOL COULD GIVE YOU AN IDEA.
A SMALL IDEA, AT LEAST.

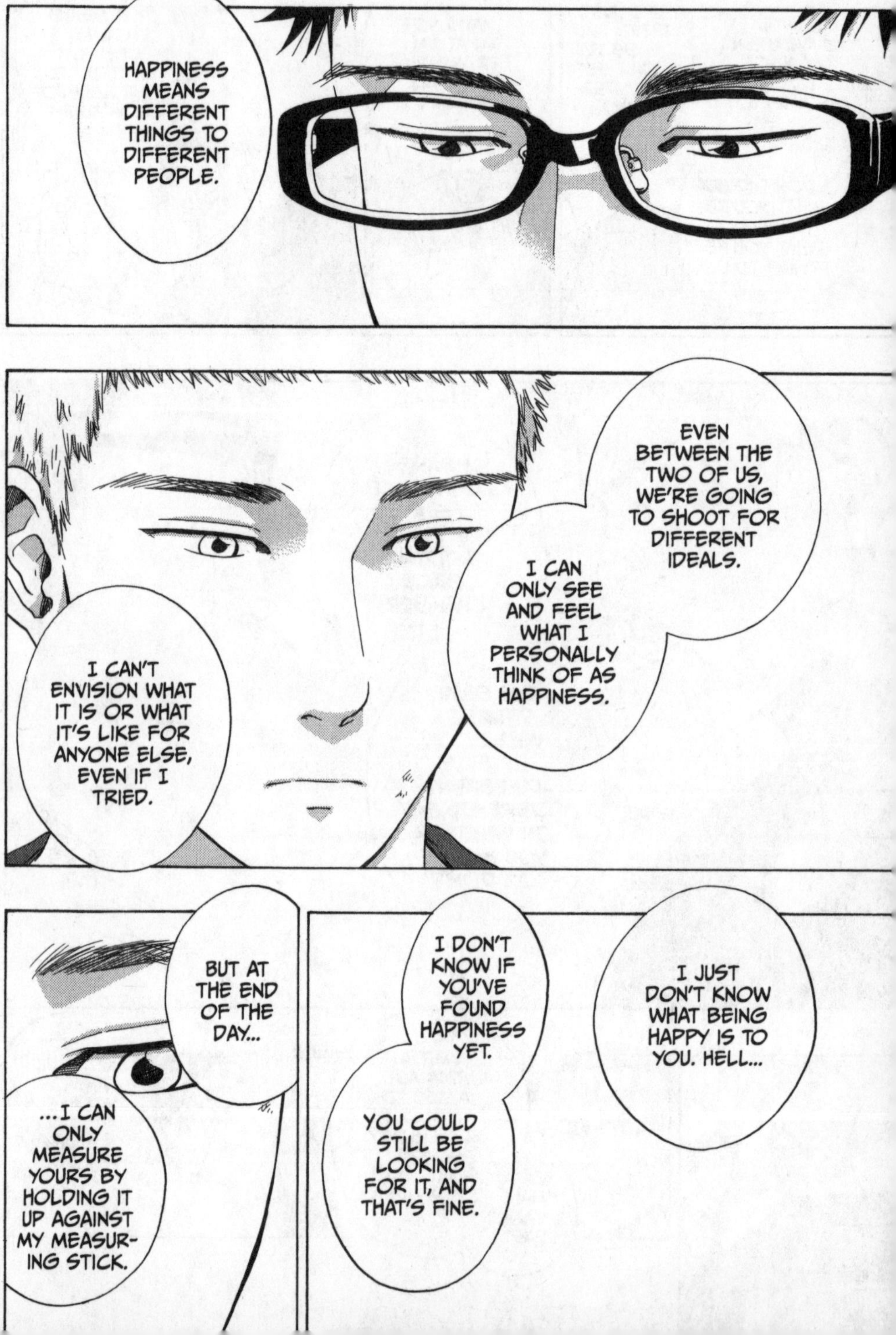
HAPPINESS MEANS DIFFERENT THINGS TO DIFFERENT PEOPLE.
EVEN BETWEEN THE TWO OF US, WE'RE GOING TO SHOOT FOR DIFFERENT IDEALS.
I CAN ONLY SEE AND FEEL WHAT I PERSONALLY THINK OF AS HAPPINESS.
I CAN'T ENVISION WHAT IT IS OR WHAT IT'S LIKE FOR ANYONE ELSE, EVEN IF I TRIED.
I JUST DON'T KNOW WHAT BEING HAPPY IS TO YOU. HELL...
I DON'T KNOW IF YOU'VE FOUND HAPPINESS YET.
YOU COULD STILL BE LOOKING FOR IT, AND THAT'S FINE.
BUT AT THE END OF THE DAY...
...I CAN ONLY MEASURE YOURS BY HOLDING IT UP AGAINST MY MEASUR-ING STICK.

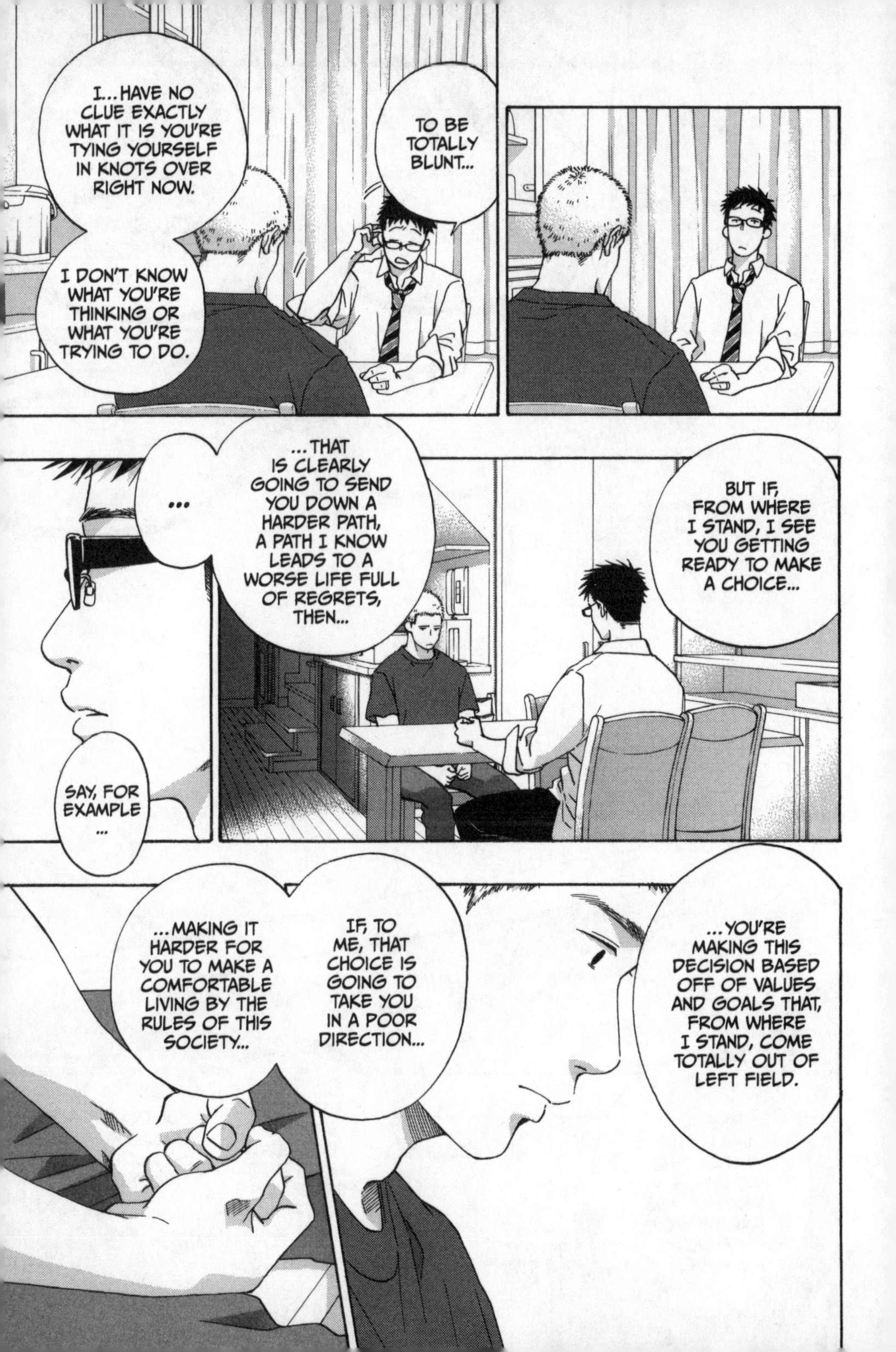
TO BE TOTALLY BLUNT...
I...HAVE NO CLUE EXACTLY WHAT IT IS YOU'RE TYING YOURSELF IN KNOTS OVER RIGHT NOW.
I DON'T KNOW WHAT YOU'RE THINKING OR WHAT YOU'RE TRYING TO DO.
BUT IF, FROM WHERE I STAND, I SEE YOU GETTING READY TO MAKE A CHOICE...
...
...THAT IS CLEARLY GOING TO SEND YOU DOWN A HARDER PATH, A PATH I KNOW LEADS TO A WORSE LIFE FULL OF REGRETS, THEN...
SAY, FOR EXAMPLE ...
...YOU'RE MAKING THIS DECISION BASED OFF OF VALUES AND GOALS THAT, FROM WHERE I STAND, COME TOTALLY OUT OF LEFT FIELD.
IF, TO ME, THAT CHOICE IS GOING TO TAKE YOU IN A POOR DIRECTION...
...MAKING IT HARDER FOR YOU TO MAKE A COMFORTABLE LIVING BY THE RULES OF THIS SOCIETY...

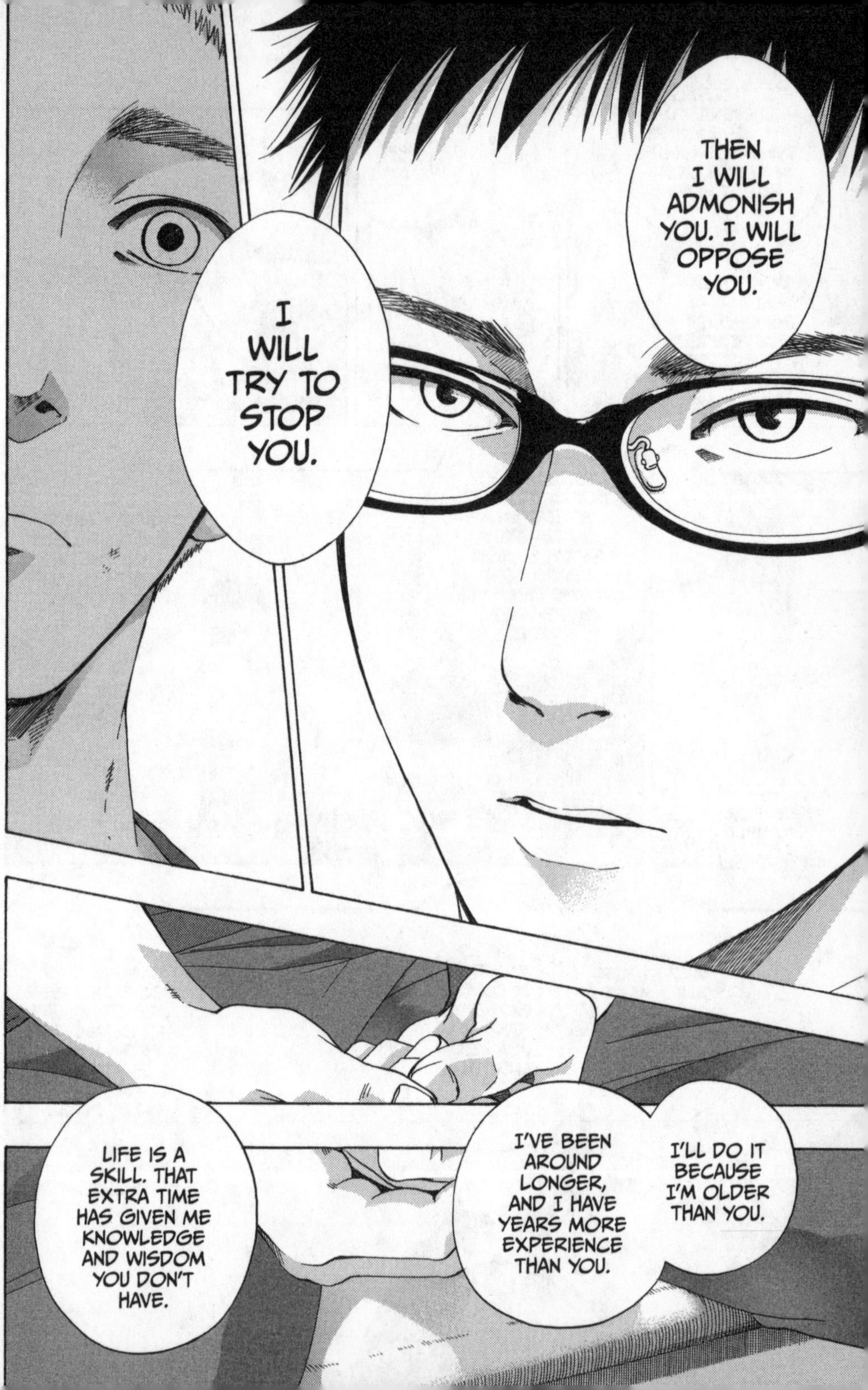
THEN I WILL ADMONISH YOU. I WILL OPPOSE YOU.
I WILL TRY TO STOP YOU.
I'LL DO IT BECAUSE I'M OLDER THAN YOU.
I'VE BEEN AROUND LONGER, AND I HAVE YEARS MORE EXPERIENCE THAN YOU.
LIFE IS A SKILL. THAT EXTRA TIME HAS GIVEN ME KNOWLEDGE AND WISDOM YOU DON'T HAVE.

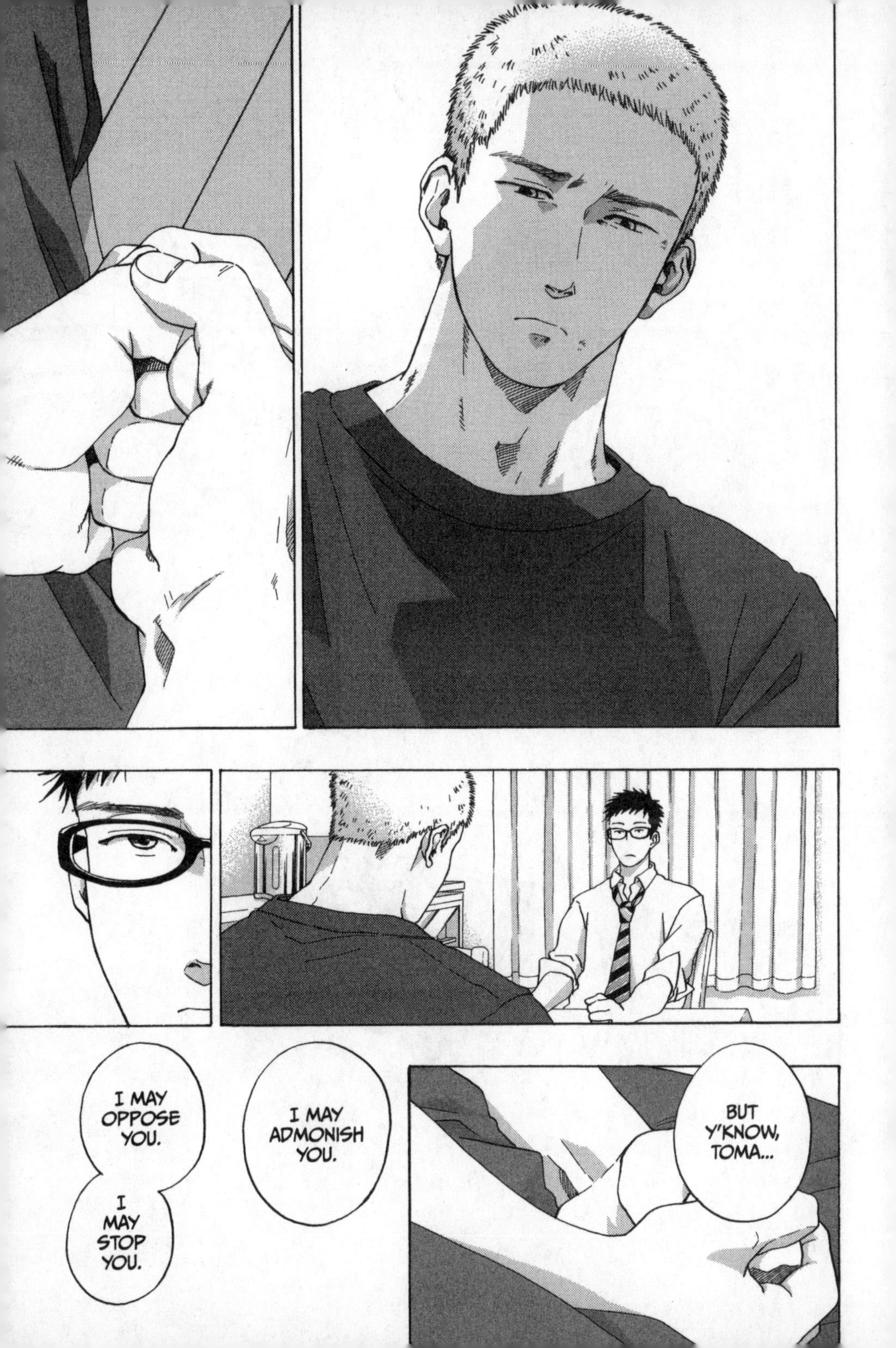

BUT Y'KNOW, TOMA...
I MAY ADMONISH YOU.
I MAY OPPOSE YOU.
I MAY STOP YOU.

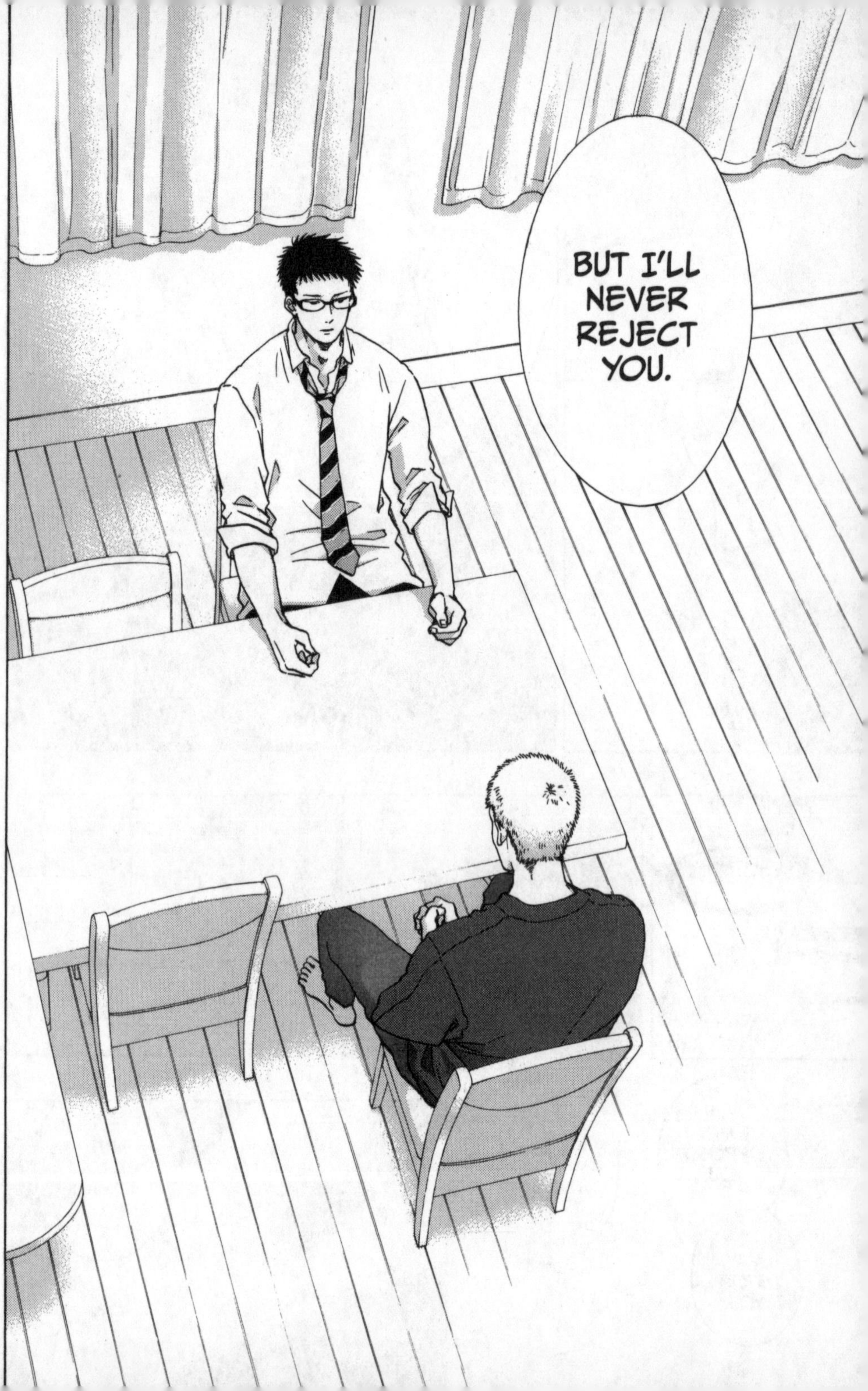
BUT I'LL NEVER REJECT YOU.

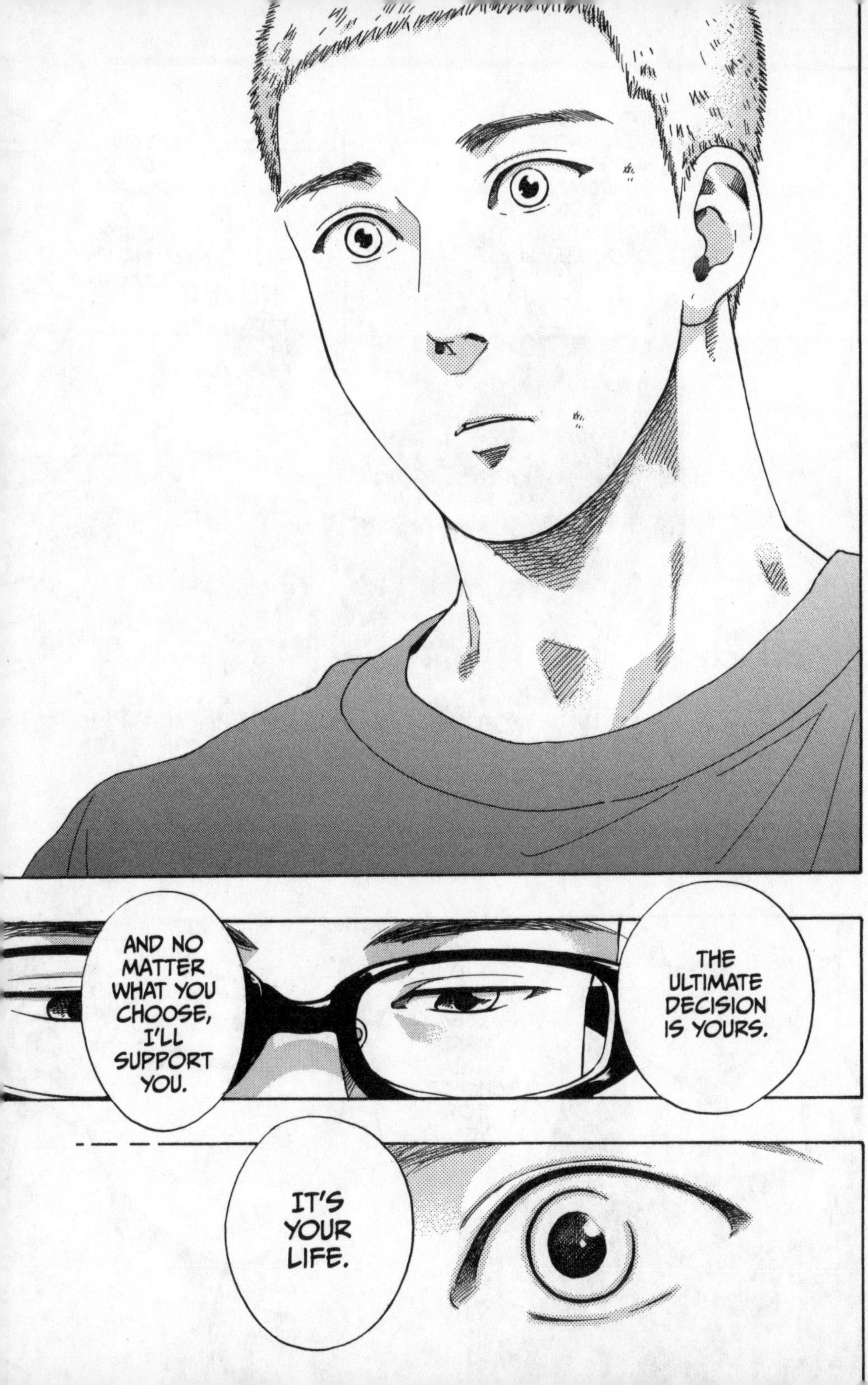
THE ULTIMATE DECISION IS YOURS.
AND NO MATTER WHAT YOU CHOOSE, I'LL SUPPORT YOU.
IT'S YOUR LIFE.

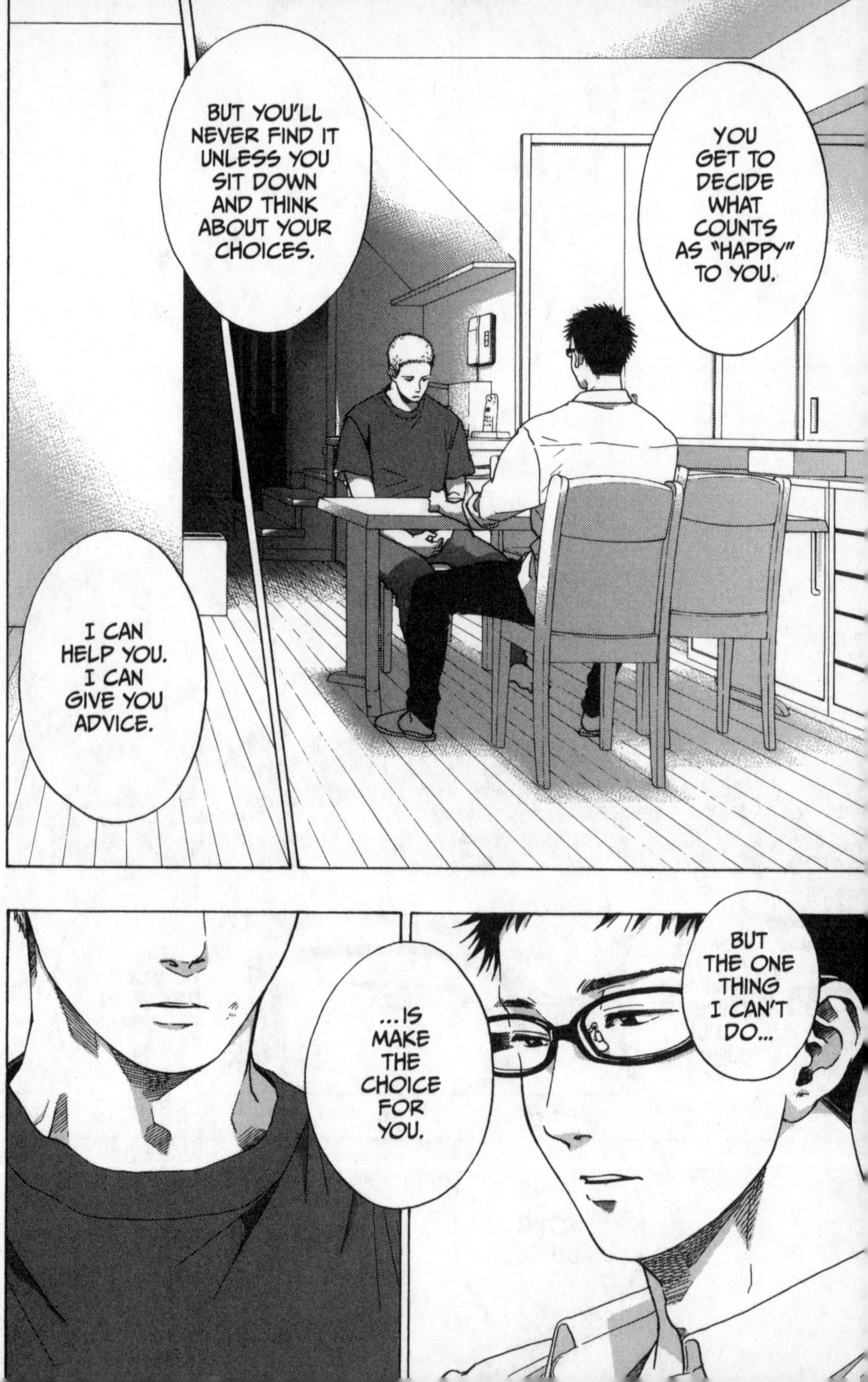
YOU GET TO DECIDE WHAT COUNTS AS "HAPPY" TO YOU.
BUT YOU'LL NEVER FIND IT UNLESS YOU SIT DOWN AND THINK ABOUT YOUR CHOICES.
I CAN HELP YOU. I CAN GIVE YOU ADVICE.
BUT THE ONE THING I CAN'T DO...
...IS MAKE THE CHOICE FOR YOU.

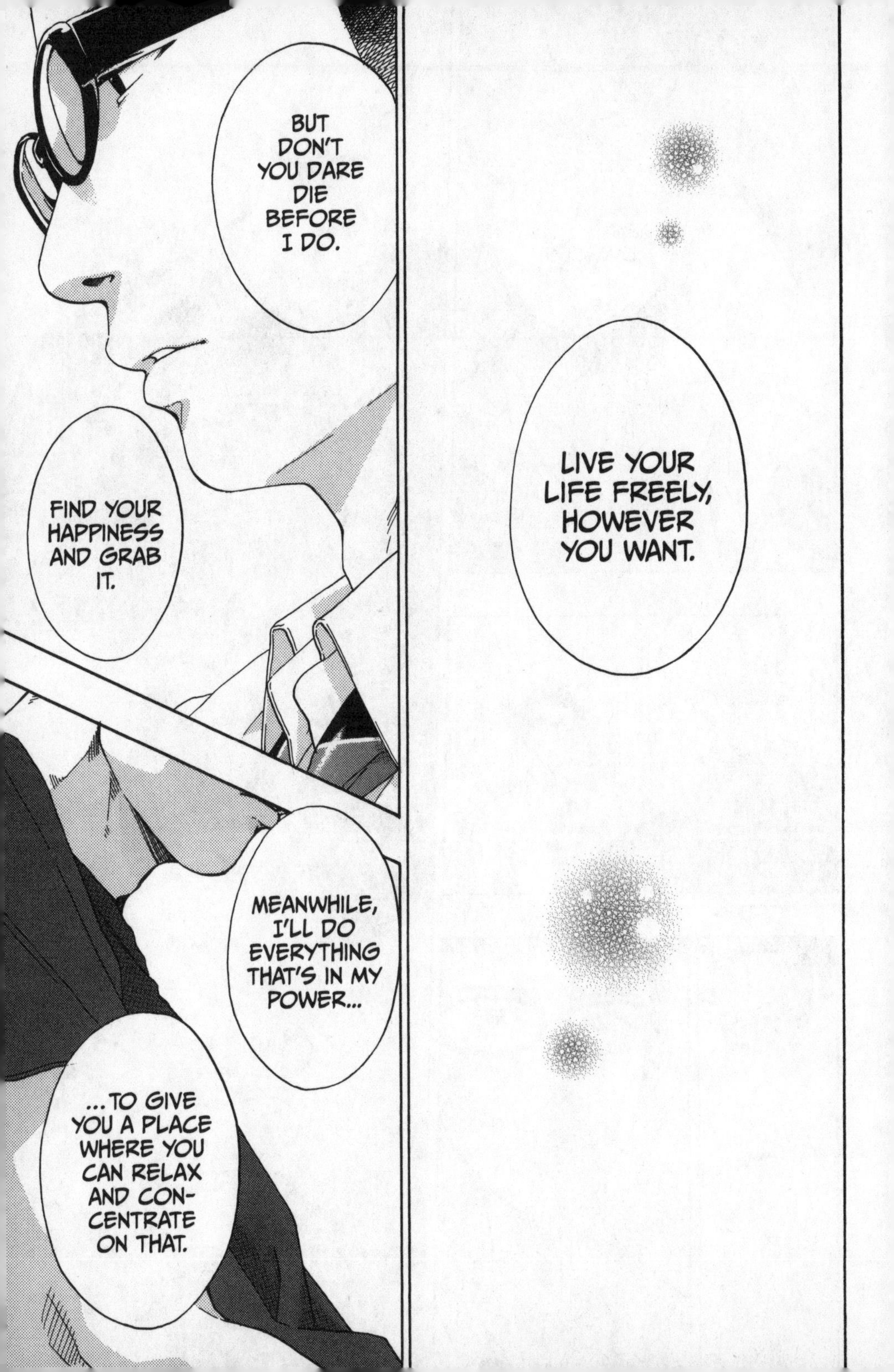
LIVE YOUR LIFE FREELY, HOWEVER YOU WANT.
BUT DON'T YOU DARE DIE BEFORE I DO.
FIND YOUR HAPPINESS AND GRAB IT.
MEANWHILE, I'LL DO EVERYTHING THAT'S IN MY POWER...
...TO GIVE YOU A PLACE WHERE YOU CAN RELAX AND CON-CENTRATE ON THAT.

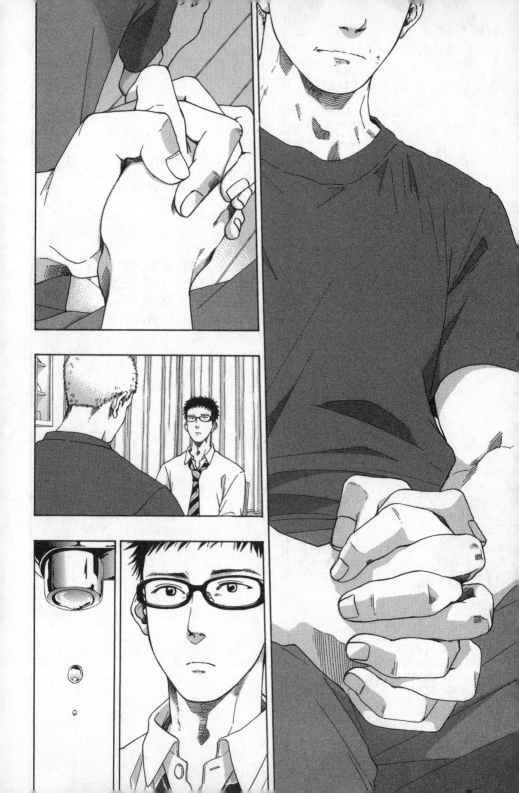

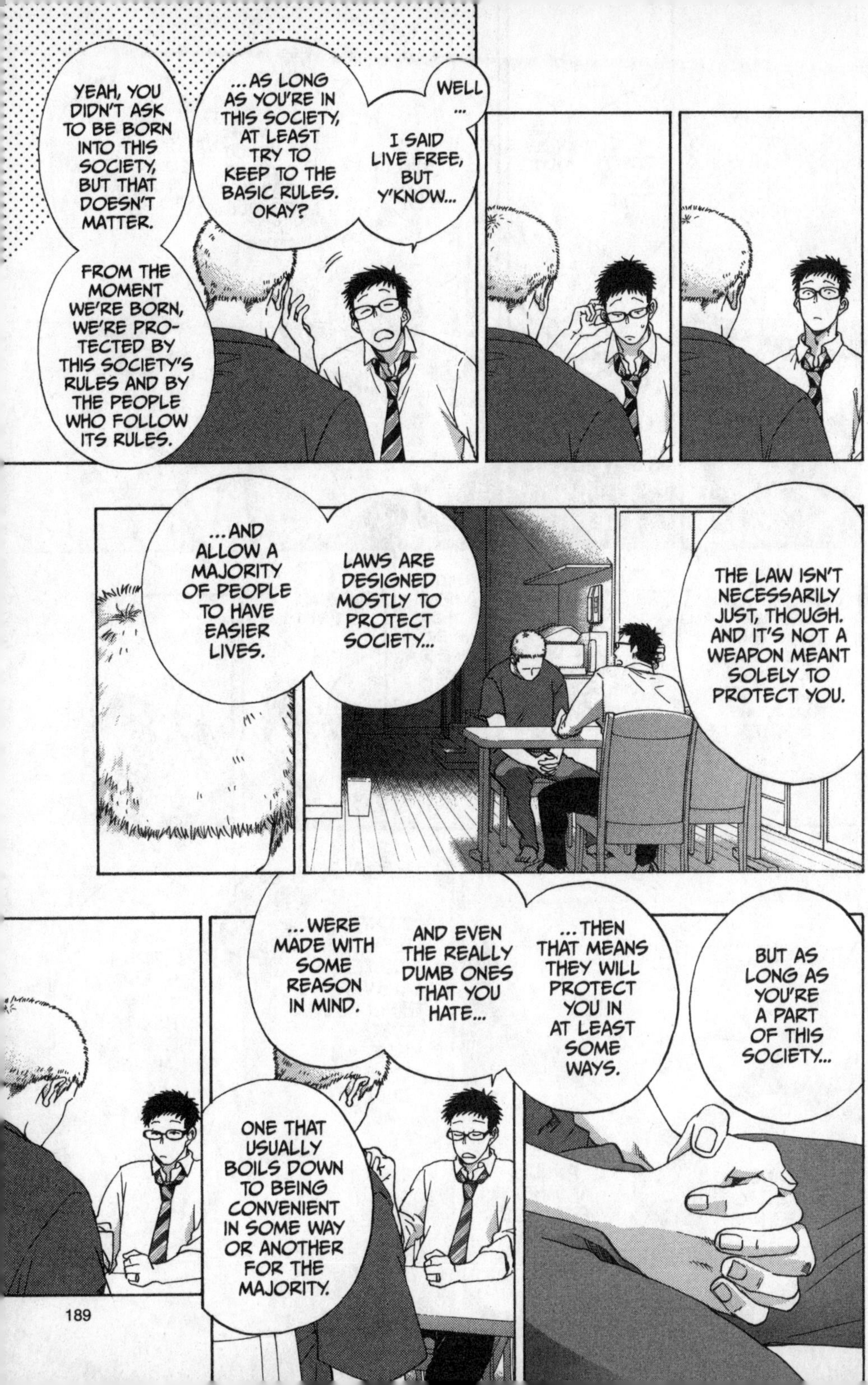
WELL... I SAID LIVE FREE, BUT Y'KNOW...
...AS LONG AS YOU'RE IN THIS SOCIETY, AT LEAST TRY TO KEEP TO THE BASIC RULES. OKAY?
YEAH, YOU DIDN'T ASK TO BE BORN INTO THIS SOCIETY, BUT THAT DOESN'T MATTER.
FROM THE MOMENT WE'RE BORN, WE'RE PROTECTED BY THIS SOCIETY'S RULES AND BY THE PEOPLE WHO FOLLOW ITS RULES.
THE LAW ISN'T NECESSARILY JUST, THOUGH. AND IT'S NOT A WEAPON MEANT SOLELY TO PROTECT YOU.
LAWS ARE DESIGNED MOSTLY TO PROTECT SOCIETY...
...AND ALLOW A MAJORITY OF PEOPLE TO HAVE EASIER LIVES.
BUT AS LONG AS YOU'RE A PART OF THIS SOCIETY...
...THEN THAT MEANS THEY WILL PROTECT YOU IN AT LEAST SOME WAYS.
AND EVEN THE REALLY DUMB ONES THAT YOU HATE...
...WERE MADE WITH SOME REASON IN MIND.
ONE THAT USUALLY BOILS DOWN TO BEING CONVENIENT IN SOME WAY OR ANOTHER FOR THE MAJORITY.

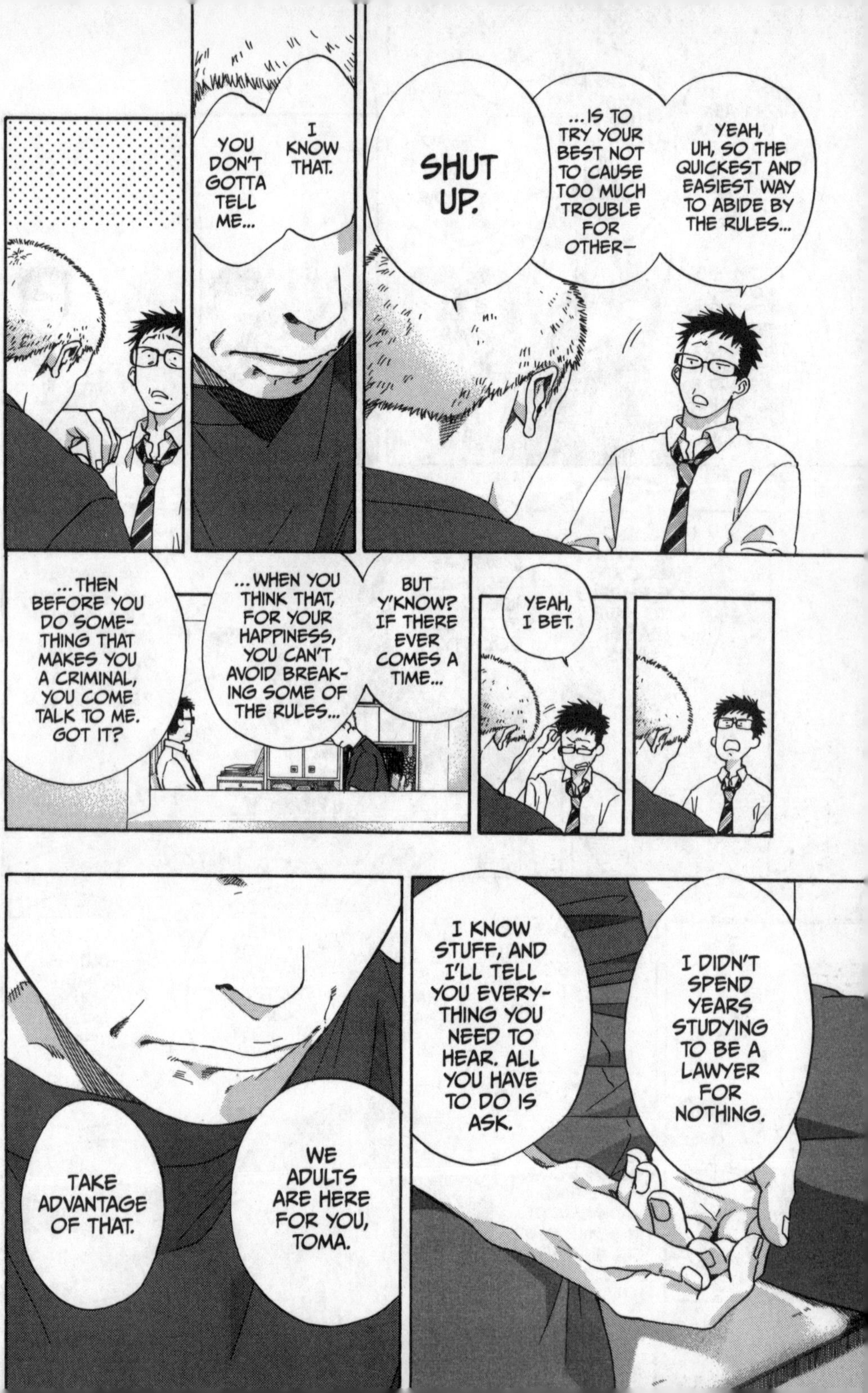

YEAH, UH, SO THE QUICKEST AND EASIEST WAY TO ABIDE BY THE RULES...
...IS TO TRY YOUR BEST NOT TO CAUSE TOO MUCH TROUBLE FOR OTHER—
SHUT UP.
I KNOW THAT.
YOU DON'T GOTTA TELL ME...
YEAH, I BET.
BUT Y'KNOW? IF THERE EVER COMES A TIME...
...WHEN YOU THINK THAT, FOR YOUR HAPPINESS, YOU CAN'T AVOID BREAKING SOME OF THE RULES...
...THEN BEFORE YOU DO SOMETHING THAT MAKES YOU A CRIMINAL, YOU COME TALK TO ME. GOT IT?
I DIDN'T SPEND YEARS STUDYING TO BE A LAWYER FOR NOTHING.
I KNOW STUFF, AND I'LL TELL YOU EVERYTHING YOU NEED TO HEAR. ALL YOU HAVE TO DO IS ASK.
WE ADULTS ARE HERE FOR YOU, TOMA.
TAKE ADVANTAGE OF THAT.

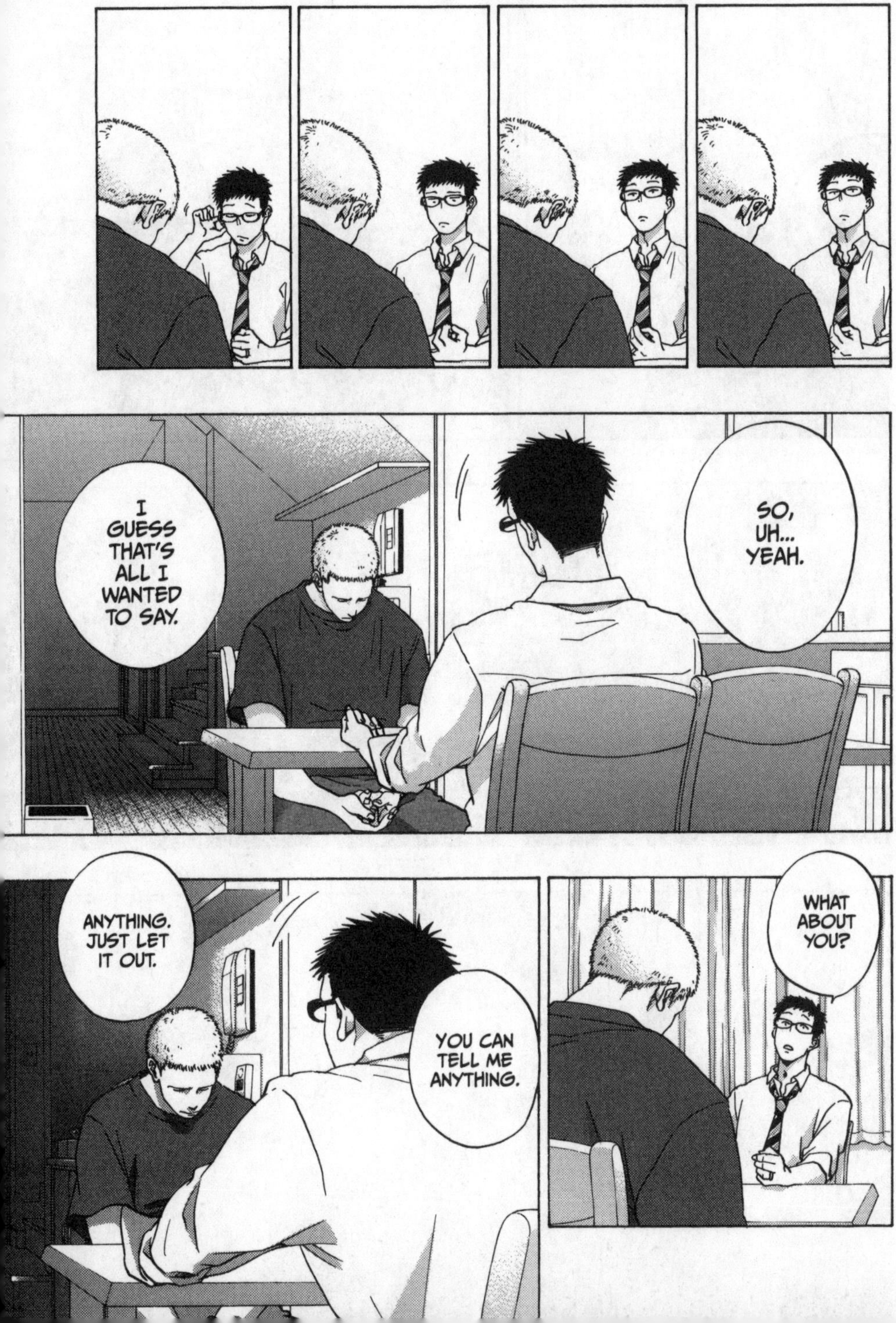
SO, UH... YEAH.
I GUESS THAT'S ALL I WANTED TO SAY.
WHAT ABOUT YOU?
YOU CAN TELL ME ANYTHING.
ANYTHING. JUST LET IT OUT.

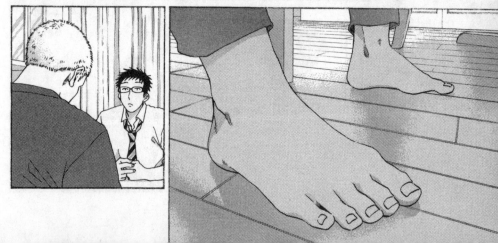

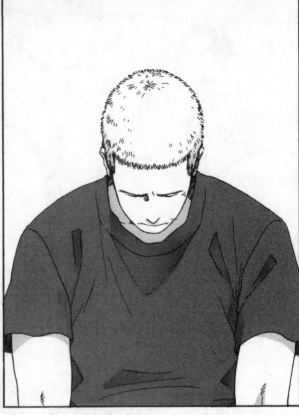

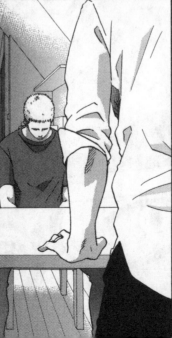

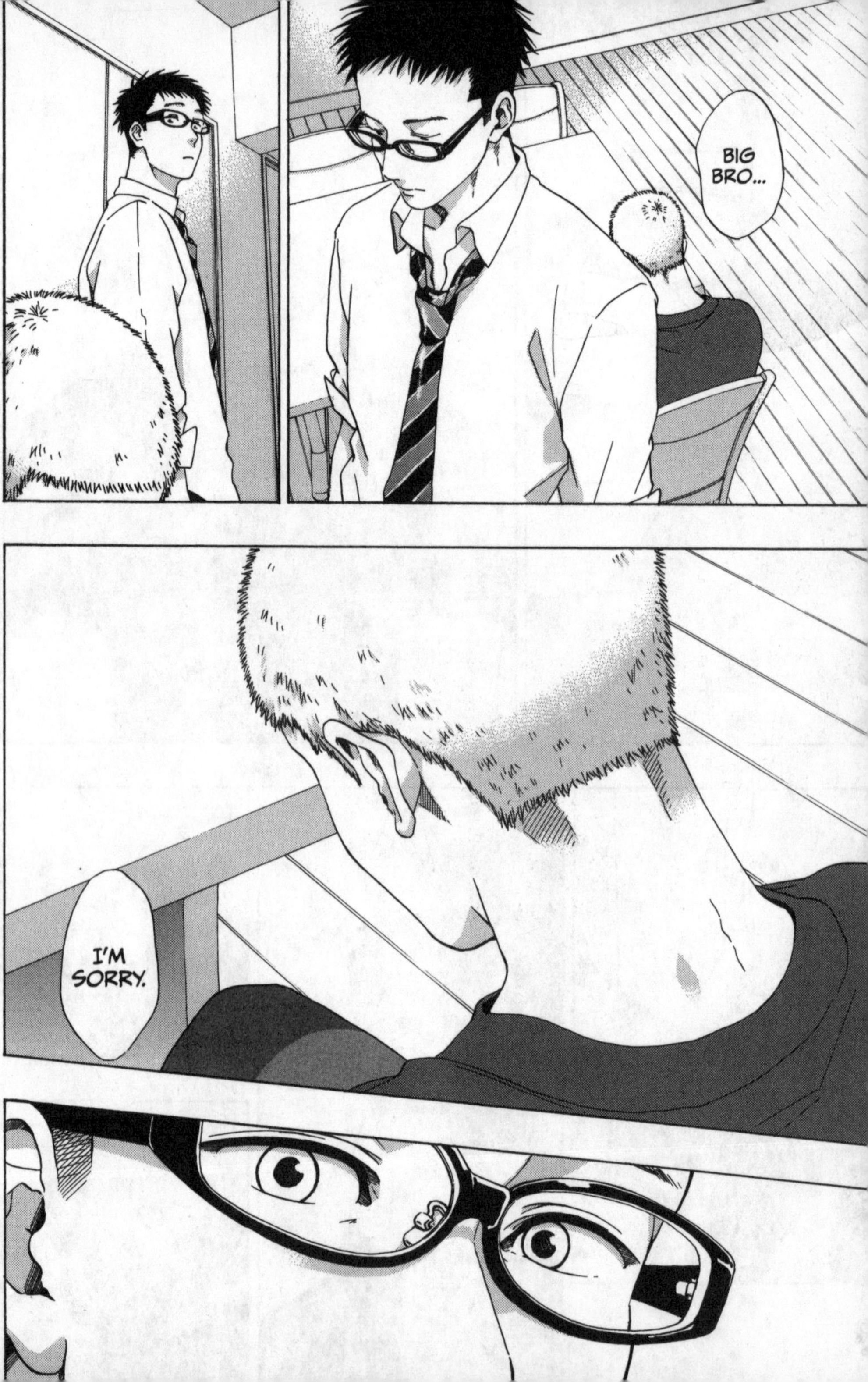
BIG BRO...
I'M SORRY.

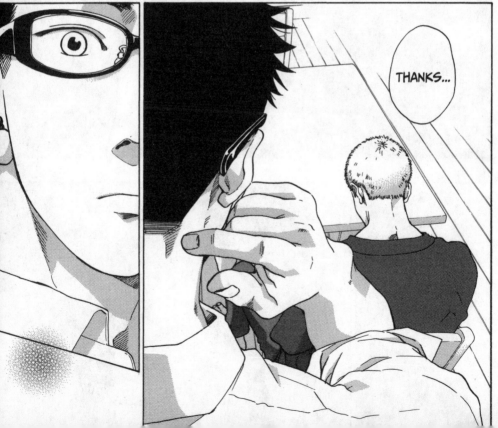

THANKS...

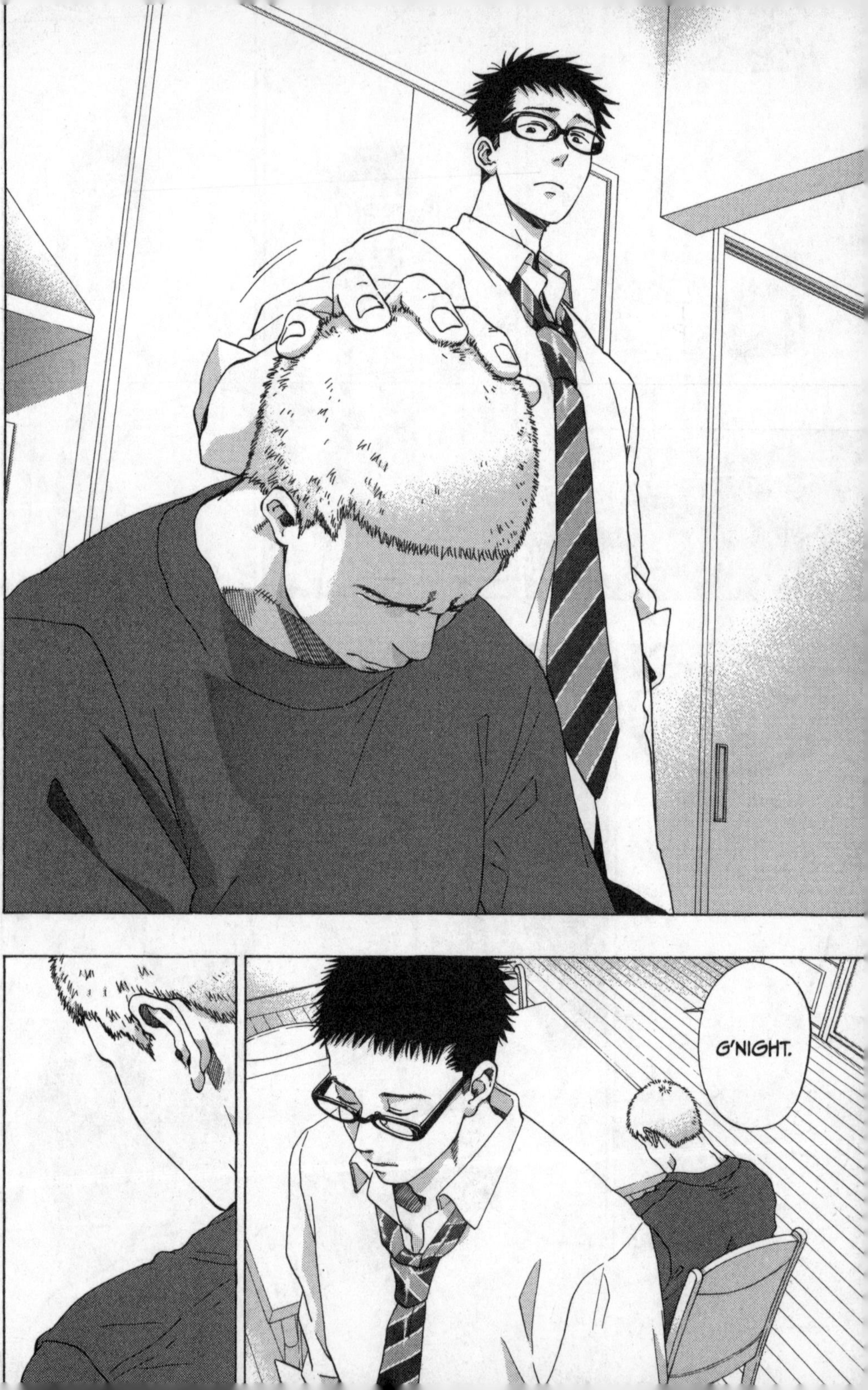
G'NIGHT.

PLIP

PLIP

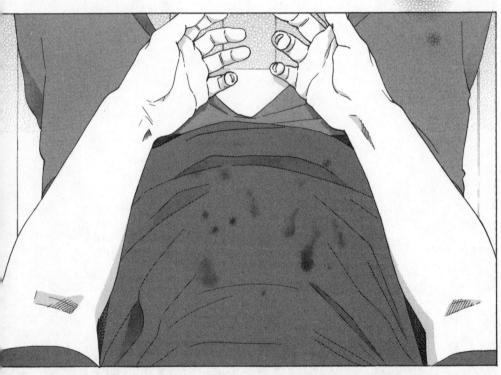

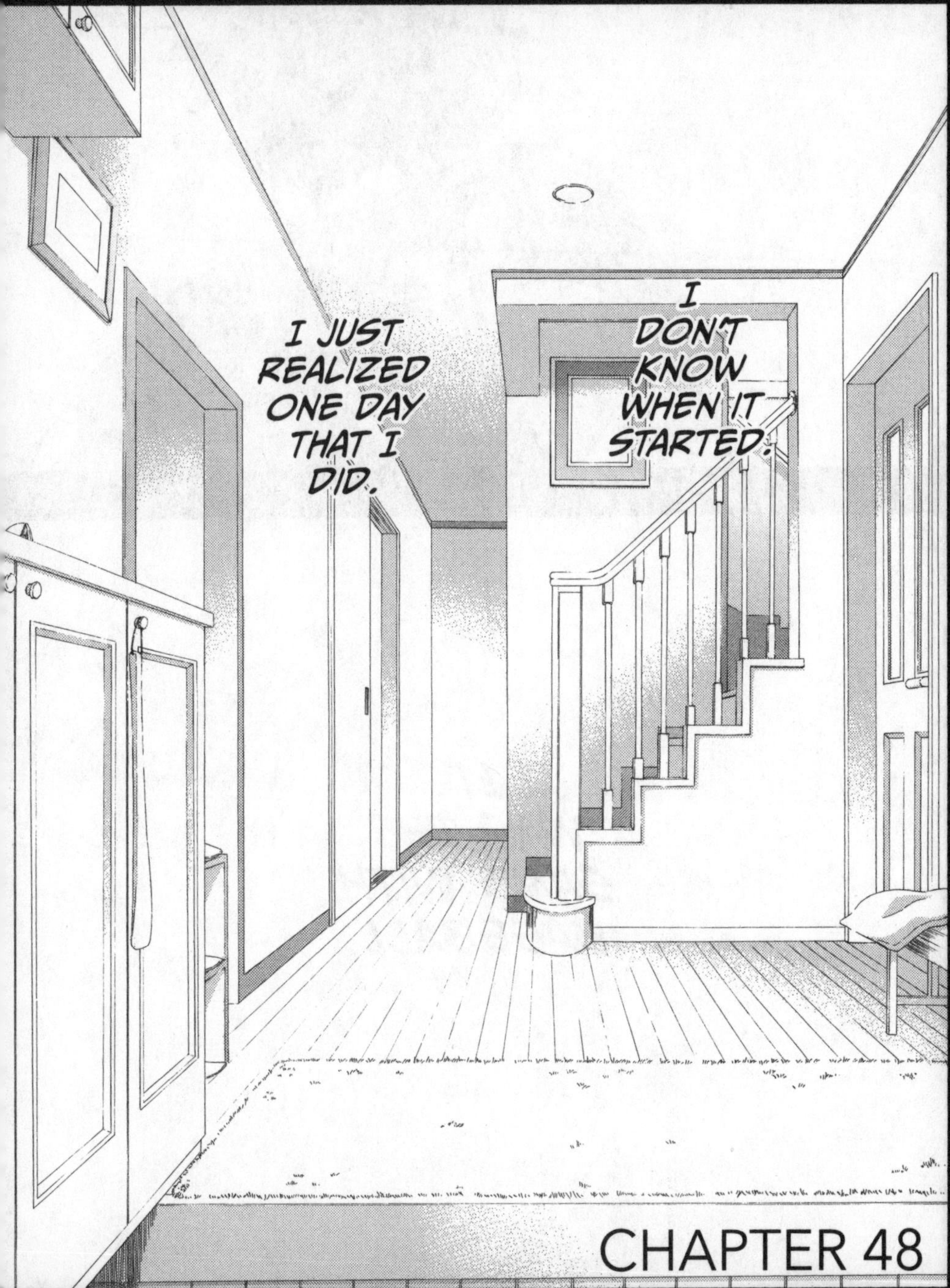
I DON'T KNOW WHEN IT STARTED.
I JUST REALIZED ONE DAY THAT I DID.

CHAPTER 48

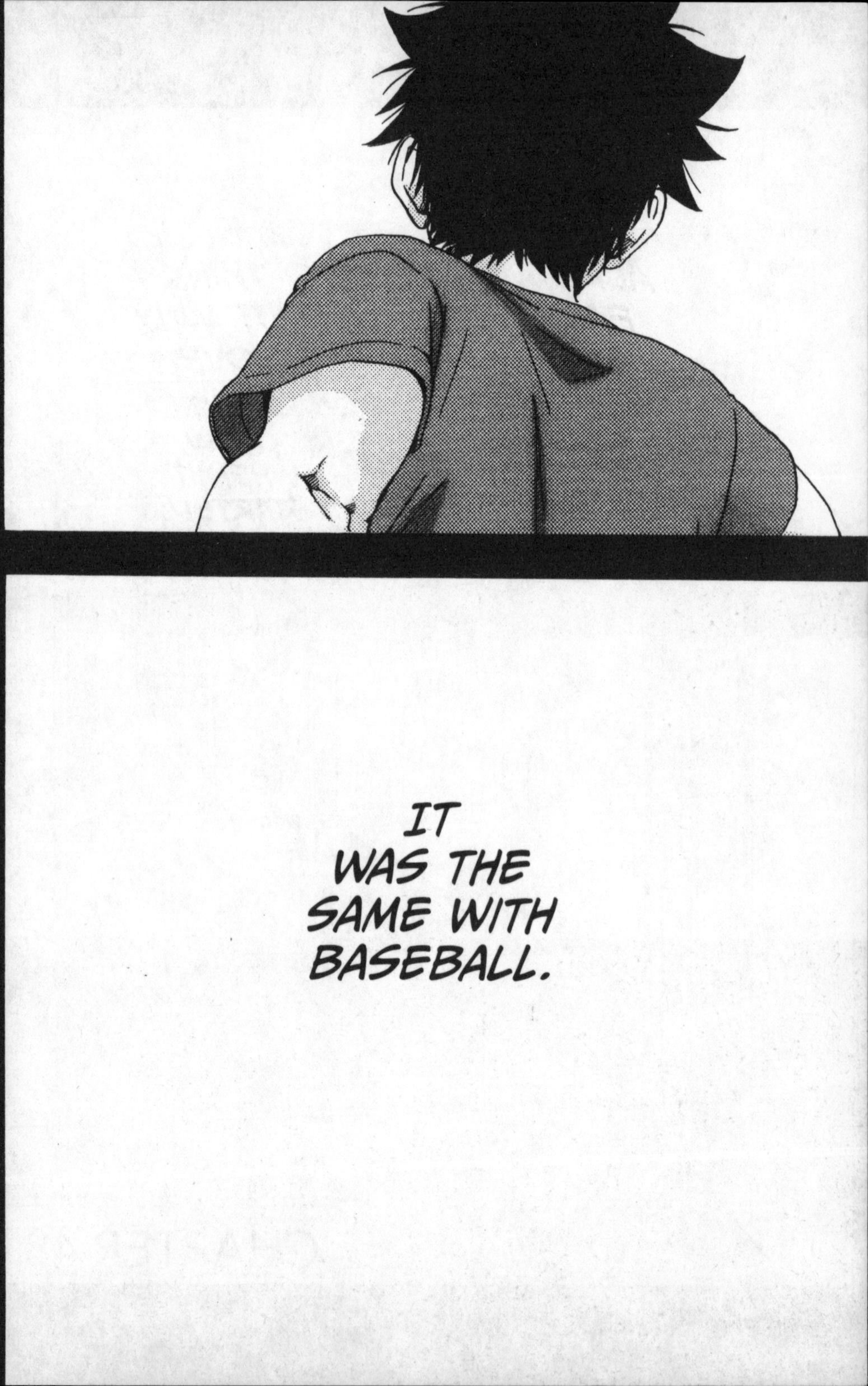
IT WAS THE SAME WITH BASEBALL.

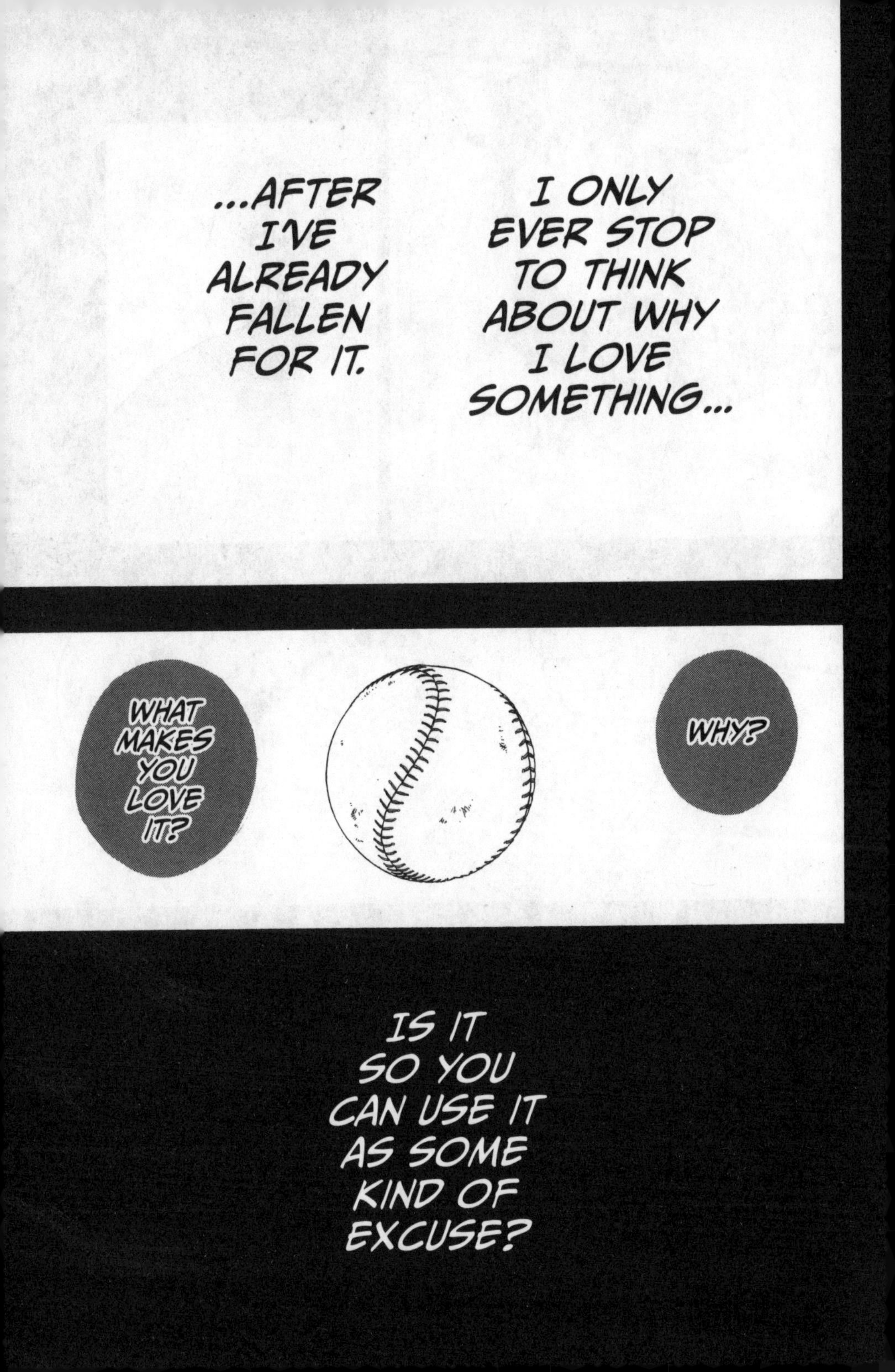
I ONLY EVER STOP TO THINK ABOUT WHY I LOVE SOMETHING...
...AFTER I'VE ALREADY FALLEN FOR IT.
WHY?
WHAT MAKES YOU LOVE IT?
IS IT SO YOU CAN USE IT AS SOME KIND OF EXCUSE?

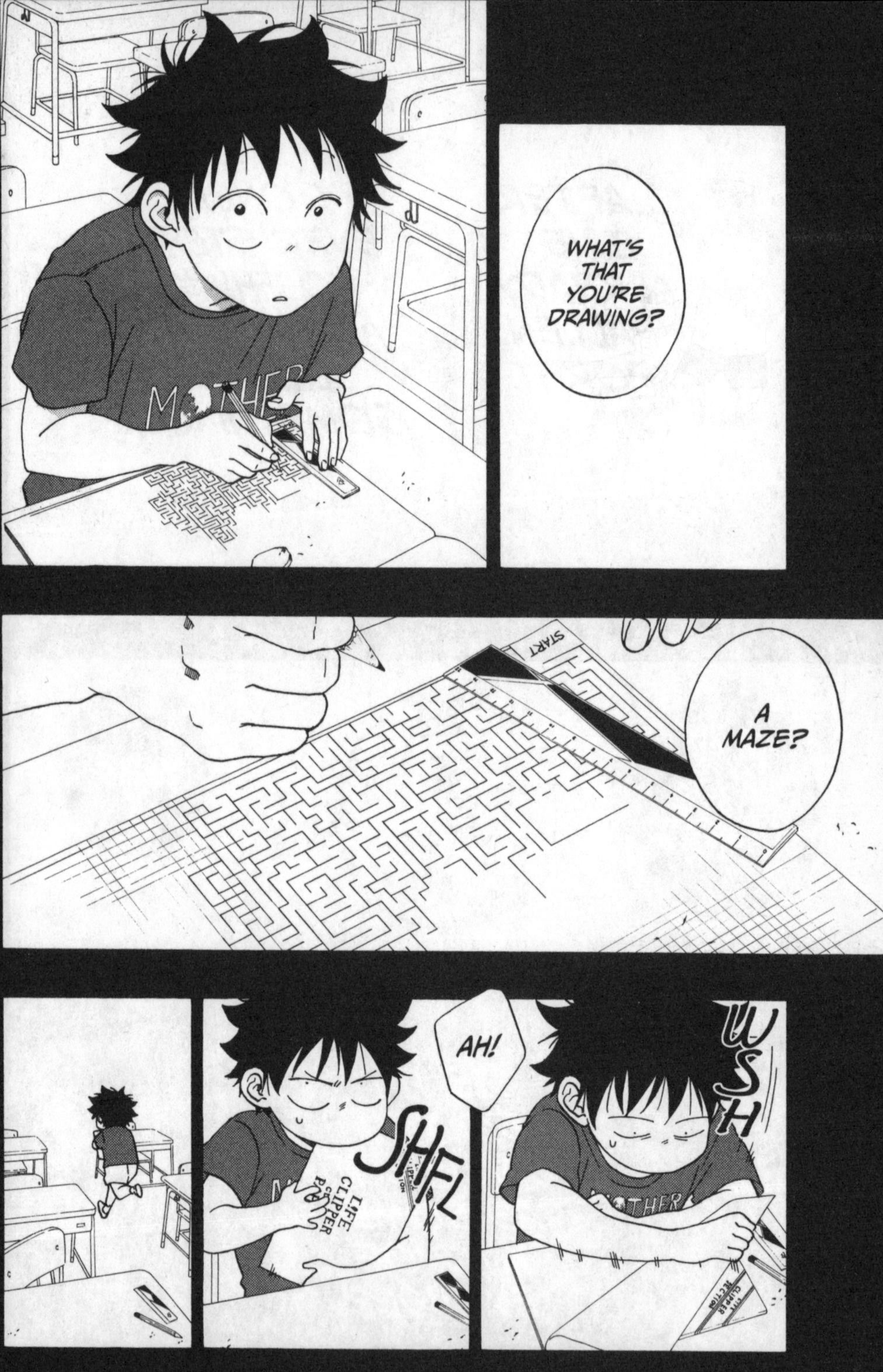
WHAT'S THAT YOU'RE DRAWING?
START
A MAZE?
WSH
AH!
SHFL

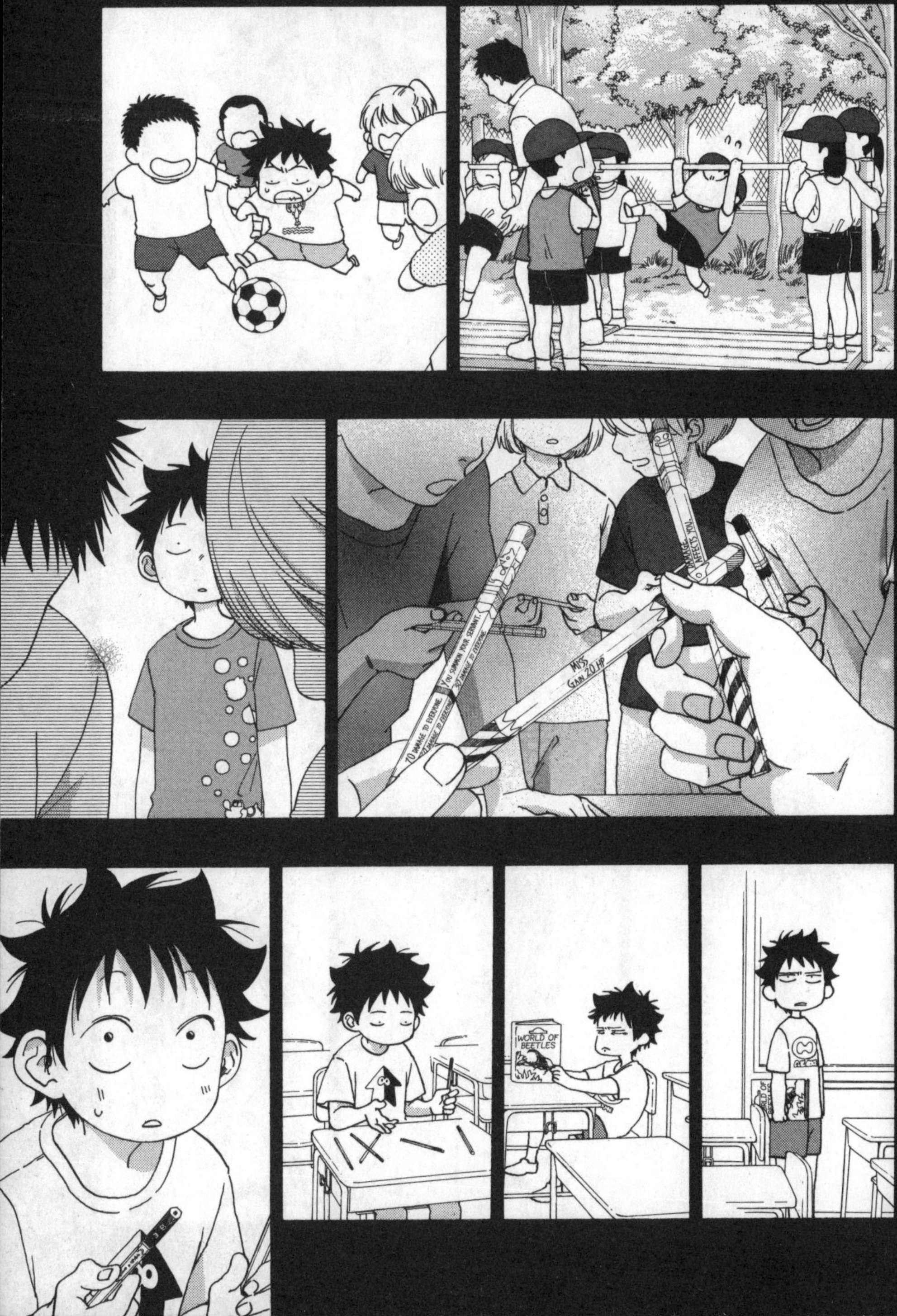
DAMAGE AFFECTS YOU.
MISS
GAIN 20 HP
YOU SUMMON YOUR SERVANT.
70 DAMAGE TO EVERYONE.
30 DAMAGE TO EVERYONE
WORLD OF BEETLES

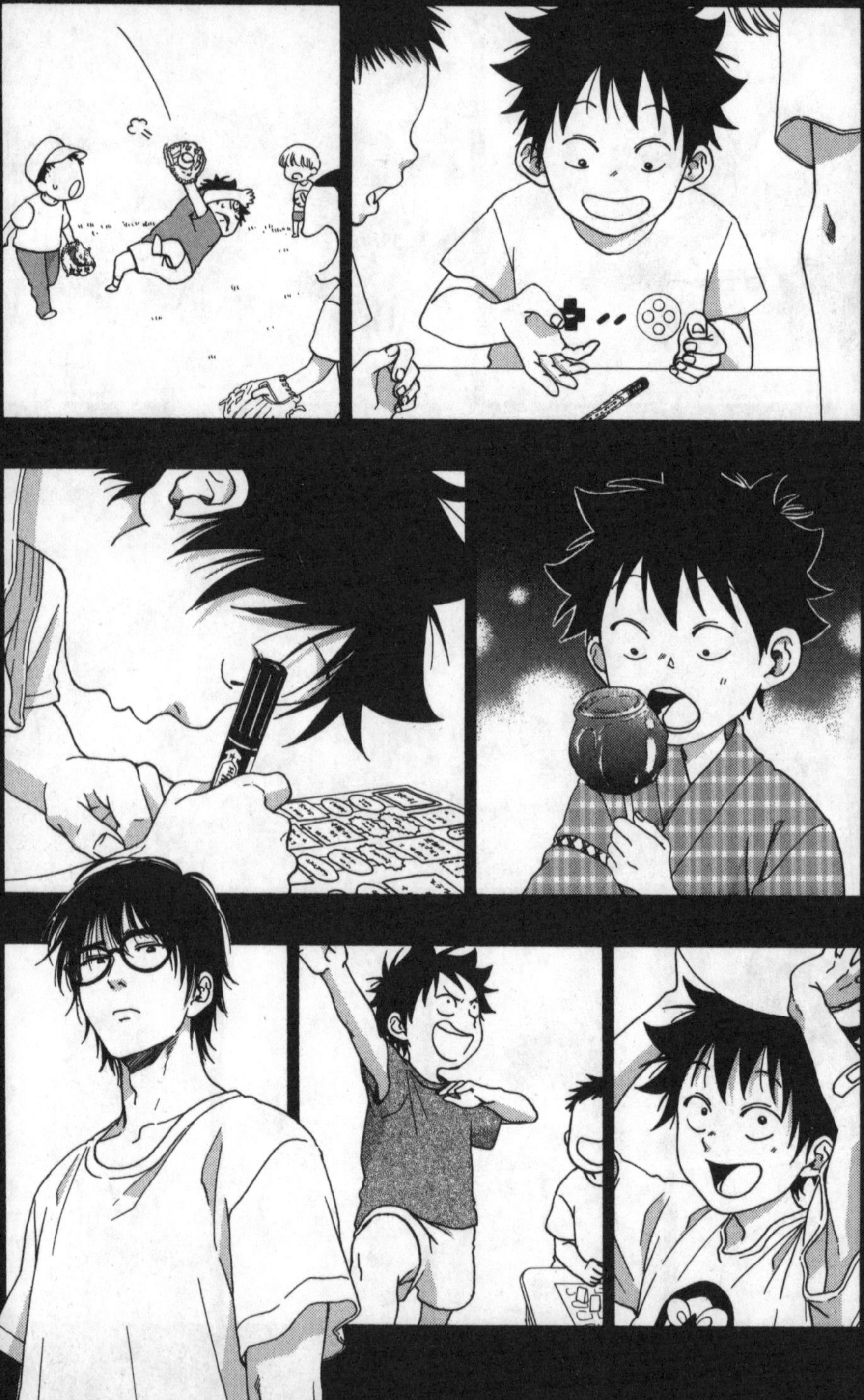

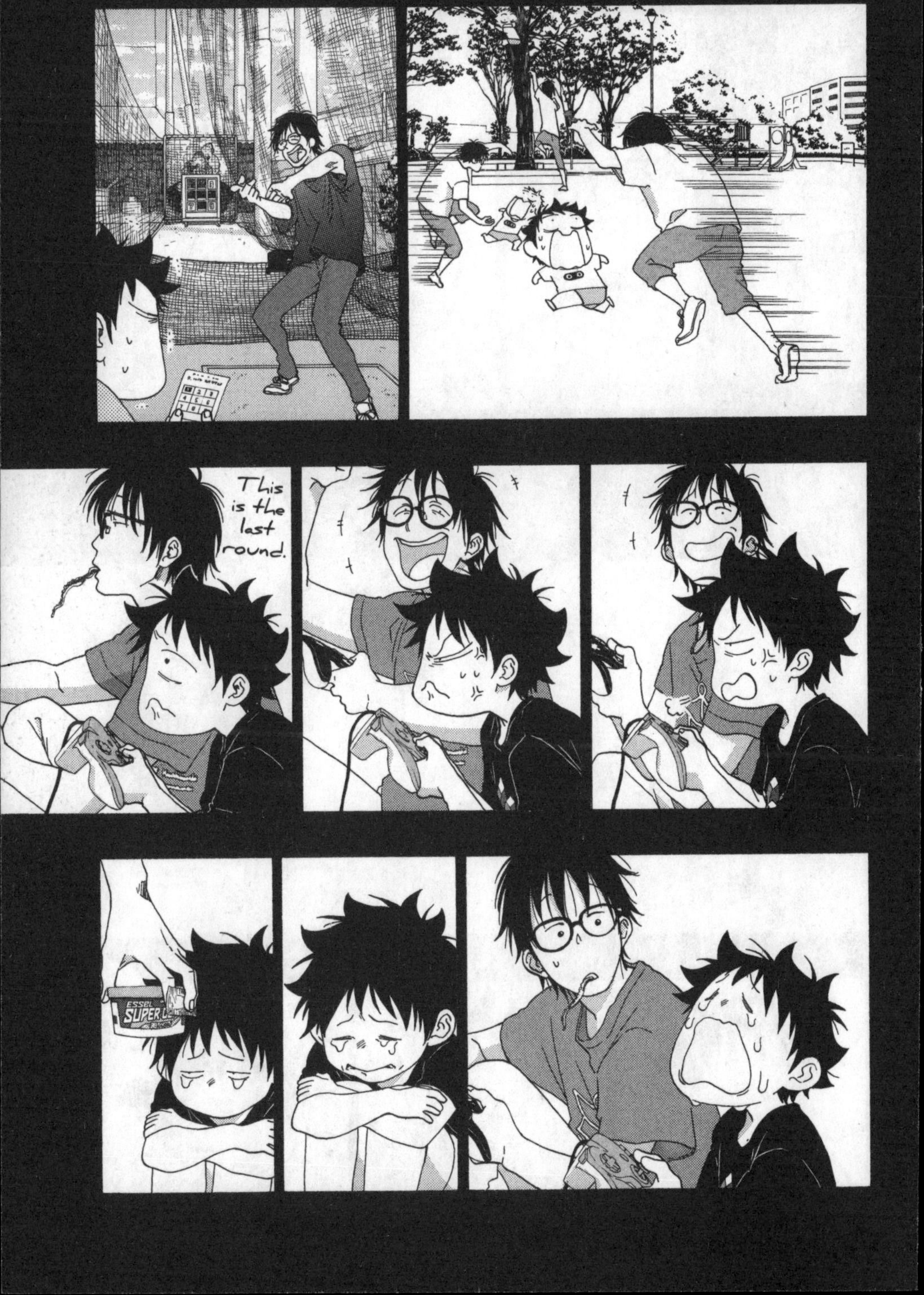
This is the last round.
ESSEL

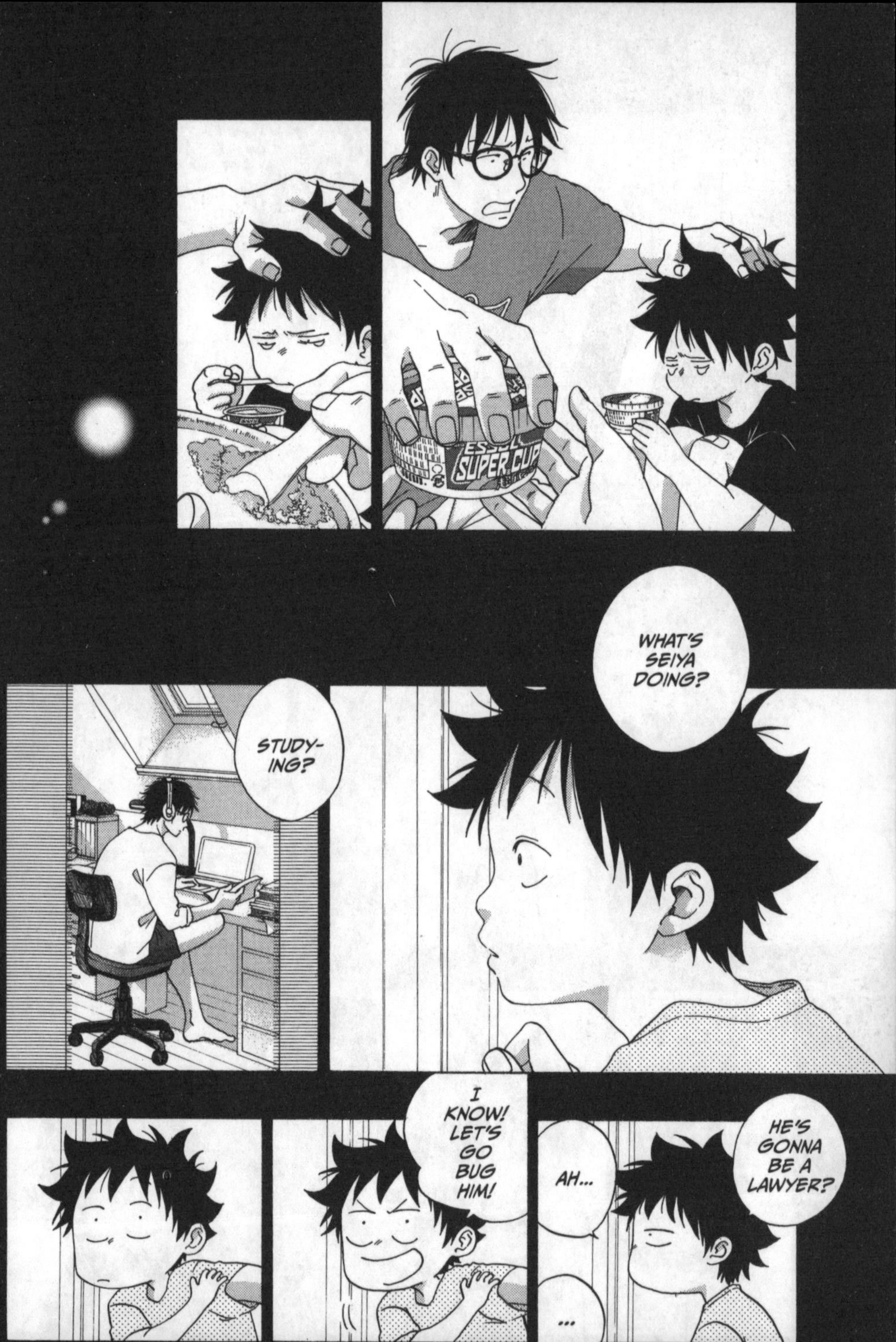
SUPER CUP
WHAT'S SEIYA DOING?
STUDY-ING?
HE'S GONNA BE A LAWYER?
AH...
...
I KNOW! LET'S GO BUG HIM!

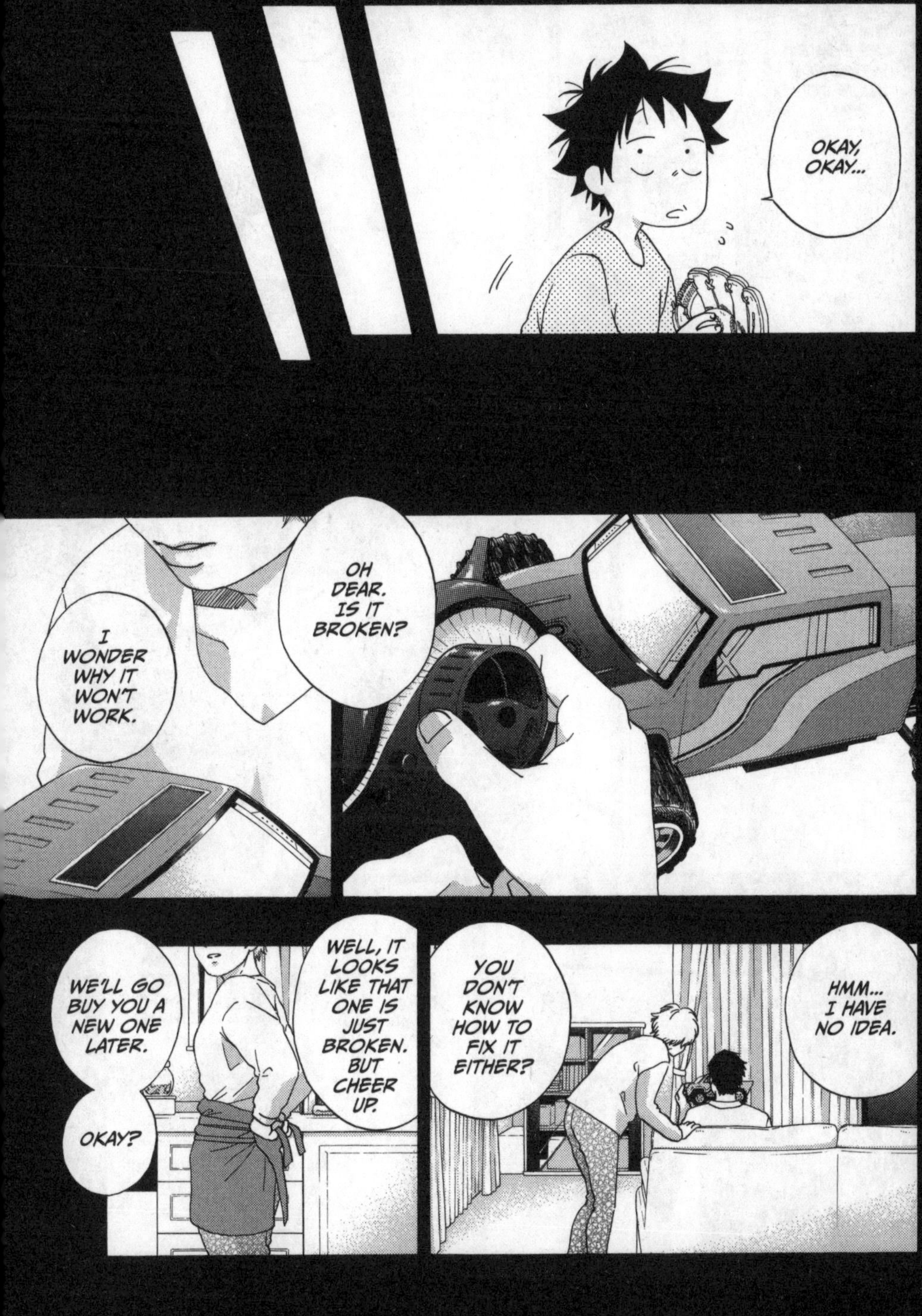
OKAY, OKAY...
OH DEAR. IS IT BROKEN?
I WONDER WHY IT WON'T WORK.
HMM... I HAVE NO IDEA.
YOU DON'T KNOW HOW TO FIX IT EITHER?
WELL, IT LOOKS LIKE THAT ONE IS JUST BROKEN. BUT CHEER UP.
WE'LL GO BUY YOU A NEW ONE LATER.
OKAY?

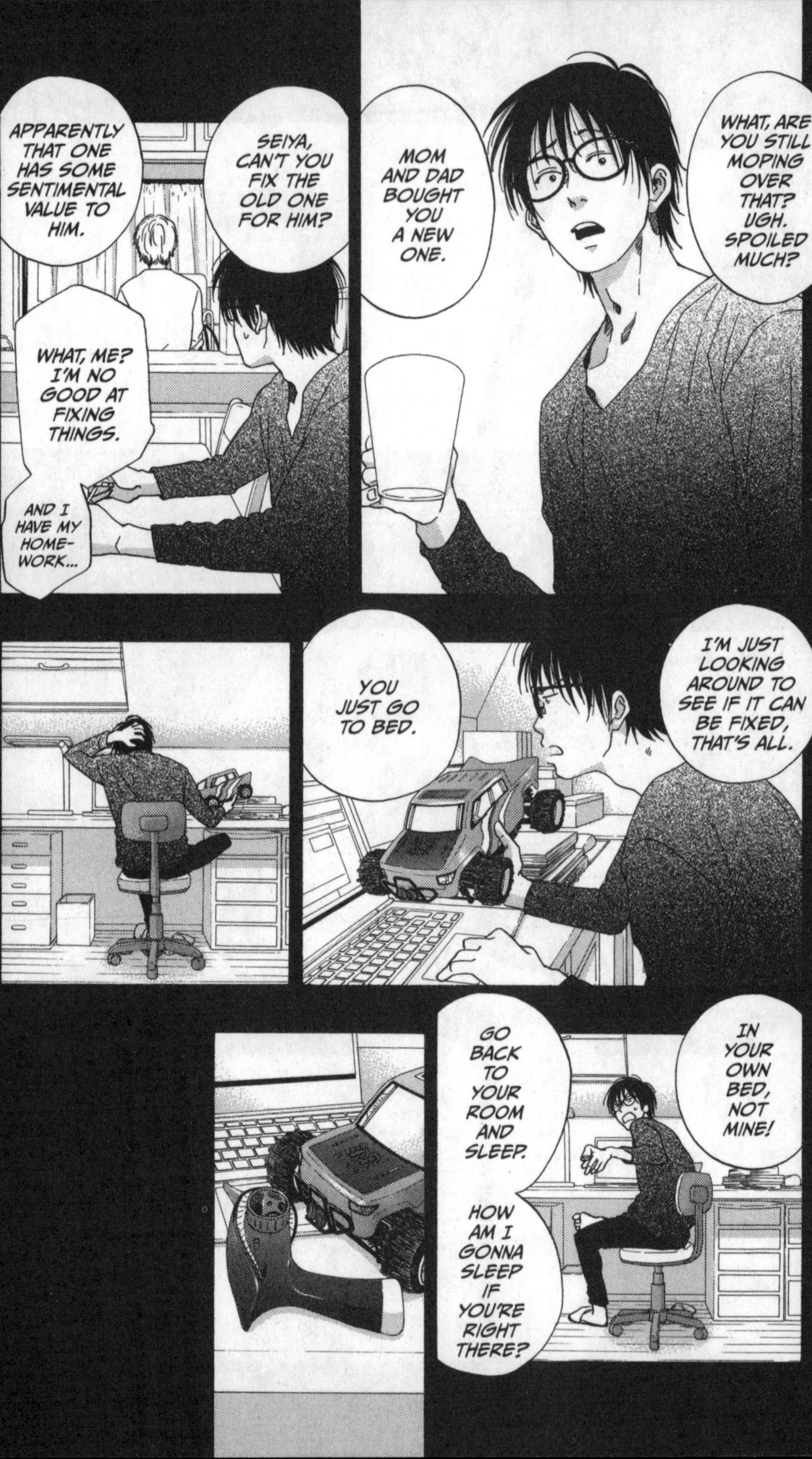
WHAT, ARE YOU STILL MOPING OVER THAT? UGH. SPOILED MUCH?
MOM AND DAD BOUGHT YOU A NEW ONE.
SEIYA, CAN'T YOU FIX THE OLD ONE FOR HIM?
APPARENTLY THAT ONE HAS SOME SENTIMENTAL VALUE TO HIM.
WHAT, ME? I'M NO GOOD AT FIXING THINGS.
AND I HAVE MY HOME-WORK...
I'M JUST LOOKING AROUND TO SEE IF IT CAN BE FIXED, THAT'S ALL.
YOU JUST GO TO BED.
IN YOUR OWN BED, NOT MINE!
GO BACK TO YOUR ROOM AND SLEEP.
HOW AM I GONNA SLEEP IF YOU'RE RIGHT THERE?

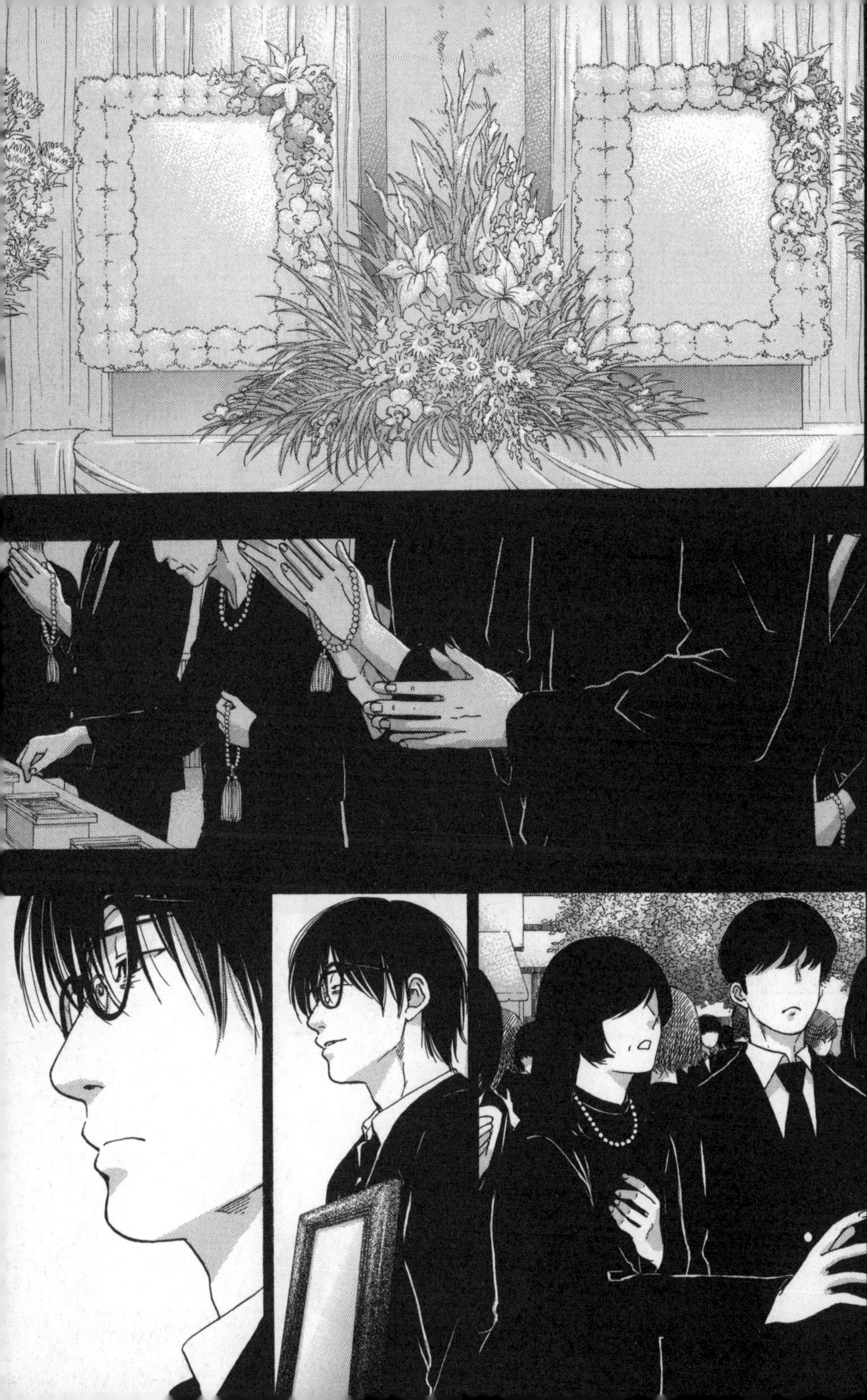

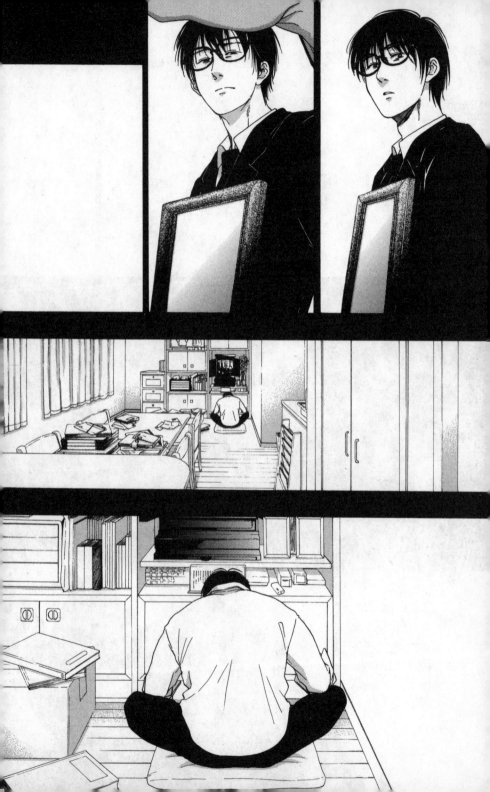

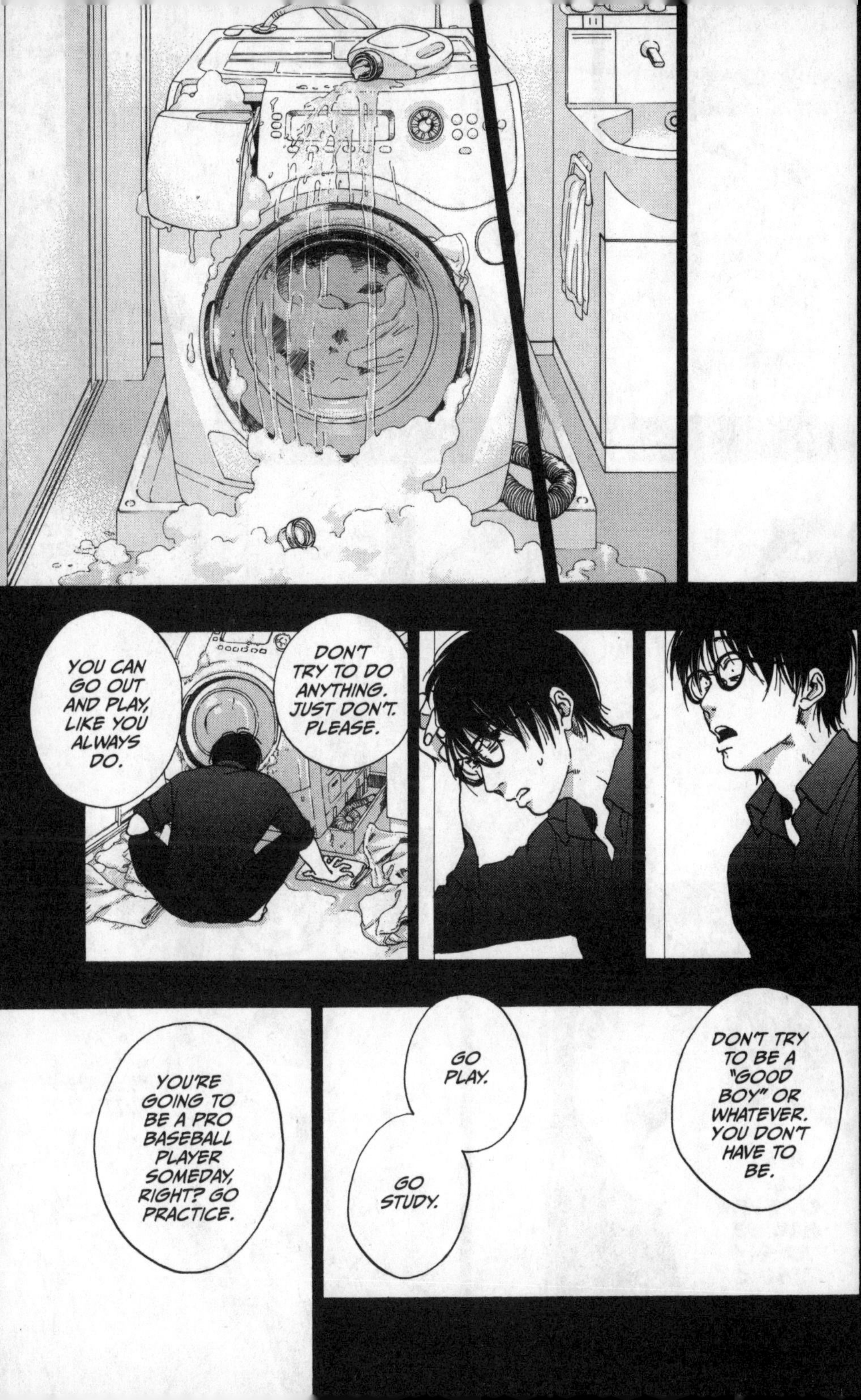
DON'T TRY TO DO ANYTHING. JUST DON'T. PLEASE.
YOU CAN GO OUT AND PLAY, LIKE YOU ALWAYS DO.
DON'T TRY TO BE A "GOOD BOY" OR WHATEVER. YOU DON'T HAVE TO BE.
GO PLAY.
GO STUDY.
YOU'RE GOING TO BE A PRO BASEBALL PLAYER SOMEDAY, RIGHT? GO PRACTICE.

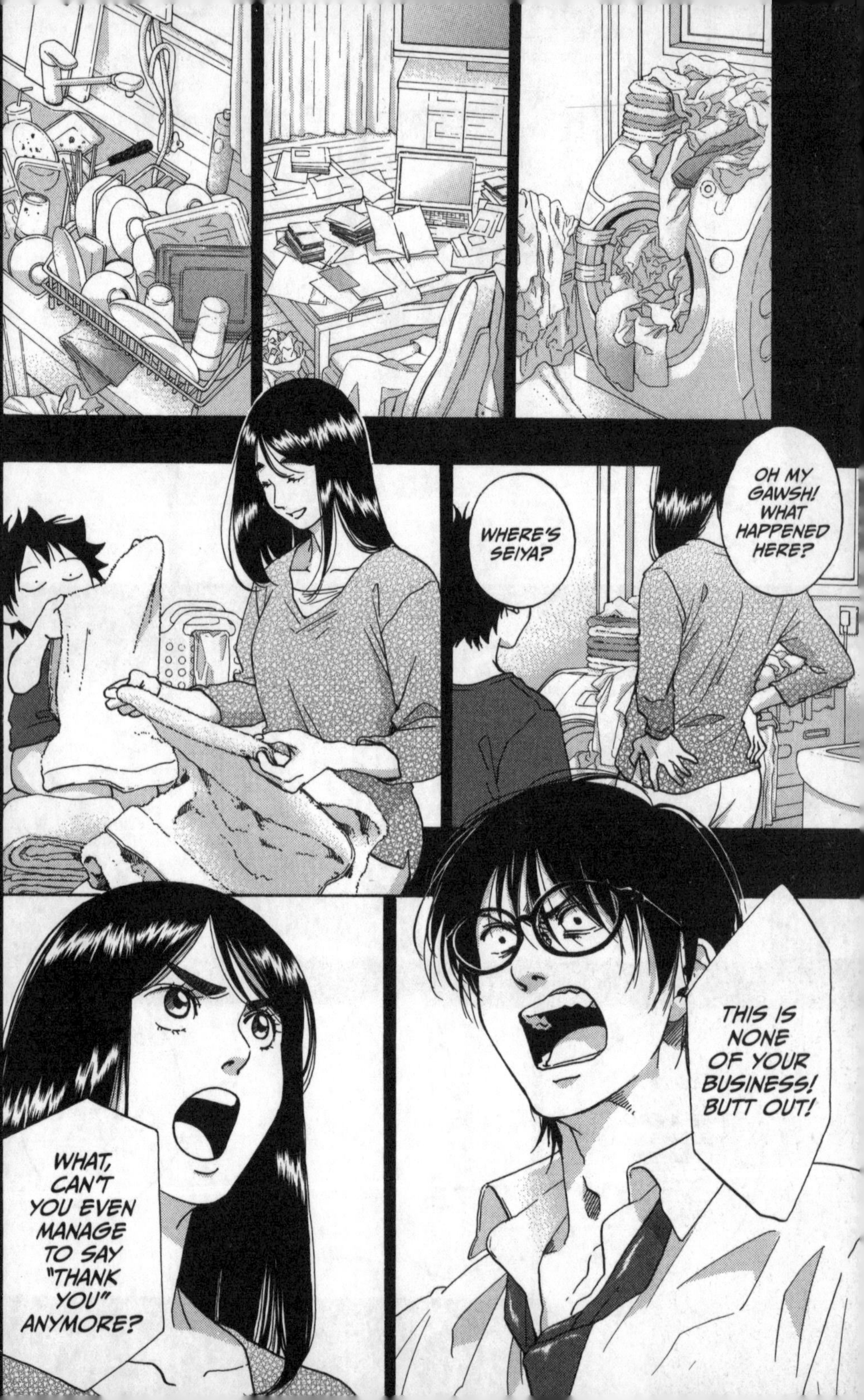
OH MY GAWSH! WHAT HAPPENED HERE?
WHERE'S SEIYA?
THIS IS NONE OF YOUR BUSINESS! BUTT OUT!
WHAT, CAN'T YOU EVEN MANAGE TO SAY "THANK YOU" ANYMORE?

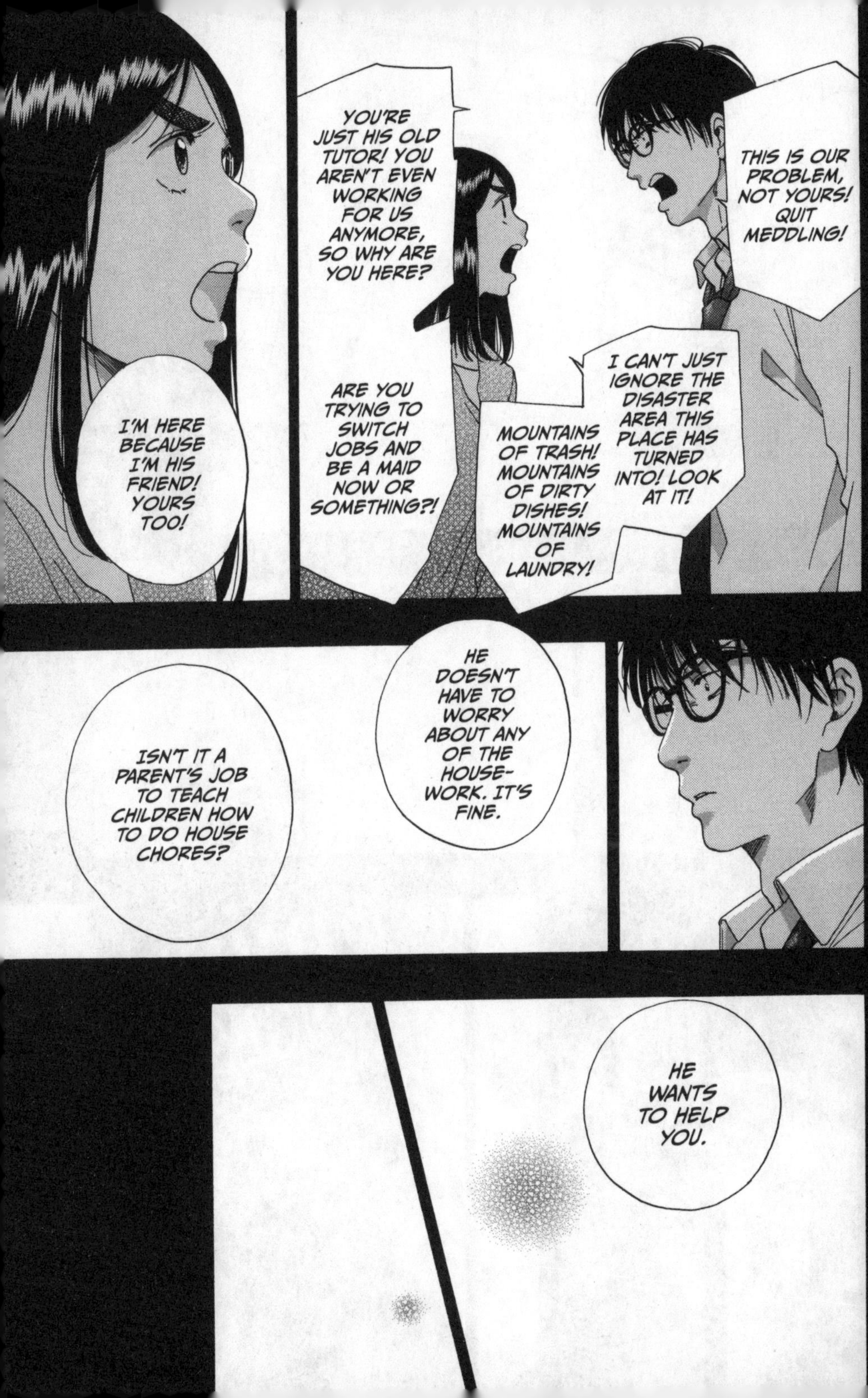

THIS IS OUR PROBLEM, NOT YOURS! QUIT MEDDLING!
YOU'RE JUST HIS OLD TUTOR! YOU AREN'T EVEN WORKING FOR US ANYMORE, SO WHY ARE YOU HERE?
I CAN'T JUST IGNORE THE DISASTER AREA THIS PLACE HAS TURNED INTO! LOOK AT IT!
MOUNTAINS OF TRASH! MOUNTAINS OF DIRTY DISHES! MOUNTAINS OF LAUNDRY!
ARE YOU TRYING TO SWITCH JOBS AND BE A MAID NOW OR SOMETHING?!
I'M HERE BECAUSE I'M HIS FRIEND! YOURS TOO!
HE DOESN'T HAVE TO WORRY ABOUT ANY OF THE HOUSE-WORK. IT'S FINE.
ISN'T IT A PARENT'S JOB TO TEACH CHILDREN HOW TO DO HOUSE CHORES?
HE WANTS TO HELP YOU.

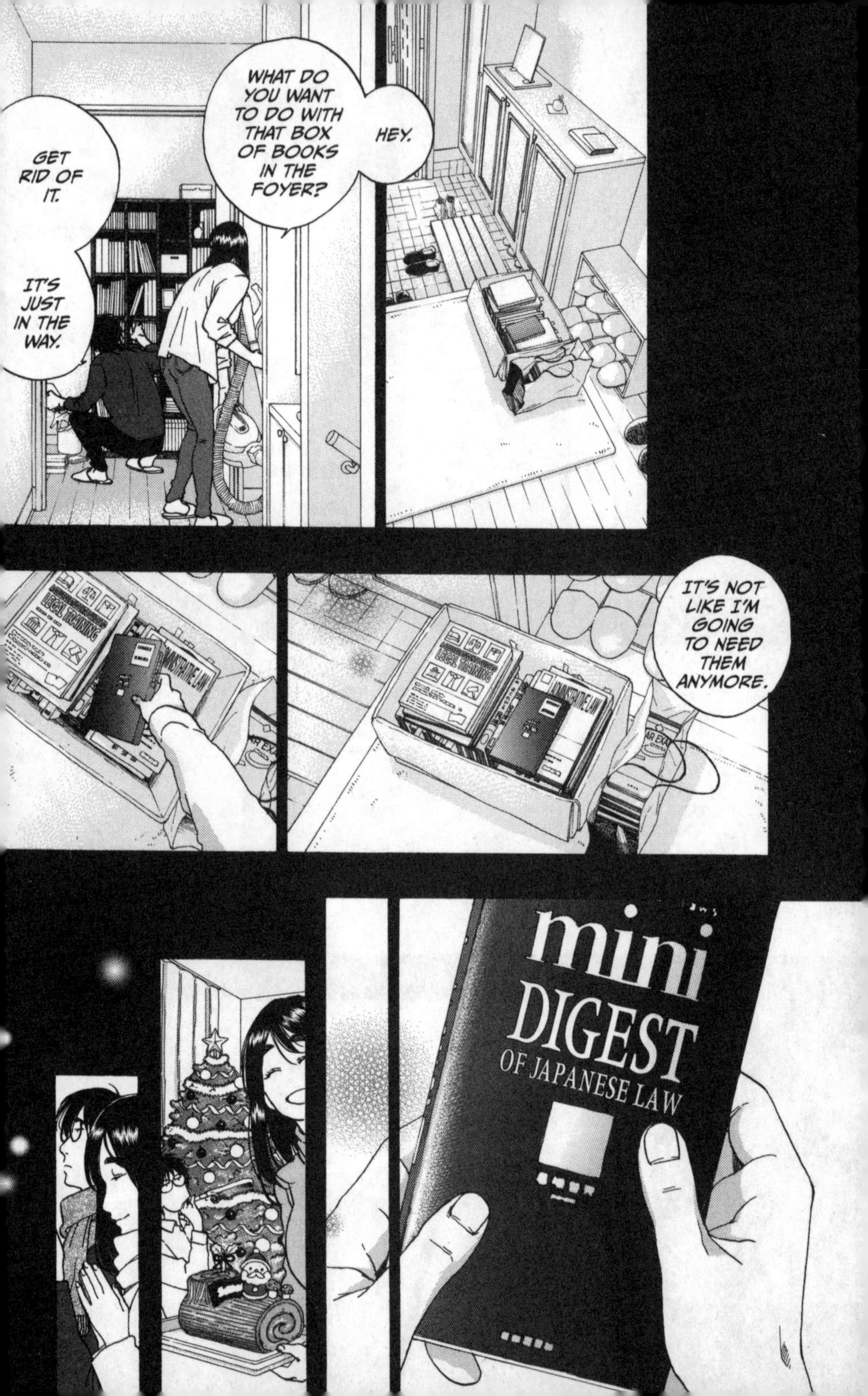
HEY.
WHAT DO YOU WANT TO DO WITH THAT BOX OF BOOKS IN THE FOYER?
GET RID OF IT.
IT'S JUST IN THE WAY.
IT'S NOT LIKE I'M GOING TO NEED THEM ANYMORE.
mini DIGEST OF JAPANESE LAW

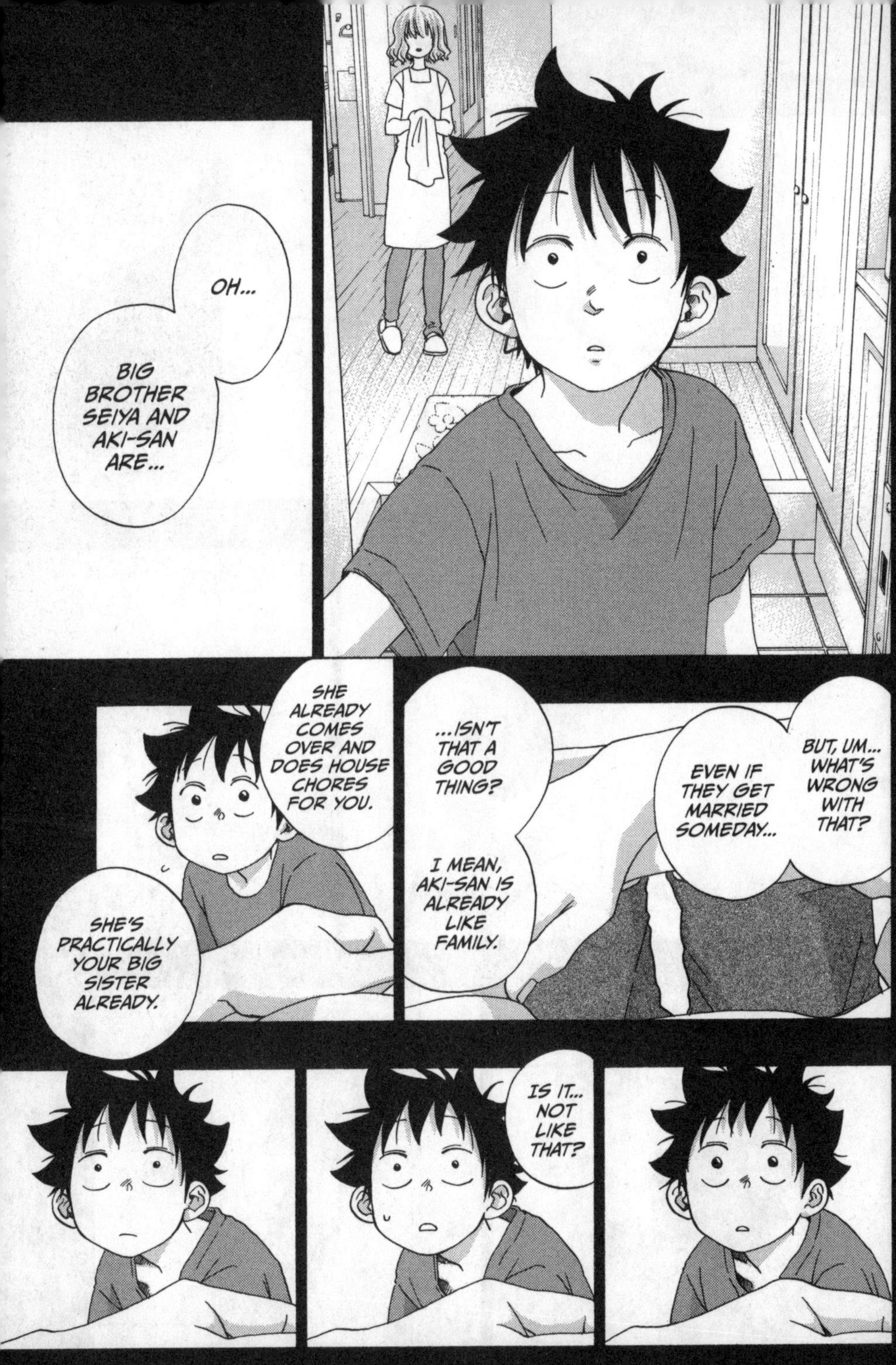
OH...
BIG BROTHER SEIYA AND AKI-SAN ARE...
BUT, UM... WHAT'S WRONG WITH THAT?
EVEN IF THEY GET MARRIED SOMEDAY...
...ISN'T THAT A GOOD THING?
I MEAN, AKI-SAN IS ALREADY LIKE FAMILY.
SHE ALREADY COMES OVER AND DOES HOUSE CHORES FOR YOU.
SHE'S PRACTICALLY YOUR BIG SISTER ALREADY.
IS IT... NOT LIKE THAT?

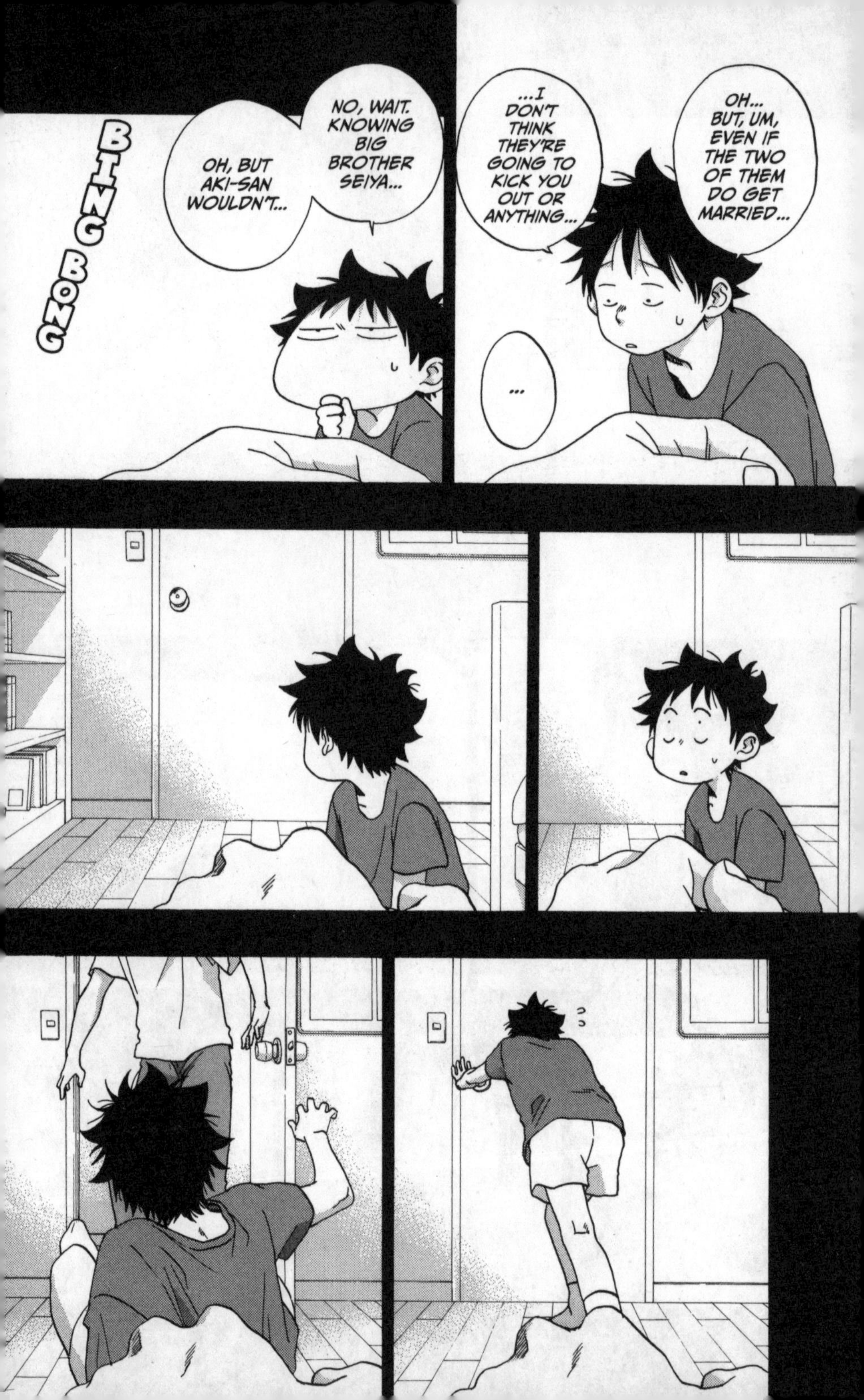
OH... BUT, UM, EVEN IF THE TWO OF THEM DO GET MARRIED...
...I DON'T THINK THEY'RE GOING TO KICK YOU OUT OR ANYTHING...
...
NO, WAIT. KNOWING BIG BROTHER SEIYA...
OH, BUT AKI-SAN WOULDN'T...
BING BONG

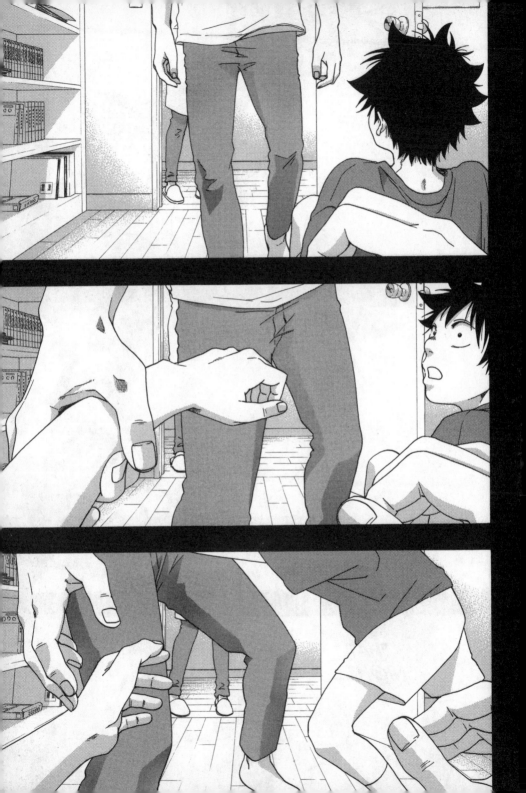

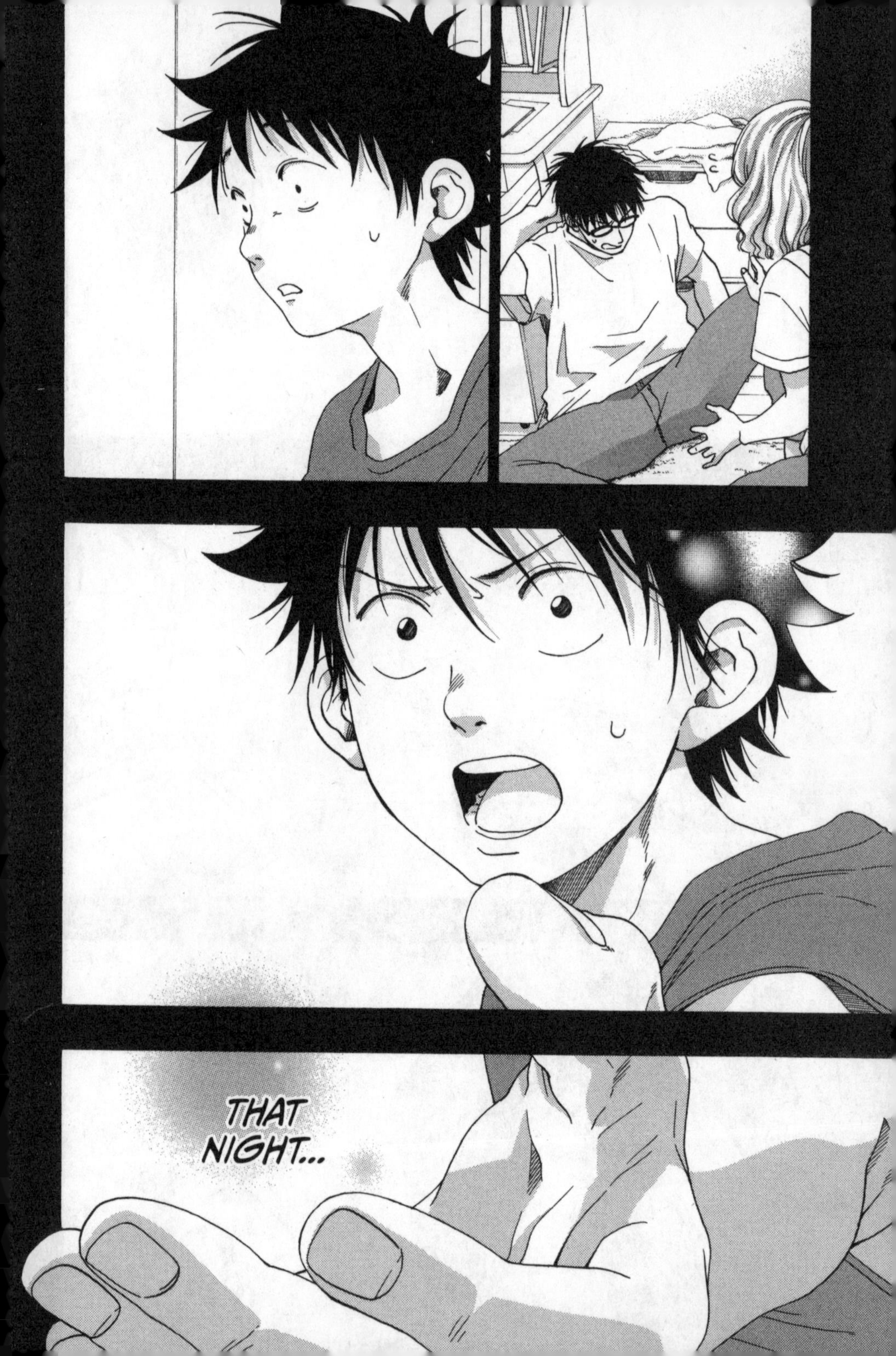
THAT NIGHT...

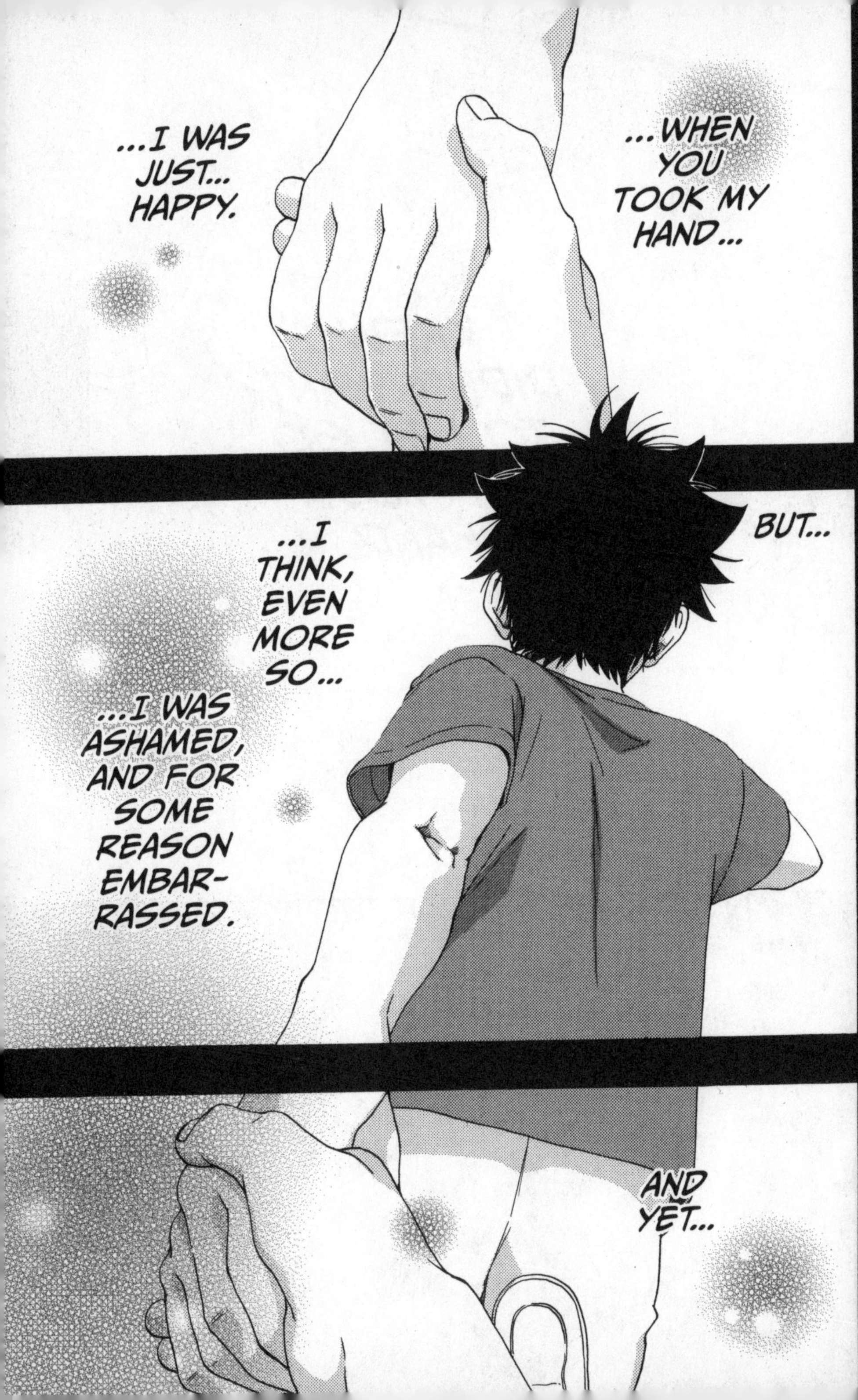
...WHEN YOU TOOK MY HAND...
...I WAS JUST... HAPPY.
BUT...
...I THINK, EVEN MORE SO...
...I WAS ASHAMED, AND FOR SOME REASON EMBAR-RASSED.
AND YET...

I KNEW I
DIDN'T WANT
TO LET GO
OF YOUR
HAND.

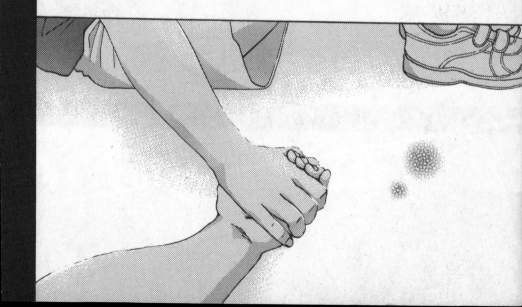

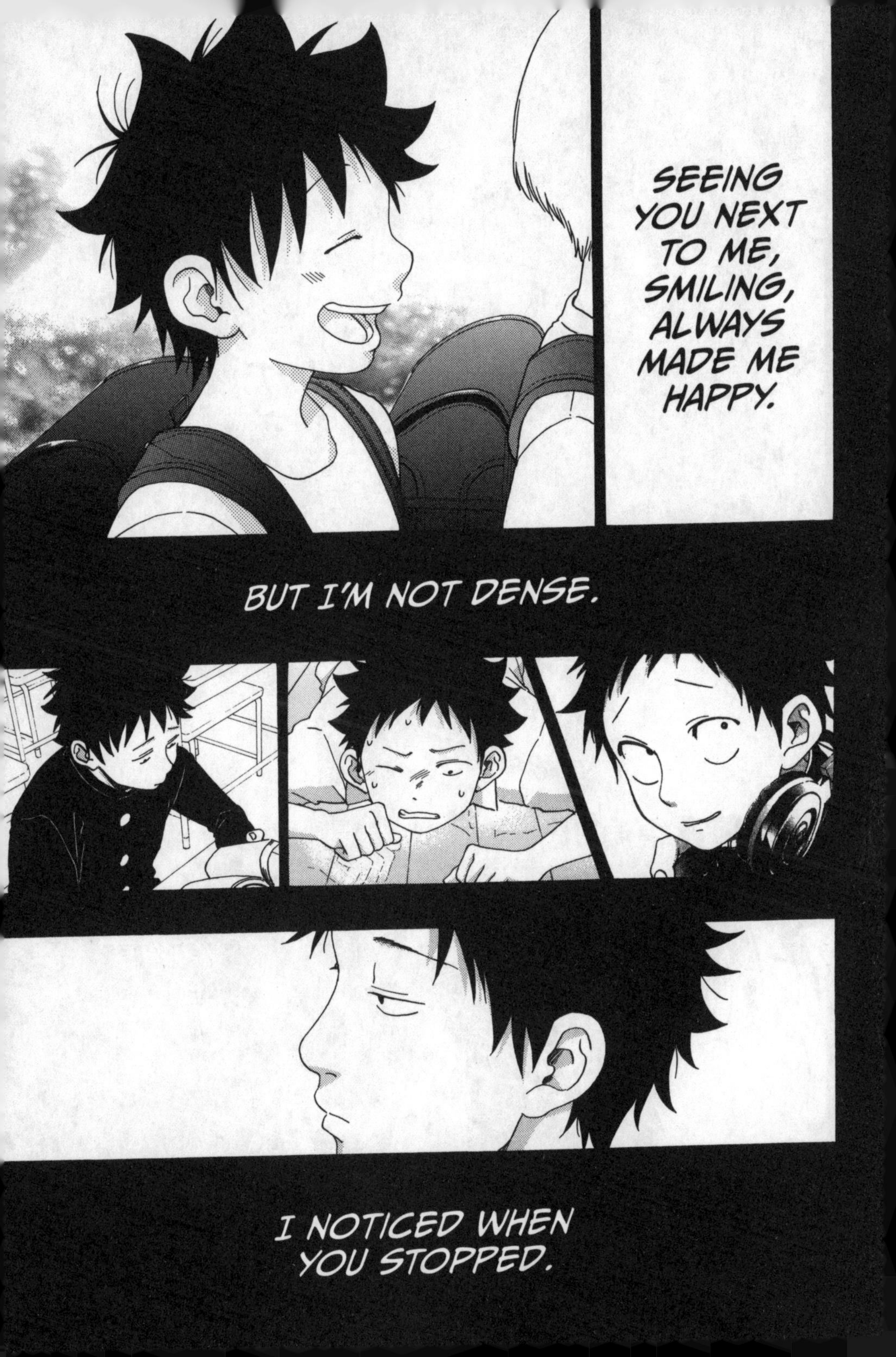
SEEING YOU NEXT TO ME, SMILING, ALWAYS MADE ME HAPPY.
BUT I'M NOT DENSE.
I NOTICED WHEN YOU STOPPED.

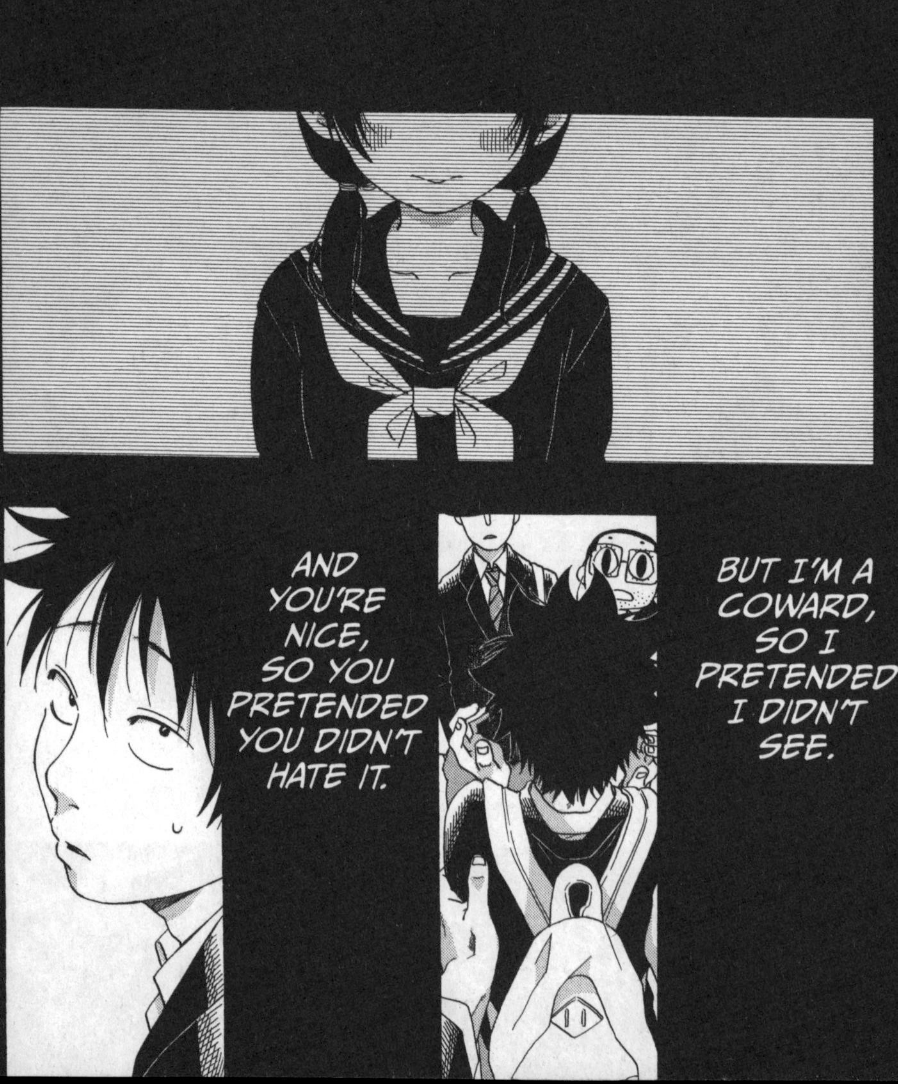
BUT I'M A COWARD, SO I PRETENDED I DIDN'T SEE.
AND YOU'RE NICE, SO YOU PRETENDED YOU DIDN'T HATE IT.

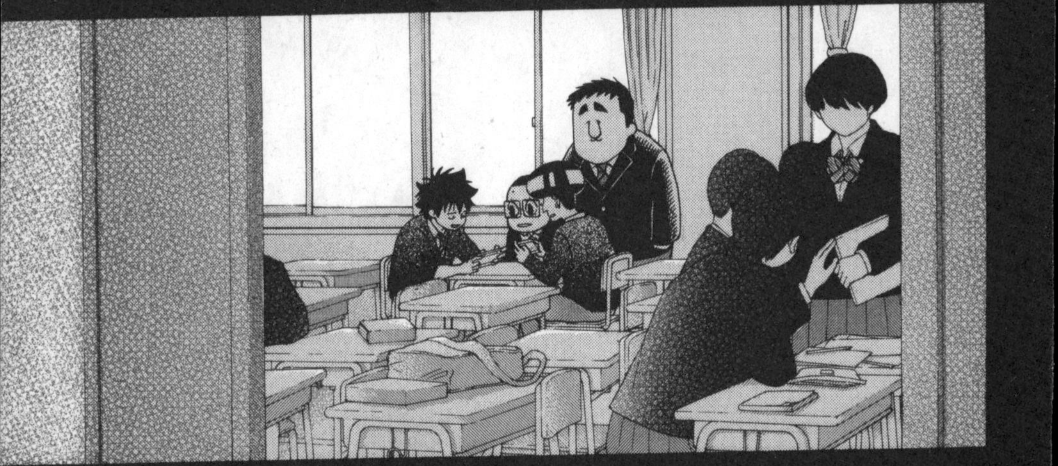

I'M SORRY.

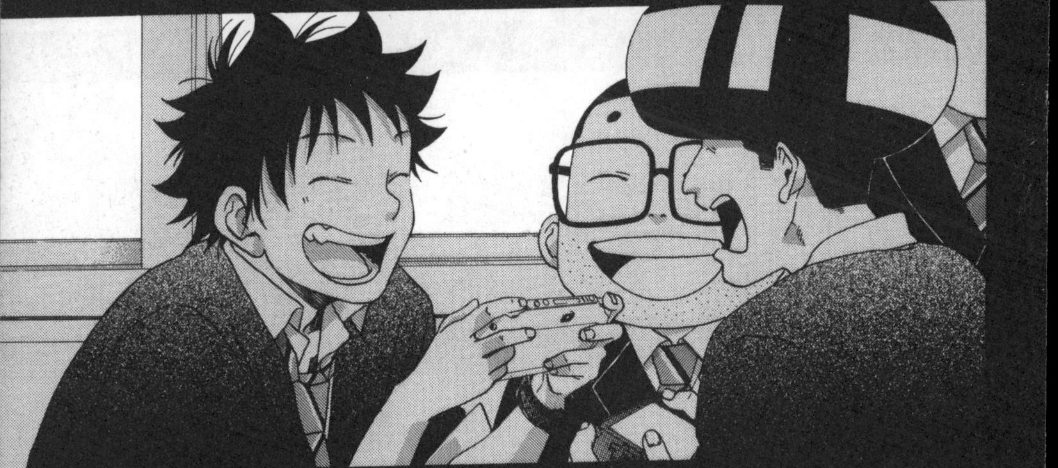

WHAT DO I HAVE TO DO...?

HOW CAN WE GO BACK TO HOW WE USED TO BE...?

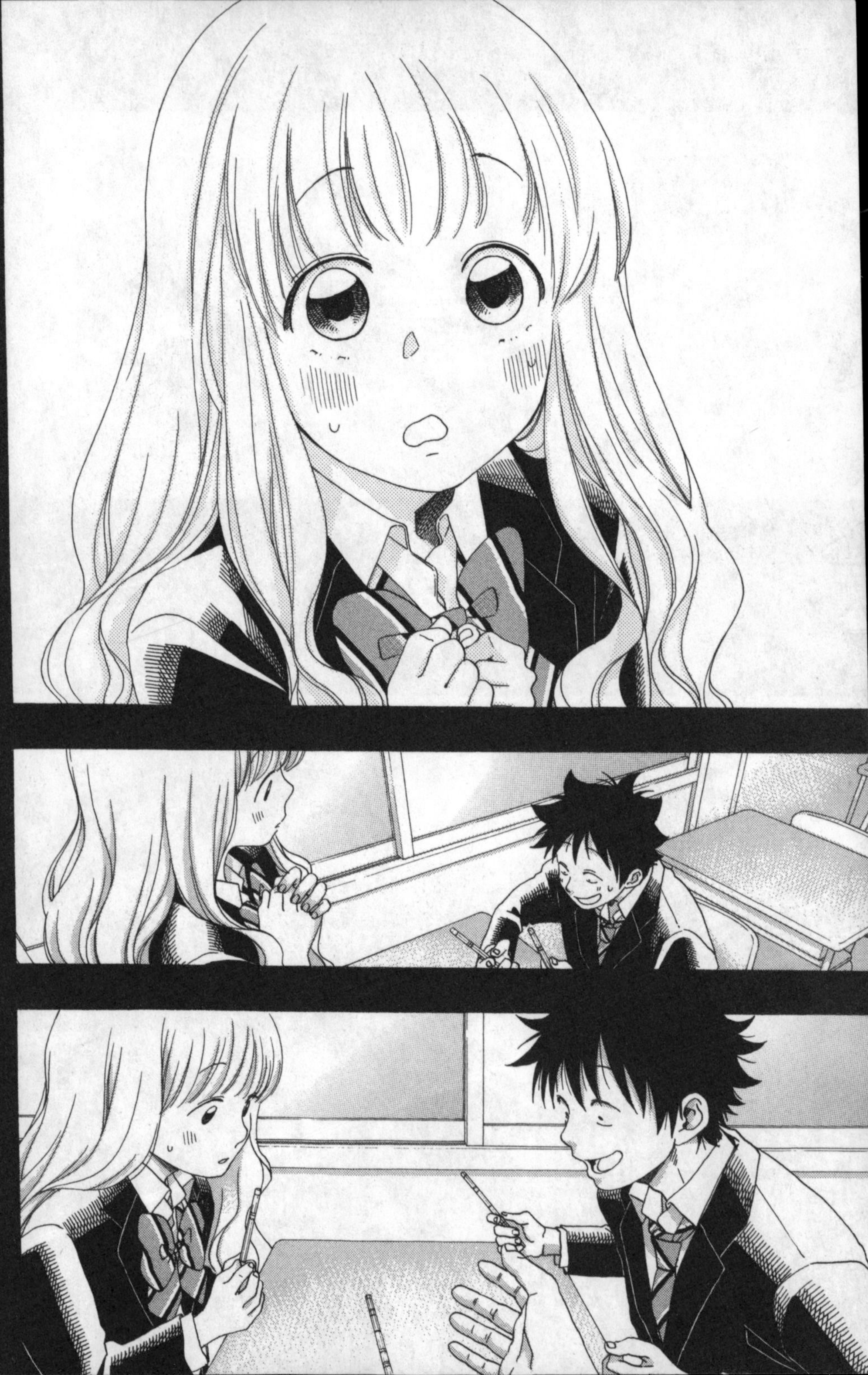

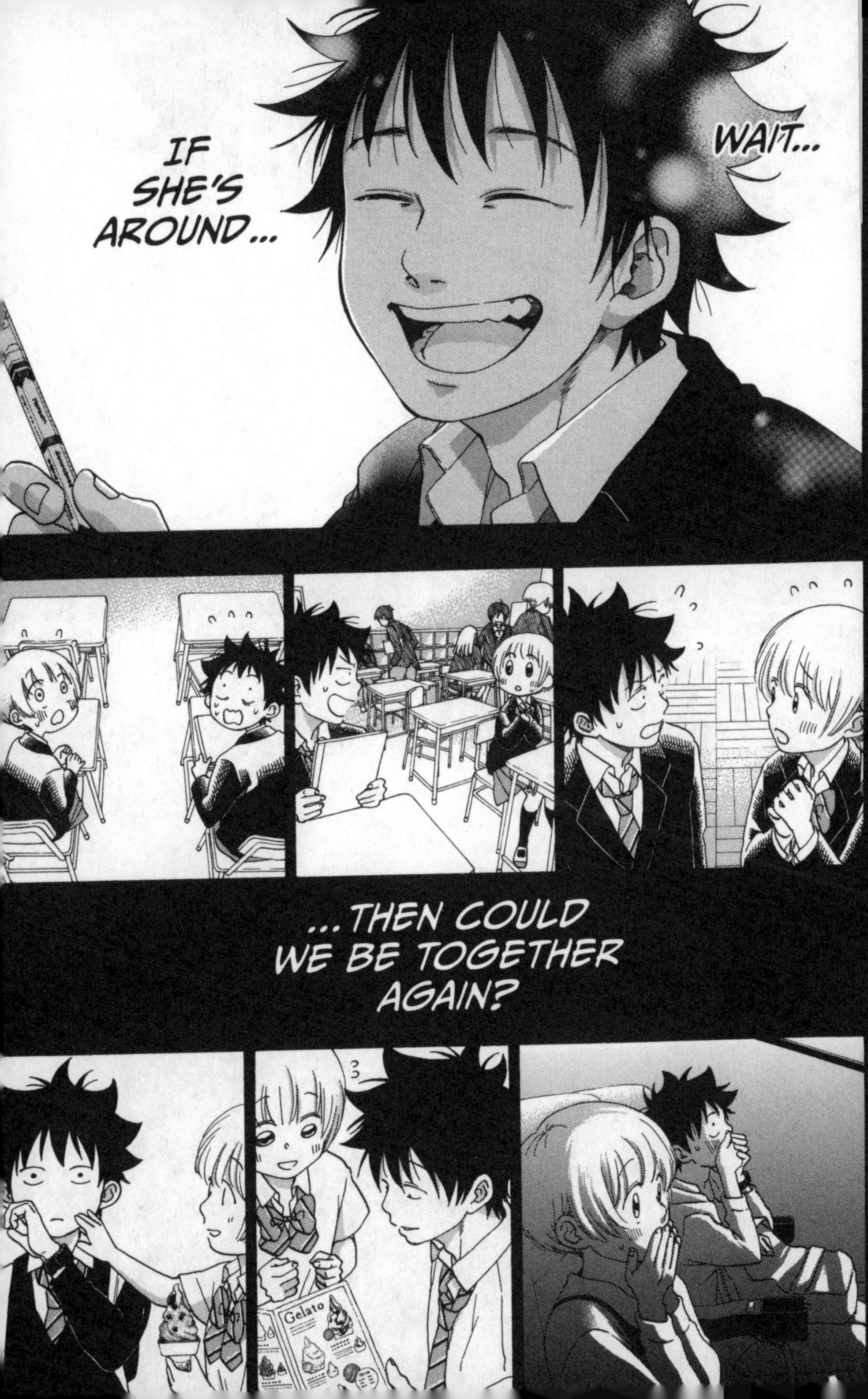
WAIT...
IF SHE'S AROUND...
...THEN COULD WE BE TOGETHER AGAIN?
Gelato

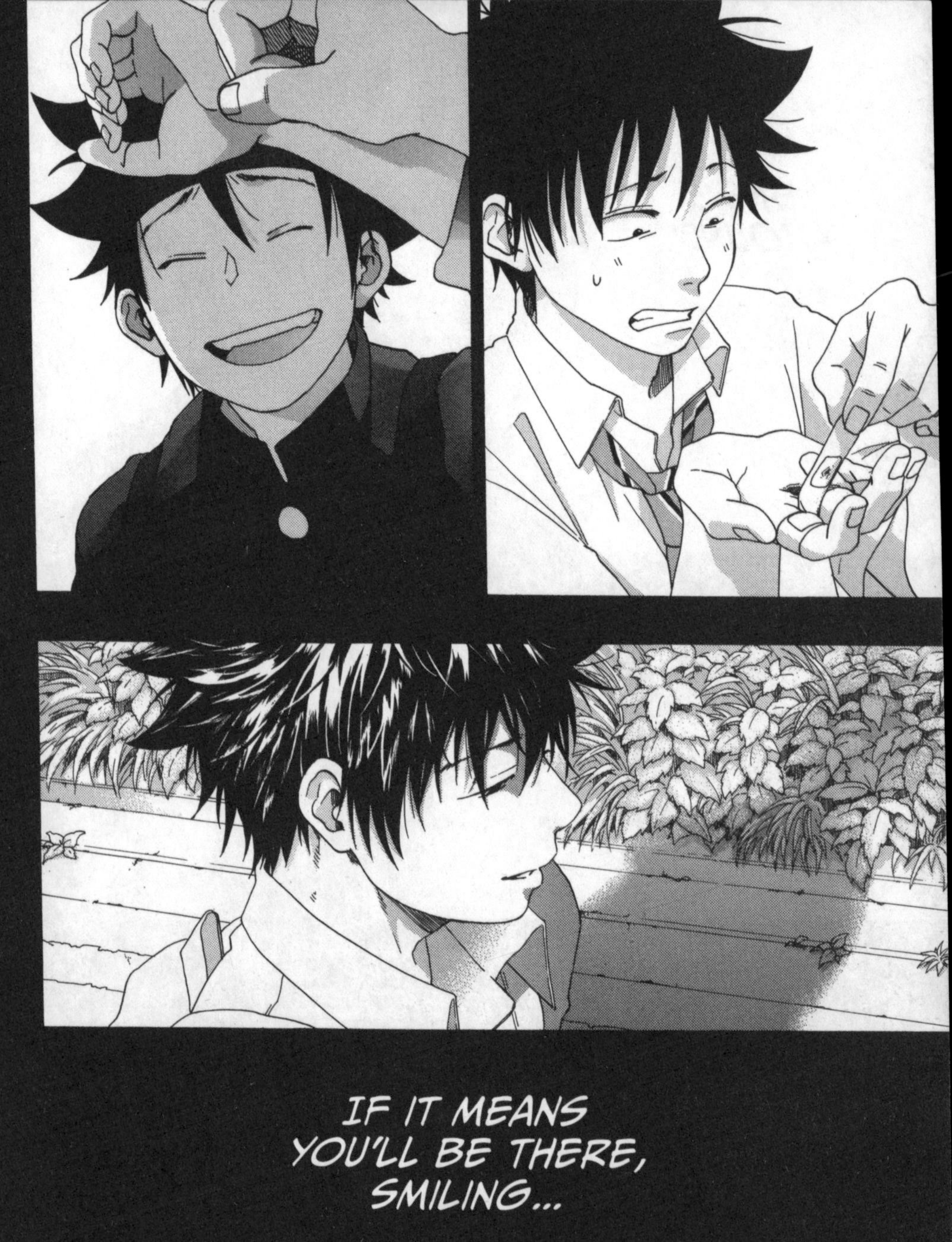
IF IT MEANS YOU'LL BE THERE, SMILING...

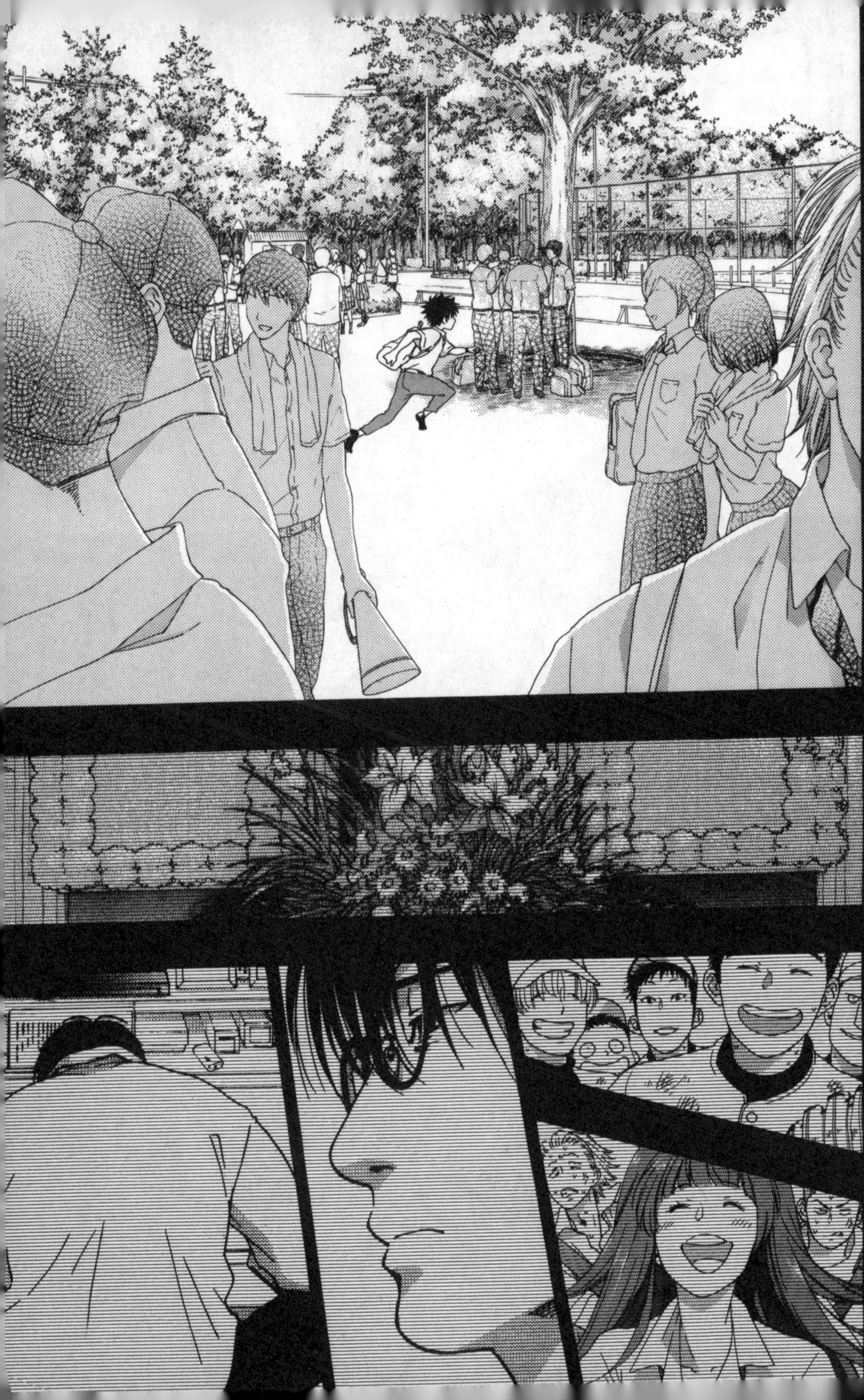

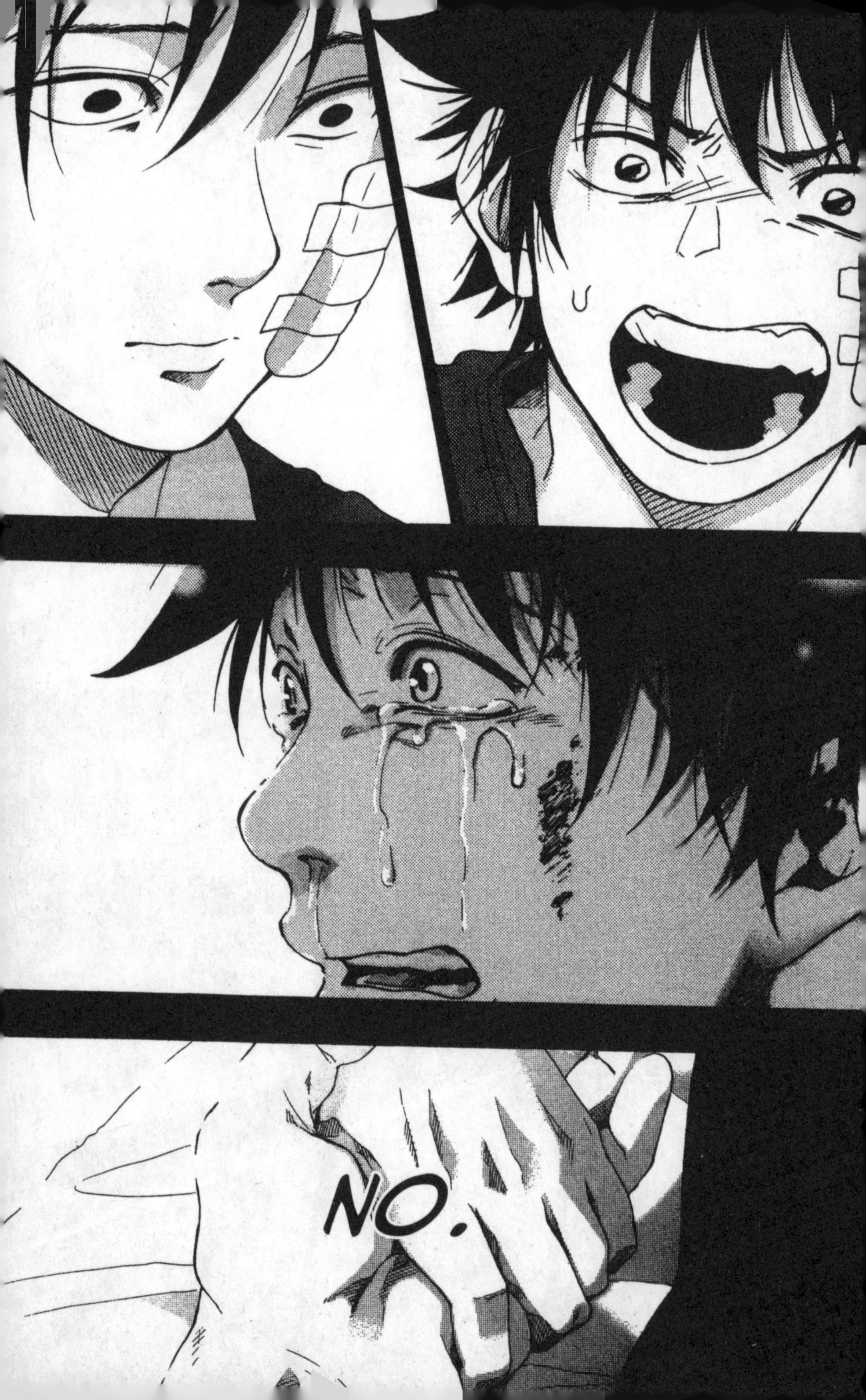
NO.

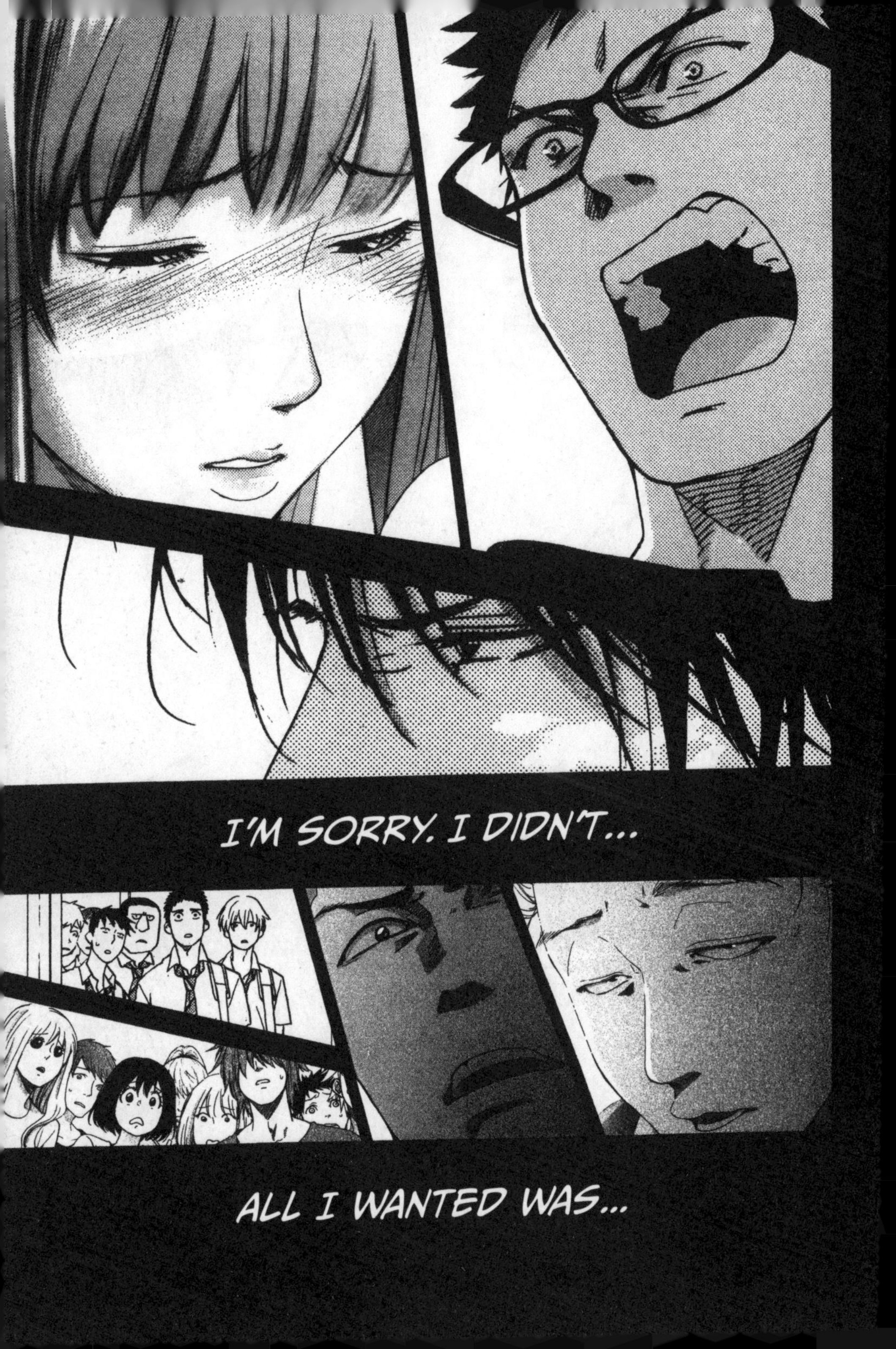
I'M SORRY. I DIDN'T...
ALL I WANTED WAS...

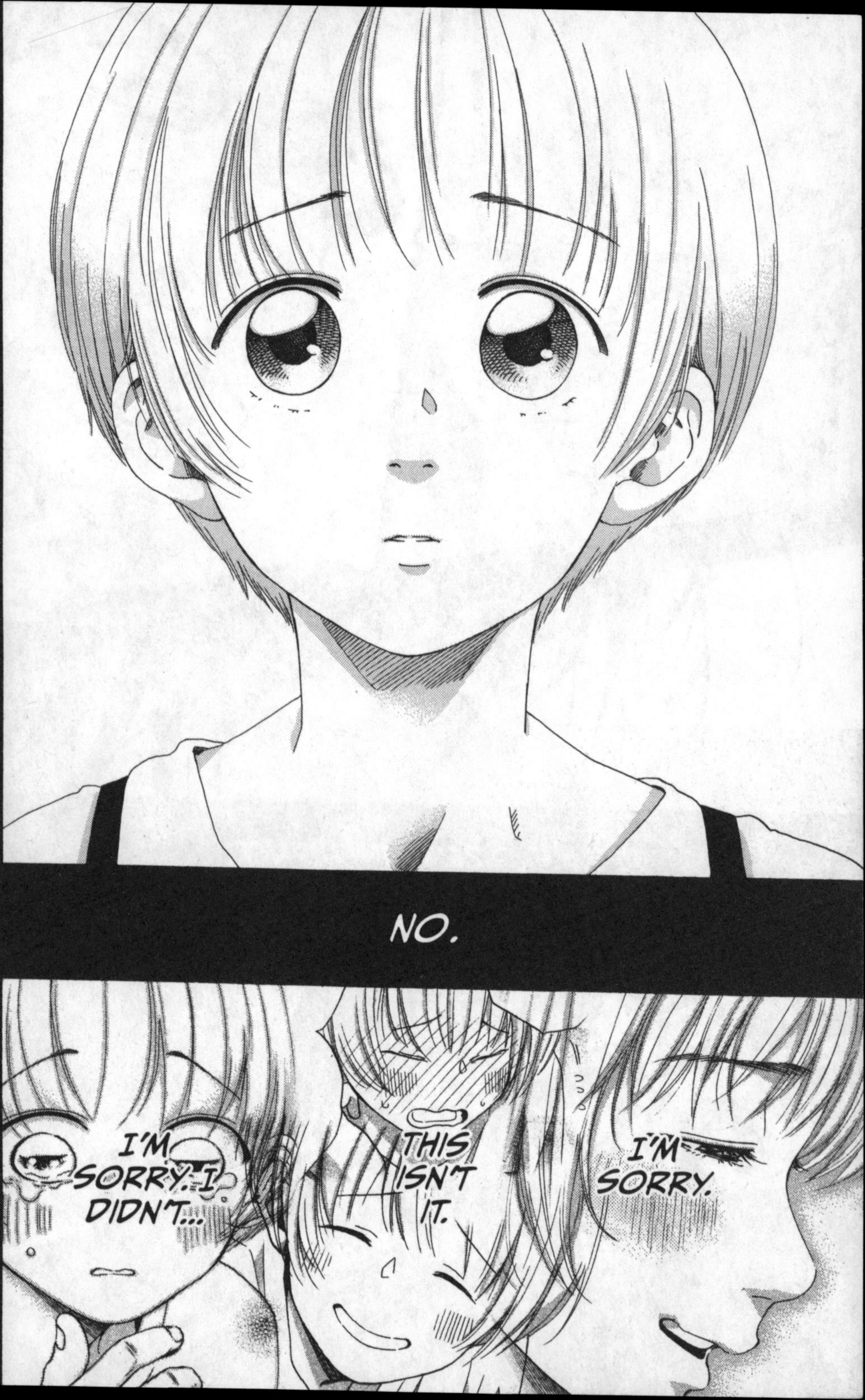
NO.
I'M SORRY.
THIS ISN'T IT.
I'M SORRY. I DIDN'T...

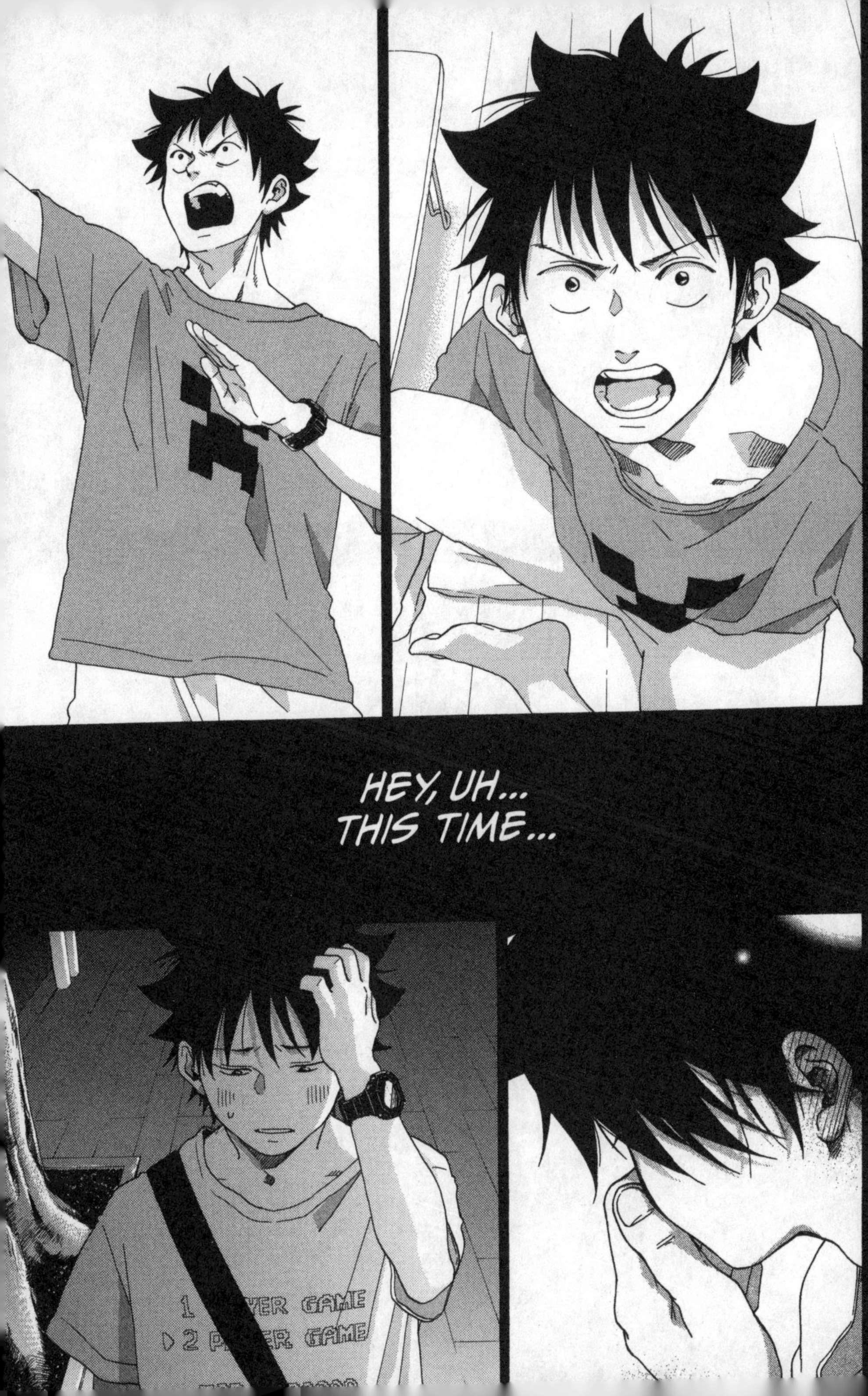
HEY, UH...
THIS TIME...

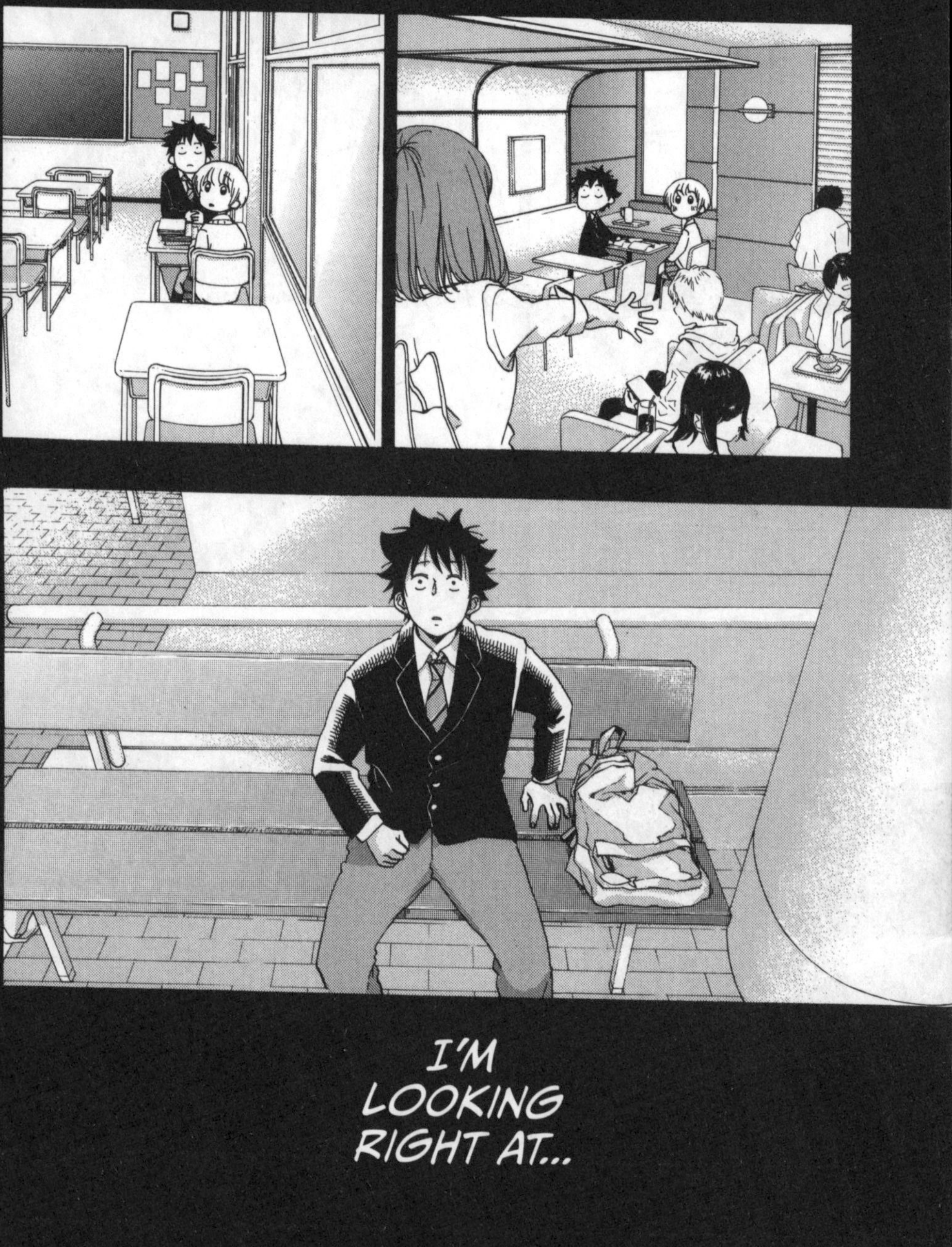
I'M LOOKING RIGHT AT...

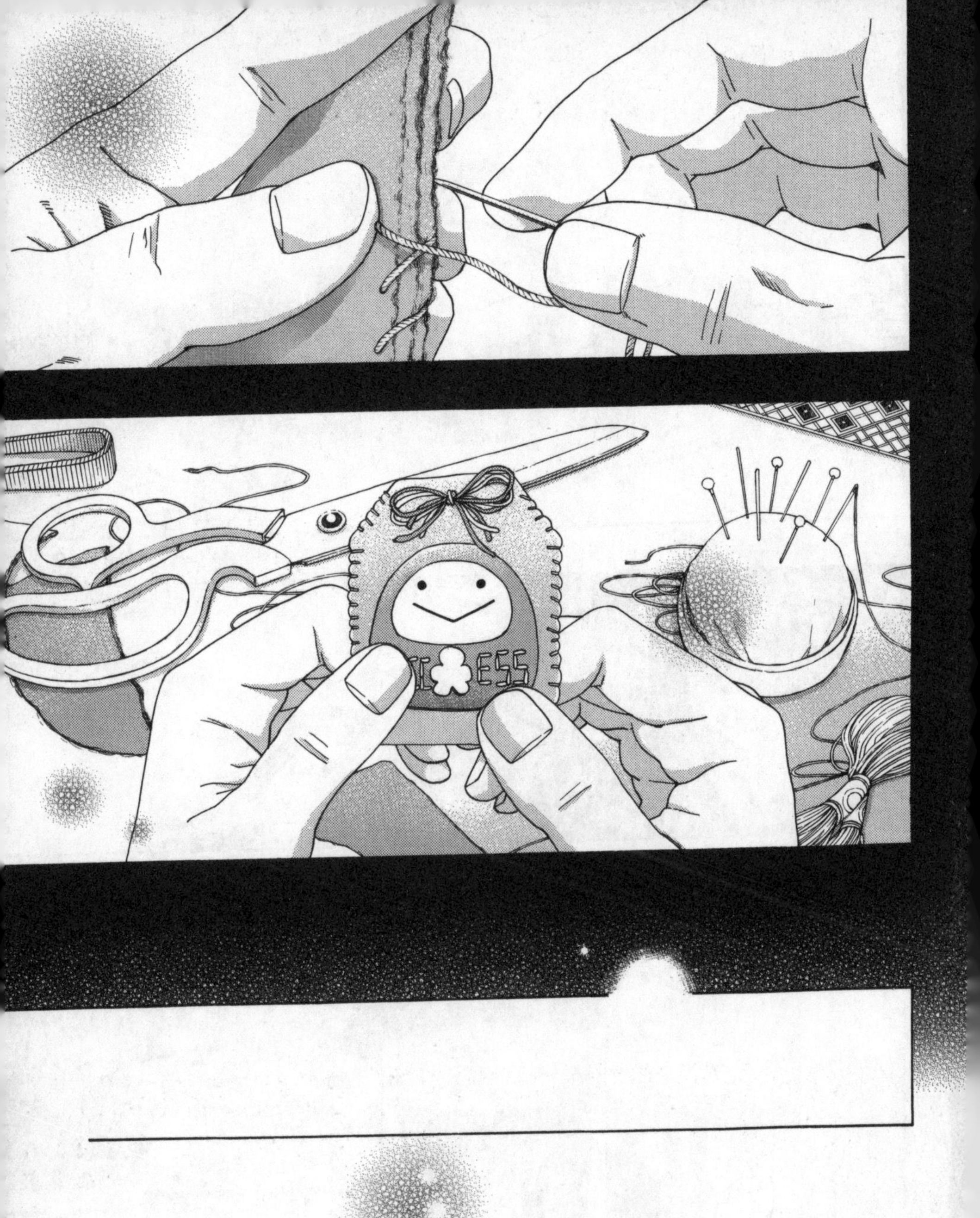

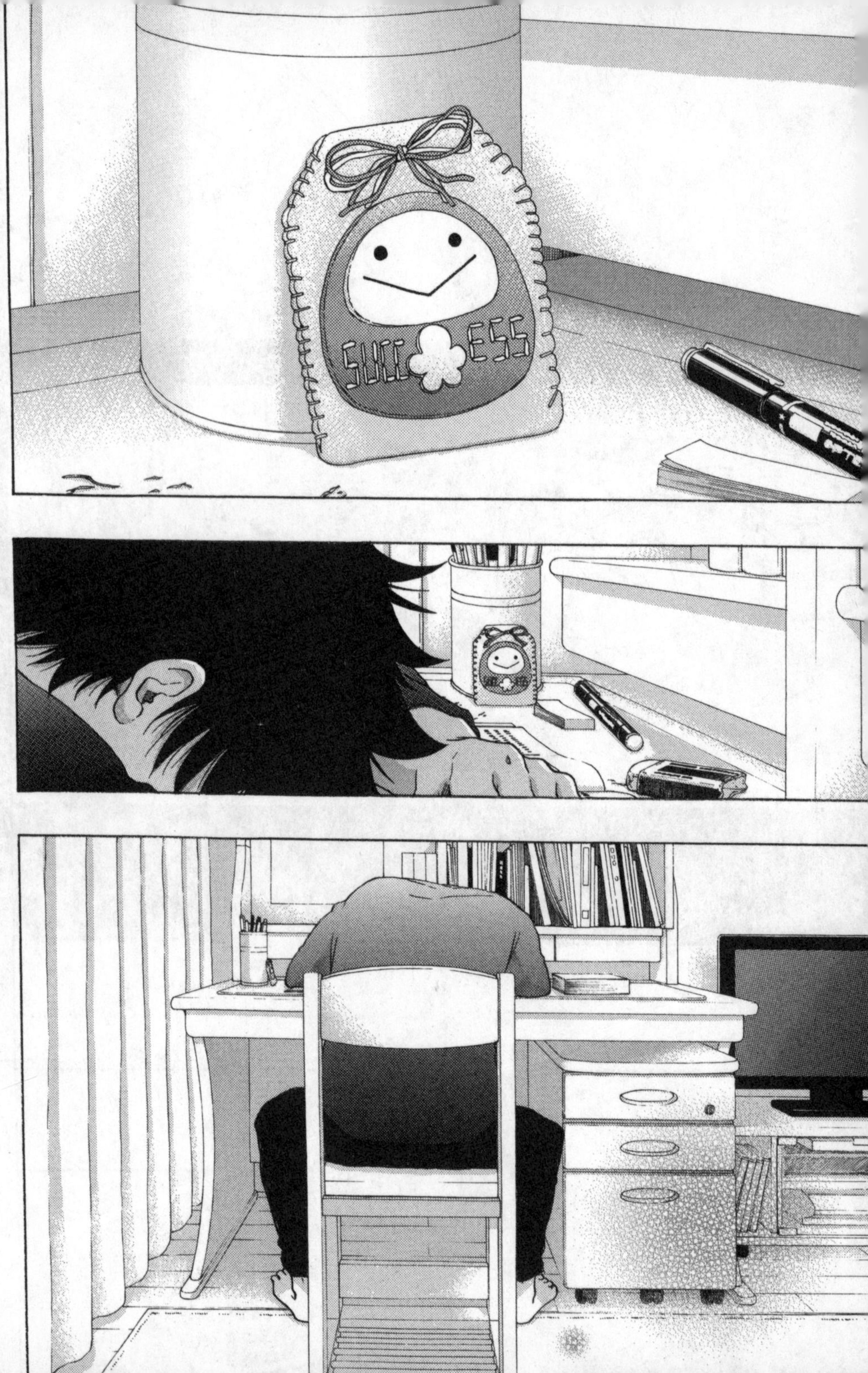
SUCC ESS

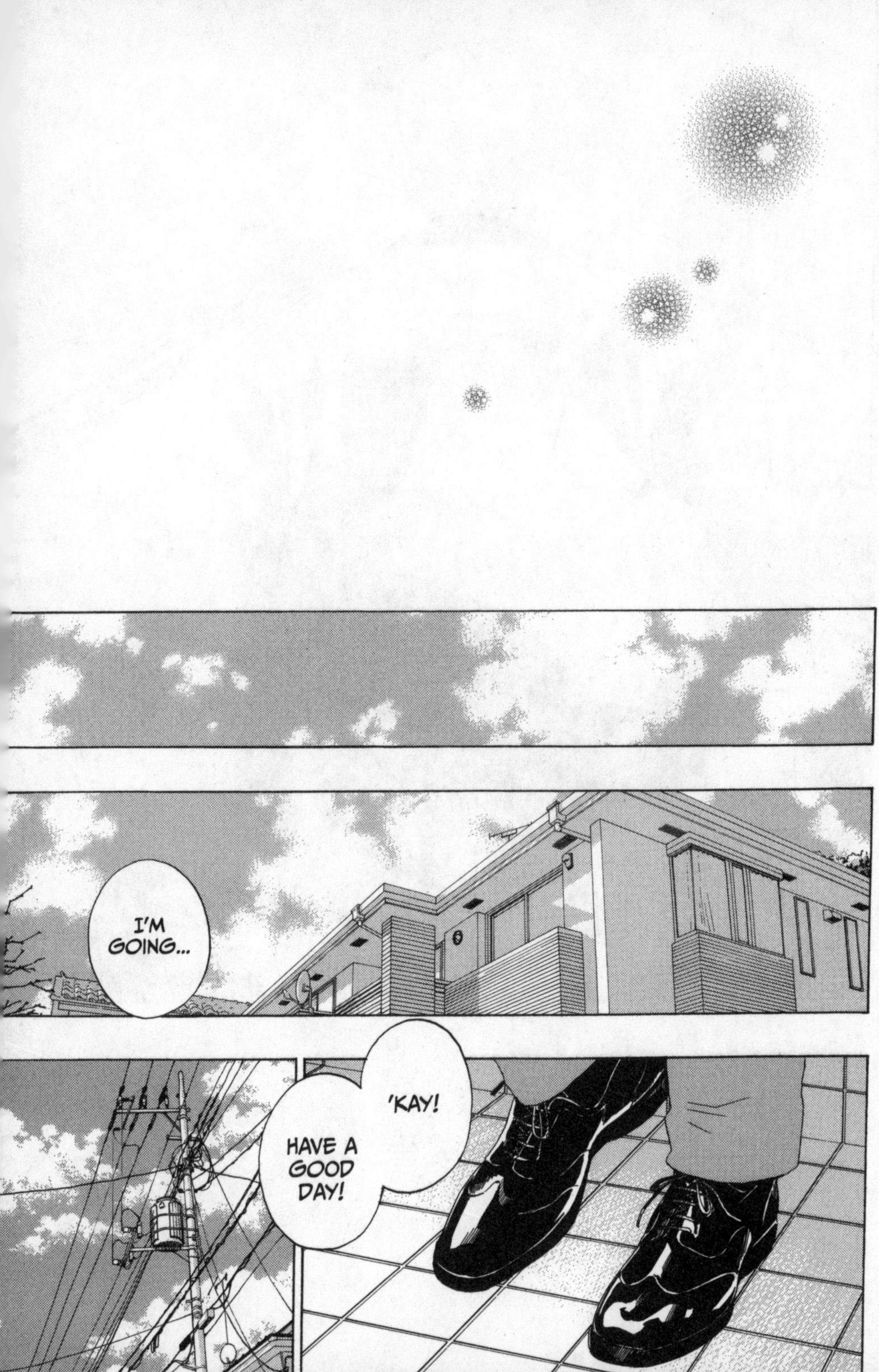
I'M GOING...
'KAY!
HAVE A GOOD DAY!

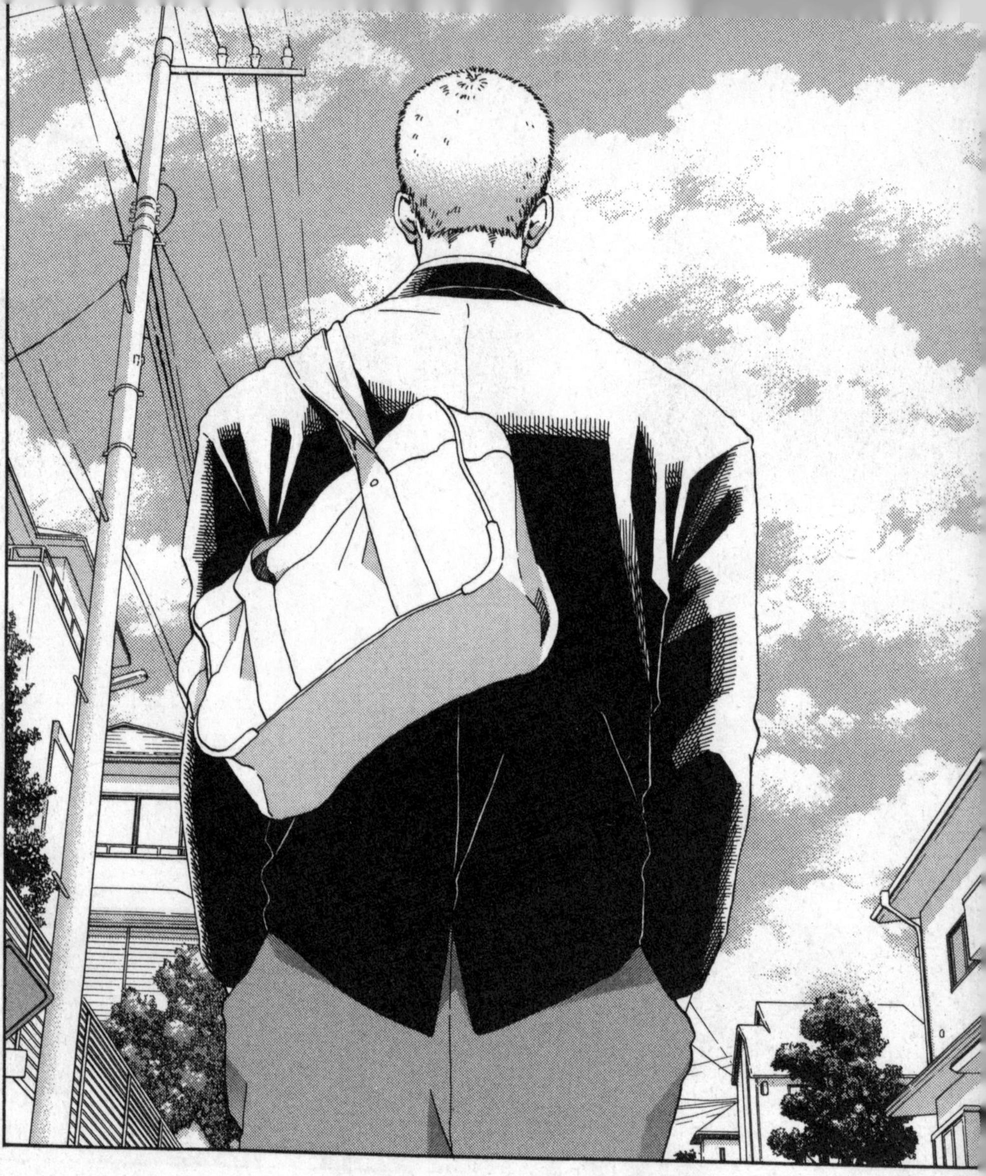

Blue Flag Vol. 7 (END)

KAITO

Until someone gave me the handicrafts above,
made with perler beads, I had no idea they even existed.
They're adorable. I want to try making something with
perler beads myself, so I'm collecting various patterns
to try out when I finally have spare time.

*KAITO began his manga career at the age of 20, when
his one-shot "Happy Magi" debuted in Weekly Shonen Jump.
He published the series Cross Manage in 2012. In 2015,
he returned to Weekly Shonen Jump with Buddy Strike.
KAITO started work on Blue Flag in Jump+ in 2017.*

BLUE FLAG

VOL. 7

VIZ SIGNATURE EDITION

story and art by

KAITO

Translation / Adrienne Beck
Lettering / Annaliese "Ace" Christman
Design / Jimmy Presler
Editor / Marlene First

First published in Japan in 2017 by SHUEISHA Inc., Tokyo.
English translation rights arranged by SHUEISHA Inc.

Printed in Canada

Published by VIZ Media, LLC
P.O. Box 77010
San Francisco, CA 94107

10 9 8 7 6 5 4 3 2 1
First printing, April 2021

ratings.viz.com RATED T+ OLDER TEEN

PARENTAL ADVISORY
BLUE FLAG is rated T+ for Older Teen and is recommended for ages 16 and up for mature themes.

VIZ MEDIA
viz.com

VIZ SIGNATURE
vizsignature.com

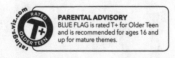

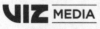

Blue Flag reads from right to left, starting in the upper-right corner. Japanese is read from right to left, meaning that action, sound effects and word-balloon order are completely reversed from English order.

YOU'RE READING THE WRONG WAY...